4th Workshop on Cognitive Aspects of the Lexicon 2014

(CogALex IV)

Held at COLING 2014

Dublin, Ireland
23 August 2014

ISBN: 978-1-63439-217-4

Printed from e-media with permission by:

Curran Associates, Inc.
57 Morehouse Lane
Red Hook, NY 12571

Some format issues inherent in the e-media version may also appear in this print version.

Printed by Curran Associates, Inc. (2014)

For permission requests, please contact the Association for Computational Linguistics
at the address below.

Association for Computational Linguistics
209 N. Eighth Street
Stroudsburg, Pennsylvania 18360

Phone: 1-570-476-8006
Fax: 1-570-476-0860

acl@aclweb.org

Additional copies of this publication are available from:

Curran Associates, Inc.
57 Morehouse Lane
Red Hook, NY 12571 USA
Phone: 845-758-0400
Fax: 845-758-2634
Email: curran@proceedings.com
Web: www.proceedings.com

Introduction to the 4th Workshop on Cognitive Aspects of the Lexicon (CogALex-IV)

1 Background[1]

Starting with a workshop devoted to electronic dictionaires at COLING, Geneva, 2004 (*Enhancing and Using Electronic Dictionaries*) we have continued to do so, by keeping it associated to this conference (2008, Manchester, 2010, Beijing , 2012, Mumbai).[2] What we did change though is the name, as CogALex captures better our mindset, i.e. the focus from which we look at the lexicon. CogALex stands for Cognitive Aspects of the Lexicon. Encouraged by the enthusiasm and interest expressed by the participants of the preceding events, it was natural to come up with a follow-up workshop.

As in the past our aim is to provide a forum for computational lexicographers, researchers in NLP, psychologists and users of lexical resources to share their knowledge and needs concerning the construction, organisation and use of a lexicon by people (lexical access) and machines (NLP, IR, datamining). Hence we invite again researchers with diverse backgrounds to address unsolved problems (see below). In addition we have added two features: One is devoted to a *shared Task*[3] where the sys-tem is meant to learn automatically how to find a word on the basis of its associated terms, the other feature is *vocabulary learning*.

While vocabulary learning is understandably not a hot topic in computational linguistics, it is nevertheless an important aspect of language learning, both in the mother tongue and in a foreign language. Having a rich stock of vocabulary is certainly an asset, but knowing the basic words and expressions is a must. Yet, people tend to forget some of the words they (thought to) have learned. This is not just a question of exercise (quantity vs. quality). Traditional word lists or flash cards are clearly not the ultimate answer. They are not only boring, but also rarely very effective. There is so much more we could do these days by using corpora and computational linguistics know-how, to extract the to-be learned words from text and to display them with their context. Hence, rather than having the user repeat sin-gle words (or word pairs) we could display them in various contexts (e.g. sentences), thereby making sure that the chosen ones correspond to the learners' level and interests.

2 Motivation

The way we look at dictionaries (their creation and use) has changed dramatically over the past 30 years. While being considered as an appendix to grammar in the past, by now they have moved to centre stage. Indeed, there is hardly any task in NLP which can be conducted without them. Also, rather than being static entities (database view), dictionaries are now viewed as dynamic networks, i.e. graphs, whose nodes and links (connection strengths) may change over time. Interestingly, properties concerning topology, clustering and evolution known from other disciplines (society, economy, human brain) also apply to dictionaries: everything is linked, hence accessible, and everything is evolving. Given these similarities, one may wonder what we can learn from these disciplines. In this 4th edition of the CogALex workshop we therefore also invited scientists working in these fields, with the goal to broaden the picture, i.e. to gain a better understanding concerning the mental lexicon and to integrate these findings into our dictionaries in order to support navigation. Given recent advances in neurosciences, it appears timely to seek inspiration from neuroscientists studying the human brain. There is also a lot to be learned from other fields studying graphs and networks, even if their object of study is something else than language, for example biology, economy or society.

[2]Workshop proceedings: see ACL Anthology: http://aclweb.org/anthology/

[3]http://pageperso.lif.univ-mrs.fr/~michael.zock/CogALex-IV/cogalex-webpage/pst.html

3 Topics of Interest

This workshop is about possible enhancements of lexical resources and electronic dictionaries. To perform the groundwork for the next generation of such resources we invite researchers involved in the building of such tools. The idea is to discuss modifications of existing resources by taking the usersí needs and knowledge states into account, and to capitalize on the advantages of the digital media. For this workshop we solicit papers including but not limited to the following topics, each of which can be considered from various points of view: linguistics, neuro- or psycholinguistics (tip of the tongue problem, associations), network related sciences (sociology, economy, biology), mathematics (vector-based approaches, graph theory, small-world problem), etc.

I) Analysis of the conceptual input of a dictionary user

- What does a language producer start from (bag of words)?
- What is in the authors' minds when they are generating a message and looking for a word?
- What does it take to bridge the gap between this input and the desired output (target word)?

II) The meaning of words

- Lexical representation (holistic, decomposed);
- Meaning representation (concept based, primitives);
- Revelation of hidden information (distributional semantics, latent semantics, vector-based approaches: LSA/HAL);
- Neural models, neurosemantics, neurocomputational theories of content representation.

III) Structure of the lexicon

- Discovering structures in the lexicon: formal and semantic point of view (clustering, topical structure);
- Creative ways of getting access to and using word associations (reading between the lines, subliminal communication);
- Evolution, i.e. dynamic aspects of the lexicon (changes of weights);
- Neural models of the mental lexicon (distribution of information concerning words, organi-sation of words).

IV) Methods for crafting dictionaries or Indexes

- Manual, automatic or collaborative building of dictionaries and indexes (crowd-sourcing, serious games, etc.);
- Impact and use of social networks (Facebook, Twitter) for building dictionaries, for organizing and indexing the data (clustering of words), and for allowing to track navigational strategies, etc.;
- (Semi-) automatic induction of the link type (e.g. synonym, hypernym, meronym, association, collocation, ...);
- Use of corpora and patterns (datamining) for getting access to words, their uses, combinations and associations.

V) Dictionary access (navigation and search strategies) and interface issues

- Search based on sound, meaning or associations;

- Search (simple query vs multiple words);
- Context-dependent search (modification of usersí goals during search);
- Recovery;
- Navigation (frequent navigational patterns or search strategies used by people);
- Interface problems, data-visualisation.

We received 30 submissions, of which seven were accepted as full papers, eight were accepted for poster presentation, and nine were accepted in the context of the shared task. While we did not get papers on all the issues mentioned in our call, we did get a quite rich panel of topics including cognitive approaches to lexical access, considerations on word meaning and ontologies, manual and automatic approaches for constructing lexicons, as well as pragmatic aspects. It was also interesting to see the variety of languages in which these issues are addressed. In sum, the community working on dictionaries is dynamic, and there seems to be a growing awareness of the importance of some of the problems presented in our call for papers.

We would like to thank Roberto Navigli for having accepted to be our invited speaker, Shishang Wang for proofreading, and the COLING organizers for providing the framework and for their support. We would also like to express our sincerest thanks to all the members of the Programme Committee whose expertise was invaluable to assure a good selection of papers, despite the tight schedule. Their reviews were helpful not only for us to make the decisions, but also for the authors, helping them to improve their work. In the hope that the results will inspire you, provoke fruitful discussions and result in future collaborations.

Dublin, Ireland, August 2014

Michael Zock, Reinhard Rapp, Chu-Ren Huang

Organizers:

Michael Zock (LIF-CNRS, Marseille, France)
Reinhard Rapp (LIF, Marseille, France and University of Mainz, Germany)
Chu-Ren Huang (The Hong Kong Polytechnic University, China)

Invited Speaker:

Roberto Navigli (Sapienza, University of Rome, Italy)

Program Committee:

Bel Enguix, Gemma (LIF Marseille, France)
Chang, Jason (National Tsing Hua University, Taiwan)
Cook, Paul (University of Melbourne, Australia)
Cristea, Dan (University A.I.Cuza, Iasi, Romania)
De Deyne, Simon (Experimental Psychology, Leuven, Belgium and Adelaide, Australia)
De Melo, Gerard (IIIS, Tsinghua University, Beijing, China)
Ferret, Olivier (CEA LIST, Gif sur Yvette, France)
Fontenelle, Thierry (CDT, Luxemburg)
Gala, Nuria (LIF-CNRS, Aix Marseille University, Marseille, France)
Granger, Sylviane (Université Catholique de Louvain, Belgium)
Grefenstette, Gregory (Inria, Saclay, France)
Hirst, Graeme (University of Toronto, Canada)
Hovy, Eduard (CMU, Pittsburgh, USA)
Hsieh, Shu-Kai (National Taiwan University, Taipei, Taiwan)
Huang, Chu-Ren (Hongkong Polytechnic University, China)
Joyce, Terry (Tama University, Kanagawa-ken, Japan)
Lapalme, Guy (RALI, University of Montreal, Canada)
Lenci, Alessandro (CNR, University of Pisa, Italy)
L'Homme, Marie Claude (University of Montreal, Canada)
Mihalcea, Rada (University of Texas, USA)
Navigli, Roberto (Sapienza, University of Rome, Italy)
Pirrelli, Vito (ILC, Pisa, Italy)
Polguère, Alain (ATILF-CNRS, Nancy, France)
Rapp, Reinhard (LIF Marseille, France and University of Mainz, Germany)
Rosso, Paolo (NLEL, Universitat Politècnica de València, Spain)
Schwab, Didier (LIG-GETALP, Grenoble, France)
Serasset, Gilles (IMAG, Grenoble, France)
Sharoff, Serge (University of Leeds, UK)
Su, Jun-Ming (University of Tainan, Taiwan)
Tiberius, Carole (Institute for Dutch Lexicology, The Netherlands)
Tokunaga, Takenobu (TITECH, Tokyo, Japan)
Tufis, Dan (RACAI, Bucharest, Romania)
Valitutti, Alessandro (Helsinki Institute of Information Technology, Finland)
Wandmacher, Tonio (IRT SystemX, Saclay, France)
Zock, Michael (LIF-CNRS, Marseille, France)

Table of Contents

Workshop Program

Saturday, August 23, 2014

9:00–9:05 **Opening Remarks**

9:05–10:30 **Session 1: Shared Task on the Lexical Access Problem**

The CogALex-IV Shared Task on the Lexical Access Problem
Reinhard Rapp and Michael Zock

A Two-Stage Approach for Computing Associative Responses to a Set of Stimulus Words
Urmi Ghosh, Sambhav Jain and Paul Soma

Deep Learning from Web-Scale Corpora for Better Dictionary Interfaces
Pavel Smrz and Lubomir Otrusina

Exploring the use of word embeddings and random walks on Wikipedia for the CogAlex shared task
Josu Goikoetxea, Eneko Agirre and Aitor Soroa

ETS Lexical Associations System for the COGALEX-4 Shared Task
Michael Flor and Beata Beigman Klebanov

Using Significant Word Co-occurences for the Lexical Access Problem
Rico Feist, Daniel Gerighausen, Manuel Konrad, Georg Richter, Thomas Eckart, Dirk Goldhahn and Uwe Quasthoff

NaDiR: Naive Distributional Response Generation
Gabriella Lapesa and Stefan Evert

Retrieving Word Associations with a Simple Neighborhood Algorithm in a Graph-based Resource
Gemma Bel Enguix

Predicting sense convergence with distributional semantics: an application to the CogaLex 2014 shared task
Laurianne Sitbon and Lance De Vine

WordFinder
Catalin Mititelu and Verginica Barbu Mititelu

Saturday, August 23, 2014 (continued)

10:30–11:00 **Coffee Break**

11:00–12:00 **Session 2: Invited Talk**

(Digital) Goodies from the ERC Wishing Well: BabelNet, Babelfy, Video Games with a Purpose and the Wikipedia Bitaxonomy
Roberto Navigli

12:00–12:30 **Session 3a: Booster Presentations for Posters**

12:03–12:06 *Measuring Similarity from Word Pair Matrices with Syntagmatic and Paradigmatic Associations*
Jin Matsuoka and Yves Lepage

12:06–12:09 *Jibiki-LINKS: a tool between traditional dictionaries and lexical networks for modelling lexical resources*
Ying Zhang, Mathieu Mangeot, Valérie Bellynck and Christian Boitet

12:09–12:12 *When Frequency Data Meet Dispersion Data in the Extraction of Multi-word Units from a Corpus: A Study of Trigrams in Chinese*
Chan-Chia Hsu

12:12–12:15 *Exploring Mental Lexicon in an Efficient and Economic Way: Crowdsourcing Method for Linguistic Experiments*
Shichang Wang, Chu-Ren Huang, Yao Yao and Angel Chan

12:15–12:18 *A Computational Approach to Generate a Sensorial Lexicon*
Serra Sinem Tekiroglu, Gözde Özbal and Carlo Strapparava

12:18–12:21 *Database Design of an Online E-Learning Tool of Chinese Classifiers*
Helena Gao

12:21–12:24 *Default Physical Measurements in SUMO*
Francesca Quattri, Pease Adam and John P. McCrae

12:24–12:27 *Lexical Access Preference and Constraint Strategies for Improving Multiword Expression Association within Semantic MT Evaluation*
Dekai Wu, Chi-kiu Lo and Markus Saers

12:30–14:00 **Lunch Break**

14:00–15:00 **Session 3b: Posters**

Saturday, August 23, 2014 (continued)

The CogALex-IV Shared Task on the Lexical Access Problem

Reinhard Rapp
Aix-Marseille Université
13288 Marseille
France
reinhardrapp@gmx.de

Michael Zock
Aix-Marseille Université
13288 Marseille
France
michael.zock@lif.univ-mrs.fr

Abstract

The shared task of the 4th Workshop on Cognitive Aspects of the Lexicon (CogALex-IV) was devoted to a subtask of the lexical access problem, namely multi-stimulus association. In this task, participants were supposed to determine automatically an expected response based on a number of received stimulus words. We describe here the task definition, the theoretical background, the training and test data sets, and the evaluation procedure used for ranking the participating systems. We also summarize the approaches used and present the results of the evaluation. In conclusion, the outcome of the competition are a number of systems which provide very good solutions to the problem.

1 Introduction

In the framework of CogALex-IV (co-located with COLING 2014 in Dublin) we invited colleagues to participate in a shared task devoted to the lexical access problem in language production. Our aim was to make a quantitative comparison between different systems based on a shared set of data and using the same evaluation metric.

The lexical access problem is very relevant for this workshop series as the quality of a dictionary depends not only on its coverage, but also on the accessibility of the information. Put differently, a crucial point of dictionary development is word access by the language producer, an often neglected aspect. Access strategies vary with the task (text understanding versus text production) and the knowledge available at the very moment of consultation (words, concepts, speech sounds). Unlike readers who look for meanings, writers start from them, searching for the corresponding words. While paper dictionaries are static, permitting only limited strategies for accessing information, their electronic counterparts promise dynamic, proactive search via multiple criteria (meaning, sound, related words) and via diverse access routes. Navigation takes place in a huge conceptual lexical space, and the results are displayable in a multitude of forms (e.g. as trees, as lists, as graphs, or sorted alphabetically, by topic, by frequency).

Given a great number of possibilities of approaching the lexical access problem, we felt that for a competition it was necessary to narrow down the choices in order to be able to come up with a clear task definition. Therefore the CogALex shared task focused on a crucial subtask, namely *multi-stimulus association*. What we mean by this is the following. Suppose we were looking for a word matching the following description: *tasty nut with hard shell originally from Australia*, but could not retrieve the corresponding and intended form *macadamia*. This is the well known tip-of-the-tongue problem where an author knows the word but fails to access its form, even though he is able to retrieve certain features of it (meaning, sound, syllables, ...). People being in the tip-of-the-tongue state always remember something concerning the elusive word (Brown & Mc Neill, 1966). This being so, it would be nice to have a system accepting this kind of information as input, and which then proposes a number of can-

Zock/Rapp/Huang (eds.): Proceedings of the 4th Workshop on Cognitive Aspects of the Lexicon, pages 1–14,
Dublin, Ireland, August 23, 2014.

didates which ideally should contain the target word. Given the above example, we might enter *tasty*, *nut*, *hard*, *shell*, and *Australia*, and the system would be supposed to come up with one or several associated words such as *macadamia*, *walnut*, *cashew*, or *coconut*.

This paper is meant to provide an overview on the shared task and on its results. It is organized as follows: Section 2 gives some background concerning the theory of word finding. Section 3 describes the task definition and Section 4 the training and the test data sets and the evaluation procedure. Section 5 lists the participating systems, tries to characterize the different approaches, and presents the results. For all systems but one, further details are given in the separate papers (in these proceedings) as provided by the members of the participating groups. Section 6 summarizes the conclusions.

2 The problem of word finding

One could imagine many kinds of shared tasks within the framework of the CogALex workshop. Yet, we have focused here on a very specific problem, namely word finding. To this end we have defined a task demanding participants to come up with a system able to compute reversed word associations. While in the standard association experiment people are asked to provide the associations coming to their mind given some stimulus (prime), we have reversed this situation. Given a set of associations, the system was supposed to predict its trigger. More concretely speaking, participants were given 2000 sets of words, each set containing five words. The task was to determine automatically the sixth element, i.e. the prime (or stimulus), evoking the five words. One could object that this task does not really address the word access problem or its solution, but this is not quite so as we will try to show.

In particular, it seems quite reasonable to claim that an association network with bi-directional links (see Rapp, 2014) is a suitable resource to support word 'finding'. Since words are connected via bi-directional links either of the connected items can be the source or the target during the search (or during navigation).

Although systems designed for the shared task can have many applications (see Section 6), a prototypical one is the tip-of-the-tongue problem, which is a special case (yet a quite frequent one) of word access. So let us briefly describe this problem and the steps needed to overcome it.

One of the most vexing problems in speaking or writing is that one knows a given word, yet fails to access it when needed. Suppose, you were looking for a word expressing the following ideas: *superior dark coffee made of beans from Arabia*, but could not retrieve the intended word *mocha*. What will you do in a case like this? You know the *meaning*, you know how or when to *use* the corresponding word, and in principle you even seem to know its spoken or written *form*, since you have used it some time ago (for more details, see Zock et al., 2010). Yet for some unknown reason you simply cannot access it at the very moment of writing or speaking. The just described situation is called *anomia* or *dysnomia*, which in less technical terms means that a person has a word finding problem. This case is often assimilated with the tip-of-the-tongue phenomenon, which technically speaking is not quite correct, but this shall not concern us here.[1]

To resolve the problem, one can think of many strategies. For example, one can ask somebody, by providing him some hints (cues) hoping that the person can guess the elusive word. Such hints could take various forms like a description (definition or circumlocution), an association or the role played by the target word, say, *instrument used for eating Chinese food* when searching for *chopsticks*. Of course, one can also search in an external resource (dictionary). Unfortunately, most dictionaries are primarily designed for the language recipient and not particularly well suited to assist the language producer. And even if there are quite a number of promising proposals,[2] a lot more could be done these days with the help of corpora, computers, and language technology.

---

[1] The tip-of-the-tongue phenomenon (http://en.wikipedia.org/wiki/Tip_of_the_tongue) is a weak form of an anomic aphasia (http://en.wikipedia.org/wiki/Anomic_aphasia). Yet, unlike the latter, it is only momentary. It is characterized by the fact that the person (speaker/writer) has only partial access to the word s/he is looking for. The typically lacking parts are phonological (syllables, phonemes). Since all information except this last one seems to be available, and since this is the one preceding articulation, we say: the word is stuck on the *tip of the tongue*.

[2] Think of *Roget's Thesaurus* (Roget, 1852), *WordNet* (Fellbaum, 1998; Miller et al., 1990), Longman's *Language Activator* (Summers, 1993), the *Oxford Reverse Dictionary* (Edmonds, 1999) or *OneLook* which combines a dictionary, WordNet, and an encyclopedia, Wikipedia (http://onelook.com/reverse-dictionary.shtml).

This being said, to build a dictionary for the language producer, certain provisions must be made, and it is easy to understand why. When searching a word form (target), the dictionary user will certainly not search in the entire resource. He will rather navigate in a substantially smaller subset (Zock, 2014; Zock & Cristea, 2014). The question is, how to build this reduced space and how to support then navigation. We will deal here mainly with this first step of search space reduction as it is crucial and this is where associations come into play (Deese, 1965; Cramer, 1968).

The experiments concerning the tip-of-the-tongue problem have systematically shown (Aitchison, 2003; Brown, 1991; Brown & McNeill, 1996) that users being in this state always know 'something' concerning the target word: fragments of the meaning, origin, number of syllables, etc. This being so, any of this could be used to guide the search.

Suppose we focused only on the semantic aspects. In such a case it is reasonable to assume that the target form can be found on the basis of its defining elements (bag of the words contained in the definition). While not being perfect, this works quite well (Dutoit & Nugues, 2002; El-Kahlout & Oflazer, 2004; Mandala et al., 1999; Michiels, 1982). Actually, even Google – although not designed for this – is able to recover in many cases the elusive word. Just try the following example, *spring, typically found in Iceland or in the Yellowstone National Park, discharging hot water and steam*, and chances are that you will find the target word *geyser*. Although not perfect, this is nevertheless quite useful. However, this represents only one kind of cognitive state (knowledge of the definition), and this is certainly neither the only one nor the most frequent one. Indeed, there are many situations where it is hard to come up with a precise definition, and in this case other types of information are used to initiate search, for example, co-occurrences, associations, etc. Hence, if our target is *mocha* it may be accessible not only via its definitional terms (*coffee*, *beverage*, ...) but also via any of its associates: *black*, *hot*, *drink*, *Java*, etc. This is the point where associations come to the centre stage.

Some of the related recently published work has been cited in Rapp (2014), and some other is mentioned by the authors participating in the shared task. Therefore, let us focus here primarily on some of the earlier and nowadays often overlooked related work.

Associative networks have been very popular in Artificial Intelligence at the end of the nineteen-seventies (Findler, 1979). They were proposed to be used for many tasks such as word sense disambiguation, finding brand names, reading between the lines, subliminal communication, brainstorming, and supporting word finding. That is, the tip-of-the-tongue problem is but one of the many possible applications.

The study of associative networks was motivated by the goal to understand the organization of the human memory and the mental lexicon. This led to the building of lexical graphs like WordNet (Fellbaum, 1998), the study of the tip-of-the-tongue problem (Brown & Mc Neill, 1966), error analysis (Fromkin, 1980, 1973) and priming experiments. Priming is said to take place if exposure to one stimulus increases significantly the response to another. Meyer and Schvaneveldt (1971) showed in their seminal experiments that people were faster in deciding that a string of letters is a word when it was followed by an associatively or semantically related word. For example, *nurse* is recognized more quickly following *doctor* than following *bread.* These findings supported also the idea of activation spreading as a method of access or search (Collins & Loftus, 1975).

Associative networks can be considered as a special type of semantic network which were introduced by Richens (1956) and by Ceccato (1956) for quite a different purpose. They were meant to serve as an interlingua for machine translation. These knowledge representation structures were then further developed in the sixties by Simmons (1963) and Quillian (1963, 1966, 1967, 1968, 1969). They finally became famous due to the work done by Quillian and two psychologistst (Collins & Quillian, 1969 & 1970 and Collins & Loftus, 1975). Note that semantic networks can represent language at various levels of granularity: word, sentence (Sowa, 1984) or discourse (Mann & Thomson, 1988). Also, and very relevant for us here is the fact that at the word level, they can represent its semantics, i.e. meaning (Nogier & Zock, 1992), or its place withing the global structure of the mental lexicon (Miller, 1995; Aitchison, 2003; Bonin, 2004). In this latter case words are connected by associations rather than by deep-case roles, and the resulting graphs show word neighborhood (Schvaneveldt, 1989). The fact that the mental lexicon exhibits 'small world' characteristics (http://en.wikipedia.org/wiki/Small-world_network) has been shown by Vitevitch (2008) and by Sporns and colleagues (2004).

For the construction of associative networks knowledge about associations is required. Such knowledge can be obtained in two different ways. One is to ask people what a given term (say *cat*) evokes in their mind (say *dog*, *mouse*, etc.). Another option is to look at word co-occurrences in corpora, and to derive the associations from them (which, strictly speaking, pre-supposes that the human brain is also doing this). For the purpose of having a gold standard for the shared task, by using the EAT, we have opted for the first possibility. In contrast, most systems constructed by the shared task participants rely on the second.

3 Task definition

The participants received lists of five given words (primes) such as *circus*, *funny*, *nose*, *fool*, and *Coco* and were supposed to compute the word most closely associated to all of them. In this case, the word *clown* would be the expected response. Table 1 shows some more examples.

Given Words	Target Word
gin, drink, scotch, bottle, soda	whisky
wheel, driver, bus, drive, lorry	car
neck, animal, zoo, long, tall	giraffe
holiday, work, sun, summer, abroad	vacation
home, garden, door, boat, chimney	house
blue, cloud, stars, night, high	sky

Table 1. Lists of given words together with their targets.

We provided a training set of 2000 sets of five input words (multiword stimuli), together with the expected target words (associative responses). The way how the datasets were produced will be described in the next section. The participants had about five weeks to train their systems on this data. After the training phase, we released a test set containing another 2000 sets of five input words, but without providing the expected target words.

The participants were given five days to run their systems on the test data,[3] with the goal of predicting the target words. For each system, we compared the results to the expected target words and computed an accuracy based on the number of exact string matches (but without taking capitalization into account). The participants were invited to submit a paper describing their approach and their results.

For the participating systems, we distinguished two categories:

1) *Unrestricted systems*. They could use any kind of data to compute their results.

2) *Restricted systems based on ukWaC*: These systems were only allowed to draw on the freely available ukWaC corpus (Ferraresi et al., 2008)[4] in order to extract information on word associations. The ukWaC corpus comprises about 2 billion words of web texts and provides also lemma and part-of-speech information.

Participants could compete in either category or in both. They were encouraged to further improve on their results outside of the competition after the deadline, and to describe these advances in their papers (in these proceedings).

4 Training and test data sets and evaluation procedure

The training and the test data sets were both derived from the *Edinburgh Associative Thesaurus* (EAT; Kiss et al., 1973). The EAT lists for each of 8400 stimulus words up to 100 associative responses as obtained from test persons who were asked to produce the word coming spontaneously to their mind.

As the EAT uses uppercase characters only, and as this might not suit everybody's needs, we decided to modify its capitalization. For this purpose, for each word occurring in the EAT, we looked up which form of capitalization showed the highest occurrence frequency in the *British National Corpus* (Burnard & Aston, 1998). By this form we replaced the respective word. E.g. *DOOR* was replaced by

[3] The exact dates were: training data release: March 27, 2014; test data release: May 5, 2014; final results due: May 9, 2014.

[4] http://wacky.sslmit.unibo.it/doku.php?id=corpora.

door, and *GOD* was replaced by *God*. This way we hoped to come close to what might have been produced during compilation of the EAT if case distinctions had been taken into account.[5] Since this method is not perfect, e.g. words often occurring in sentence initial position might be falsely capitalized, we did some manual checking, but cannot claim to have achieved perfection.

Next, for each stimulus word, only the top five associations (i.e. the associations produced by the largest number of test person) were retained, and all other associations were discarded. The decision to keep only a small number of associations was motivated by the results of Rapp (2013) which indicate that associations produced by very few test persons tend to be of arbitrary nature. We also wanted to avoid unnecessary complications, which is why we decided on a fixed number, although the exact choice of five is of course somewhat arbitrary.

From the remaining dataset we removed all items which contained non-alphabetical characters. We also removed items which contained words that did not occur in the BNC. The reason for this is that quite a few of them are misspellings. By these measures, the number of items was reduced from initially 8400 to 7416.

From these we randomly selected 4000 items. 2000 of these were used as our training data set. The remaining 2000 were used as our test data set, but of course for the test set we removed the stimulus words. Tables 2 and 3 show the alphabetically first 20 items in each data set.[6]

The participating teams were asked to submit a list of 2000 words reflecting their predictions concerning the 2000 items of the test data set. For evaluation, we simply compared these 2000 words to the expected results (as taken from the EAT) by counting the number of exact matches, with the only flexibility that word capitalization was not taken into account.

There are a number of reasons why it was very difficult for the teams to get the target words exactly right:

1) In many cases, the given words might almost quite as strongly point to other target words. For example, when given the words *gin*, *drink*, *scotch*, *bottle*, and *soda*, instead of the target word *whisky* the alternative spelling *whiskey* should also be fine, and possibly some other beverages might also be acceptable.

2) The target vocabulary was not restricted in any way, so in principle hundred thousands of words had to be considered.

3) Although most of the target words were base forms, the training and the test sets also contain a good number of cases where the target words were inflected forms. Of course it is almost impossible to get these inflected forms exactly right.

Because of these difficulties we expected low performance figures (e.g. below 10%) in the competition[7] and were positively surprised by some of the actual results (see Section 5).

Concerning point 1 (other acceptable solutions) our data source did not provide any, so it was not practical for us to try to come up with alternative solutions in the chosen reverse association framework.

Concerning point 2 (restriction of target vocabulary), of course all teams had to make assumptions about the underlying vocabulary, as it is already difficult to fix boundaries for the English vocabulary, and occasionally even foreign words or names might occur as associations. In this respect all results have to be taken with caution, as some teams might have been more lucky than others in making good guesses concerning the target vocabulary.[8]

---

[5] Note that the participants of the shared task were nevertheless free to discard all case distinctions if their approach would not require them. During evaluation, case distinctions were not taken into account.

[6] From http://pageperso.lif.univ-mrs.fr/~michael.zock/CogALex-IV/cogalex-webpage/pst.html the full data sets can be downloaded

[7] Note that the results of up to 54% reported in Rapp (2014) were obtained using different data sets and severely restricted vocabularies, so these cannot be used for comparison.

[8] For such reasons we had requested to include such information in the papers. We concede that a competition with a pre-defined target vocabulary might have been more fair by reducing the influence of chance. But we were also very interested in the approaches on how to limit this vocabulary, so this was an important part of the shared task.

Target Word	Given Words
a	B the alphabet an man
abound	plenty many lots around leap
about	around turn round now time
above	below high over sky all
abrasive	rough sandpaper rub cutting hard
absence	away fonder illness leave presence
absent	away minded gone present ill
absurdity	stupid ridiculous mad stupidity clown
accents	dialects language foreign speech French
accordion	music piano play player instrument
accountant	money chartered clerk office turf
accrue	gather gain money acquire collect
achieve	nothing attain gain success win
acids	alkalis alkali bases burn science
acknowledged	letter receipt accepted received replied
acquaintance	friend know person friends casual
acquired	got obtained gained taste bought
acrid	smell bitter acid smoke dry
actions	words deeds movement movements reactions
actual	real fact happening truth exact

Table 2: Extract from the training set.

Given Words
able incapable brown clever good
able knowledge skill clever can
about near nearly almost roughly
above earth clouds God skies
above meditation crosses passes rises
abuse wrong bad destroy use
accusative calling case Latin nominative
ache courage blood stomach intestine
ache nail dentist pick paste
aches hurt agony stomach period
action arc knee reaction jerk
actor theatre door coach Act
actress stage play man theatre
addict pot store hash medicine
Africa Bible priest abroad doctor
again fresh afresh old morning
against angry bad fight hostile
age time epoch period years
aid assistant kind mother good
aid eyes aids see eye

Table 3: Extract from the test set. The respective (undisclosed) target words are shown in Table 4.

Concerning point 3 (matches of inflected forms) the ETS team had correctly pointed out that performance figures would significantly improve if matches with alternative inflected forms of the same word would also be counted as correct. For this purpose, the team kindly provided expanded versions of the target words for the training and for the test data set which were obtained using an in-house morphological tool. Table 4 shows the respective data for the alphabetically first 20 target words of the test data set. As we assumed that only the absolute but not the relative performance of the systems (ranking in competition) would be affected by this measure, we decided not to include this in the standard procedure, but nevertheless forwarded the data to all teams and encouraged them to conduct such an evaluation by themselves outside of the competition (and some actually did so). Let us nevertheless point out our main concerns:

1) Many target words are ambiguous, and in some cases the range of inflected forms depends on the way how the ambiguity is resolved. Assume, for example, that the target word form is *can* which might be an auxiliary verb or a noun. In this case, the inflected form *cans* in the expanded list would only be correct if the target word *can* referred to the noun, but not if it referred to the auxiliary verb (see also Lezius et al., 1998). Of course one could try to disambiguate the target words based on the given words. But this is a non trivial task likely to be error prone and possibly controversial.

2) In principle, such considerations might also apply to the given words, i.e. they could also be expanded. But in this case the disambiguation task is even more difficult as it is not clear what should be considered as context (i.e. as clues for disambiguation).

Although point 2 could be left to the participants, our aim was to avoid any such complications, in order to keep the focus on the core part of the shared task. So, as far as we as organizers were concerned, we decided not to consider inflectional variation.

Let us now comment on the overall character of the shared task. It should be noted that this task is actually the *reverse association task* as described in Rapp (2013, 2014). That is, the shared task participants were supposed to consider the associations from the EAT as their given words, and their task was to determine the original stimulus words.

Word	**Morphological expansions**
capable	
ability	abilities
approximately	
heavens	heaven
transcends	transcending, transcend, transcended
misuse	misusing, misused, misuses
vocative	vocatives
guts	gut, gutted, gutting
tooth	tooths
pains	pain, paining, pained
reflex	reflexes
stage	staging, staged, stages
actor	actors
drug	drugging, drugs, drugged
missionary	missionaries
anew	
antagonistic	
era	eras
helper	helpers
visual	visuals

Table 4: Morphological expansions of the first 20 words in the test data set.

However, we had not disclosed the nature of the data until after the competition mainly for the following reasons:

1) To avoid reverse engineering approaches based on the EAT or similar association norms.
2) To avoid leading participants in a particular direction. For us it seemed most important to obtain approaches as diverse as possible. And as this was the first shared task devoted to multi-stimulus associations, we thought that this would be a unique opportunity to obtain contributions as unbiased as possible.

On the other hand we had concerns about the fairness of not disclosing the nature of the data. Firstly, some of the participants might discover its origin and thus possibly have an advantage. Secondly, it is not clear in how far the reverse association task is prototypical enough for the lexical access problem as to assume that in terms of relative system performance the two tasks are comparable. In any case, concerning the lexical access problem we saw no chance of acquiring large scale data sets within the given time frame, so it was clear that this was not feasible.

When, after the competition, we disclosed the nature of the data, we invited the participants to comment on these issues in their papers, and it was very interesting for us to learn about the different views.

5 Participating systems and results

Altogether 15 teams expressed their interest to participate in the shared task. Of these, ten teams actually submitted results, of which one (BRNO) participated in both tracks (ukWaC and unrestricted), and another (SAAR) provided two solutions for the unrestricted track. The teams who submitted results are listed in Table 5, where each team is assigned a short Team ID which is derived from the institution names. In Table 6 for each team we make an attempt to give short characterizations of the approaches and the resources used.

Most approaches are variants of analyzing word co-occurrence statistics as derived from large text corpora. Several teams, among them the best performing ones, use for this purpose the open source tool *Word2Vec* which provides two neural network-based model architectures for computing continuous vector representations of words from very large data sets (Mikolov, 2013a; Mikolov, 2013b). In contrast, the RACAI team uses WordNet relation chains, a method which makes absolutely sense, but seems to severely suffer from data sparseness issues (i.e. there are much fewer WordNet relations between words than there are non-random word co-occurrences within large corpora). This finding is confirmed by the BRNO and UBC teams who tried out both approaches (corpus-based and WordNet-based) and came to the conclusion that the corpus-based approach performed considerably better.

Let us emphasize that we consider this type of findings a valuable output of the shared task and therefore are very grateful to the teams who pursued the WordNet-based approach that they shared these results although they were all well aware that, despite excellent scientific work, the respective performance figures were not very competitive.

Table 7 shows the results of the competition, ranked according to the accuracy of the results, and indicating the respective track (ukWAC or unrestricted). As some teams (AMU, QUT, SOEN, ranks 7 to 9) could not quite make it for the deadline, they were granted an extension of three days. On the top four positions are submissions who all used the above mentioned Word2Vec tool, indicating that this software is well suited for this task. Note that the winning system (IIITH) opted for the CBOW (continuous bag-of-words) architecture, whereas the other three opted for the skip-gram architecture. This might be an explanation for the differences in the results. However, this must be further analyzed as there are also other differences, including the assumptions constraining the target vocabulary, which, as described in Section 4, is an important issue. For example, the IIITH team used a frequency threshold of 25 while making word vectors using Word2Vec. In addition, when calculating PMI (pointwise mutual information) associations, a frequency threshold (for bigrams) of 3 was used (see sections 4.1 and 4.2 of their paper).

It should be mentioned that, like some others (see e.g. the papers by the ETS and by the RACAI teams), the IIITH team was able to improve on their results after the shared task deadline. Whereas for their submission they had used a re-ranking procedure based on point-wise mutual information (PMI), later on they used weighted PMI as their association measure. This improved their results from

30.45% to 34.9%. Likewise, the ETS team could improve their results from 14.95% to 18.90%. And the RACAI team (who used a WordNet-based approach) was able to almost double their results from 1.50% to 2.95%.

Team ID	Affiliation	Team members / Authors of papers
AMU	Aix-Marseille University, France	Gemma Bel-Enguix
BRNO	Brno University of Technology, Czech Republic	Lubomir Otrusina, Pavel Smrz
ETS	Educational Testing Service, Princeton, USA	Michael Flor, Beata Beigman Klebanov
IIIT	International Institute of Information Technology (IIIT), Hyderabad, India	Urmi Gosh, Sambhav Jain, Soma Paul
LEIPZIG	University of Leipzig, Germany	Rico Feist, Daniel Gerighausen, Manuel Konrad, Georg Richter, Thomas Eckart, Dirk Goldhahn, Uwe Quasthoff
QUT	Queensland University of Technology, Brisbane, Australia	Laurianne Sitbon, Lance De Vine
RACAI	Romanian Academy Research Institute for Artificial Intelligence, Bukarest, Romania	Catalin Mititelu, Verginica Barbu Mititelu
SAAR	Saarland University, Germany	Asad Sayeed (no paper)
SOEN	Universities of Stuttgart, Osnabrück, and Erlangen-Nürnberg, Germany	Gabrielle Lapesa, Stefan Evert
UBC	University of the Basque Country, Spain	Josu Goikoetxea, Eneko Agirre, Aitor Soroa

Table 5: Participating teams.

Team ID	Approach	Resources used
AMU	Co-occurrence-based lexical graph	British National Corpus
BRNO	Word2Vec from Python package GenSim (skip-gram architecture)	ukWaC, ClueWeb12, WordNet
ETS	Aggregating co-occurrence-based association strengths to individual cue words	English Gigaword 2003, ETS in-house corpus
IIITH	Word2Vec using CBOW architecture and re-ranking	ukWaC
LEIPZIG	Sum of co-occurrence-based significance values	Leipzig corpora collection
QUT	Own implementation similar to the Word2Vec package (skip-gram architecture)	ukWaC
RACAI	Shortest WordNet relations chain and maximum entropy modeling	Princeton WordNet, Google n-gram corpus
SAAR	Co-occurrence-based	ukWaC and others
SOEN	Ranking according to average (co-occurrence-based) association strength or according to distributional similarity	ukWaC
UBC	Word2Vec (skip-gram architecture), random walks, personalized PageRank	Google news corpus, Wikipedia, WordNet

Table 6: Overview on approaches and resources.

To give a rough idea on how much the results can be improved when inflectional variants are tolerated during evaluation (see Section 4), let us mention that the IIITH team did so. This way their results improved from 34.90% (as obtained after the deadline) to 39.55. Likewise, in the case of the ETS team the results improved from 14.95% to 20.25%. (For details see the respective contributions in these proceedings.)

Concerning the two tracks of the competition, namely ukWaC and unrestricted, it appears that the ukWaC corpus contains already enough information to solve the task. Evidence for this is provided by the BRNO team which submitted results in both tracks and where the improvements were minimal (19.85% vs. 19.65%). Another indication is that, unexpectedly, the winning IIITH team was in the ukWaC track.

For details on all other approaches (except SAAR) see the papers provided by the participating teams in these proceedings. Ideas that occurred when discussing the shared task with other colleagues were that Adam Kilgarriff's SketchEngine might be a useful tool for solving the lexical access problem (thanks to Eva Schaeffer-Lacroix for pointing this out), and that it may be useful to take syntax into account (thanks to Eric Wehrli and Luka Nerima). The latter would be in analogy to the generation of distributional thesauri where working with parsed rather than raw corpora has been shown to lead to very good quality (see e.g. Pantel & Lin, 2002). This way, rather than taking all word co-occurrences into account, the focus can be laid on selected relations between words, such as e.g. head-modifier or subject-object relations.

Rank	Team ID	Accuracy (%)	Track
1	IIITH	30.45	ukWAC
2	BRNO	19.85	unrestricted
3	BRNO	19.65	ukWaC
4	UBC	16.35	unrestricted
5	ETS	14.95	unrestricted
6	LEIPZIG	14.05	unrestricted
7	SOEN	13.10	ukWaC
8	AMU	9.10	unrestricted
9	QUT	4.25	ukWaC
10	SAAR	3.50	unrestricted
11	SAAR	2.60	unrestricted
12	RACAI	1.50	unrestricted

Table 7: Results of the shared task.

6 Discussion and conclusions

For the shared task of finding associations to multiple stimuli, by the participants accuracies of up to 30% (35% after the deadline) were reported. Given the very conservative evaluation procedure (see Section 4) which relies on exact matches and does not give any credit to alternative solutions, this is a very good result which considerably exceeded our expectations. Although we do not have comparative figures on human performance, our guess is that humans would not be able to do much better on this. So, in some sense, it seems that we have rather perfect results.

But what does this mean? Is there any psycholinguistic relevance? And is the task which we addressed here of any relevance for practical work in computational linguistics?

Let us first discuss the question of psycholinguistic relevance. In Rapp (2011) we have argued that human language intuitions are based on the detection, memorization, and reproduction of statistical regularities in perceived language. But we have only discussed this for single words. Now we can do so for multiword stimuli. And it seems that the same mechanisms that apply to single word stimuli are also valid in the case of multiwords. Apparently, from a relatively limited corpus such as ukWaC, intuitively plausible associations to an almost unlimited number of multiword stimuli can be derived. This is in analogy to human language acquisition: Due to limitations of the input channel a person can only perceive a few hundred million words during lifetime. But this limited information seems to suffice to have intuitions on almost anything that is language related.

This is a contradiction only on first glance: Apparently, language is a highly compressed form of information where all co-occurrences of words or word-sequences count (and were literally counted by most algorithms!). Therefore its information content is far higher than it may appear, and this provides a solution to the often discussed argument concerning the poverty of the stimulus (Landauer & Dumais, 1997). With regard to language, it seems there simply is no poverty of the stimulus, but instead the human language is a highly condensed form of extremely rich information. As the capacities of the input and the output channels are very limited, evolution was probably forced to optimize on this.

As the systems participating in the shared task can simulate human intuitions concerning zillions of possible multiword stimuli, it is likely that their algorithms grasp some of the essence that governs the respective inference processes taking place in human memory. In particular, they provide evidence that human association processing is also co-occurrence based, and that this not only applies to associations to single stimulus words as shown by Wettler et al. (2005), but also to associations concerning multiple stimuli.

Concerning the practical relevance of the work, our feeling is that such systems will be useful additions to many language-related tasks requiring human-like intuitions for the reason that human language intuitions seem to be based on associative learning. Let us come up with some examples of possible applications:

1) Augment associative resources such as the EAT.
2) Tip-of-the-tongue problem: Recall elusive words.
3) Lexical access: Rather than relying on alphabetical order, encyclopedias and dictionaries can be accessed associatively (e.g. *president of Poland → Bronislaw Komorowski*).
4) Generating thesauri of related words: Related words in the sense of Pantel & Lin (2002) are second order associations. The words related to a given word can be determined by computing its associations, and by then computing the multi-stimulus associations to these.
5) Question answering: Questions can be considered as multiword stimuli, answers as their associations (e.g. *height of Eiffel Tower → 324 m*).
6) Paraphrasing: The meaning of a phrase can be characterized by the associations resulting from its content words. Paraphrases are likely to lead to similar associations.
7) Search word generation in information retrieval: Keywords used in search queries can be augmented with relevant other keywords.
8) Advertising: The effect of an advertisement can be described by the associations evoked by the words that are used in it.
9) Word sense induction and disambiguation: Word contexts can be replaced by their multi-stimulus associations. This way the effects of word choice will be reduced when clustering contexts.
10) Machine translation: Translations can be seen as associations across languages (seed dictionary is required, see below).

Of course, most of the above has already been dealt with using other approaches. But, when looking at the respective (statistical) algorithms more closely, it seems often the case that researchers have intuitively chosen statistics which show some analogy to multi-stimulus associations. So what we suggest here is not entirely new. We nevertheless hope that the current framework can be useful. Firstly, it draws a connection to psycholinguistic evidence. And secondly, as done in the shared task, it allows to optimize the core algorithm independently of particular applications.

To be a bit more explicit, let us try to sketch a possible agenda of some future work which we would be happy to see: Let us start from the hypothesis that the meaning of a short sentence or phrase can be characterized by the vector resulting from taking its content words as multiword stimuli, and by computing their associations. For example, given the sentence *John laughed in the circus*, we would take *John*, *laugh*, and *circus* as our stimulus words, and the resulting association vector could be expected to have high values at its positions corresponding to *clown*, *nose*, and *fun*. For conciseness, let us call this type of vector *meaning vector.*[9] Now let us look at the sentences *Someone walks across the border* and *A person passes customs*. The two sentences do not share a single word. But the associations derived from them should be nevertheless similar, because associations such as *toll*, *officer*, or *country* can be expected to come up in both cases. That is, their meaning vectors should be similar, and this similarity can be quantified e.g. by computing the cosine similarity between them. We thus have a method which allows us to measure the similarity between sentences in a way that to some extend takes their meanings into account.

Finally, we can try to cross language barriers and make the step to association-based machine translation (ABMT). To translate a source language phrase, we compute its meaning vector. Presupposing that we have a basic dictionary, in analogy to Rapp (1999) we can translate this meaning vector into the target language.[10] Further assuming that we already know the meaning vectors of a very large number of target language phrases, we next select the target language meaning vector which is most similar to the source language meaning vector. The respective target language phrase can be considered to be the translation of the source language phrase. Optionally, to improve translation quality, the target language phrase can be modified by adding, removing, substituting, or reordering words with the aim of improving the similarity between the meaning vectors of the source and target language phrases.

Acknowledgments

This work was supported by a Marie Curie Intra European Fellowship within the 7th European Community Framework Programme. We would like to thank George R. Kiss and colleagues for creating the Edinburgh Associative Thesaurus, and Michael Wilson for making it publicly available. Many thanks also to Adriano Ferraresi and colleagues for providing the ukWaC corpus, and to the participants of the shared task for their contributions and comments, as well as for the pleasant cooperation.

References

Aitchison, J. (2003). *Words in the Mind: an Introduction to the Mental Lexicon*. Oxford, Blackwell.

Bonin, P. (2004). *Mental Lexicon: Some Words to Talk about Words*. Nova Science Publishers.

Brown, A. (1991). A review of the *tip of the tongue* experience. *Psychological Bulletin*, 10, 204–223.

Brown, R. & Mc Neill, D. (1966). The tip of the tongue phenomenon. *Journal of Verbal Learning and Verbal Behavior*, 5: 325–337.

Burnard, L.; Aston, G. (1998): The BNC Handbook: Exploring the British National Corpus with Sara. Edinburgh: University Press.

Ceccato, S. (1956). La grammatiea insegnata alle machine. *Civiltà delle Machine*, Nos. 1 & 2.

Collins, A.M. & Quillian, M.R. (1969). Retrieval time from semantic memory. *Journal of verbal learning and verbal behavior* 8 (2): 240–247.

Collins, A.M. & Quillian, M.R. (1970). Does category size affect categorization time? *Journal of verbal learning and verbal behavior* 9 (4): 432–438.

Collins, A.M. & Loftus, E.F. (1975). A spreading-activation theory of semantic processing. *Psychological Review* 8.

Cramer, P. (1968). *Word Association*. Academic Press, New York.

Deese, J. (1965). The structure of associations in language and thought. Johns Hopkins Press. Baltimore

[9] As this is a bag-of-words approach which does not take syntax into account, of course we do not claim that such a vector can grasp all of a sentence's meaning.

[10] Note that gaps in dictionary coverage can be typically tolerated in such a setting as associations tend to be common words. That is, in principle the method allows to correctly translate words which are not in the dictionary. This is a property giving it some plausibility as a model for the cognitive processes underlying human translation.

Dutoit, D. and P. Nugues (2002): A lexical network and an algorithm to find words from definitions. In Frank van Harmelen (ed.): *ECAI2002, Proceedings of the 15th European Conference on Artificial Intelligence*, Lyon, 450–454.

Edmonds, D. (ed.), (1999). *The Oxford Reverse Dictionary*, Oxford University Press, Oxford, 1999.

El-Kahlout, I. D. and K. Oflazer. (2004). Use of Wordnet for Retrieving Words from Their Meanings. *Proceedings of the 2nd Global WordNet Conference*, Brno, 118–123.

Fellbaum, C. (1998). WordNet: An Electronic Lexical Database and some of its Applications. MIT Press.

Ferraresi, A.; Zanchetta, E.; Baroni M.; Bernardini, S. (2008). Introducing and evaluating ukWaC, a very large web-derived corpus of English. In: S. Evert, A. Kilgarriff and S. Sharoff (eds.): *Proceedings of the 4th Web as Corpus Workshop (WAC-4) – Can we beat Google?*, Marrakech.

Findler, N. (editor). (1979). Associative Networks: The Representation and Use of Knowledge by Computers. Academic Press, Inc., Orlando, FL, USA.

Fromkin V. (ed.). (1980). Errors in linguistic performance: Slips of the tongue, ear, pen and hand. New York: Academic Press.

Fromkin, V. (ed.) (1973): *Speech errors as linguistic evidence*. The Hague: Mouton Publishers

Kiss, G., Armstrong, C., Milroy, R. & Piper, J. (1973). An associative thesaurus of English and its computer analysis. In: A. Aitken, R. Beiley and N. Hamilton-Smith (eds.): *The Computer and Literary Studies*. Edinburgh: University Press.

Landauer, T.K.; Dumais, S.T. (1997). A solution to Plato's problem: The latent semantic analysis theory of acquisition, induction, and representation of knowledge. *Psychological Review* 104 (2), 211–240.

Lezius, W.; Rapp, R.; Wettler, M. (1998). A freely available morphology system, part-of-speech tagger, and context-sensitive lemmatizer for German. In: *Proceedings of COLING-ACL 1998,* Montreal, Vol. 2, 743–748.

Mandala, R., Tokunaga, T. & Tanaka, H. (1999). Complementing WordNet with Roget's and Corpus-based Thesauri for Information Retrieval. *Proceedings of EACL.*

Mann, W. C. Thompson, S. A. (1988). Rhetorical structure theory: Toward a functional theory of text organization. *Text* 8(3), 243–281.

Meyer, D.E. & Schvaneveldt, R.W. (1971). Facilitation in recognizing pairs of words: Evidence of a dependence between retrieval operations. *Journal of Experimental Psychology* 90: 227–234.

Michiels, A. (1982). Exploiting a Large Dictionary Database. *PhD Thesis, University of Liège*, mimeographed.

Mikolov, T.; Chen, K.; Corrado, G.; Dean, J. (2013a). Efficient estimation of word representations in vector space. *CoRR*, abs/1301.3781.

Mikolov, T.; Sutskever, I.; Chen, K.; Corrado, G.S.; Dean, J. (2013b). Distributed representations of words and phrases and their compositionality. *Advances in Neural Information Processing Systems*, 3111–3119.

Miller, G. A. (1995). WordNet : A lexical database for english. *Communications of the ACM*, 38 (11), 39–41.

Miller, G.A. (ed.) (1990): WordNet: An On-Line Lexical Database. *International Journal of Lexicography*, 3(4), 235–244.

Nogier, J.F. & Zock, M. (1992) Lexical choice by pattern matching. *Knowledge Based Systems*, Vol. 5, No 3, Butterworth.

Pantel, P.; Lin, D. (2002): Discovering Word Senses from Text. *Proceedings of ACM Conference on Knowledge Discovery and Data Mining (KDD-02).* Edmonton, Canada , 613–619.

Quillian, M. R. (1967). Word concepts: A theory and simulation of some basic semantic capabilities. *Behavioral Science*, 12(5), 410–430.

Quillian, M. R. (1968). Semantic memory. *Semantic Information Processing*, 227–270.

Quillian, M. R. (1969). The teachable language comprehender: a simulation program and theory of language. *Communications of the ACM*, 12(8), 459-476.

Quillian, R. (1963). A notation for representing conceptual information: An application to semantics and mechanical English paraphrasing. SP-1395, System Development Corporation, Santa Monica.

Quillian, R. (1966). *Semantic Memory*. Unpublished doctoral dissertation, Carnegie Institute of Technology.

Rapp, R. (1999). Automatic identification of word translations from unrelated English and German corpora. In: *Proceedings of the 37th Annual Meeting of the Association for Computational Linguistics 1999,* College Park, Maryland. 519–526.

Rapp, R. (2011). Language acquisition as the detection, memorization, and reproduction of statistical regularities in perceived language. *Journal of Cognitive Science*, Vol. 12, No. 3, 297–322.

Rapp, R. (2013). From stimulus to associations and back. Proceedings of the 10th Workshop on Natural Language Processing and Cognitive Science, Marseille, France.

Rapp, R. (2014). Corpus-based computation of reverse associations. Proceedings of the Ninth International Conference on Language Resources and Evaluation (LREC 2014), Reykjavik, Island.

Richens, R. H. (1956) Preprogramming for mechanical translation, *Mechanical Translation* 3 (1), 20–25.

Roget, P. (1852). Thesaurus of English Words and Phrases. Longman, London.

Schvaneveldt, R. (ed.) (1989). Pathfinder Associative Networks: studies in knowledge organization. Ablex. Norwood, New Jersey, US.

Simmons, R. (1963). Synthetic language behavior. *Data Processing Management* 5 (12): 11–18.

Sowa, John F. (1984). Conceptual Structures: Information Processing in Mind and Machine, Addison-Wesley, Reading, MA.

Sporns, O., Chialvo, D. R., Kaiser, M., & Hilgetag, C. C. (2004). Organization, development and function of complex brain networks. *Trends in Cognitive Sciences*, 8, 418–425.

Summers, D. (1993). Language Activator: the world's first production dictionary. Longman, London.

Vitevitch, M. (2008). What can graph theory tell us about word learning and lexical retrieval? *Journal of Speech, Language, and Hearing Research* , 51:408–422.

Wettler, M.; Rapp, R.; Sedlmeier, P. (2005). Free word associations correspond to contiguities between words in texts. *Journal of Quantitative Linguistics* 12(2), 111–122.

Zock, M. (2014). How to overcome the tip-of-the-tongue problem with the help of a computer. Proceedings *of CogALex-IV*, COLING, Dublin, Ireland

Zock, M.; Cristea, D. (2014). You shall find the target via its companion words: specification of tools and resources to overcome the tip-of-the-tongue problem. *Proceedings of the 11th International Workshop on Natural Language Processing and Cognitive Science (NLPCS)*, Venice.

Zock, M.; Ferret, O.; Schwab, D. (2010). Deliberate word access : an intuition, a roadmap and some preliminary empirical results. *International Journal of Speech Technology*, 13(4), 107–117.

A Two-Stage Approach for Computing Associative Responses to a Set of Stimulus Words

Urmi Ghosh, Sambhav Jain and Soma Paul
Language Technologies Research Center
IIIT-Hyderabad, India
{urmi.ghosh, sambhav.jain}@research.iiit.ac.in,
soma@iiit.ac.in

Abstract

This paper describes the system submitted by the IIIT-H team for the CogALex-2014 shared task on multiword association. The task involves generating a ranked list of responses to a set of stimulus words. The two-stage approach combines the strength of neural network based word embeddings and frequency based association measures. The system achieves an accuracy of 34.9% over the test set.

1 Introduction

Research in psychology gives evidence that word associations reveal the respondents' perception, learning and verbal memories and thus determine language production. Hence, it is possible to simulate human derived word associations by analyzing the statistical distribution of words in a corpus. Church and Hanks (1990) and Wettler and Rapp (1989) were amongst the first to devise association measures by utilizing frequencies and co-occurrences from large corpora. Wettler and Rapp (1993) demonstrate that corpus-based computations of word associations are similar to association norms collected from human subjects.

The CogALex-2014 shared task on multi-word association involves generating a ranked list of response words for a given set of stimulus words. For example, the stimulus word *bank* can invoke associative responses such as *river*, *loan*, *finance* and *money*. Priming[1] *bank* with *bed* and *bridge*, results in strengthening association with the word *river* and it emerges as the best response amongst the aforementioned response choices. This task is motivated by the tip-of-the-tongue problem, where associated concepts from the memory can help recall the target word. Other practical applications include query expansion for information retrieval and natural language generation where missing words can be predicted from their context.

The participating systems are distinguished into two categories - *Unrestricted* systems that allows usage of any kind of data and *Restricted* systems that can only make use of the *ukWaC* (Baroni et al., 2009) corpus, consisting of two billion tokens. Our proposed system falls in the *restricted* track since we only used *ukWaC* for extracting information on word associations. It follows a two-staged approach: *Candidate Response Generation*, which involves selection of words that are semantically similar to the primes and *Re-ranking by Association Measure*, that re-ranks the responses using a proposed weighted Pointwise Mutual Information ($wPMI$) measure. Our system was evaluated on test-datasets derived from the Edinburgh Associative Thesaurus (Kiss et al., 1972) and it achieved an accuracy of 34.9%. When ignoring the inflectional variations of the response word, an accuracy of 39.55% was achieved.

2 Observations on Training Data

The training set consists of 2000 sets of five words (multiword stimuli or primes) and the word that is most closely associated to all of them (associative response). For example, a set of primes such as *wheel*, *driver*, *bus*, *drive* and *lorry* are given along with the expected associative response - *car*.

In this section, our initial observations on the given training data are enlisted.

[1]The phenomenon of providing multiple stimulus words is called *priming*.

Zock/Rapp/Huang (eds.): Proceedings of the 4th Workshop on Cognitive Aspects of the Lexicon, pages 15–21,
Dublin, Ireland, August 23, 2014.

2.1 Relation between the Associative Response and the Prime Words

It is observed that a response largely exhibits two kind of relations with a priming word.

Primes	Associative Response
presents, Christmas, birthday, shops, present	gifts
butterfly, light, ball, fly, insect	moth
mouse, cat, catcher, race, tail	rat

Table 1: Some examples of primes and their associative responses from the training set

Type A relation depicts a synonymous/antonymous behavior or "of the same kind" nature. Word pairs with paradigmatic relation are highly semantically related and belong to the same part of speech. And hence, they tend to show a substitutive nature amongst themselves without affecting the grammar of the sentence. From Table - 1, we observe that *present/presents* , *butterfly/insect* and *mouse/cat* can be substituted in place of *gifts*, *moth* and *rat* respectively. *Type B* relation depicts contextual co-occurrence, where the words tend to occur together or form a collocation. This kind of relationship can be demonstrated by taking examples from Table - 1, such as *Christmas gifts*, *gift shops*, *birthday gifts*, *moth ball*, *rat catcher*, *rat race* and *rat tail*. In theory, the above have been formally categorized as paradigmatic (*Type A*) and syntagmatic (*Type B*) relations by De Saussure et al. (1916) and we will be referring to them accordingly in rest of the paper.

Type C relation, depicting associations based on the phonological component of the words was also observed. According to McCarthy (1990), responses can be affected by phonological shapes and orthographic patterns especially when instantaneous paradigmatic or syntagmatic association is difficult. Examples from the training data set include *ajar-Ajax*, *hypothalamus-hippopotamus* and *cravat-caravan*. Such examples were very few and hence, have not been dealt with in this paper.

2.2 Context Window Size

Words exhibiting syntagmatic associations often occur in close proximity in the corpus. We tested this phenomenon on 500 randomly chosen sets of primes by calculating the distance of each prime from the associative responses in the corpus. Figure - 1 testifies that a majority of primes occur within a context window size of ± 2 from the associative response.

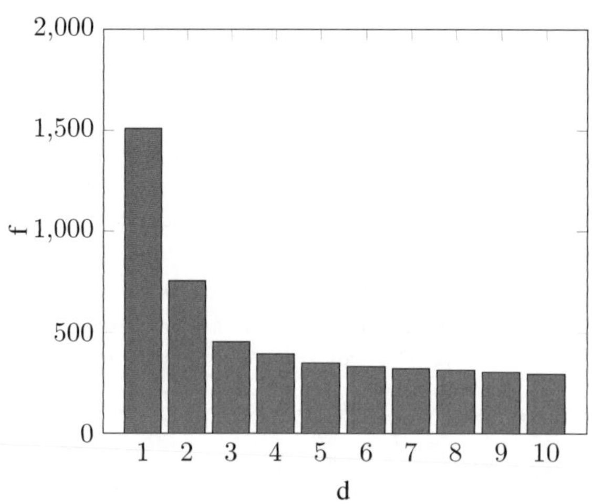

Figure 1: Co-occurrence frequency *f* of an association at distance *d* from the response, averaged over the 2500 stimulus word and response word pairs from randomly chosen 500 training datasets

Next, a mechanism to interpret the above associations in a quantitative manner is required.

3 Word Representation

In order to have a quantitative comparison of association, first we need a representation for words in a context. Traditionally co-occurrence vectors serve as a simple mechanism for such a representation. However, such vectors are unable to effectively capture deeper semantics of words and also tend to suffer from sparsity due to high dimensional space (equal to the vocabulary size). Several efforts have been made to represent word vectors in a lower dimensional space. Largely, these can be categorized into:

1. **Clustering**: Clustering algorithms like Brown et al. (1992), are used to form clusters and derive a vector based representation for each cluster, where semantically similar clusters are closer in distance.

2. **Topic Modeling**: In this approach a word (or a document) is represented as a distribution of topics. Latent Semantic Analysis (LSA) (Deerwester et al., 1990; Landauer and Dutnais, 1997) , which falls in this category, utilizes SVD (Singular Value Decomposition) to produce a low rank representation of a word. Latent Dirichlet Allocation (Blei et al., 2003) is an improvement with dirichlet priors over the probabilistic version of LSA (Hofmann, 1999).

3. **Neural Network based Word Embeddings**: Here, a neural network is trained to output a vector corresponding to a word which effectively signifies its position in the semantic space. There has been different suggestions on the nature of the neural-net and how the context needs to be fed to the neural-net. Some notable works include Collobert and Weston (2008), Mnih and Hinton (2008), Turian et al. (2010) and Mikolov et al. (2013a).

4 Methodology

Our system follows a two-staged approach, where we first generate response candidates which are semantically similar to prime words, followed by a re-ranking step where we give weightage to the responses likely to occur in proximity.

4.1 Candidate Response Generation

The complete vocabulary (of *ukWaC* Corpus) is represented in a semantic space by generating word embeddings induced by the algorithm described in Mikolov et al. (2013a). Our choice is motivated by the fact that this approach models semantic similarity and outperforms other approaches in terms of accuracy as well as computational efficiency(Mikolov et al., 2013a; Mikolov et al., 2013c).

The *word2vec*[2] utility is used to learn this model and thereby create 300-dimensional word embeddings. *word2vec* implements two classification networks - the Skip-gram architecture and the Continuous Bag-of-words (CBOW) architecture. We applied CBOW architecture as it works better on large corpora and is significantly faster than Skip-gram(Mikolov et al., 2013b). The CBOW architecture predicts the current word based on its context. The architecture employs a feed forward neural network, which consists of:

1. An *input layer*, where the context words are fed to the network.
2. A *projection layer*, which projects words onto continuous space and reduces number of parameters that are needed to be estimated.
3. An *output layer*.

This log-linear classifier learns to predict words based on its neighbors in a window of ± 5. We also applied a minimum word count of 25 so that infrequent words are filtered out.

With the vector representation available, a response r to a set of primes S, is searched in the vocabulary by measuring its cosine similarity with each prime x_i in S. The overall similarity of the response r, with the prime word set S, is defined as the average of these similarities.

[2] *word2vec* : https://code.google.com/p/word2vec/

$$sim(r,S) = \frac{1}{|S|} \times \sum_{i=1}^{|S|} \frac{x_i.r}{|x_i|.|r|}$$

Using the best similarity score as the selection criterion for response, the approach resulted in an accuracy of 20.8% over the test set. Error analysis revealed that the above approach is biased towards finding a paradigmatic candidate. However, it is further observed that much of the correct answers ($> 80\%$) exist in a k-best(k=500) list but with a relatively lower similarity score. This confirmed that our broader selection is correct but a better re-ranking approach is required.

4.2 Re-ranking by Association Measures

To give due weightage to responses with high syntagmatic associativity, we utilize word co-occurrences from the corpus. Since we are dealing with semantically related candidates, applying even a basic lexical association measure like Pointwise Mutual Information (PMI) (Church and Hanks, 1990) tend to improve the results.

PMI

For each prime word, we calculate co-occurrence frequency information for its neighbors within a window of ± 2 as mentioned in Section 2. Also, a threshold of 3 is set to the observed frequency measures as PMI tends to give very high association score to infrequent words.

For each candidate response r, we calculate its PMI_i with each of the primes (x_i) in the set S. The total association score $Score_{PMI}$ for a candidate is defined as the average of the individual measures.

$$PMI_i = \frac{p(x_i r)}{p(x_i)p(r)} \qquad\qquad Score_{PMI} = \frac{1}{|S|} \times \sum_{i \in S} PMI_i$$

Ranking the candidates based on PMI improved the results to 30.45%

Weighted PMI

It should be duly noted that only some primes exhibit a syntagmatic relation with the response, while the rest exhibit a paradigmatic relation. For example, the expected response for primes *Avenue*, *column*, *dimension*, *sixth*, *fourth* is *fifth*. The first three words share a syntagmatic relation with the response while the last two words share a paradigmatic relation with the response. As PMI deals with word co-occurrences, ideally, only primes exhibiting syntagmatic associations should be considered for re-ranking. However, a clear distinction between the two categories of primes is a difficult task as the target response is unknown.

In order to take effective contribution of each prime, we propose a weighed extension of PMI which gives more weightage to syntagmatic primes as to the paradigmatic ones. Since, primes sharing a paradigmatic relation with the response word are highly semantically related, they are expected to be closer in the semantic space too. On the other hand, the primes showcasing syntagmatic relations are expected to be distant.

Using the vector representation described in Section 4.1, we calculate an average vector of the five primes, p_{avg}, and compute its cosine distance from individual primes. The cosine distance thus obtained is used as the weight w for the PMI associativity of a prime. In a nutshell, larger the distance of a prime from p_{avg}, the greater is its contribution in the PMI based re-ranking score. This ranking schema assumes that the prime set consists of at least two words demonstrating paradigmatic relation with the target response. Table - 2 displays the primes along with their distance from p_{avg}.

$$Score_{wPMI} = \frac{1}{|S|} \times \sum_{i \in S} w_i PMI_i$$

Next, a ranked list of candidate responses for each set is generated by sorting the previously ranked list according to the new score. The new ranking scheme based on weighted PMI ($wPMI$) improves the results to 34.9%. Table -3 displays some sets which show improvement upon implementing the $wPMI$

Primes	Cosine Distance
Avenue	0.612
column	0.422
dimension	0.390
sixth	0.270
fourth	0.212

Table 2: An example demonstrating Cosine Distance between the primes and the p_{avg} of the prime set

ranking scheme. Taking a case from Table - 3, we observe that the correct response *skeleton* is generated for primes *cupboard, body, skull, bone* and *bones* when ranked according to the $wPMI$ scheme. This is due to larger weights being assigned to primes *cupboard* and *body* which have a closer proximity to the word *skeleton* than the word *vertebral* which is generated by the simple PMI ranking scheme.

Primes(with weights)	cupboard	0.615	pit	0.553	boat	0.499
	body	0.410	band	0.549	sailing	0.476
	skull	0.248	hand	0.426	drab	0.338
	bone	0.244	limb	0.0.340	dark	0.318
	bones	0.172	leg	0.270	dull	0.307
PMI	vertebral		amputated		drizzly	
$wPMI$	skeleton		arm		dingy	
Expected Response	skeleton		arm		dingy	

Table 3: Comparison between results from PMI and wPMI re-ranking approaches

5 Results and Evaluation

The system was evaluated on the test set derived from the Edinburgh Associative Thesaurus (EAT) which lists the associations to thousands of English stimulus words as collected from native speakers. For example, for the stimulus word *visual* the top associations are *aid, eyes, aids, see, eye, seen* and *sight.* For the shared task, top five associations for 2000 randomly selected stimulus words were provided as prime sets and the system was evaluated based on its ability to predict the corresponding stimulus word for each set. Table - 4 displays the top ten responses generated by our system for some prime sets and their corresponding stimulus word.

Primes	*knight, plate, soldier, protection, sword*	*ants, flies, fly, bees, bite*	*babies, baby, rash, wet, washing*	*butterfly, moth, caterpillar, cocoon, insect*
Top 10 Responses	armor armour helmet shield guard bulletproof guards warrior enemy gallant	mosquitoes wasps beetles insects spiders sting moths butterflies arachnids bedbugs	nappy shaving nappies clothes skin bathing dry eczema bedding dirty	larva larvae pupa species pests beetle silkworm wings pupate pollinated
Target	*armour*	*insects*	*nappies*	*chrysalis*

Table 4: Top ten responses for some prime sets and their corresponding target response

As we have considered exact string match(ignoring capitalization), the evaluation does not account for spelling variations. For example, the response output *armor* instead of the expected response *armour* results in counting it as incorrect.

We achieved an accuracy of 34.9% by considering the top response for each list of ranked responses. However, it was observed that the correct response was present within the top ten responses in 59.8% of the cases. For example, the primes *ants, flies, fly, bees, bite* generate the response output *mosquitoes*. The expected output *insects* ranks 4th in our list of responses.

For primes *babies, baby, rash, wet, washing*, our system outputs *nappy* while the expected response is *nappies*. Such inflected forms of the responses are challenging to predict and hence, another evaluation is presented which ignores the inflectional variation of the response word. Under this evaluation, we achieved an accuracy of 39.55% for the best response and 63.15% if the expected response occurs in the top ten responses. Table - 5 displays accuracy of our system when the target response lies within the top-n responses for both evaluation methods.

	Exact Match	**Ignoring Inflections**
n=**1**	34.9	39.55
n=**3**	48.15	49.65
n=**5**	53.2	55.45
n=**10**	59.8	63.15

Table 5: Evaluation results in %

6 Conclusion

There exist some word associations that are *asymmetric* in nature. Rapp (2013) observed that the primary response of a given stimulus word may have stronger association with another word and need not generate the stimulus word back. For example, the strongest association to *bitter* is *sweet* but the strongest association to *sweet* is *sour*. Therefore, the EAT data set chosen for evaluation, may not be the best judge for certain cases. Taking a case from our test data, for primes *butterfly, moth, caterpillar, cocoon, insect*, our system outputs *larva* instead of the original stimulus word *chrysalis* which does not feature even in the top ten responses (Refer Table - 4).

In this work, we proposed a system to generate a ranked list of responses for multiple stimulus words. Candidate responses were generated by computing its semantic similarity with the stimulus words and then re-ranked using a lexical association measure, PMI. This system scored 34.9% when the top ranked response was considered and 59.8% when the top ten responses were taken into account. When ignoring inflectional variations, the accuracy improved to 39.55% and 63.15% for the two evaluation methods respectively.

In future, a more sophisticated re-ranking approach in place of PMI measure can be used such as product-of-rank algorithm (Rapp, 2008). Since, the re-ranking methodologies discussed by far, take into account word co-occurrences, it is biased towards syntagmatic responses. A better trade-off can be worked out to give due weightage to paradigmatic responses too.

References

Marco Baroni, Silvia Bernardini, Adriano Ferraresi, and Eros Zanchetta. 2009. The wacky wide web: a collection of very large linguistically processed web-crawled corpora. *Language resources and evaluation*, 43(3):209–226.

David M. Blei, Andrew Y. Ng, and Michael I. Jordan. 2003. Latent dirichlet allocation. *the Journal of machine Learning research*, 3:993–1022.

Peter F. Brown, Peter V. Desouza, Robert L. Mercer, Vincent J. Della Pietra, and Jenifer C. Lai. 1992. Class-based n-gram models of natural language. *Computational linguistics*, 18(4):467–479.

Kenneth Ward Church and Patrick Hanks. 1990. Word association norms, mutual information, and lexicography. *Comput. Linguist.*, 16(1):22–29, March.

Ronan Collobert and Jason Weston. 2008. A unified architecture for natural language processing: Deep neural networks with multitask learning. In *Proceedings of the 25th international conference on Machine learning*, pages 160–167. ACM.

Ferdinand De Saussure, Charles Bally, Albert Sechehaye, and Albert Riedlinger. 1916. *Cours de linguistique générale: Publié par Charles Bally et Albert Sechehaye avec la collaboration de Albert Riedlinger*. Libraire Payot & Cie.

Scott Deerwester, Susan T. Dumais, George W. Furnas, Thomas K. Landauer, and Richard Harshman. 1990. Indexing by latent semantic analysis. *JOURNAL OF THE AMERICAN SOCIETY FOR INFORMATION SCIENCE*, 41(6):391–407.

Thomas Hofmann. 1999. Probabilistic latent semantic analysis. In *Proceedings of the Fifteenth conference on Uncertainty in artificial intelligence*, pages 289–296. Morgan Kaufmann Publishers Inc.

George R. Kiss, Christine A. Armstrong, and Robert Milroy. 1972. *An associative thesaurus of English*. Medical Research Council, Speech and Communication Unit, University of Edinburgh, Scotland.

Thomas K. Landauer and Susan T. Dutnais. 1997. A solution to platos problem: The latent semantic analysis theory of acquisition, induction, and representation of knowledge. *Psychological review*, pages 211–240.

Michael McCarthy. 1990. *Vocabulary*. Oxford University Press.

Tomas Mikolov, Kai Chen, Greg Corrado, and Jeffrey Dean. 2013a. Efficient estimation of word representations in vector space. *CoRR*, abs/1301.3781.

Tomas Mikolov, Quoc V. Le, and Ilya Sutskever. 2013b. Exploiting similarities among languages for machine translation. *arXiv preprint arXiv:1309.4168*.

Tomas Mikolov, Wen-tau Yih, and Geoffrey Zweig. 2013c. Linguistic regularities in continuous space word representations. *Proceedings of NAACL-HLT*, pages 746–751.

Andriy Mnih and Geoffrey E. Hinton. 2008. A scalable hierarchical distributed language model. In *NIPS*, pages 1081–1088.

Reinhard Rapp. 2008. The computation of associative responses to multiword stimuli. In *Proceedings of the workshop on Cognitive Aspects of the Lexicon*, pages 102–109. Association for Computational Linguistics.

Reinhard Rapp. 2013. From stimulus to associations and back. *Natural Language Processing and Cognitive Science*, page 78.

Joseph Turian, Lev Ratinov, and Yoshua Bengio. 2010. Word representations: a simple and general method for semi-supervised learning. In *Proceedings of the 48th Annual Meeting of the Association for Computational Linguistics*, pages 384–394. Association for Computational Linguistics.

Manfred Wettler and Reinhard Rapp. 1989. A connectionist system to simulate lexical decisions in information retrieval. *Pfeifer, R., Schreter, Z., Fogelman, F. Steels, L.(eds.), Connectionism in perspective. Amsterdam: Elsevier*, 463:469.

Manfred Wettler and Reinhard Rapp. 1993. Computation of word associations based on the co-occurrences of words in large corpora.

Deep Learning from Web-Scale Corpora for Better Dictionary Interfaces

Pavel Smrz
Brno University of Technology
Faculty of Information Technology
Bozetechova 2, 612 66 Brno
Czech Republic
smrz@fit.vutbr.cz

Lubomir Otrusina
Brno University of Technology
Faculty of Information Technology
Bozetechova 2, 612 66 Brno
Czech Republic
iotrusina@fit.vutbr.cz

Abstract

This paper explores advanced learning mechanisms – neural networks trained by the Word2Vec method – for predicting word associations. We discuss how the approach can be built into dictionary interfaces to help tip-of-the-tongue searches. We also describe our contribution to the CogALex 2014 shared task. We argue that the reverse response-stimulus word associations chosen for the shared task are only mildly related to the motivation idea of the lexical access support system. The methods employed in our contribution are briefly introduced. We present results of experiments with various parameter settings and show what improvement can be expected if more than one answer is allowed. The paper concludes with a proposal for a new collective effort to assemble real tip-of-the-tongue situation records for future, more-realistic evaluations.

1 Introduction

Human memory is fundamentally associative. To focus just on lexical access issues, it is often the case that people cannot immediately recall a word expressing a specific concept but they can give one or more words referring to concepts associated with the desired one in their minds. The failure to retrieve a word from memory, combined with partial recall and the feeling that retrieval is imminent, is generally referred to as the tip-of-the-tongue phenomenon (TOT), sometimes called presque vu (Brown, 1991).

Before one starts to think about automatic means supporting the lexical access, it is important to distinguish various situations in which TOT appears. First, the personal state of the language producer (writer/speaker) plays a crucial role. Fatigue or lack of attention can increase frequency of TOT situations. Specific problems come with mild cognitive impairments (incipient dementia) which is more frequent in elders. The communication mode (written or spoken language) also needs to be taken into account – it often helps to recollect an intended word if one just says associated words aloud. Consequently, people can prefer expressing the hesitation over a TOT word as a question to a family member, a friend or an automatic assistant. The spoken communication generally brings longer, more specific and detailed clues that can potentially lead to better identification of the word to be reminded. The language (mother tongue v. foreign language) and producer's familiarity and proficiency also need to be considered. Language learners would frequently associate a word with others that sound similar but are not related semantically, they could combine clues in their native language and the target one, misspell/mispronounce words, etc. Although the search across languages is not typically considered as a kind of the TOT phenomenon, we include this situation in the considered scenario.

Research prototypes of automatic assistants have to consider the above-mentioned settings and clearly identify in what types of TOT they can help. The primary decision a tool designer needs to make relates to the appropriate interface. The ultimate goal of the work described in this paper consists in integrating a TOT-aware assistants into natural user interfaces. Rather than on a desktop or tablet computer with a standard keyboard or (hand)written input, we focus on smart-phones or even wearable interfaces (smart watches, glasses), intelligent home/office infrastructure components, or robotic companions that can communicate in natural (spoken) language and that help users in their language producing tasks.

Zock/Rapp/Huang (eds.): Proceedings of the 4th Workshop on Cognitive Aspects of the Lexicon, pages 22–30,
Dublin, Ireland, August 23, 2014.

Although the current research deals strictly with explicitly expressed requests for a TOT-situation help, there is a possibility of automatic detection of TOT-related hesitations and immediate generation of word suggestions. In any case, the state of the art on this topic is at the beginning and these types of automatic assistants are mostly research prototypes.

To be able to evaluate the ongoing development work, the first author of this paper started to document and collect real TOT events. This includes personal experiences but also cases appearing during his communication with colleagues, family members, etc. In a relatively short time of three months, 19 documented cases were recorded. This shows that a collective effort in this area could easily lead to a new reasonably-large resource that would help to direct future research (see the concluding section). As we aim at a general TOT setting, the collected data include full descriptions of the clues, not just keyword-based TOT searches. For written-only interfaces, we provide a list of extracted keywords too. Thus, there would the full sentence: *It is like racism but on women* (the correct answer – *discrimination*) and the set of two keywords – *racism, women* – for the written case.

Although its current limited size does not allow deriving statistically-significant results (only 3 out of 19 TOT cases can be correctly retrieved by our method if we allow 4 suggestions), the resource can be used to demonstrate crucial differences between the task of TOT- and reverse-association predictions (see the next section).

In addition to this discussion, the paper presents methods used for the stimulus-response association prediction submitted as our contribution to the CogALex 2014 shared task and their results. Section 3 introduces the methods, while Section 4 summarizes results under varying parameters. We conclude with future directions of our research and a proposal for a joint TOT-related activity.

2 Related Work

There is a long-term interest in intelligent dictionary interfaces that reflect natural lexical-access needs. Yet, advanced mechanisms of the access by meaning are rarely implemented as their integration presents significant challenges. Zock and Bilac (2004) discuss lookup mechanisms on the basis of word associations. Sinopalnikova and Smrz (2004) introduce lexical access-supporting dictionary enhancements based on various language resources – corpora, Wordnets, explanatory dictionaries and word association norms.

Free-word associations are frequently used as testing data for word relatedness experiments. Church and Hanks (1990) estimate word associations by a corpus-based association ratio. Word association thesauri or norms, representing a collection of empirical data obtained through large-scale psycholinguistic free-association tests, often define a gold standard. In particular, Zesch and Gurevych (2007) employ the University of South Florida word association, rhyme, and word fragment norms (Nelson et al., 1998) to compare characteristics of its graph representation to that of Wikipedia. Rapp (2008) experiments with associative responses to multiword stimuli on the Edinburgh Associative Thesaurus.

The CogALex 2014 shared task is very close to the experimental setting discussed in (Rapp, 2013) which also aims at computing a stimulus word leading to responses given in EAT. A fixed-window size to count word co-occurrences is used first. Log-likelihood ratios are employed to rank candidate words and products of the ranks then define the winner. Providing 7 responses (as compared to 5 in the CogALex 2014 shared task), the stimulus word is predicted with 54 % accuracy. However, only a specific subset (Kent and Rosanoff, 1910) of EAT is used which comprises 100 words. It is also not fully clear from which set of potential words target answers are chosen. This is a crucial aspect that influences accuracy. For example, Rapp (2014) took into account only primary associative responses from EAT, i. e,. only 2,792 words. Obviously, it is far simpler to choose the correct answer from a limited set than from all existing words.

Other word association resources are also frequently used as test data. In addition to the Wordnet itself, they include TOEFL (Landauer and Dumais, 1997) and ESL synonym questions (Turney, 2001), RG-65 (Rubenstein and Goodenough, 1965) and WordSimilarity-353 (Finkelstein et al., 2001) test collections for degree of synonymy or SAT analogy questions (Turney et al., 2003) for the relational similarity.

Additionaly, Heath et al. (2013) evaluate their association model in word guessing games (games with a purpose).

3 Free word associations v. TOT – similarities and differences

The CogALex 2014 shared task was motivated by natural lexical access but it was defined as computing reversed free-word associations. Participating automatic systems were employed to determine the most probable stimulus leading to given five most frequent responses from a free association test. For example, given words *circus*, *funny*, *nose*, *fool*, and *fun*, participating systems were supposed to compute word *clown* as the answer.

Training and test datasets came from the Edinburgh Associative Thesaurus (EAT)[1] (Kiss et al., 1972). EAT comprises about 100 associative responses given by British students for each of 8,400 stimuli. Items containing multi-word units and non-alphabetical characters were filtered out from the CogALex 2014 experimental data.

Although it has been shown that free word association norms and thesauri provide a valuable source of information for TOT-assisting (Sinopalnikova and Smrz, 2006), the two corresponding phenomena are not identical. Indeed, available data and experience clearly point out similarities but also significant differences.

Both, individual free associations as well as TOT can be full of idiosyncrasies. However, while association norms and thesauri try to present prototypical, generalized, most frequent associations, TOT assistants need to cope with personal specificity. Ideally, a system should be able to help its user remind a word given the clue *it was mentioned by Mary during our yesterday's conversation*.

Both the phenomena are also strongly culturally-dependent. Among others, this can make some resources such as large-scale corpora for particular language variants unusable. For example, let us consider the very first item from the CogALex test set – word *capable* is to be guessed as the stimulus for responses *able, incapable, brown, clever, good*. Putting aside the first two response words sharing their roots with the stimulus for a while (see the related discussion below), we come to word *brown*. This refers to *Lancelot Brown*, more commonly known as *Capability Brown* – an 18th century English landscape architect. This association is specific for the U.K. and it is hardly known to Americans. For example, the two words never collocate in the 450 million Corpus of Contemporary American English (COCA)[2], while *Capability Brown* is mentioned 36 times in the 100 million British National Corpus (BNC)[3].

This observation led us to the question what is the overlap between two distinct word association thesauri/norms. To explore this, we compared EAT to the University of South Florida Word Association Norm (SFWAN)[4] (Nelson et al., 1998). SFWAN consists of 5,019 normed words and their 72,176 responses. EAT and SFWAN have 3,545 stimulus terms in common. There are 11,788 words used as one or more responses in both the sets. Despite the substantial overlap of the stimulus and response sets, responses for same stimulus words in SFWAN rarely correspond to those given in EAT. Using a simple algorithm of the highest overlap among response sets, only 106 stimuli from the CogALex test set (out of 2,000) can be correctly determined from SFWAN. It can be partially explained by the cultural differences between the U.K. and the U.S.A., but also by relatively distant times of collecting/publishing the resources (1972 v. 1998), slightly different settings of the experiments and non-uniform presentation of the results. In any case, this finding casts doubts upon suitability of EAT for the shared task if no available (large) corpus data reflects the time and the setting of corresponding word association experiments (reflecting the background of students in 1972).

It can be also argued that observed associations corresponding to TOT clue words are of different nature than (reversed) free-word associations. Definitely, numbers of given clues vary, sometimes, there are two or three words only, sometimes, there are full sentences giving more than 5 keywords to associate

[1] `http://www.eat.rl.ac.uk/`
[2] `http://corpus.byu.edu/coca/`
[3] `http://www.natcorp.ox.ac.uk/`
[4] `http://web.usf.edu/FreeAssociation/`

with. Spoken clues also frequently explicitly state the kind of relation of the search word to a clue (e.g., *it is an opposite to..., it is used for...*).

Subjects are usually instructed to give the first response in their mind to the stimulus in free word association tests. On the other hand, TOT clues are usually related to the searched word in much more subtle way. At least, it is usually enough to mention any word of the same root/stem as a candidate and the subject finds the word in TOT situations. Thus, testing free associations such as *choler-cholera, capable-incapable, misuse-abuse, actor-actress* is completely irrelevant for vocabulary access problems.

Native speakers have usually no problem to retrieve a word from memory if it forms a part of an idiom and the other part of the idiom is suggested. Thus, predicting either word of *tooth a nail* is not relevant for TOT situations (in any language that lexicalizes Latin *dentibus et vnguibus*). Considering lexical access in a foreign language, the reason for the same conclusion can be opposite – an idiom can be unknown to a learner so that it is not probable that a part will be given as a clue.

In languages naturally conceptualizing different parts of speech, writers or speakers always know what word category they search for. The collected data as well as intuition also suggest that TOT clues would not mix various senses of a word to be recalled. Consequently, free associations such as *stage – theatre/coach* or *March – April/Hare* have also nothing to do with TOT.

4 Methods

This section introduces methods used to compute multi-word reversed associations in our experiments. The primary method applied in the submitted system takes advantage of deep learning from web-scale corpora. To be sure that computed word associations automatically derived from large textual data cannot be matched by those resulting from a manually created resource, associations predicted by various Wordnet-based measures were also considered.

The Word2Vec technique[5] available in Python package GenSim[6] (Řehůřek and Sojka, 2010) was primarily utilized to predict a stimulus word from a list of most frequent responses. Word2Vec defines an efficient way to work with continuous bag-of-word (CBOW) and skip-gram (SG) architectures computing vector representations from very large data sets (Mikolov et al., 2013). The CBOW and SG approaches are both based on distributed representations of words learned by neural networks. The CBOW architecture predicts a current word based on contexts, while the SG algorithm predicts surrounding words given a current word. Mikolov et al. (2013) showed that the SG algorithm achieves better accuracies in tested cases. We have therefore applied only this architecture in our experiments. Various parameters of the training model need to be set – the dimensionality of feature vectors, the maximum distance between a current and a predicted word within a sentence or the initial learning rate. Consequently, we built various instances of the stimulus predictor varying values of the parameters. Their detailed evaluation is given in the next section.

The CogALex 2014 shared task was divided into two categories. Unrestricted systems could use any kind of data to compute results, while restricted systems were allowed only to draw on the freely available UKWaC corpus (Ferraresi et al., 2008) in order to predict word associations. We implemented systems for both the categories. Our unrestricted system employs the ClueWeb12 corpus.[7] UKWaC comprises about 2 billion words and has size of about 30 GB (including annotations). The ClueWeb12 dataset consists of more than 733 million English web pages (collected between February and May 2012). The size of the complete ClueWeb12 data is 1.95 TB. To speed-up the process of training, only a fraction of the ClueWeb12 dataset was used to compute the Word2Vec models. It consists of about 8.7 billion words and has size of 131 GB. The ClueWeb12 data was pre-processed by removing web-page boilerplates and content duplication. The original UKWaC dataset already contains POS and lemma annotations. TreeTagger[8] was used to produce the same input for the ClueWeb12 dataset. Some models were created from identified lemmata rather than individual tokens.

[5]https://code.google.com/p/Word2Vec/

[6]http://radimrehurek.com/gensim/

[7]http://lemurproject.org/clueweb12/

[8]http://www.cis.uni-muenchen.de/~schmid/tools/TreeTagger/

We took advantage of the nltk[9] toolkit to experiment with Wordnet-based measures. A candidate list of all possible Wordnet-related words that could be considered as potential stimuli was computed for each of five given responses first. The word with the highest sum of similarities to all five response words was returned as the best stimulus candidate.

To populate the set of all possibly related words, standard Wordnet relations (Fellbaum, 1998) were considered – hypernyms/hyponyms, instances, holonyms/meronyms (including members and substances), attributes, entailments, causes, verb groups, see-also and similar-to relations. As the similarity measures, we used the path similarity based on the shortest path that connects the senses in the is-a (hypernym/hyponym) taxonomy, Wu-Palmer's similarity (Wu and Palmer, 1994) based on the depth of word/sense pairs in the taxonomy and that of their Least Common Subsumer, Leacock-Chodorow's similarity (Leacock and Chodorow, 1998) based on the shortest path that connects the senses (as above) and the maximum depth of the taxonomy in which the senses occur, Resnik's similarity (Resnik, 1995) based on the Information Content (IC) of the least common subsumer, Jiang-Conrath' similarity (Jiang and Conrath, 1997) based on the Information Content (IC) of the least common subsumer and that of the two input synsets and Lin's Similarity (Lin, 1998) based on the Information Content (IC) of the least common subsumer and that of the two input synsets.

5 Evaluation

5.1 Word2Vec approach

There are various parameters to tune up when creating the models for the SG algorithm. We experimented with three of them – values *100*, *300* and *500* were tested as dimensionalities of feature vectors, values *3*, *5* and *7* for maximum distances between current and predicted words within a sentence, and the lemmatization was switched on or off. Value *word* means that original lowercased tokens were used for the computation of models, whereas value *lemma* means we used lowercased lemmata corresponding to original words. Resulting models are named accordingly: *size-window-token* (e.g., *100-3-lemma*, *500-3-word*), where *size* denotes the dimensionality of the feature vectors, *window* the maximum distance between the current and a predicted word within a sentence and *token* determines whether original words or lemmata were used for a given model. We restricted the parameters to these values mainly to cope with computational requirements. Although the Word2Vec toolkit supports multi-threaded computation, it took significant time to build all the models. For example, 60 hours in 8 threads were needed to compute the *500-7-lemma* model for the ClueWeb12 data. Although higher values for *size* and *window* parameters would probably bring better accuracies, they were not tested due to time constraints. Results for various combinations of parameters are summarized in Table 1.

EAT sometimes gives inflectional variants of words (e.g., plurals) as stimuli or responses. A strict evaluation comparing exact strings can then harm systems that do not try to match particular wordforms. To quantify the effect we compared results of our system on two versions of the test sets expanded target word lists which allow all wordforms for each target word[10] and the original lists. Results are given in Table 1 in columns denoted *inflectional* in the case of the expanded lists and *non-inflectional* for the original data.

As can be seen, model *500-5-lemma* reaches the best accuracy for the unrestricted task and models *300-7-word* and *500-5-word* win in the restricted task. As only one set of results was allowed to be submitted for each task, we employed the *500-5-word* model in our submission.

Although, the CogALex 2014 shared task was defined as to predict exactly one stimulus word for five given responses, lexical access helpers can easily accommodate more suggestions. This can be evaluated by checking how frequently a gold standard stimulus appears among top n predicted words. Figures 1 and 2 compare results of our unrestricted and restricted systems, respectively, for up to 10 suggestions (the inflectional case). As expected, the accuracy increases with the number of candidate words taken into account. The best value of 0.4865 for the unrestricted system is reached using model *500-5-lemma*, while the best accuracy of 0.4575 for the restricted system comes from model *500-7-word*.

[9] `http://www.nltk.org/`

[10] Provided by Michael Flor and Beata Beigman Klebanov (ETS Princeton).

model	non-inflectional		inflectional	
	unrestricted	restricted	unrestricted	restricted
100-3-lemma	0.11	0.083	0.1215	0.0865
100-3-word	0.1005	0.098	0.11	0.1015
100-5-lemma	0.1055	0.1	0.1165	0.1045
100-5-word	0.1115	0.1165	0.1195	0.1225
100-7-lemma	0.1235	0.1035	0.1345	0.108
100-7-word	0.112	0.1265	0.1235	0.137
300-3-lemma	0.178	0.1395	0.1945	0.1475
300-3-word	0.1605	0.157	0.1705	0.163
300-5-lemma	0.179	0.1525	0.196	0.161
300-5-word	0.175	0.183	0.19	0.193
300-7-lemma	0.1875	0.158	0.206	0.167
300-7-word	0.17	**0.195**	0.1885	0.207
500-3-lemma	0.188	0.1395	0.203	0.1465
500-3-word	0.174	0.176	0.1845	0.1845
500-5-lemma	**0.1975**	0.161	**0.219**	0.1685
500-5-word	0.1795	**0.195**	0.1955	0.2065
500-7-lemma	0.193	0.169	0.2075	0.1795
500-7-word	0.191	0.194	0.209	**0.2085**

Table 1: Accuracies of Word2Vec-based methods with varying parameters

Together with their original Word2Vec implementation, Mikolov et al. (2013) made available also word vectors resulting from training on a part of the Google News dataset (consisting of 100 billion words). The model contains 300-dimensional vectors for 3 millions of words and phrases (no lemmatization was performed). We repeated CogALex 2014 shared task experiments with this pre-trained model as well. The resulting accuracy was 0.1375. The lower value is probably caused by the fact that the model is trained on the specific dataset with different pre-processing.

5.2 Wordnet-based measures

The Wordnet-based approach was evaluated in the same way as the Word2Vec one. Result for all six similarity measures are listed in Table 2. As in the previous case, accuracies for top n ($1 \leq n \leq 10$) predicted responses are considered. The best performing Wordnet similarity measure for the task showed to be Lin's similarity based on the Information Content of the least common subsumer and that of the two input synsets. Yet, the best values are far from accuracies of the Word2Vec-based methods, especially when only few predicted responses are allowed. This confirms our hypothesis that approaches deriving their lexical knowledge from large textual corpora overcome those based only on Wordnet.

6 Conclusions and future directions

The CogALex 2014 shared task focused on computing reversed multi-word response-stimulus relations extracted from the Edinburgh Association Thesaurus. We showed that this setting is only weakly related to computer-aided lexical access problems, namely to the tip-of-the-tongue phenomenon.

The submitted results were obtained with a system based on the Word2Vec distributional similarity model. Best of the implemented systems reaches accuracy of 0.1975 when trained on a subset of the ClueWeb12 dataset. Unfortunately, in time of writing this paper, official results of other teams are not published. Hence, no comparison with other participants could be included.

Section 2 also mentions our experience in collecting real TOT data. We believe that a collective effort could lead to a much larger resource better reflecting nature of the TOT phenomenon. We propose to establish a task force aiming at this goal. During discussions at the workshop, we could focus on actual

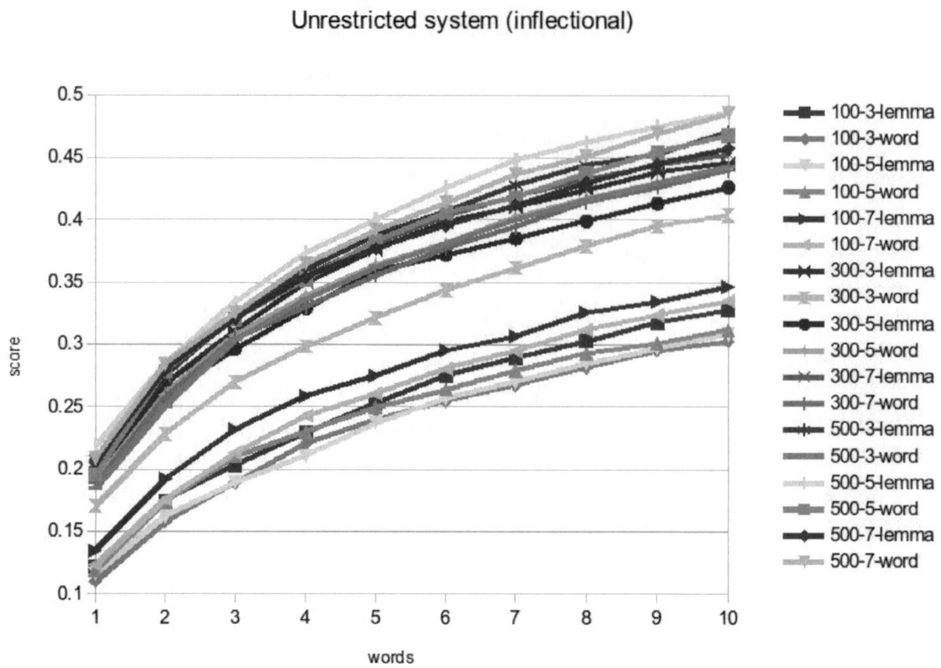

Figure 1: Accuracies growing with the number of suggestions for the unrestricted system

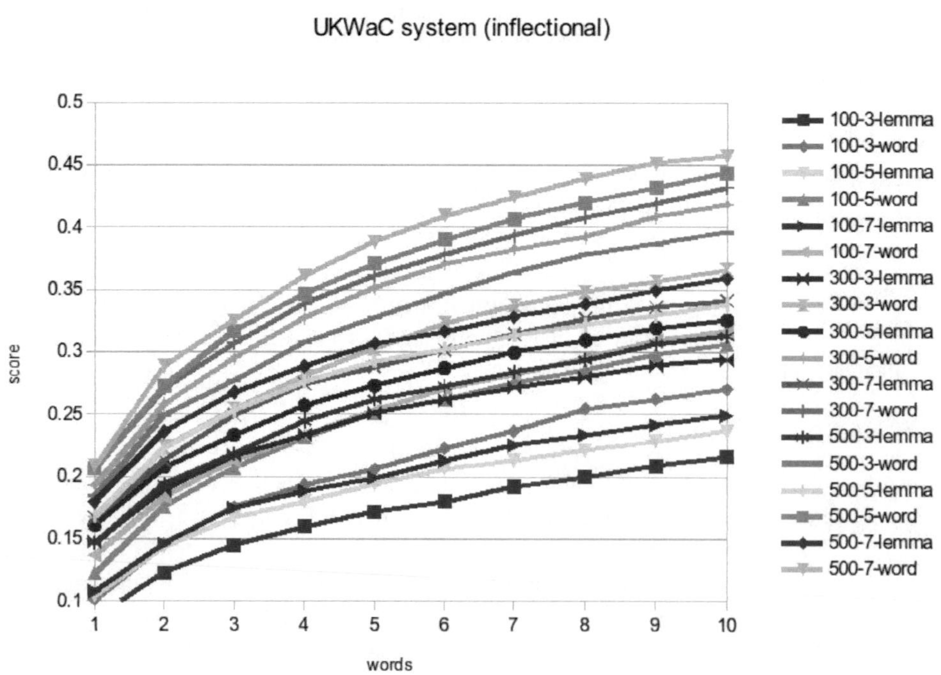

Figure 2: Accuracies growing with the number of suggestions for the restricted system

sim.	top n predicted responses are considered									
	1	2	3	4	5	6	7	8	9	10
path	0.0085	0.0175	0.024	0.0325	0.0395	0.044	0.0525	0.057	0.063	0.066
wup	0.012	0.03	0.0455	0.057	0.068	0.0745	0.0875	0.095	0.1025	0.1075
lch	0.003	0.0085	0.015	0.0195	0.0215	0.028	0.034	0.0375	0.04	0.042
res	0.008	0.0205	0.031	0.0435	0.048	0.061	0.0715	0.0785	0.0845	0.09
jcn	0.0135	0.029	0.042	0.0575	0.065	0.0825	0.098	0.1105	0.12	0.1295
lin	**0.022**	**0.044**	**0.068**	**0.091**	**0.1045**	**0.1265**	**0.1485**	**0.1675**	**0.1805**	**0.1955**

Table 2: Results of Wordnet-based methods (*path* stands for the path similarity, *wup* for Wu-Palmer's similarity, *lch* for Leacock-Chodorow's similarity, *res* for the Resnik's similarity, *jcn* for the Jiang-Conrath's similarity and *lin* for Lin's similarity).

procedures and technical support means (through a web-based system) to build the resource within the next year. The collected dataset could then be used for future shared tasks in the domain.

Acknowledgements

The research leading to these results has received support from the IT4Innovations Centre of Excellence project, Reg. No. CZ.1.05/1.1.00/02.0070, supported by Operational Programme "Research and Development for Innovations" funded by Structural Funds of the European Union and the state budget of the Czech Republic.

References

Alan S. Brown. 1991. A review of the tip-of-the-tongue experience. *Psychological Bulletin*, 109(2):204–223, March.

Kenneth Ward Church and Patrick Hanks. 1990. Word association norms, mutual information, and lexicography. *Computational Linguistics*, 16(1):22–29, March.

Christiane Fellbaum. 1998. *WordNet: An Electronic Lexical Database*. The MIT Press, Cambridge, MA; London, May. ISBN 978-0-262-06197-1.

Adriano Ferraresi, Eros Zanchetta, Marco Baroni, and Silvia Bernardini. 2008. Introducing and evaluating ukwac, a very large web-derived corpus of english. In *Proceedings of the 4th Web as Corpus Workshop (WAC-4) Can we beat Google*, pages 47–54.

Lev Finkelstein, Gabrilovich Evgenly, Matias Yossi, Rivlin Ehud, Solan Zach, Wolfman Gadi, and Ruppin Eytan. 2001. Placing search in context: the concept revisited. In *Proceedings of the Tenth International World Wide Web Conference*.

Derrall Heath, David Norton, Eric K. Ringger, and Dan Ventura. 2013. Semantic models as a combination of free association norms and corpus-based correlations. In *ICSC*, pages 48–55. IEEE.

J.J. Jiang and D.W. Conrath. 1997. Semantic similarity based on corpus statistics and lexical taxonomy. *Arxiv preprint cmp-lg/9709008*.

Grace Helen Kent and Aaron Joshua Rosanoff. 1910. *A study of association in insanity*. American Journal of Insanity.

GR Kiss, Christine A Armstrong, and R Milroy. 1972. *An associative thesaurus of English*. Medical Research Council, Speech and Communication Unit, University of Edinburgh, Scotland.

T. K. Landauer and S. T. Dumais. 1997. A solution to Plato's problem: The latent semantic analysis theory of acquisition, induction, and representation of knowledge. *Psychological review*, 104(2):211–240.

C. Leacock and M. Chodorow. 1998. Combining local context and WordNet similarity for word sense identification. *WordNet: An electronic lexical database*, 49(2):265–283.

D. Lin. 1998. An information-theoretic definition of similarity. In *Proceedings of the 15th International Conference on Machine Learning*, volume 1, pages 296–304. Citeseer.

Tomas Mikolov, Ilya Sutskever, Kai Chen, Greg S Corrado, and Jeff Dean. 2013. Distributed representations of words and phrases and their compositionality. In *Advances in Neural Information Processing Systems*, pages 3111–3119.

D. L. Nelson, McEvoy, C. L., and T. A. Schreiber. 1998. The University of South Florida word association, rhyme, and word fragment norms. `http://w3.usf.edu/FreeAssociation/`.

Reinhard Rapp. 2008. The computation of associative responses to multiword stimuli. In *Proceedings of the Workshop on Cognitive Aspects of the Lexicon*, COGALEX '08, pages 102–109. Association for Computational Linguistics.

Reinhard Rapp. 2013. From stimulus to associations and back. *Natural Language Processing and Cognitive Science*, page 78.

Reinhard Rapp. 2014. Using word association norms to measure corpus representativeness. In *Computational Linguistics and Intelligent Text Processing*, pages 1–13. Springer.

Radim Řehůřek and Petr Sojka. 2010. Software Framework for Topic Modelling with Large Corpora. In *Proceedings of the LREC 2010 Workshop on New Challenges for NLP Frameworks*, pages 45–50, Valletta, Malta, May. ELRA. `http://is.muni.cz/publication/884893/en`.

P. Resnik. 1995. Using information content to evaluate semantic similarity in a taxonomy. *Arxiv preprint cmp-lg/9511007.*

Herbert Rubenstein and John B. Goodenough. 1965. Contextual correlates of synonymy. *Communications of the ACM*, 8(10):627–633.

Anna Sinopalnikova and Pavel Smrz. 2004. Word association norms as a unique supplement of traditional language resources. In *Proceedings of the 4th International Conference on Language Resources and Evaluation (LREC)*, pages 1557–1561, Lisbon. European Language Resources Association.

Anna Sinopalnikova and Pavel Smrz. 2006. Knowing a word vs. accessing a word: Wordnet and word association norms as interfaces to electronic dictionaries. In *Proceedings of the Third International WordNet Conference*, pages 265–272.

Peter D. Turney, Michael L. Littman, Jeffrey Bigham, and Victor Shnayder. 2003. Combining independent modules to solve multiple-choice synonym and analogy problems. *CoRR*, cs.CL/0309035.

Peter D. Turney. 2001. Mining the web for synonyms: Pmi-ir versus lsa on toefl. In *Proceedings of the 12th European Conference on Machine Learning*, EMCL '01, pages 491–502. Springer-Verlag.

Z. Wu and M. Palmer. 1994. Verbs semantics and lexical selection. In *Proceedings of the 32nd annual meeting on Association for Computational Linguistics*, pages 133–138. Association for Computational Linguistics.

Torsten Zesch and Iryna Gurevych. 2007. Analysis of the wikipedia category graph for nlp applications. In *Proceedings of the TextGraphs-2 Workshop (NAACL-HLT).*

Michael Zock and Slaven Bilac. 2004. Word lookup on the basis of associations: From an idea to a roadmap. In *Proceedings of the Workshop on Enhancing and Using Electronic Dictionaries*, ElectricDict '04, pages 29–35. Association for Computational Linguistics.

Exploring the Use of Word Embeddings and Random Walks on Wikipedia for the CogAlex Shared Task

Josu Goikoetxea, Eneko Agirre, Aitor Soroa
IXA NLP Group, University of the Basque Country, Basque Country
jgoicoechea009@ikasle.ehu.es, e.agirre@ehu.es, a.soroa@ehu.es

Abstract

In our participation on the task we wanted to test three different kinds of relatedness algorithms: one based on embeddings induced from corpora, another based on random walks on WordNet and a last one based on random walks based on Wikipedia. All three of them perform similarly in noun relatedness datasets like WordSim353, close to the highest reported values. Although the task definition gave examples of nouns, the train and test data were based on the Edinburgh Association Thesaurus, and around 50% of the target words were not nouns. The corpus-based algorithm performed much better than the other methods in the training dataset, and was thus submitted for the test.

1 Introduction

Measuring semantic similarity and relatedness between terms is an important problem in lexical semantics (Budanitsky and Hirst, 2006). It has applications in many natural language processing tasks, such as Textual Entailment, Word Sense Disambiguation or Information Extraction, and other related areas like Information Retrieval. Most of the proposed techniques are evaluated over manually curated word similarity datasets like WordSim353 (Finkelstein et al., 2002), in which the weights returned by the systems for word pairs are compared with human ratings.

The techniques used to solve this problem can be roughly classified into two main categories: those relying on pre-existing knowledge resources (thesauri, semantic networks, taxonomies or encyclopedias) (Alvarez and Lim, 2007; Yang and Powers, 2005; Hughes and Ramage, 2007; Agirre et al., 2009; Agirre et al., 2010) and those inducing distributional properties of words from corpora (Sahami and Heilman, 2006; Chen et al., 2006; Bollegala et al., 2007; Agirre et al., 2009; Mikolov et al., 2013).

Our main objective when participating in the CogAlex shared task was to check how a sample of each kind of technique would cope with the task. We thus selected one of the best corpus-based models to date and another approach based on random walks over WordNet and Wikipedia.

2 Word Embeddings

Neural Networks have become quite a useful tool in NLP on the last years, specially in semantics. A lot of models have been developed, but all of them share two characteristics: they learn meaning from non-labeled corpora and represent meaning in a distributional way. These models learn the meaning of words from corpora, and they represent it distributionally by the so-called embeddings. This embeddings are low-dimensional and dense vectors composed by integers, where the dimensions are latent semantic features of words.

We have used the Mikolov model (Mikolov et al., 2013) for this task, due to its effectiveness in similarity experiments (Baroni et al., 2014). This neural network reduces the computational complexity of previous architectures by deleting the hidden layer, and also, it's able to train with larger corpora (more than 10^9 words) and extract embeddings with larger dimensionality.

Zock/Rapp/Huang (eds.): Proceedings of the 4th Workshop on Cognitive Aspects of the Lexicon, pages 31–34,
Dublin, Ireland, August 23, 2014.

The Mikolov model has two variants: Continuous Bag of Words (CBOW) and Skip-gram. The first one is quite similar to the feedforward Neural Net Language Model, but instead of a hidden layer it has a projection layer; so, all the words are projected in the same position. Word order has thus no influence in the projection. Training criterion is as follows: knowing past and future words, it will predict the one in the middle.

The Skip-gram model is related to the previous one. The main difference is that it uses each current word as an input to a log-linear classifier with a continuous projection layer, and predicts words within a certain range before and after the current word.

In order to participate in this shared task, we have used the *word2vec* tool[1]. On the one hand, we have used embeddings trained with the Skip-gram model on part of Google News corpus (about 100 billion words). The vectors have 300 dimensions and are publicly available[2]. On the other hand, we have adapted the *distance* program in *word2vec*, so that its input is the test-set file of the shared task. The way *distance* works is as follows:

- Reads all the vectors from the embeddings file, and stores them in memory.
- Reads the test-set file, and line by line
  - Saves the five entry words if they exist in vocabulary.
  - Dimension by dimension, sums five entries' embeddings into one vector, and normalizes it.
  - Calculates the semantic distance from the normalized vector to all words in vocabulary, and selects the closest ones.
  - Writes in output file the closest words along with their distances, writing the closest word first.

3 Random Walks on Wikipedia

In the last year there have been many attempts to apply graph based techniques to many NLP problems, including word sense disambiguation (Agirre et al., 2014) or measuring semantic similarity and relatedness between terms (Agirre et al., 2009). Those techniques consider a given Knowledge Base (KB) as a graph, where vertices represent KB concepts and relations among concepts are represented by edges.

For this particular task we represented WikiPedia as a graph, where articles are the vertices and links between articles are the edges. Contrary to other work using Wikipedia links (Gabrilovich and Markovitch, 2007; Milne and Witten, 2008), the use of the whole graph allows to apply algorithms that take into account the whole structure of Wikipedia. We applied PageRank and Personalized PageRank on the Wikipedia graph using freely available software (Agirre and Soroa, 2009; Agirre et al., 2014)[3].

The PageRank algorithm (Brin and Page, 1998) ranks the vertices in a graph according to their relative structural importance. The main idea of PageRank is that whenever a link from v_i to v_j exists in a graph, a vote from node i to node j is produced, and hence the rank of node j increases. Besides, the strength of the vote from i to j also depends on the rank of node i: the more important node i is, the more strength its votes will have. Alternatively, PageRank can also be viewed as the result of a random walk process, where the final rank of node i represents the probability of a random walk over the graph ending on node i, at a sufficiently large time. *Personalized PageRank* (Haveliwala, 2002) is a variant of the PageRank algorithm which biases the computation to prefer certain nodes of the graph.

Our method also needs a dictionary, an association between strings and Wikipedia articles. We construct the dictionary using article titles, redirections, disambiguation pages, and anchor text extracted from a Wikipedia dump[4]. Mentions are lowercased and all text between parenthesis is removed. If the mention links to a disambiguation page, it is associated with all possible articles the disambiguation page points to. Each association between a string and article is scored with the prior probability, estimated as the number of times that the mention occurs in the anchor text of an article divided by the total number of occurrences of the mention.

[1] `http://word2vec.googlecode.com/svn/trunk/`

[2] `https:\/\/docs.google.com/uc?id=0B7XkCwpI5KDYNlNUTTlSS21pQmM\&export=download`

[3] `http://ixa2.si.ehu.es/ukb`

[4] we used a 2013 Wikipedia dump to build the dictionary

The method to compute the answer for a given set of words is very simple. We just compute the Personalized PageRank algorithm over Wikipedia, initializing the walk using the set of given words, obtaining a probability distribution over all Wikipedia articles. We then choose the article with maximum probability, and return the title of the article as the expected answer.

Regarding PageRank implementation details, we chose a damping value of 0.85 and finish the calculation after 30 iterations. Some preliminary experiments on a related Word Sense Disambiguation task indicated that the algorithm was quite robust to these values, and we did not optimize them.

4 Development results

After running the random walks algorithms on the development data, it was clear that WordNet and Wikipedia were not sufficient resources for the task, and they were performing poorly. The embeddings, on the other hand, were doing a good job (accuracy of 14.1%, having returned a word on 1907 of the 2000 train instances). This is in contradiction with the results obtained in word relatedness datasets: for instance, in the WordSim353 dataset (Gabrilovich and Markovitch, 2007) we obtain Spearman correlations of 68.5 using random walks on WordNet, 72.8 using random walks on Wikipedia, and 71.0 using the embeddings.

One important difference between datasets like WordSim353 and the CogCalex data, is that in WordSim353, all words are nouns in singular. From a small sample of the CogaLex training data, on the contrary, we saw that only around 50% of the target words[5] are nouns, with many occurrences of grammatical words, and words in plural. Wikipedia only contains nouns, and even if WordNet contains verbs and adjectives, the semantic relations that we use are not able to check whether a meaning should be lexicalized as an adjective (absent in the dataset) or noun (absence). Note also that the random walk algorithm does not use co-occurrence data, and as such it is not able to capture that absent and minded are closely related as in "absent minded".

These differences between the WordSim 353 and the CogaLex data would explain the different behaviour of the algorithms. We would also like to mention that the definition of the task mentioned examples which are closer to the capabilities of WordNet and Wikipedia (e.g. given a set of words like "*gin, drink, scotch, bottle and soda*" the expected answer would be *whisky*). From the definition of the task, it looked as if the task was about recovering a word given a definition (as in dictionaries), but the actual data was based on the Edinburgh Association Thesaurus, which is a different kind of resource.

5 Test results

Given the development much better results of the embeddings, we submitted a run based on those. We obtained 16.35% accuracy, ranking fourth in the evaluation of all twelve submissions.

6 Conclusions

We tested three different kinds of relatedness algorithms: one based on embeddings induced from corpora, another based on random walks on WordNet and a last one based on random walks based on Wikipedia. All three of them perform similarly in noun relatedness datasets like WordSim353. Although the task definition gave examples of content nouns alone, the train and test data were based on the Edinburgh Association Thesaurus, and only around 50% of the target words were nouns. The embedding performed much better than the other methods in this dataset.

Acknowledgements

This material is based in part upon work supported by MINECO, in the scope of the CHIST-ERA READERS (PCIN-2013-002-C02-01) and SKATER (TIN2012-38584-C06-02) projects.

[5] The words that need to be predicted.

References

E. Agirre and A. Soroa. 2009. Personalizing PageRank for Word Sense Disambiguation. In *Proceedings of 14th Conference of the European Chapter of the Association for Computational Linguistics*, Athens, Greece.

E. Agirre, A. Soroa, E. Alfonseca, K. Hall, J. Kravalova, and M. Pasca. 2009. A Study on Similarity and Relatedness Using Distributional and WordNet-based Approaches. In *Proceedings of annual meeting of the North American Chapter of the Association of Computational Linguistics (NAAC)*, Boulder, USA, June.

E. Agirre, M. Cuadros, G. Rigau, and A. Soroa. 2010. Exploring Knowledge Bases for Similarity. In *Proceedings of the Seventh conference on International Language Resources and Evaluation (LREC'10)*, Valletta, Malta, May. European Language Resources Association (ELRA).

Eneko Agirre, Oier Lopez de Lacalle, and Aitor Soroa. 2014. Random walks for knowledge-based word sense disambiguation. *Computational Linguistics*, 40(1):57–88.

M.A. Alvarez and S.J. Lim. 2007. A Graph Modeling of Semantic Similarity between Words. *Proceedings of the Conference on Semantic Computing*, pages 355–362.

Marco Baroni, Georgiana Dinu, and Germn Kruszewski. 2014. Don't count, predict! A systematic comparison of context-counting vs. context-predicting semantic vectors. In *Proceedings of ACL.*

D. Bollegala, Matsuo Y., and M. Ishizuka. 2007. Measuring Semantic Similarity between Words using Web Search Engines. In *Proceedings of WWW'2007.*

S. Brin and L. Page. 1998. The Anatomy of a Large-scale Hypertextual Web Search Engine. In *Proceedings of the seventh international conference on World Wide Web 7*, WWW7, pages 107–117, Amsterdam, The Netherlands, The Netherlands. Elsevier Science Publishers B. V.

A. Budanitsky and G. Hirst. 2006. Evaluating WordNet-based Measures of Lexical Semantic Relatedness. *Computational Linguistics*, 32(1):13–47.

H. Chen, M. Lin, and Y. Wei. 2006. Novel Association Measures using Web Search with Double Checking. In *Proceedings of COCLING/ACL 2006.*

L. Finkelstein, E. Gabrilovich, Y. Matias, E. Rivlin, Z. Solan, G. Wolfman, and E. Ruppin. 2002. Placing Search in Context: The Concept Revisited. *ACM Transactions on Information Systems*, 20(1):116–131.

E Gabrilovich and S Markovitch. 2007. Computing semantic relatedness using wikipedia-based explicit semantic analysis. In *Proceedings of IJCAI 2007*, pages 1606–1611, Hyderabad, India.

T.H. Haveliwala. 2002. Topic-sensitive PageRank. In *Proceedings of the 11th international conference on World Wide Web (WWW'02)*, pages 517–526, New York, NY, USA.

T. Hughes and D. Ramage. 2007. Lexical Semantic Relatedness with Random Graph Walks. In *Proceedings of EMNLP-CoNLL-2007*, pages 581–589.

Tomas Mikolov, Wen-tau Yih, and Geoffrey Zweig. 2013. Linguistic regularities in continuous space word representations. In *Proceedings of NAACL-HLT*, pages 746–751.

D. Milne and I.H. Witten. 2008. An effective, low-cost measure of semantic relatedness obtained from wikipedia links. In *In Proceedings of the first AAAI Workshop on Wikipedia and Artifical Intellegence (WIKIAI'08)*, Chicago, I.L.

M. Sahami and T.D. Heilman. 2006. A Web-based Kernel Function for Measuring the Similarity of Short Text Snippets. *Proc. of WWW*, pages 377–386.

D. Yang and D.M.W. Powers. 2005. Measuring Semantic Similarity in the Taxonomy of WordNet. *Proceedings of the Australasian conference on Computer Science.*

ETS Lexical Associations System for the COGALEX-4 Shared Task

Michael Flor
Educational Testing Service
Rosedale Road
Princeton, NJ, 08541, USA
mflor@ets.org

Beata Beigman Klebanov
Educational Testing Service
Rosedale Road
Princeton, NJ, 08541, USA
bbeigmanklebanov@ets.org

Abstract

We present an automated system that computes multi-cue associations and generates associated-word suggestions, using lexical co-occurrence data from a large corpus of English texts. The system performs expansion of cue words to their inflectional variants, retrieves candidate words from corpus data, finds maximal associations between candidates and cues, computes an aggregate score for each candidate, and outputs an *n*-best list of candidates. We present experiments using several measures of statistical association, two methods of score aggregation, ablation of resources and applying additional filters on retrieved candidates. The system achieves 18.6% precision on the COGALEX-4 shared task data. Results with additional evaluation methods are presented. We also describe an annotation experiment which suggests that the shared task may underestimate the appropriateness of candidate words produced by the corpus-based system.

1 Introduction

The COGALEX-4 shared task is a multi-cue association task: finding a target word that is associated with a set of cue words. The task is motivated, for example, by a tip-of-the-tongue search application, as described by the organizers: "Suppose, we were looking for a word expressing the following ideas: 'superior dark coffee made of beans from Arabia', but could not remember the intended word 'mocha'. Since people always remember something concerning the elusive word, it would be nice to have a system accepting this kind of input, to propose then a number of candidates for the target word. Given the above example, we might enter 'dark', 'coffee', 'beans', and 'Arabia', and the system would be supposed to come up with one or several associated words such as 'mocha', 'espresso', or 'cappuccino'."

The data for the shared task were sampled from the Edinburgh Associative Thesaurus (**EAT** - http://www.eat.rl.ac.uk). For each of about 8,000 stimulus words, the EAT lists the associations (words) provided by human respondents, sorted according to the number of respondents who provided the respective word. Generally, when more people provided the same response, the underlying association is considered to be stronger (Kiss et al., 1973). For the COGALEX-4 shared task, the cues were the five strongest responses to an unknown stimulus word, and the task was to recover (guess) the stimulus word (henceforth, **target** word). The data for the task consisted of a training set of 2000 items (for which target words were provided), and a test set of 2000 items. The origin of the data was not disclosed before or during the system development and evaluation phases of the shared task competition.

The ETS entry consisted of a system that uses corpus-based distributional information about pairs of words in English. No use was made of human association data (EAT or other), nor of any other information such as the order of importance of the cue words, or any special preference for the British spelling often used in the EAT.

Zock/Rapp/Huang (eds.): Proceedings of the 4th Workshop on Cognitive Aspects of the Lexicon, pages 35–45, Dublin, Ireland, August 23, 2014.

2 The ETS system for computing multi-cue association

Our system is defined by the following components.

1. Corpus from which the distributional information about word pairs is learned, along with preprocessing steps (database generation).
2. The kind of distributional information collected from the corpus (collocation & co-occurrence).
3. A measure of association between two words.
4. An algorithm for generating candidate associates using the resources above.
5. An algorithm for scoring candidate associates.

2.1 Corpus

Our corpus is composed of two sources. One part is the English Gigaword 2003 corpus (Graff and Cieri, 2003), with 1.7 billion tokens. The second part is an ETS in-house corpus containing texts from the genres of fiction and popular science (Sheehan et al., 2006), with about 430 million tokens.

2.2 Types of distributional information

From this combined corpus we have built two specific lexical resources. One resource is a bigram repository, which stores counts for sequences of two words. The other resource is a first-order co-occurrence word-space model (Turney and Pantel, 2010), also known as a Distributional Semantic Model (**DSM**) (Baroni and Lenci, 2010). In our implementation of DSM, we counted non-directed co-occurrence of tokens in a paragraph, using no distance coefficients (Bullinaria and Levy, 2007). Counts for 2.1 million word-form types, and the sparse matrix of their co-occurrences, are efficiently compressed using the TrendStream toolkit (Flor, 2013), resulting in a database file of 4.7GB.

The same toolkit supports both n-grams and DSM repositories, and allows fast retrieval of word probabilities and statistical associations for pairs of words.[1] It also supports retrieval of co-occurrence vectors. When generating these two resources, we used no lemmatization and no stoplist. All tokens were converted to lowercase. All punctuation was retained and counted as tokens. The only significant filtering was applied to numbers: all digit-based numbers (e.g. 5, 2.1) were converted to the symbol '#' and counted as such. Tokenization was performed by an internal module of the TrendStream toolkit.

The lexical resources described above were not generated for the COGALEX-4 shared task. Rather, those are general-purpose large-scale lexical resources that we have used in previous research, for a variety of NLP tasks. This is an important aspect, as our intention was to find out how well those general resources would perform on this novel task. Our bigrams repository is actually part of a 5-gram language model that is used for context-aware spelling correction. The algorithms for that application are described by Flor (2012). The DSM has been used for spelling correction (Flor, 2012), for essay scoring (Beigman Klebanov and Flor, 2013a), for readability estimation (Flor and Beigman Klebanov, in press; Flor et al., 2013), as well as for a study on quality of machine translation (Beigman Klebanov and Flor, 2013b).

2.3 Measures of association

For the shared task, we used three measures of word association.

Pointwise Mutual Information (Church & Hanks, 1990):

$$PMI(a,b)=\log_2\frac{P(a,b)}{P(a)P(b)}$$

Normalized Pointwise Mutual Information (Bouma, 2009):

$$NPMI(a,b)=(\log_2\frac{P(a,b)}{P(a)P(b)})/(-\log_2 P(a,b))$$

[1] The TrendStream toolkit provides compression and storage for large-scale n-gram models, and for large-scale co-occurrence matrices. In all cases, actual counts are stored and values for statistical association measures are computed on the fly during data retrieval.

Simplified log-Likelihood (Evert, 2008):

$$SLL(a,b)=2\cdot P(a,b)\cdot \log\frac{P(a,b)}{P(a)P(b)}-P(a,b)+P(a)P(b)$$

P(a,b) signifies probability of joint co-occurrence. For bigrams, that is joint co-occurrence in a specific sequential order (e.g. AB vs. BA) ; for DSM data the co-occurrence is order-independent.

2.4 Procedure for generating candidate multi-cue associates

Our general procedure for generating target candidates is as follows. For each of the five cue words, candidate targets are generated separately, from the corpus-based resources:

1. From the DSM (generally associated words)
2. Left words from bigrams (words that, in the corpus, appeared immediately to the left of the cue)
3. Right words from bigrams (words that appeared immediately to the right of the cue)

Retrieved lists of candidates can be quite large, with hundreds and even thousands of different neighbors. One specific filter implemented at this stage was that only word-forms (alphabetic strings) were allowed, and any punctuation or '#' strings were filtered out.

Since our resources are not lemmatized, we extended the candidate retrieval procedure by expanding the cue words to their inflectional variants. This provides richer information about semantic association. We used an in-house morphological analyzer/generator. Inflectional expansions were not constrained for part of speech or word sense. For example, given the cue set {*1:letters 2:meaning 3:sentences 4:book 5:speech*} (from the training set of the shared task, target: *'words'*), after expansion the set of cues is {*1:letters, lettered, letter, lettering 2:meaning, means, mean, meant, meanings 3:sentences, sentence, sentenced, sentencing 4:book, books, booking, booked 5:speech, speeches*}. The vector of right neighbors for the cue '*letters*', brings such words as {*sent, from, between, written, came, addressed, ...*}. The vector of left neighbors for same cue word brings such candidates as {*write, send, love, capital, review, ...*}. From the DSM, the vector of co-occurrence may bring some of the same words (but with different values of association), as well as words that do not generally occur immediately before or after the cue word, e.g. {*time, people, word, now,...*}.

Next, we apply filtering that ensures the minimal requirement for multi-word association – a candidate must be related to all cues. The candidate must appear (at least once) on the list of words generated from each cue family. A candidate word that does not meet this requirement is filtered out.[2]

2.5 Scoring of candidate associates

Scoring of candidate associate-words is a two-stage process. First, for each candidate, we look for the strongest association value it has with each of the five cue families. Then, the five strongest values are combined into an aggregated score.

For a given cue family, several instances of the same candidate associate might be retrieved, with various values of association score (from DSM and n-grams, and also for each specific inflectional form of the cue). We pick the highest score, siding with the source that provides the strongest evidence of connection between the cue and the candidate associate. The maximal association value is stored as the best score for this candidate with the given cue family. We note that since the same measure of association is used, the scores from the different sources are numerically comparable.[3] For example, when PMI is used as the association measure, the following values were obtained for candidate '*capital*' with cue family '*letters, lettered, letter, lettering*' (expanded from '*letters*'). General co-occurrence (DSM): *capital & letters*: 0.477, *capital & letter*: 0.074, etc.; left bigrams: *capital letters*: 5.268, *capital letter*: 2.474, etc. The strongest association here is the bigram '*capital letters*', and the value 5.268 is the best association of the candidate '*capital*' with this cue family.

Next, for each candidate we compute an aggregate score that represents its overall association with all five cues. In current study, we experimented with two forms of aggregation: 1) sum of best scores

[2] This is 'baseline' filtering, applied in all experiments. Experiments with additional filtering are described in section 4.2.

[3] In any single experimental run we consistently use the same measure of association (no mixing of different formulae).

(SBS), and 2) product (multiplication) of ranks (MR). Sum of best scores is simply the sum of best association scores that a candidate has with each of the five cues (families). To produce a final ranked list of candidate targets, candidates are sorted by their aggregate sum value (better candidates have higher values). Multiplication of ranks has been proposed as an aggregation procedure by Rapp (2014, 2008). In this procedure, all candidates are sorted by their association scores with each of the five cues (families) separately, and five rank values are registered for each candidate. The five rank values are then multiplied to produce the final aggregate score. All candidates are then sorted by the aggregate score, and in such ranking better candidates have lower aggregate scores. Multiplication of ranks is computationally more intensive than sum of scores – for a given set of candidate words from five cues, multiplication of ranks requires six calls for sorting, while aggregation via sum-of-best-scores performs sorting only once.

Finally, all candidates are sorted by their aggregate score and top N are outputted for the calculation of *precision@N*, to be described below.

3 Results

Our system ran with several different configuration settings, using various association measures and score aggregation procedures. Under any given configuration, the system produces, for each item (i.e. a set of five cue words), a ranked list of candidates. According to the rules of the shared task, official results are computed by selecting the single best candidate for the item as the suggested target word. If the suggested word strictly matches the gold-standard word (ignoring upper/lower case), it is considered a match. If the two strings differ even slightly, it is considered a mismatch. The reported result is precision (percent matches) over the test set of 2000 items.

With strict-matching, our best result for the test-set was precision of 18.6% (372 correctly suggested targets). This was obtained by using NPMI as the association measure, product of ranks as the score aggregation procedure, and with filtering of candidates using a stoplist and a frequency filter.[4]

The shared task was described as multi-cue association for finding a sought-after 'missing' word, a situation not unlike a tip-of-the-tongue phenomenon. In such situation, a person looking for an associated word, might find it useful if the system returns not just one highest-ranked suggestion (which would often be a miss), but a list of several top-ranked suggestions – the target word might be somewhere on such list[5]. Thus, we also present our results in terms of precision for *n*-best suggestions – i.e. in how many cases the target word was among the top *n* returned by the system, with *n* ranging from 1 up to 25.

A similar consideration applies to inflectional variants. A person looking for a word associated with a set of cue words, might be satisfied when a system returns either a base-form or an inflected variant of the target word. Thus, we report our results both in terms of strict matches to gold-standard targets and under a condition of 'inflections-allowed'.[6] On the test set, our best result for precision@1, with inflections allowed, is 24.35% (487 matching suggestions).

First, we present our baseline results. Figure 1 presents the results of our system for the training set of 2000 items, using the NPMI association measure. Panel 1A presents data obtained using aggregation via sum-of-best-scores (SBS). Panel 1B presents data obtained using aggregation via multiplication of ranks (MR). Figure 2 presents similar breakdown for results of the test set. Both sets of results are quite similar. Thus, we restrict our attention to just the results of the test set. [7]

---

[4] We initially submitted a result of 14.95% strict-match precision@1 (see Figure 2A). This was improved to 16.1% (Figure 2B), and with additional filters – to 18.6% (see section 4.2).

[5] A list of *n*-best suggestions is standard approach for presenting candidate corrections for misspellings (Flor, 2013; Mitton, 2008). Also, precision "at *n* documents" is a well known evaluation approach in information retrieval (Manning et al., 2008). A recent use of *n*-best suggestions in an interactive NLP system is illustrated by Madnani and Cahill (2014).

[6] Each target word form, both in the training set and the test set, was automatically expanded to all its inflectional variants, using our morphological analyzer/generator. In our evaluations, a candidate target is considered a 'hit' if it matches the gold-standard target or one of its inflectional variants.

[7] We did not use the training set for any training or parameter tuning. We used it to select the optimal association measures for this task – we also experimented with t-score, weighted PMI and conditional probability, but PMI and NPMI performed much better than others.

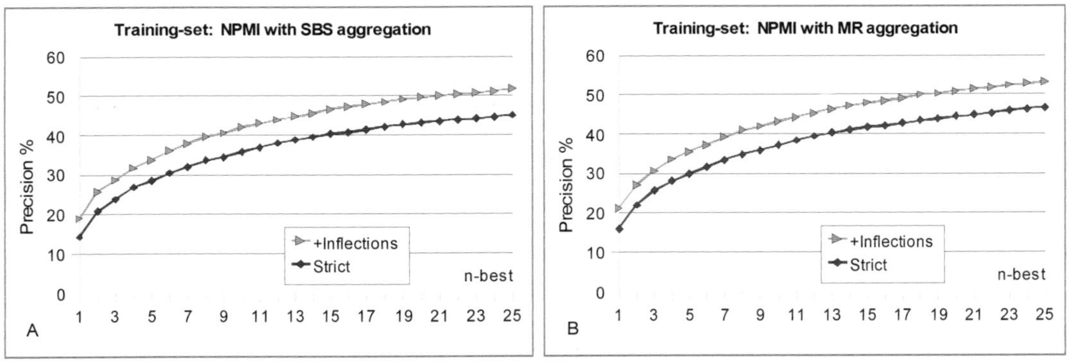

Figure 1. System performance on the training-set (percent correct out of 2000 items), for various values of *n*. Panel A: using sum-of-best-scores aggregation; Panel B: using multiplication-of-ranks aggregation. 'Strict': evaluation uses strict matching to gold-standard target, '+Inflections': inflectional variants are allowed in matching to gold-standard target.

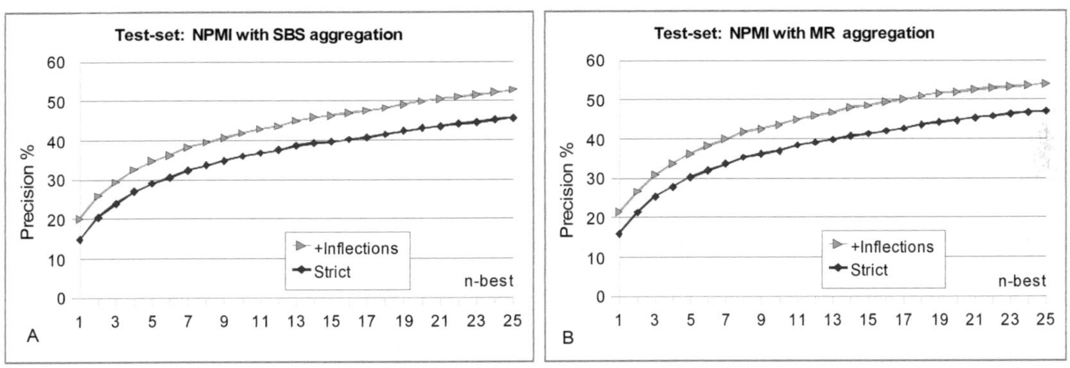

Figure 2. System performance on the test-set (percent correct out of 2000 items).

We found, as expected, that performance improves when the target is sought among the *n*-best candidates produced by the system. With NPMI and MR aggregation, strict-match precision improves from 16.1% for precision@1 to 30.3% for precision@5, 37% for precision@10, and 46.9% for precision@25 (Figure 2B).

Another expected result is that performance is better when matching of targets allows inflectional variants. This is clearly seen on the charts, as the difference between the two lines. With NPMI and MR aggregation, precision@1 improves from 16.1% to 21.45%, precision@5 improves from 30.3% to 36.3%, and precision@25 improves from 46.9% to 54%, Similar improvement is observed when using aggregation via sum-of-best-scores.

Our third finding is that multiplication of ranks achieves slightly better results than sum-of-best-scores (Figure 2, panel B vs. panel A). For precision@1 with strict matches, using NPMI, MR achieves 16.1% and with inflectional variants 21.45%, while SBS achieves 14.95% and 20.25% respectively. For precision@10, MR achieves 37% (43.55%), while SBS achieves 36% (42%). Notably, MR is consistently superior to SBS for all values of *n*-best, from 1 to 25, under both strict or inflections-allowed matching, with both NPMI and PMI (see Figure 3). However, the advantage is consistently rather small – about 1-1.5%. Since MR is computationally more intensive, SBS emerges as a viable alternative.

We have also conducted experiments with three different measures of association. Results are presented in Figure 3. With MR aggregation, NPMI achieves better results than the PMI measure. Both measures clearly outperform the Simplified log-Likelihood. Similar results are obtained with SBS aggregation. For each association measure, allowing inflections provides better results than strict matching to gold-standard targets.

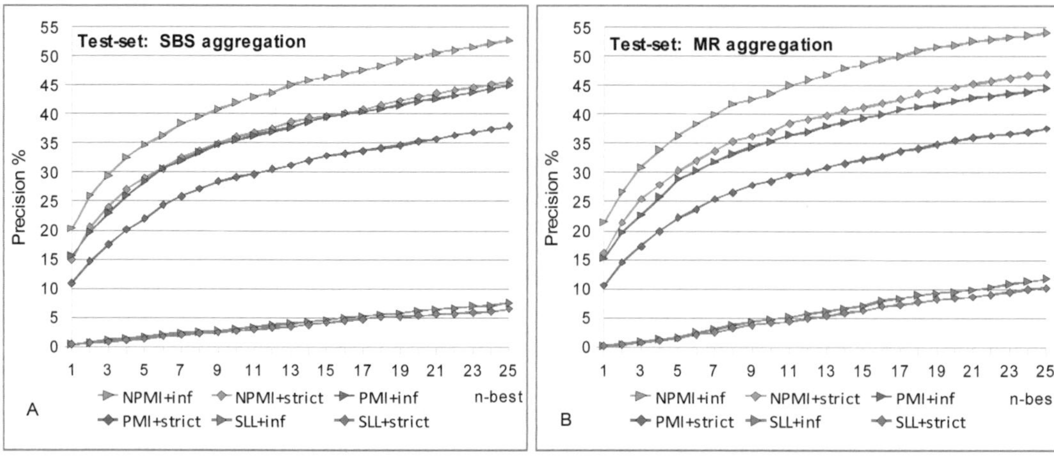

Figure 3. System performance on the test-set (2000 items) with three different association measures. Panel A: using sum-of-best-scores aggregation; Panel B: using multiplication-of-ranks aggregation. Legend: PMI: pointwise mutual information, NPMI: Normalized PMI, SLL: simplified log-likelihood, 'Strict': evaluation uses strict matching to gold-standard target, '+Inf': inflectional variants are allowed in matching to gold-standard target.

4 Additional studies

In several additional experiments we looked at the contribution of different factors to overall performance. We tried several variations of resource combination and also tested filtering of candidates by frequency and by using a list of stopwords.

4.1 Ablation experiments

We investigated how the restriction of resources impacts the performance on this task. Specifically we restricted the resources as follows. In one condition we used only the bigrams data, retrieving candidates only from the vectors of left co-occurring words (immediate preceding words) of each cue word (condition **NL** – n-grams left). A similar restriction is when candidates are retrieved only from right (immediate successor) words (condition **NR** – n-grams right). A third condition still uses only bigrams, but admits candidates from both left and right vectors (condition NL+NR). Under the fourth condition (DSM), n-grams data is not used at all, only the DSM resource is used. In the fifth and sixth conditions we combine candidates from DSM with n-gram candidates (left or right vectors only – respectively). The seventh condition is our standard – candidates from DSM and both left and right neighbors from bigrams are admitted. For those experiments, we used NPMI association measure with MR aggregation, and included inflections in evaluation. The results are presented in Figure 4.

Using only right-hand associates (typical textual successors of cue words) provides very low performance (precision@1 is 2.95%). Using only left-hand associates (typical textual predecessors of cue words) provides slightly better performance (precision@1 is 4.5%). However, it is notable that there are some items in the EAT data where all cues are strong bigrams with the target, e.g. {*orange, fruit, lemon, apple, tomato*} with target '*juice*'. Combining these two resources (condition NL+NR) provides much better performance: precision@1 is 8.5%. Using just the DSM, the system achieves 10.5% precision@1, which may seem rather close to the combined NL+NR 8.5%. However, with DSM, for *n*-best lists precision rises quite sharply (e.g. 24.35% for precision@5), while for the NL+NR setting precision tends to be under 17% for all values of *n* up to 25.

Since our DSM and bigrams resources are built on the same corpus of text, for any given set of cues the DSM produces all the candidates that the bigrams resource does (but with different association values) and a lot of other candidates. However, results for DSM+NR and DSM+NL settings (which are better than DSM alone) indicate that association values from bigrams contribute substantially to overall performance. The best result in this experiment is achieved by a setting that combines candidates (and association values) from all three resources, indicating further that associations from sequential word combinations (bigrams) provide a substantial contribution to performance in this task.

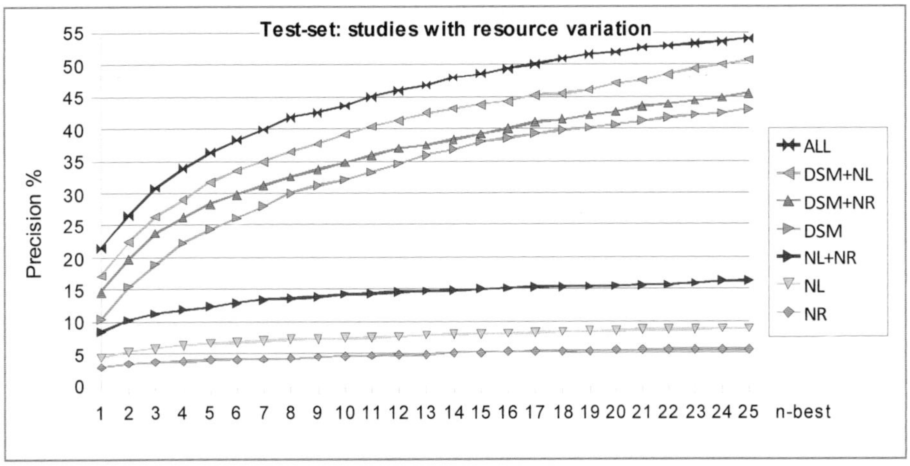

Figure 4. System performance on the test-set (2000 items), with various resource restrictions. All runs used NPMI association measure and MR aggregation. Evaluation allowed inflections. NL/NR – left/right neighbors from bigrams.

4.2 Applying filters on retrieved candidates

We also experimented with applying some filters on the retrieved candidates for each item. One of the obvious filters to use is to filter out stopwords. For general tip-of-the-tongue search cases, common stopwords are rarely useful as target words; thus presenting stopwords as candidates makes little sense. We used a list of 87 very common English stopwords, including the articles {*the, a, an*}, common prepositions, pronouns, wh-question words, etc. However, since the data of the shared task comes from EAT, common stopwords are actually targets in some cases in that collection. Therefore, we used the following strategy. For a given item, if at least one of the five cue words is a stopword, then we assume that the target might also be a stopword, and so we do not use the stoplist to filter candidates for this item. However, if none of the cues is a stopword, we do apply filtering – any retrieved candidate word is filtered out if it is on the stoplist. An additional filter, applied with the stoplist, was defined as follows: if a candidate word is strictly identical to one of the cue words, the candidate is filtered out (to allow for potentially more suitable candidates).[8]

The other filter considers frequency of words. The PMI measure is known to overestimate the strength of pair association when one of the words is a low-frequency word (Manning & Schütze, 1999). Normalized PMI is also sensitive to this aspect, although less than PMI. Thus, we use a frequency filter to drop some candidate words. For technical reasons, it was easier for us to apply a cutoff on the joint frequency of a candidate and a cue word. We used a cutoff value of 10 – a candidate is dropped if corpus data indicates it co-occurs with the cue words fewer than 10 times in the corpus data.

We applied the stoplist filter, the frequency filter and a combination of those two filters, always using NPMI as our association measure, aggregating scores via multiplication-of-ranks, and allowing inflections in evaluation. No ablation of resources was applied. The results are presented in Figure 5. The baseline condition is when neither of the two filters is applied. The frequency filter with cutoff=10 provides a very small improvement for precision@1, and for higher values of best-*n* it actually hurts performance. Application of a stoplist provides a very slight improvement of performance. The combination of a stoplist and frequency cutoff=10 provides a sizable improvement of performance (precision@1 is 24.35% vs. baseline 21.45%, and precision@10 is 44.55% vs. baseline 43.55%). However, for *n*-best lists of size 15 and above, performance without filters is slightly better than with those filters. For the shared task (using strict matching – no inflections), our best result is 18.6% precision@1 with two filters (16.1% without filters).

[8] Cases when a candidate word is identical to one of the cues do occur when associate candidates are harvested from corpus data. Such candidates have little utility for a missing-word-search task. Notably, however, the training-set for the shared task did have one item where the target word was identical to one of the cues: *Yeah ~ Yeah no Yes Beatles Oh.*

Given that the gold-standard targets in the shared task are original stimulus words form the EAT collection, we can use a special restriction – restrict the candidates to just the EAT stimuli word-list (Rapp, 2014). Notably, this is a very specific restriction, suited to the specific dataset, and not applicable to the general case of multi-cue associations or tip-of-the-tongue word searches. We used the list of 7913 single-word stimuli from EAT as a filter in our system – generated candidates that were not on this list were dropped from consideration. The results (Figure 5) indicate that this restriction (EATvocab) provides a substantial improvement over the baseline condition. For precison@1, using EATvocab (24.55%) is comparable to using a stoplist+cutoff10 (24.35%). However, for larger n-best lists, EATvocab filter provides substantially better performance.

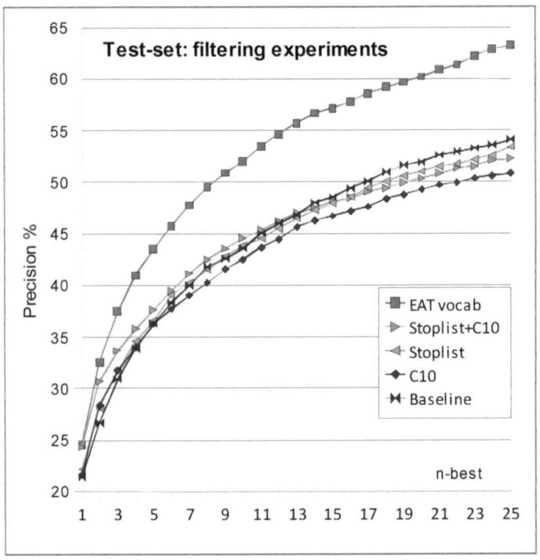

Condition	Precision@1	Precision@10
EAT Vocabulary	24.55%	52.00%
Stoplist & Cutoff10	24.35%	44.55%
Stoplist	22.15%	43.85%
Cutoff10	21.70%	42.50%
Baseline (no filters)	21.45%	43.55%

Figure 5. System performance on the test set with different filtering conditions. All runs use NPMI association and MR aggregation. Inflections allowed in evaluation. C10: frequency cutoff=10.

5 Small-scale evaluation using direct human judgments

Inspecting results from training-set data, we observed a number of cases where the system produced very plausible targets which however were struck down as incorrect (not matching the gold-standard). For example, for the cue set {*music, piano, play, player, instrument*} the gold-standard target was '*accordion*'. But why not '*violin*' or '*trombone*'? To provide a more in-depth evaluation of the results, we sampled 180 items at random from the test set, along with the candidate targets produced by our system,[9] and submitted those to evaluation by two research assistants. For each item, evaluators were given the five cue words and the best candidate target generated by the system. They were told that the word is supposed to be a common associate of the five cues, and asked to indicate, for each item, whether the candidate was (a) *Just Right*; or (b) *OK*; or (c) *Inadequate;* (a,b,c are on ordinal scale).

Out of the 180 items, 80 were judged by both annotators. Table 1 presents the agreement matrix between the two annotators. Agreement on the 3 classes was kappa=0.49. If *Just Right* and *OK* are collapsed, the agreement is kappa=0.60. The discrepancy is largely due to a substantial number of instances that one annotator judged *OK* and the other – *Just Right*.

	Inadequate	OK	Just Right	TOTAL
Inadequate	17	6	1	24
OK	6	25	10	41
Just Right	0	3	12	15
TOTAL	23	34	23	80

Table 1. Inter-annotator agreement matrix for a subset of items from the test-set.

[9] Using all resources, NPMI association measure, MR aggregation, and with the general stoplist filter.

We note that one annotator commented on a difficulty making a decision in a number of cases where the cues are a list of mostly adjectives or possessives, and the target produced by the system is an adverb. For example, the cue set {*busy, house, vacant, engaged, empty*} with the proposed candidate target '*currently*'; the cue set {*food, thirsty, tired, empty, starving*} with the proposed candidate '*perpetually*'; the cue set {*fat, short, build, thick, built*} with the proposed candidate '*slightly*'; the cue set {*mine, yours, his, is, theirs*} with the proposed target '*rightfully*'. This annotator felt that these responses were *OK*, while the other annotator rejected them.

We merged the two annotations to provide a single annotation for the full set of 180 items by taking one annotator's judgment on single-annotated cases and taking the lower of the two judgments for the double annotated disagreed cases (thus, *OK* and *Inadequate* are merged to *Inadequate*; *Just Right* and *OK* are merged to *OK*). We next compare these annotations to the EAT gold standard. Table 2 shows the confusion matrix between the "gold label" from EAT and our annotation. We observe that the totals for *Just Right* and EAT-match are almost identical (43 vs 42); however, only 17 items were both *Just Right* and EAT-matches. There were 24 EAT matches that were judged as *OK* by the annotators (presumably, these did not quite create the "just right" impression for at least one annotator). Examples include: the cue set {*beer, tea, storm, ale, bear*} with the proposed correct target '*brewing*' (one annotator commented that the relationship with "*bear*" was unclear); the cue set {*exam, match, tube, try, cricket*} with the proposed correct target '*test*' (one annotator commented that the relationship with '*cricket*' was unclear); the cue set {*school, secondary, first, education, alcohol*} with the proposed correct target '*primary*' (one annotator commented that the relationship with '*alcohol*' was unclear). These results might reflect cultural differences between original EAT respondents (British undergraduates circa year 1970) and present-day American young adults who, e.g. might not know much about cricket. Another possibility is that in the EAT collection, the 5th cue sometimes corresponds to a very weak associate provided by just a single respondent out of 100, as in *brewing-bear* and *primary-alcohol* cases. Interestingly, the weak cues did not confuse the system, but replicability of the human judgments for such cases is doubtful.

	Just Right	**OK**	**Inadequate**	**Total**
EAT match	17	24	1	**42**
EAT mismatch	26	58	54	**138**
Total	**43**	**82**	**55**	**180**

Table 2. Annotated data vs. gold-standard matches for a set of 180 items.

There were also 26 instances that were judged as *Just Right* yet were not EAT-matches. Three of these were derivationally related, like '*build*' (EAT target) vs '*buildings*' (proposed) for the cue set {*house, up, construct, destroy, bricks*}, the others were '*dwell*' vs '*dwellings*', '*collector*' vs '*collecting*'. In the rest of the cases, the generated candidates seemed as good as, or better, than the EAT words. For example, the cue set {*ships, boat, sea, ship, ocean*} had '*liners*' as the EAT target, whereas the system proposed '*cruise*'. For the cue set {*natural, animal, nature, birds, fear*}, the gold-standard EAT target is '*instinct*', whereas the system proposed '*predatory*'. For the cue set {*sound, speak, sing, noise, speech*} the gold-standard EAT target is '*voice*', while the system produced '*louder*'. For the cue set {*music, band, noise, club, folk*} the target was '*jazz*', whereas the system proposed '*dance*'. For the cue set {*violin, music, orchestra, bow, instrument*} the target was '*cello*', while the system produced '*stringed*'. Furthermore, in as many as 58 cases (32%) the response produced by the system did not match the target from EAT, but was OK-ed by the annotators. Some examples include: the cue set {*fool, loaf, idiot, lout, lazy*} with proposed candidate '*ignorant*'; the cue set {*hard, problems, work, hardship, trouble*} with proposed candidate '*economic*'; {*interesting, intriguing, amazing, book, exciting*} with proposed candidate '*discoveries*'; {*lazy, chair, about, lying, sitting*} with proposed candidate '*motionless*'. In all, if the system were evaluated by counting *Just Right* and *OK* annotations as correct, the precison@1 would have been (43+82)/180 = 69%. The estimation of performance based on gold-standard EAT data for this set is 42/180 = 23%, exactly one-third of what annotators found to be reasonable responses. This suggests that evaluation of multi-cued retrieval on targets from EAT rejects many good semantic associates, and thus might be considered too harsh.

6 Conclusions

This paper presented an automated system that computes multi-cue associations and generates associated-word suggestions, using lexical co-occurrence data from a large corpus of English texts. The system uses pre-existing resources – a large *n*-ngram database and a large word-co-occurrence database, which have been previously used for a range of different NLP tasks. The system performs expansion of cue words to their inflectional variants, retrieves candidate words from corpus data, finds maximal associations between candidates and cues, and then computes an aggregate score for each candidate. The collection of candidates is then sorted and an *n*-best list is presented as output. In the paper we presented experiments using various measures of statistical association and two methods of score aggregation. We also experimented with limiting the lexical resources, and with applying additional filters on retrieved candidates.

For test-set evaluation, the shared task requires strict-matches to gold-standard targets. Our system, in optimal configuration, was correct in 372 of 2000 cases, that is precision of 18.6%. We have also suggested a more lenient evaluation, where a candidate target is also considered correct if it is an inflectional variant of the gold-standard word. When inflections are allowed, our system achieves precision of 24.35%. Performance improves dramatically when evaluation considers in how many cases the gold-standard target (or its inflectional variants) are found among the *n*-best suggestions provided by the system. For example, with a list of 10-best suggestions, precision rises to 45%, and to 54% with a list of 25-best. Using an *n*-best list of suggestions makes sense for applications like tip-of-the-tongue situation.

We note that the specific data set used in COGALEX-4 shared task, i.e. the Edinburgh Associative Thesaurus, might be sub-optimal for evaluation of multi-cue associative search. With the EAT dataset, the gold-standard words were the original stimuli from EAT, and the cue words were the associated words that were most frequently produced by respondents in the original EAT experiment (Kiss et al., 1973). Rapp (2014) has argued that corpus-based computation of reverse-associations is a reasonable test case for multi-cued word search. However, Rapp also notes that in many cases, suggestions provided by a corpus-based system are quite reasonable, but are not correct for the EAT dataset. We have conducted pilot human annotation on a small subset of the test-set – judging how reasonable the top suggestion of our system is in general, and not whether it matched EAT targets. In this experiment, 69% of the system's first responses were judged acceptable by humans, while only 23% matched targets. This provides a quantitative confirmation that EAT-based evaluation underestimates the quality of results produced by a corpus-based multi-cue association system.

The use of data from EAT hints at the following direction for future research. In the original EAT data, the first cue is actually the strongest associate of the target word (original stimulus), while other cues are much weaker associates. In our current implementation, we treated all cues as equally important. Future research may include consideration for relative importance or relevance of the different cues. In potential applications, like the tip-of-the-tongue word search, a user may be able to specify which cues are more relevant than others.

Acknowledgments

Special thanks to Melissa Lopez and Matthew Mulholland for their help with the evaluation study. We also thank Mo Zhang, Paul Deane and Keelan Evanini at ETS, and three anonymous COGALEX reviewers, for comments on earlier drafts of this paper.

References

Marko Baroni and Allesandro Lenci. 2010. Distributional Memory: A General Framework for Corpus-Based Semantics. *Computational Linguistics*, 36(4), 673-721

Beata Beigman Klebanov and Michael Flor. 2013a. Word Association Profiles and their Use for Automated Scoring of Essays. In Proceedings of the 51st Annual Meeting of the Association for Computational Linguistics, pages 1148–1158, Sofia, Bulgaria.

Beata Beigman Klebanov and Michael Flor. 2013b. Associative Texture Is Lost In Translation. In Proceedings of the Workshop on Discourse in Machine Translation (DiscoMT), pages 27–32. ACL 2013 Conference, Sofia, Bulgaria.

Gerlof Bouma. 2009. Normalized (Pointwise) Mutual Information in Collocation Extraction. In: Chiarcos, Eckart de Castilho & Stede (eds), From Form to Meaning: Processing Texts Automatically, Proceedings of the Biennial GSCL Conference 2009, Tübingen, Gunter Narr Verlag, p. 31–40.

John A. Bullinaria and Joseph P. Levy. 2007. Extracting semantic representations from word co-occurrence statistics: A computational study. *Behavior Research Methods*, 39:510–526.

Kenneth Church and Patrick Hanks. 1990. Word association norms, mutual information and lexicography. *Computational Linguistics*, 16(1), 22–29.

David Graff and Christopher Cieri. 2003. English Gigaword. LDC2003T05. Philadelphia, PA, USA: Linguistic Data Consortium.

Stefan Evert. 2008. Corpora and collocations. In A. Lüdeling and M. Kytö (eds.), Corpus Linguistics: An International Handbook, Mouton de Gruyter: Berlin.

Michael Flor. 2013. A fast and flexible architecture for very large word n-gram datasets. *Natural Language Engineering*, 19(1), 61-93.

Michael Flor. 2012. Four types of context for automatic spelling correction. *Traitement Automatique des Langues* (TAL), 53:3 (Special Issue: Managing noise in the signal: error handling in natural language processing), 61-99.

Michael Flor and Beata Beigman Klebanov. (in press) Associative Lexical Cohesion as a factor in Text Complexity. Accepted for publication in the International Journal of Applied Linguistics.

Michael Flor, Beata Beigman Klebanov and Kathleen M. Sheehan. 2013. Lexical Tightness and Text Complexity. In Proceedings of the 2th Workshop of Natural Language Processing for Improving Textual Accessibility (NLP4ITA), p.29–38. NAACL 2013 Conference, Atlanta, Georgia.

G.R. Kiss, C. Armstrong, R. Milroy and J. Piper. 1973. An associative thesaurus of English and its computer analysis. In Aitken, A.J., Bailey, R.W. and Hamilton-Smith, N. (Eds.), The Computer and Literary Studies. Edinburgh: University Press.

Nitin Madnani and Aoife Cahill. 2014. An Explicit Feedback System for Preposition Errors based on Wikipedia Revisions. To appear in Proceedings of the 9th Workshop on Innovative Use of NLP for Building Educational applications (BEA-9). ACL 2014 Conference, Baltimore, MD.

Christopher D. Manning, Prabhakar Raghavan, and Hinrich Schütze. 2008. *Introduction to Information Retrieval*. Cambridge University Press.

Christopher D. Manning, and Hinrich Schütze. 1999. *Foundations of Statistical Natural Language Processing*, 1999, Cambridge, Massachusetts, USA: MIT Press.

Roger Mitton. 2008. Ordering the suggestions of a spellchecker without using context. *Natural Language Engineering*, 15(2), 173–192.

Reinhard Rapp. 2014. Corpus-Based Computation of Reverse-Associations. Proceedings of LREC.

Reinhard Rapp. 2008. The computation of associative responses to multiword stimuli. In Proceedings of the Workshop on Cognitive Aspects of the Lexicon (COGALEX) at COLING-2008, p.102–109. Manchester, UK

Kathleen M. Sheehan, Irene Kostin, Yoko Futagi, Ramin Hemat and Daniel Zuckerman. 2006. Inside SourceFinder: Predicting the Acceptability Status of Candidate Reading-Comprehension Source Documents. ETS research report RR-06-24. Educational Testing Service: Princeton, NJ.

Peter Turney and Patrick Pantel. 2010. From Frequency to Meaning: Vector Space Models of Semantics. *Journal of Artificial Intelligence Research*, 37, 141-188.

Using Significant Word Co-occurences for the Lexical Access Problem

Rico Feist and **Daniel Gerighausen** and **Manuel Konrad** and **Georg Richter** and
Department of Computer Science,
University of Leipzig,
Germany
rf@ricofeist.de, daniel@bioinf.uni-leipzig.de
manuel.konrad, georg.richter @studserv.uni-leipzig.de

Thomas Eckart and **Dirk Goldhahn** and **Uwe Quasthoff**
Natural Language Processing Group,
University of Leipzig,
Germany
teckart, dgoldhahn, quasthoff
@informatik.uni-leipzig.de

Abstract

One way to analyse word relations is to examine their co-occurrence in the same context. This allows for the identification of potential semantic or lexical relationships between words. As previous studies showed word co-occurrences often reflect human stimuli-response pairs. In this paper significant sentence co-occurrences on word level were used to identify potential responses for word stimuli based on three automatically generated text corpora of the Leipzig Corpora Collection.

1 Introduction

Conventional dictionaries have very limited possibilities for retrieving information. By contrast electronic dictionaries offer a much wider and more dynamic range of access strategies. One important task in dictionary lookup is to retrieve a word starting just with the corresponding meaning. For this purpose the flexibility of electronic dictionaries should be advantageous. In the following the related task of retrieving a word based just on a stimulus of five related input words is addressed. Based on the assumption that word co-occurrences in the same context can be used to analyse word relations and to identify potential semantic or lexical relationships between words an automatic system is built based on an electronic dictionary extracted from Web corpora. As previous studies showed word co-occurrences often reflect human stimuli-response pairs (Spence, 1990; Schulte im Walde, 2008). In this paper significant sentence co-occurrences on word level were used to identify potential responses for word stimuli based on three automatically generated text corpora of the Leipzig Corpora Collection (LCC).

2 Used Methods and Resources

2.1 Used Corpora

The text corpora of the Leipzig Corpora Collection (Biemann, 2007; Goldhahn, 2012) were used as data basis. As the origin of the stimuli data was unknown corpora based on different text material were exploited:

- eng_wikipedia_2010: a corpus based on the English Wikipedia generated in 2010 containing 23 million sentences
- eng_news_2008: 49 million sentences from English newspaper articles collected in 2008
- eng_web_2002: 57 million sentences of English Web text crawled in 2002

Zock/Rapp/Huang (eds.): Proceedings of the 4th Workshop on Cognitive Aspects of the Lexicon, pages 46–49,
Dublin, Ireland, August 23, 2014.

All of these corpora were generated by the standard preprocessing toolchain of the LCC. This toolchain contains different procedures to ensure corpus quality like language identification and pattern based removal of invalid text material (Goldhahn, 2012). Furthermore all corpora were annotated with statistical information about word co-occurrences based on co-occurrence in the same sentence or direct neighbourhood. These word relations were generated by using the log-likelihood ratio (Buechler, 2006) as measure of significance. Complete sentences were used as co-occurrence window.

2.2 Raw Results Generation

For each of the five stimulus words and every corpus all co-occurrent words were extracted. For extracted terms that significantly co-occurred with more than one of the stimulus words the significance of co-occurrence were combined. Based on the sum of the significance values a ranking of the most relevant terms for every stimulus was created for every corpus. The most significant 15 words were considered as raw result for every corpus and stimulus 5-tuple.

2.3 Postprocessing

The raw results were combined by replacing the result ranks in the three intermediate result lists l_i $(1 <= i <= 3)$ with a weight $(weight_i(w) = 16 - rank_i(w))$. These weights were merged by generating the combined weight for all three corpora $c\_weight(w) = \sum_{i=1}^{3} weight_i(w)$. The word with the highest combined weight was chosen as response for a stimulus tupel.

The same procedure was used in two variations:

- Rankings were generated based on the combination of all inflected terms of the same word stem (by using the Porter stemmer(Porter, 1980)).
- Stop words were removed from the result lists to reduce the influence of high frequent function words[1].

For some stimuli only stop words were extracted as response. Here not only the 15 most significant terms were extracted from every corpus but the 45 most significant terms. This lead to more useful results in most cases.

2.4 Results

All three variants were evaluated on the training data set. The evaluation lead to the conclusion that a stop word filter is a useful preprocessing step, whereas stemming lead to unsatisfactory results (cp. table 1). As a consequence only the stop word filter (without stemming) was used for the test data set where 281 (14.05%) of the responses were correctly predicted.

Used Data	Correctly Predicted	Percentage
Original corpus data (incl. stop words, unstemmed)	61	3.05%
Removed stop words	262	13.1%
Stemmed	43	2.15%

Table 1: Evaluation of the different approaches based on the training data set

3 Conclusion

It is noteworthy that corpora where solely stop words were removed yielded better results than corpora where additional stemming took place. One reason for this observation is most likely that by using the Porter algorithm an overstemming occurred. Some word pairs were reduced to identical word stems

[1]For this purpose the stop word list of the database management system MySQL was used (https://dev.mysql.com/doc/refman/5.5/en/fulltext-stopwords.html).

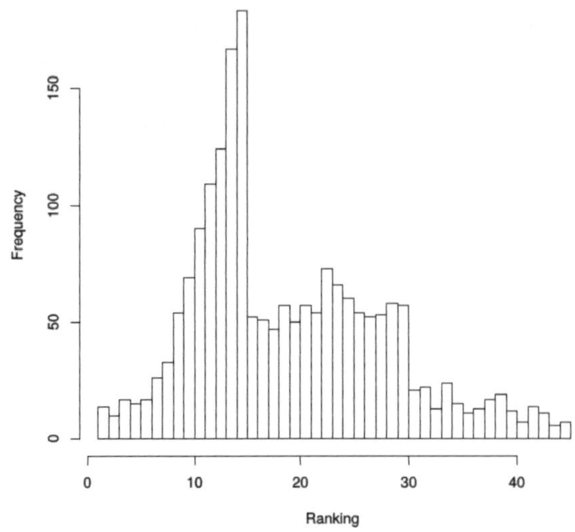

Figure 1: Histogramm of the combined weights for the training data set

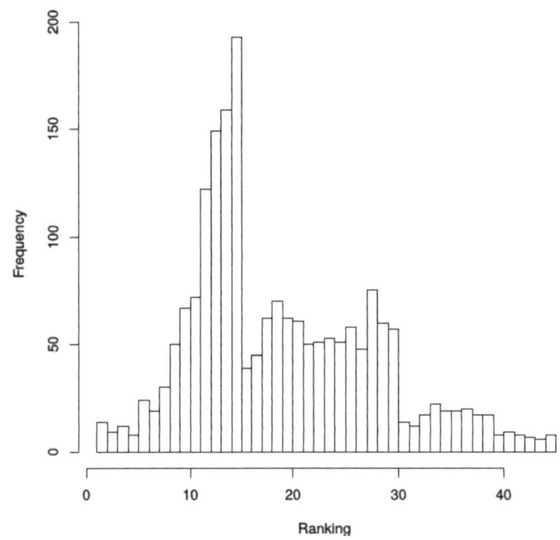

Figure 2: Histogramm of the combined weights for the test data set

although having no semantic relationship.
The final results also contained a disproportionately high number of specific terms. As an example the word "god" was chosen 38 times as response. An analysis of the corpora showed that the word "god" was especially frequent in the Web corpus (330,276 of 56,523,369 sentences (0.59%)) and the Wikipedia-based corpus (58,605 of 22,675,331 sentences (0.26%)). In contrast, the newspaper corpus had only 29 occurrences of the term "god" (in 48,903,372 sentences (0.00006%)).

The evaluation for both the training (figure 1) and the test data set (figure 2) shows that there is a peak for the combined weight of 15. This behaviour originates in terms that have the maximum rank in one of the three corpora but being no significant co-occurrent term in the other two.

4 Further Improvements

The evaluation showed that the used corpora generated results of different quality. This was especially demonstrated at the example of the term "god". As a consequence a stricter selection of the corpus material combined with a weighting of the specific results from each corpus could improve the predictions.

The used corpora reflect a specific selection of input material (in this case written text material from different sources of the years 2002 to 2010). A corpus that reflects more of the details of the test data (most notably being significantly older) would very likely enhance the results. This is especially the case as words that became prominent over the last decades (like technical terms or words strongly related to more recent political developments) would not have occurred in the generated results. A deeper analysis of the input material and the availability of a comparable corpus would have been the prerequisites.

An examination of the results also showed that in many cases a synonym of the correct response was identified. Hence the usage of a synonym database could also lead to further improvements. Furthermore using part of speech information could be beneficial for the weighting of intermediate results. The basic idea is that part of speech of stimulus and response are very likely to be the same. This would have eliminated parts of the generated result sets. Furthermore a deeper analysis of the ranking procedure may have reduced the effect which manifests in many terms having a weight of 15 in the results.

References

Chris Biemann, Gerhard Heyer, Uwe Quasthoff, and Matthias Richter. 2007. The Leipzig Corpora Collection - Monolingual corpora of standard size. *Proceedings of Corpus Linguistic 2007*, Birmingham, UK.

Marco Buechler. 2006. Flexibles Berechnen von Kookkurrenzen auf strukturierten und unstrukturierten Daten. *Diploma Thesis*, University of Leipzig.

Dirk Goldhahn, Thomas Eckart, and Uwe Quasthoff. 2012. Building Large Monolingual Dictionaries at the Leipzig Corpora Collection: From 100 to 200 Languages. *Proceedings of the Eighth International Conference on Language Resources and Evaluation (LREC 2012).*

Martin F. Porter. 1980. An algorithm for suffix stripping. *electronic library and information systems*, 14.3 (1980): 130-137.

Donald P. Spence, and Kimberley C. Owens. 1990. Lexical co-occurrence and association strength. *Journal of Psycholinguistic Research*, Volume 19(5):317–330.

Sabine Schulte im Walde, and Alissa Melinger. 2008. An in-depth look into the co-occurrence distribution of semantic associates. *Italian Journal of Linguistics, Special Issue on From Context to Meaning: Distributional Models of the Lexicon in Linguistics and Cognitive Science.*

NaDiR: Naive Distributional Response Generation

Gabriella Lapesa
Institut für Maschinelle Sprachverarbeitung, Universität Stuttgart
Institut für Kognitionswissenschaft, Universität Osnabrück
glapesa@uos.de

Stefan Evert
Professur für Korpuslinguistik
FAU Erlangen-Nürnberg
stefan.evert@fau.de

Abstract

This paper describes *NaDiR* (Naive DIstributional Response generation), a corpus-based system that, from a set of word stimuli as an input, generates a response word relying on association strength and distributional similarity. *NaDiR* participated in the CogALex 2014 shared task on multiword associations (restricted systems track), operationalizing the task as a ranking problem: candidate words from a large vocabulary are ranked by their average association or similarity to a given set of stimuli. We also report on a number of experiments conducted on the shared task data, comparing first-order models (based on co-occurrence and statistical association) to second-order models (based on distributional similarity).

1 Introduction

This paper describes *NaDiR*, a corpus-based system designed for the *reverse association task*. NaDiR is an acronym for Naive Distributional Response generation. NaDiR is naive because it is based on a very simple algorithm that operationalizes the multiword association task as a ranking problem: candidate words from a large vocabulary are ranked by their average statistical association or distributional similarity to a given set of stimuli, then the highest-ranked candidate is selected as NaDiR's response.

We compare models based on collocations (first-order models, see Evert (2008) for an overview) to models based on distributional similarity (second-order models; see Sahlgren (2006), Turney and Pantel (2010), and reference therein for a review). Previous work on this task showed that co-occurrence models outperform distributional semantic models (henceforth, DSMs), and that using rank measures improves performance because it accounts for directionality of the association/similarity (e.g., the association from stimulus to response may be larger than the association from response to stimulus). Our results corroborate both claims.

The paper is structured as follows: section 2 provides an overview of the task and of the problems we encountered in its implementation; section 3 summarizes related work; section 4 describes NaDiR in detail; section 5 reports the results of our experiments on the shared task training and test data; section 6 describes ongoing and future work on NaDiR.

2 The Task and its Problems

The shared task datasets are derived from the Edinburgh Associative Thesaurus (Kiss et al., 1973)[1]. The Edinburgh Associative Thesaurus (henceforth, EAT) contains free associations to approximately 8000 English cue words. For each cue (e.g., *visual*) EAT lists all associations collected in the survey (e.g., *aid*, *eyes*, *aids*, *see*, *eye*, *seen*, *sight*, etc.) sorted according to the number of subjects who responded with the respective word. The CogALex shared task on multiword association is based on the EAT dataset, and is in fact a *reverse association task* (Rapp, 2014). The top five responses for a target word are provided as stimuli (e.g., *aid*, *eyes*, *aids*, *see*, *eye*), and the participating systems are required to generate the original cue as a response (e.g., *visual*). The training and the test sets are random extracts of 2000 EAT

[1] http://www.eat.rl.ac.uk/

Zock/Rapp/Huang (eds.): Proceedings of the 4th Workshop on Cognitive Aspects of the Lexicon, pages 50–59, Dublin, Ireland, August 23, 2014.

items each, with minimal pre-processing (only items containing multiword units and non-alphabetical characters were discarded).

A key problem we had to tackle while developing our system was the unrestricted set of possible responses in combination with a discrete association task, which requires the algorithm to pick exactly the right answer out of tens of thousands of possible responses. This feature makes this task much more difficult than the multiple-choice tasks often used to evaluate distributional semantic models. The problem is further complicated by the fact that the response may be an inflected form and only a prediction of the exact form was accepted as a correct answer. The need for a solution to these issues motivates various aspects of the NaDiR algorithm, described in section 4.

3 Related Work

Previous studies based on free association norms differ considerably in terms of the type of task (regular free association task – one stimulus, one response vs. multiword association task – many stimuli, one response), gold standards, and key features of the evaluated models (e.g., source corpora used and choice of a candidate vocabulary from which responses are selected).

In regular free association tasks (one stimulus, one response), responses are known to contain both paradigmatically and syntagmatically related words. Rapp (2002) proposes to integrate first-order (co-occurrence lists) and second-order (bag-of-words DSMs) information to distinguish syntagmatic from paradigmatic relations by exploiting the comparison of most salient collocates and nearest neighbors.

A task derived from the EAT norms was used in the ESSLLI 2008 shared task[2]. Results from first-order co-occurrence data turned out to be much better than those from second-order DSMs, in line with the findings made by Rapp (2002) and Wettler et al. (2005).

A similar picture emerges from studies on the multiword association task. Models based on first-order co-occurrence (collocations) outperform models based on vector similarity. This superiority, however, is not validated via a direct comparison: results were obtained by studies with different features and goals (see Rapp (2014) for a review; see Griffiths et al. (2007) and Smith et al. (2013) for evaluations of models based on Latent Semantic Analysis). A specific feature of successful studies on the multiword association task is that they introduce an element of directionality (Rapp, 2013; Rapp, 2014), which allows a correct implementation of the directionality of the modeled effects (from stimulus to response).

Our survey of related studies motivated the choice to base NaDiR on first-order or second-order co-occurrence statistics, and to use collocate or neighbor rank to account for directionality. Our main contribution to research on the reverse association task is a systematic experimental comparison of first-order and second-order models (using the same gold standard, same source corpus, and same candidate vocabulary), which enables us to give a sound answer to the question whether first-order models are indeed superior for multiword association tasks.

4 NaDiR

NaDiR operationalizes the multiword association task as a ranking problem. For each set of stimuli, the possible response words ("candidates") are ranked according to their average association strength or distributional similarity to the stimulus words. The top-ranked candidate is selected as NaDiR's response. One advantage of the ranking approach is that it provides additional insights into the experimental results: if the model prediction is not correct, the rank of the correct answer can be used as a measure how "close" the model came to the human associations.

Since neither a fixed set of response candidates nor an indication of the source of the training and test data were available (and we did not google for the training sets), we compiled a large vocabulary of possible responses. We believe that restricting the vocabulary to the 8,033 cue words in the EAT would have improved our results considerably. More details concerning the choice of the candidate vocabulary are reported in section 4.1.

[2] `http://wordspace.collocations.de/doku.php/data:esslli2008:correlation_with_free_association_norms`

NaDiR uses either first-order or second-order co-occurrence statistics to predict the association strength between stimuli and responses. In the first case ("collocations"), we apply one of several standard statistical association measures to co-occurrence counts obtained from a large corpus. In the second case, association is quantified by cosine similarity in a distributional semantic model built from the same corpus. Both first-order and second-order statistics were collected from UKWaC in order to compete in the constrained track of the shared task.

Recent experiments (Hare et al., 2009; Lapesa and Evert, 2013; Lapesa et al., to appear) suggest that semantic relations are often better captured by neighbour ranks rather than direct use of statistical association measures or cosine similarity values. Therefore, NaDiR can alternatively quantify association strength by collocate rank and similarity by neighbour rank. In our experiments (section 5), we compare the different approaches.

NaDiR is designed for the multiword association task, and it contains additional features related to the particular design of the CogALex shared task:

- We reduce the number of candidates by selecting the most likely response POS with a machine-learning algorithm (section 4.1);
- NaDiR operates on lemmatized data in order to reduce sparseness. We lemmatize stimuli using a heuristic method (section 4.1), predict a response lemma, and then use machine-learning techniques to generate a plausible word form (section 4.3).

4.1 Pre-processing and Vocabulary

Our experiments were conducted on the UKWaC[3] corpus. UKWaC contains 2 billion words, web-crawled from the `.uk` domain between 2005 and 2007. The release of UKWaC also contains linguistic annotation (pos-tagging and lemmatization) performed with Tree Tagger[4].

To assign a part-of-speech tag and a lemma to every word in the dataset without relying on external tools, we adopted the following mapping strategy based on the linguistic annotation already available in UKWaC:

1. We extracted all attested wordform/part of speech/lemma combinations from UKWaC, together with their frequency;
2. Every word form in the training set was assigned to the most frequent part of speech/lemma combination attested in UKWaC.

We believe that the advantages of constructing distributional models based on lemmatized words overcome the drawbacks of this type of out-of-context lemmatization and part-of-speech assignment.

The part-of-speech information added to every word in the dataset by the mapping procedure was used to train a classifier that, given the parts of speech of the stimuli, predicts the part of speech of the response. We trained a support-vector machine, using the `svm` function from the R package `e1071`[5], with standard settings.

The part-of-speech classifier is based on a coarse part-of-speech tagset with only five tags: `N` (noun), `J` (adjective), `V` (verb), `R` (adverb), `other` (closed-class words). We considered each row of the dataset as an observation, with the part of speech of the response as predicted value, and the part of speech of the stimulus words as predictors. Every observation is represented as a bag of tags, i.e., a vector listing for each of the five tags how often it occurs among the stimuli. For example, if a set of stimuli contains 3 nouns, one verb and one adjective, the corresponding bag-of-tags vector looks as follows: $\{\mathtt{N} = 3; \mathtt{V} = 1; \mathtt{J} = 1; \mathtt{R} = 0; \mathtt{other} = 0\}$. On the training set, the part-of-speech classifier achieves an accuracy of 72%.

The vocabulary of our models only contains lemmatized open-class words (this information is available in the annotation of the corpus). By inspecting the frequencies of stimuli and response words in the training dataset, we established a reasonable minimum frequency threshold for candidate words of 100 occurrences in UKWaC. With this threshold, only 10 response words and 16 stimulus words from the

[3] `wacky.sslmit.unibo.it/doku.php?id=corpora`
[4] `http://www.ims.uni-stuttgart.de/projekte/corplex/TreeTagger/`
[5] `http://cran.r-project.org/web/packages/e1071/index.html`

training dataset are excluded from the vocabulary. Given the large size of the dataset, we decided that a minimal loss in coverage would be justified by the reduced computational complexity. The resulting candidate vocabulary contains 155,811 words.

4.2 First- and Second-order Statistics

The aim of this section is to describe the parameters involved in the collection of first-order and second-order statistics from UKWaC. All models have been built and evaluated using the UCS toolkit[6] and the `wordspace` package for R (Evert, to appear)[7].

First-order Models

Collocation data are compiled from UKWaC based on the vocabulary described in section 4.1. Both nodes (rows of the co-occurrence matrix) and collocates (columns of the co-occurrence matrix) are chosen from this vocabulary. Collection of first-order models involved the manipulation of a number of parameters, briefly summarized below.
We adopted three different **window sizes**:

- symmetric window, 2 words to the left and to the right of the node;
- asymmetric window, 3 words to the left of the node;
- asymmetric window, 3 words to the right of the node.

We tested the following **association scores** (Evert, 2008):

- co-occurrence frequency;
- simple log-likelihood (similar to local MI used by Baroni and Lenci (2010));
- conditional probability.

Our experiments involved a third parameter, the **index of association strength**, which determines alternative ways of quantifying the degree of association between targets and contexts in the first-order model. Given two words *a* and *b* represented in a first-order model, we propose two alternative ways of quantifying the degree of association between *a* and *b*. The first option (and standard in corpus-based modeling) is to compute the *association score* between *a* and *b*. The alternative choice is based on *rank among collocates*. Given two words *a* and *b*, in our task *stimulus* and *potential response*, we consider:

- forward rank: the rank of the potential response among the collocates of the stimulus;
- backward rank: the rank of the stimulus among the collocates of the potential response;
- average rank: the average of forward and backward rank.

Second-order Models

Based on the results of a large-scale evaluation of DSM parameters (Lapesa and Evert, under review) and the modeling of semantic priming effects (Lapesa and Evert, 2013; Lapesa et al., to appear), we identified a robust configuration of parameters for second-order models that we decided to adopt in this study. Second-order models involved in our experiments share the following parameter settings:

- The target words (rows) are defined by the vocabulary described in section 4.1.
- The context words (columns) are the 50,000 most frequent context words in the respective co-occurrence matrices. The 50 most frequent words in UKWaC are discarded.
- Co-occurrence vectors are scored with a sparse version of simple-log likelihood, in which negative values clamped to zero in order to preserve the sparseness of the co-occurrence matrix. Scored vectors are rescaled by applying a logarithmic transformation.
- We reduce the scored co-occurrence matrix to 1000 latent dimensions using randomized SVD (Halko et al., 2009).
- We adopt *cosine distance* (i.e. the angle between vectors) as a distance metric for the computation of vector similarity.

[6] `http://www.collocations.de/software.html`
[7] `http://r-forge.r-project.org/projects/wordspace/`

Our experiments on second-order models involved the manipulation of two parameters: **window size** and **index of association strength**.

The size of the context window quantifies the amount of shared context involved in the computation of similarity. We expect the manipulation of window size to be crucial in determining model performance, as different context windows will enable the model to capture different types of relations between response and stimulus words (Sahlgren, 2006; Lapesa et al., to appear). In our experiments with NaDiR, we adopted three different **window sizes**:

- symmetric window, 2 words to the left and to the right of the target;
- symmetric window, 4 words to the left and to the right of the target;
- symmetric window, 16 words to the left and to the right of the target.

The values for **index of association strength** are the same as for the first-order models, computing ranks among the nearest neighbors of the stimulus or response word. The use of rank-based measures is of particular interest, because: (i) it allows us to model directionality (while, for example, cosine distance is symmetric); (ii) it already proved successful in modeling behavioral data (Hare et al., 2009; Lapesa and Evert, 2013); (iii) since the vocabulary of first-order and second-order models are identical, rank-based measures allow a direct comparison between the two classes of models, as well as experiments based on their combination.

4.3 Response Generation

To generate a response for a set of stimuli in the training/test dataset, we apply the following procedure:

1. For each set of stimuli, we compute association strengths or similarities between each stimulus and each response candidate, adopting one of the measures described in section 4.2.
2. From the set of potential responses, we select the words whose POS agrees with the predictions of the classifier described in section 4.1. Stimulus words are discarded from the potential answers.
3. We compute the average association strength or similarity across all five stimuli; if a stimulus does not appear in the model, it is simply omitted from the average.
4. The top-ranked candidate is the POS-disambiguated lemma suggested as a response by NaDiR.
5. We generate a suitable word form by inverting the heuristic lemmatization; if the full Penn tag (e.g., `NNS`: noun, common, plural; `NN`: noun, common, singular or mass, etc.) of the response is known, this step can be implemented as a deterministic lookup (since a word form is usually determined uniquely by lemma and Penn tag). We therefore trained a second SVM classifier that predicts the full Penn tag of the response based on the full tags of the stimuli. On the training set, this part-of-speech classifier reaches an accuracy of 68%.

5 Experiments

In our experiments, we compared first-order (collocations) and second-order (DSM) models; for each class of models, we evaluated the different parameter values described in section 4.2. Table 1 summarizes the evaluated parameters for first-order and second-order models.

Model	Window	Score	Relatedness Index
first-order	symmetric, 2	frequency	association score
	left 3, right 0	simple log-likelihood	forward rank
	left 0, right 3	conditional probability	backward rank
			average rank
second-order	symmetric, 2	simple log-likelihood	distance
	symmetric, 4		forward rank
	symmetric, 16		backward rank
			average rank

Table 1: Evaluated Parameters for First- and Second-order Models

Tables 2 to 5 display the results of our experiments on the training data, separately for first-order (tables 2-4) and second-order models (table 5). Parameter configurations are reported in the *Parameter* column[8]. The number of correct responses in the lemmatized version is reported in the column *Lemma* (showing how often our system predicted the correct lemma). The column *Wordform* reports the number of correct responses for which, before inverting the lemmatization, the inflected form was already identical to the lemma. As the task of predicting exactly one word is particularly difficult, we further characterize the performance of our evaluated models by reporting the number of cases in which the correct answer from the training set was among the first 10 (< 10), 50 (< 50), or 100 (< 100) ranked candidates. In the last column, we report the average rank of the correct responses (*Avg_correct*).

The results reported in tables 2 to 5 allowed us to identify best parameter configurations for the first-order (symmetric 2 words window, frequency, backward rank) and second-order models (2 words window, distance). We evaluated these configurations on the test data (table 6). Table 7 compares the performance of the best first-order and the best second-order model on the training and test datasets, both for lemmatized response (*Training-Lemma*, *Test-Lemma*) and generation of the correct word form (*Training-Inflected*, *Test-Inflected*).

A considerable portion of the experiments reported in this paper were conducted after the submission deadline of the CogALex shared task. As a consequence, our submitted results do not correspond to the best overall configuration found in the evaluation study. The submission was based on a second order model, a 4-word window, and cosine distance as index of distributional similarity. In this configuration, NaDiR generated 262 correct responses, corresponding to an accuracy of 13%.

Parameters	Lemma	Wordform	< 10	< 50	< 100	Avg_correct
Freq_{ass}	2	2	85	372	561	1400
Freq_{fwd}	0	0	77	359	550	6258
Freq_{bwd}	**555**	464	973	1269	1369	1546
Freq_{avg}	424	322	677	848	934	5969
Simple-ll_{ass}	33	28	237	721	985	933
Simple-ll_{fwd}	405	319	760	916	947	12031
Simple-ll_{bwd}	531	444	914	1141	1253	1971
Simple-ll_{avg}	490	388	785	918	950	11645
Cond.prob_{ass}	18	16	329	746	970	978
Cond.prob_{fwd}	0	0	77	359	550	6258
Cond.prob_{bwd}	422	359	856	1129	1255	1719
Cond.prob_{avg}	343	256	611	860	971	5948

Table 2: First Order Models - Symmetric Window: 2 words to the left/right of the node - Training Data

5.1 Discussion

The results of our experiments are in line with the tendencies identified in the literature (see section 3). First-order models based on direct co-occurrence (high scores are assigned to words that co-occur), outperform second-order models based on distributional similarity (smaller distances between words that occur in similar contexts).

For the first-order models, the best index of association strength is backward rank (the rank of the stimulus among the collocates of the potential response), fully congruent with the experimental setting (in the EAT norm, subjects produced the stimuli as free associations of the expected response). Surprisingly, frequency outperforms simple-log likelihood (which is usually considered to be among the best association measures for the identification of collocations). In line with the results achieved by Rapp (2014), a symmetric window of 2 words to the left and to the right of the target achieves best results.

For the second-order models, the smallest context window (2 words) achieves the best performance.

[8]Abbreviations used in the tables: *ass* = association score; *dist* = distance; *fwd* = forward rank; *bwd* = backward rank; *avg* = average rank.

Parameters	Lemma	Wordform	< 10	< 50	< 100	Avg_correct
Freq_{ass}	1	1	63	279	450	1733
Freq_{fwd}	0	0	32	219	395	7575
Freq_{bwd}	358	292	789	1124	1247	1974
Freq_{avg}	277	191	515	690	793	7251
Simple-ll_{ass}	23	18	196	618	878	1259
Simple-ll_{fwd}	271	196	605	789	842	14177
Simple-ll_{bwd}	369	296	737	1002	1135	2848
Simple-ll_{avg}	346	251	636	798	845	13760
Cond.prob_{ass}	7	6	209	588	806	1234
Cond.prob_{fwd}	0	0	32	219	395	7575
Cond.prob_{bwd}	284	230	659	974	1109	2318
Cond.prob_{avg}	201	137	462	711	851	7230

Table 3: First Order Models – Asymmetric Window: 3 words to the left of the node – Training Data

Parameters	Lemma	Wordform	< 10	< 50	< 100	Avg_correct
Freq_{ass}	1	1	63	279	450	1733
Freq_{fwd}	0	0	32	219	395	7575
Freq_{bwd}	358	292	789	1124	1247	1974
Freq_{avg}	277	191	515	690	793	7251
Simple-ll_{ass}	25	22	220	643	891	1168
Simple-ll_{fwd}	321	250	708	895	936	12244
Simple-ll_{bwd}	507	424	884	1142	1246	2223
Simple-ll_{avg}	402	314	740	901	939	11868
Cond.prob_{ass}	26	20	279	665	864	1282
Cond.prob_{fwd}	0	0	59	298	498	7543
Cond.prob_{bwd}	381	319	791	1094	1201	1981
Cond.prob_{avg}	278	209	535	800	922	7214

Table 4: First Order Models – Asymmetric Window: 3 words to the right of the node – Training Data

Parameters	Lemma	Wordform	< 10	< 50	< 100	Avg_correct
2_{dist}	**264**	208	686	1077	1224	936
2_{fwd}	127	83	380	703	849	1560
2_{bwd}	73	56	275	584	720	3524
2_{avg}	157	106	436	750	911	1507
4_{dist}	255	200	665	1037	1195	997
4_{fwd}	108	73	338	651	824	1750
4_{bwd}	77	57	254	545	694	3843
4_{avg}	129	87	397	710	862	1694
16_{dist}	206	158	546	910	1062	1433
16_{fwd}	63	40	252	512	667	2481
16_{bwd}	49	37	188	449	581	4949
16_{avg}	79	56	282	560	713	2416

Table 5: Second order models – Training data

Considering the good results from collocation-based models, we would have expected a better performance from larger windows, traditionally considered to be more sensitive to syntagmatic relations. A significant difference between first-order and second-order models is the fact that neighbor rank works less well than the distance between vectors, while collocate rank outperformed the association scores.

Model	Lemma	Wordform	< 10	< 50	< 100	Avg_correct
first-order	572	490	1010	1303	1408	1366
second-order	304	246	734	1119	1256	569

Table 6: Best models (first order and second order) – Performance on test data

Model	Training-Lemma	Training-Inflected	Test-Lemma	Test-Inflected
first-order	27.7% (555)	26.9% (538)	28.6% (572)	27.7% (554)
second-order	13.2% (264)	12.0% (241)	15.0% (304)	14.0% (279)

Table 7: Performance (% accuracy and number of correct responses) of the best first-order and second-order model on training vs. test dataset (lemmatized response vs. response with restored inflection)

The observation for second-order models contrasts with previous work showing that rank consistently outperforms distance in modeling priming effects (Lapesa and Evert, 2013; Lapesa et al., to appear) and also in standard tasks such as prediction of similarity ratings and noun clustering (Lapesa and Evert, under review). Among the standard tasks, the only case in which the use of neighbor rank did not produce significant improvements with respect to vector distance was the TOEFL multiple-choice synonymy task. Despite clear differences, the TOEFL task and the reverse association task share the property that they involve multiple stimuli. The results presented in this paper, together with those achieved on the TOEFL task, seem to suggest that a better strategy for the use of neighbor rank needs to be developed when multiple stimuli are involved.

6 Conclusions and Future Work

The results of the evaluation reported in this paper confirmed the tendencies identified in previous studies: first-order models, based on direct co-occurrence, outperform second-order models, based on distributional similarity. We consider the experimental results described in this paper as a first exploration into the dynamics of the reverse association task, and we believe that our systematic evaluation of first- and second-order models represents a good starting point for future work, which targets improvements of NaDiR at many levels.

The first point of improvement concerns the size of the vocabulary. We aim at finding a more optimal cutoff on the training data, for example by implementing a frequency bias similar to Wettler et al. (2005). We are confident that NaDiR will significantly benefit from a smaller range of potential responses (compared to the 155,811 lemmatized candidate words in the current version).

We are also conducting experiments using log ranks instead of plain ranks: since we compute an arithmetic mean of the rank values, a single very high rank (from a poorly matched stimulus) will dominate the average. We therefore assume that log ranks will improve results and make NaDiR's responses more robust.

An interesting research direction targets the integration of first- and second-order statistics in the process of response generation. The evaluation results reported in this paper revealed that a very small context window achieves the best performance for second-order models: as widely acknowledged in the literature (Sahlgren, 2006; Lapesa et al., to appear), smaller context windows highlight paradigmatic relations. First-order models, on the other hand, highlight syntagmatic relations (Rapp, 2002). The best second-order and first-order models from the evaluation reported in this paper are likely to focus on different types of relations between response and stimulus words: this leads us to believe that an integration of the two sources may produce improvements in NaDiR's performance.

At a general level, we plan to make more elaborate use of the training data. In the experiments presented in this paper, training data were used to set a frequency threshold for potential responses, train the part-of-speech classifiers, and find the best configuration for first- and second-order models.

A possible new application of NaDiR is the modeling of datasets containing semantic norms or concept properties, such as the McRae norms (McRae et al., 2005) or BLESS (Baroni and Lenci, 2011). Those datasets are standard in DSM evaluation, and their modeling can be implemented in terms of a reverse association task, with the additional advantage that the relations between concepts and properties in those datasets are labelled with property types for the McRae norms (e.g., encyclopedic, taxonomic, situated) or semantic relations (e.g., hypernymy, meronymy, event-related) for BLESS. This allows a specific evaluation for each property type or semantic relation, which will in turn give new insights into the semantic knowledge encoded in the different corpus-based representations (first order vs. second order vs. hybrid) and how model parameters affect these representations (e.g., window size in the comparison of syntagmatic vs. paradigmatic relations).

Acknowledgments

Gabriella Lapesa's research is funded by the DFG Collaborative Research Centre SFB 732 (University of Stuttgart).

References

Marco Baroni and Alessandro Lenci. 2010. Distributional memory: A general framework for corpus-based semantics. *Computational Linguistics*, 36(4):1–49.

Marco Baroni and Alessandro Lenci. 2011. How we BLESSed distributional semantic evaluation. In *Proceedings of the GEMS 2011 Workshop on GEometrical Models of Natural Language Semantics*, GEMS '11, pages 1–10. Association for Computational Linguistics.

Stefan Evert. 2008. Corpora and collocations. In Anke Lüdeling and Merja Kytö, editors, *Corpus Linguistics. An International Handbook*, chapter 58. Mouton de Gruyter, Berlin, New York.

Stefan Evert. to appear. Distributional semantics in R with the wordspace package. In *Proceedings of COLING 2014: System Demonstrations.*

Thomas L. Griffiths, Mark Steyvers, and Joshua B. Tenenbaum. 2007. Topics in semantic representation. *Psychological Review*, 114:211–244.

Nathan Halko, Per-Gunnar Martinsson, and Joel A. Tropp. 2009. Finding structure with randomness: Stochastic algorithms for constructing approximate matrix decompositions. Technical Report 2009-05, ACM, California Institute of Technology.

Mary Hare, Michael Jones, Caroline Thomson, Sarah Kelly, and Ken McRae. 2009. Activating event knowledge. *Cognition*, 111(2):151–167.

G. R. Kiss, C. Armstrong, R. Milroy, and J. Piper. 1973. An associative thesaurus of English and its computer analysis. In *The Computer and Literary Studies*. Edinburgh University Press.

Gabriella Lapesa and Stefan Evert. 2013. Evaluating neighbor rank and distance measures as predictors of semantic priming. In *Proceedings of the ACL Workshop on Cognitive Modeling and Computational Linguistics (CMCL 2013)*, pages 66–74.

Gabriella Lapesa, Stefan Evert, and Sabine Schulte im Walde. to appear. Contrasting syntagmatic and paradigmatic relations: Insights from distributional semantic models. In *Proceedings of the 3rd Joint Conference on Lexical and Computational Semantics (*SEM). Dublin, Ireland, August 2014.*

Ken McRae, George Cree, Mark Seidenberg, and Chris McNorgan. 2005. Semantic feature production norms for a large set of living and nonliving things. *Behavior Research Methods*, 4(37):547—559.

Reinhard Rapp. 2002. The computation of word associations: Comparing syntagmatic and paradigmatic approaches. In *Proceedings of the 19th International Conference on Computational Linguistics - Volume 1*, pages 1–7.

Reinhard Rapp. 2013. From stimulus to associations and back. In *Proceedings of the 10th Workshop on Natural Language Processing and Cognitive Science.*

Reinhard Rapp. 2014. Corpus-based computation of reverse associations. In *Proceedings of the Ninth International Conference on Language Resources and Evaluation (LREC'14).*

Magnus Sahlgren. 2006. *The Word-Space Model: Using distributional analysis to represent syntagmatic and paradigmatic relations between words in high-dimensional vector spaces.* Ph.D. thesis, University of Stockolm.

Kevin A. Smith, David E. Huber, and Edward Vul. 2013. Multiply-constrained semantic search in the remote associates test. *Cognition*, 128(1):64–75.

Peter D. Turney and Patrick Pantel. 2010. From frequency to meaning: Vector space models of semantics. *Journal of Artificial Intelligence Research*, 37:141–188.

Manfred Wettler, Reinhard Rapp, and Peter Sedlmeier. 2005. Free word associations correspond to contiguities between words in texts. *Journal of Quantitative Linguistics*, 1(12):111–122.

Retrieving Word Associations with a Simple Neighborhood Algorithm in a Graph-Based Resource

Gemma Bel-Enguix
LIF
Aix Marseille Université,
13288 Marseille
gemma.belenguix@gmail.com

Abstract

The paper explains the procedure to obtain word associations starting from a graph that has not been specifically built for that purpose. Our goal is being able to simulate human word associations by using the simplest possible methods, including the basic tools of a co-occurrence network from a non-annotated corpus, and a very simple search algorithm based on neighborhood. The method has been tested in the Cogalex shared task, revealing the difficulty of achieving word associations without semantic annotation.

1 Introduction

Building annotated computational resources for natural language is a difficult and time-consuming task that not always produces the desired results. A good alternative to semantic annotation by hand could be using statistics and graph-based operations in corpora. In order to implement a system capable to work with such methods we have designed co-occurrence networks from large existing corpora, like Wikipedia or the British National Corpus (Burnard & Aston, 1998). The underlying idea is that systems based on mathematics and statistics can achieve comparable results to the ones obtained with more sophisticated methods relying on semantic processing.

Non-annotated networks have been suggested and implemented, for example, by Ferrer-i-Cancho and Solé (2001). The authors suggested non-semantically annotated graphs, building exclusively syntagmatic networks. By this method, they reduced the syntagmatic-paradigmatic relations. The authors used the BNC corpus to build two graphs G1 and G2. First, a so-called co-occurrence graph G1 in which words are linked if they co-occur in at least one sentence within a span of maximal three tokens. Then a collocation graph G2 is extracted in which only those links of G1 are retained whose end vertices co-occur more frequent than expected by chance.

A non-annotated graph built from a large corpus (Bel-Enguix and Zock, 2013) is a good representation to allow for the discovery of a large number of word relationships. It can be used for a number of tasks, one of them being computing word associations. To test the consistence of the results obtained by our method, they will be compared with the Edinburgh Association Thesaurus, a collection of 8000 words whose association norms were produced by presenting each of the stimulus words to about 100 subjects each, and by collecting their responses. The subjects were 17 to 22 year old British students. To perform the tests, we take a sample (EAT: http://www.eat.rl.ac.uk/) consisting in 100 words.

For building a network to deal with the specific task of producing word associations we have used the British National Corpus (BNC) as a source.

The way the network has been constructed has also some interest and impact in the final results. Firstly, for the sake of simplicity, we removed all words other than Nouns and Adjectives. Nouns have been normalized to singular form. After this pre-processing, a graph has been built where the nouns

Zock/Rapp/Huang (eds.): Proceedings of the 4th Workshop on Cognitive Aspects of the Lexicon, pages 60–63,
Dublin, Ireland, August 23, 2014.

and adjectives in the corpus are the nodes, and where the edges between these nodes are zero at the beginning, and are incremented by 1 whenever the two respective words co-occur in the corpus as direct neighbors (i.e. more distant neighborhood was not taken into account). That is, after processing the corpus the weight of each edge represents the number of times the respective words (nodes) co-occur.

To build the graph our system runs through a pipeline of four modules:

- document cleaning (deletion of stop-words), extracting only 'Nouns' and 'Adjectives';
- lemmatisation of word forms to avoid duplicates (horse, horses);
- computation of the (un-directed) graph's edges. Links are created between direct neighbours;
- computation of the edges' weights. The weight of an edge is equal to the number of its occurrences. We only use absolute values.
- computation of the node's weights. As in the edges, the weight of a node is the number of it occurrences.

The graph has been implemented with Python.

The resultant network has 427668 nodes (different words). Of them, 1894 are happax (occur only once), only the 0,5%. There are 13654814 edges. From them, 9836987 with weight one; and 3817827 have a weight higher than one, on a percentage relation 72/28. The average degree of the nodes of the network is 31, 92.

2 Searching method

The search of the target word in the graph has two different steps:

1. Determining the set of common neighbors of the clues,
2. Ranking the set of nodes obtained in 1, and picking the 'best result'.

2.1 Search of neighbors

The search of the target word T in a graph G, is done via some clues $c_1, c_2, \ldots, c_n$, which act as inputs. G=(V, E) stands for the graph, with V expressing the set of vertices (words) and E the set of edges (co-occurrences). The clues $c_1, c_2, \ldots, c_n \in V$. N(i) expresses the neighbourhood of a node $i \in V$, and is defined as 'every $j \in V \mid e_{i,j} \in E$. The search algorithm is as follows:

- Define the neighbourhood of $c_1, c_2, \ldots, c_n$ as $N(c_1), N(c_2), \ldots, N(c_n)$;
- Get the set of nodes $V_T = N(c_1) \cap N(c_2) \cap \ldots \cap N(c_n)$ and consider $V_c=\{c_1, c_2, \ldots, c_n\}$ to be the set of nodes representing the clues. We define a subgraph of G, G_T, that is a complete bipartite graph, where every element of V_T is connected to every element of V_c;

In the Cogalex shared task, five clues have been given, belonging to any grammatical category, and in different inflected forms (ie., am, be, been or horse, horses). Since the graph has the limitation of containing only Nouns and Adjectives, the system dismisses every word not belonging to the set of nodes V and uses only the remaining clues. And being the words lemmatized, inflected forms are reduced to only one. Therefore, the application will never find 'be' from 'am', 'been', 'is'.

To build the graph and perform the search, a Python module has been used, Networkx (https://networkx.github.io/), that is extremely fast and efficient.

2.2 Ranking the nodes

This task has been designed with a very simple algorithm. Let's consider C the number of final stimulus words; $wc_1, wc_2, \ldots, wc_n$ is the weight in the graph of every node $c \in V_C$; $wt_1, wt_2, \ldots, wt_n$ the weight in the graph of every one of the nodes $t \in V_T$; we_{tc} the weight for every edge of G_T, where $c \in V_C$ and $t \in V_T$.

The nodes of the graph are gathered in groups in a logarithmic scale: up to 10^1, 10^2, 10^3, 10^4, 10^5, 10^6. We name a the power of 10, ie., for 10^6, a=6.

The nodes of VT are ranked with a simple algorithm, consisting in calculating W_t for every $t \in V_T$, so as $W_t = \frac{(we_{tc1} + we_{tc2} + \cdots + we_{tcn})/C}{a}$

The nodes are ranked according to the values of W.

3 Results

In some initial tests, the results were compared with the ones obtained in a sample of the Edinburgh Association Thesaurus (EAT: http://www.eat.rl.ac.uk/) consisting in 100 words. The EAT (Kiss et al., 1973) has 8000 words, and the 100 selected for the test were all of them nouns or adjectives, what made the working easier for our system. There were 15 words that match the ones observed in the Edinburgh Associative Thesaurus (EAT) as Primary Response (PR). There is a partial coincidence – the word given has not a 0 in the EAT – in 54 of the outputs. This means that in more than 50% of the cases the method retrieves a word corresponding to the one produced by a human in the association experiment. This does not imply though that it is the most popular one.

Some other methods of evaluation (Evert & Krenn, 2001) have been applied to the system (Bel-Enguix et al., 2014), showing that the outcomes provided by the graph-based method are quite consistent with human responses, and even optimize them in some specific classes.

In contrast with these results, the ones obtained in the Cogalex shared task were clearly worse. From a total of 200 items, the number of matches was 182, which means an accuracy of the 9,10%.

There are several reasons for that: a) some of the targets were not Nouns or Adjectives, what makes them not retrievable for the system, b) many stimulus words were not Nouns or Adjectives, what makes the algorithm weaker, because such words are dismissed as clues, c) stimulus were not lemmatized and the lemmatization process for words without a context is not easy for the python lemmatization module, d) probably many of the words of the first tested sample were very well-known relations, while the ones in the Cogalex shared task could be less well-connected nodes, e) the ranking algorithm can be clearly improved in order to retrieve the best word, not only one in the list, because we have been asked only full matches.

4 Conclusions: strengths and weakness of the method

Even though the results obtained were not good, there are several strengths that make this system worth to be improved in the future.

Firstly, the network is easy to built and program is very fast. We have used the python package 'networkx' to build the graph, integrating its commands into the python script. The result is that in less than one minute the system can compute the two thousand associations that were required. Therefore, while an important improvement is needed in the ranking algorithm, there is room for it, because the performance of the method can afford it.

Secondly, the system works with any co-occurrence graph made from any corpus. This allows us to use specialized corpora as a basis, as well as collections of texts closer to the time the human associations have been produced.

However, there are important weaknesses in the procedure. In the first place, it is necessary to use a network resource including other grammatical categories, at least verbs and adverbs. Even though such graph exists, the difficulty in the application of the current ranking algorithm makes it not-usable so far for this specific task. There is still another clear difficulty in the method, related to the one we just stated: the lack of clustering. Not using semantic annotations is one of our axioms, because it makes the system heavier. Nevertheless, a way to detect which words are more related is needed. This is currently the strongest weakness of this graph-based algorithm. We propose for the future a very simple clustering based on WordNet *synsets* (Miller, 1990), in a way the search can be oriented towards the best choices for every word connection, even though their weight in the graph is lower.

5 Aknowledgements

I am very grateful to my colleagues Michael Zock and Reinhard Rapp for their expertise, comments and constant support.

This work has been supported by the European Commission under a Marie Curie Fellowship, project DynNetLAc.

References

Bel-Enguix, G., Rapp, R. and Zock, M. (2014) A Graph-Based Approach for Computing Free Word Associations, Proceedings of LREC 2014, Ninth International Conference on Language Resources and Evaluation, 3027-3033.

Bel-Enguix, G. and Zock, M. (2013). Lexical Access via a Simple Co-occurrence Network, Proceedings of TALN-RECITAL 2013, 596-603.

Burnard, L. and Aston, G. (1998). *The BNC Handbook: Exploring the British National Corpus*. Edinburgh: Edinburgh University Press

Evert, S. and Krenn, B. (2001). Methods for qualitative evaluation of lexical association measures. In *Proceedings of the 39th Annual Meeting of the Association of Computational Linguistics,* Toulouse, France, 188-915.

Ferrer-Cancho, R., Solé, R. (2001). The small-world of human language. *Proceedings of the Royal Society of London. Series B, Biological Sciences* 268 (2001) 2261-2265.

Kiss, G.R., Armstrong, C., Milroy, R., and Piper, J. (1973). An associative thesaurus of English and its computer analysis. In: A. Aitken, R. Beiley, N. Hamilton-Smith (eds.): *The Computer and Literary Studies*. Edinburgh University Press.

Miller, G. (1990). Wordnet: An on-line lexical database. *International Journal of Lexicography*, 3(4).

Predicting sense convergence with distributional semantics: an application to the CogALex-IV 2014 shared task

Laurianne Sitbon
School of Electrical Engineering and Computer Science
Queensland University of Technology
Brisbane, Australia
laurianne.sitbon@qut.edu.au

Lance De Vine
School of Electrical Engineering and Computer Science
Queensland University of Technology
Brisbane, Australia
l.devine@student.qut.edu.au

Abstract

This paper presents our system to address the CogALex-IV 2014 shared task of identifying a single word most semantically related to a group of 5 words (queries). Our system uses an implementation of a neural language model and identifies the answer word by finding the most semantically similar word representation to the sum of the query representations. It is a fully unsupervised system which learns on around 20% of the UkWaC corpus. It correctly identifies 85 exact correct targets out of 2,000 queries, 285 approximate targets in lists of 5 suggestions.

1 Introduction

How humans draw associations between words or concepts has been the object of many studies by psychologists, and for many years computer scientists have attempted to model this human mental lexicon by means of symbolic methods (Enguix et al., 2014) or statistical models (Baroni and Lenci, 2013). These models and methods have in turn been used to improve natural language processing systems (Lewis and Steedman, 2013), search technologies (Deerwester et al., 1990) and have since been evaluated in the view of supporting such systems more than helping users directly. The Shared Task CogALex-IV 2014 aims to evaluate how these models can support a user with deficiencies in their lexical access. The task is set as one of retrieving one target word when being presented with 5 cue (associated) words. After submissions of all systems, the organisers revealed that the cue words were the 5 words most often associated with the target words. They have been collected from a large number of users who were presented with the target word and invited to produce one associate. In this paper we present our preliminary investigations to address the task with a neural net language model learning representations for words on the UkWaC corpus (M. Baroni and Zanchetta, 2009). We propose a strict evaluation (accuracy of finding the target word) as well as a retrieval based evaluation that we believe is closer to the aim of helping user find their words.

2 Approach and methodology

2.1 Neural Net Language Model

In 2003 Bengio et. al. (Bengio et al., 2003) introduced a neural net based method for language modelling that learns simultaneously 1) a distributed representation for each word and 2) the probability function for word sequences, expressed in terms of the distributed representations. Generalization to unseen word sequences is obtained because such sequences receive a high probability if they are composed of words that are similar to words from an already seen sequence. An outcome of this approach is the learning of "word embeddings", which are vectors representing the meanings of words relative to other words (via a mechanism akin to word distribution). For this task, we used our own implementation of the continuous Skip-Gram neural language model introduced by (Mikolov et al., 2013). We refer to this model hereafter as skip-gram. The implementation is similar to the word2vec software package. Neither

Zock/Rapp/Huang (eds.): Proceedings of the 4th Workshop on Cognitive Aspects of the Lexicon, pages 64–67, Dublin, Ireland, August 23, 2014.

sub-sampling nor negative sampling were used. A small context term window radius of size two and a vector dimensionality of 128 were used. We use the cosine between the word embedding representations (vectors) to estimate the similarity between the words in the evaluation task. The parameters were not tuned for the task and so it is probable that further improvements can be made.

2.2 Combined similarity

Once semantic vectors are created with skip-gram it allows us to measure the distances between words and retrieve the words most similar to another word, or those with a vector most similar to any vector, such as the sum of several word vectors.

In the CogALex-IV shared task, we are provided with 5 words (cues) associated to a target word to be found. If we consider that these words are effectively a unique semantic context for the word to be found, then it makes sense to add their vectors and find the unique word most similar. This approach is of course inspired by vectorial models of information retrieval and adopted widely when testing distributional models for more than single words (see for example (Deerwester et al., 1990)).

However we found that this strategy has limitations, because in the case of some polysemous words, some of the cues were from radically different contexts, and therefore summing up the vector did not necessarily make sense. For such situations, it makes more sense to find the lists of words most related to each of the cues, and then combine these lists. To do this we first selected 10 candidate targets for each cue, which are the 10 words with a representation most similar to the cue, according to the cosine between their words embeddings and that of the cue. We then ranked the words according to their number of occurrences in the 5 lists. We did not consider the distance as measured by cosine similarity (the actual value) because while cosine is a good measure to rank terms by similarity, we do not believe that this leads to an absolute estimate for actual semantic similarity. Additionally, we chose not to assign weights to the terms depending on which cue they were associated to as there was no reason to believe that the cues were ordered in any way (that is, by manual inspection, we did not find that cues early in the lists were most likely to lead to the target than cues later in the list were). The results were not as good then as those with the summed vectors. We then adopted a third strategy, which was to consider the sum of the cues as a 6th cue when generating the lists of candidates, but also to decide on priority when selecting a unique target in case there are several candidates ranked first with an equal number of occurrences in the 6 lists. On the training set, this allowed us to find 92 correct answers for the 2,000 cases.

court	law	judge	judges	courts	SUM
courts	laws	judges	appellants	court	court
sheriff	legislation	pettiti	judge	rackets	courts
tribunal	jurisprudence	court	defendants	**magistrates**	judge
prosecution	statutes	**sheriff**	respondents	badminton	judges
judge	statute	prosecutor	panellists	sharia	**sheriff**
justiciary	litigation	dredd	jury	squash	law
judicature	antiunion	jury	organizers	tribunals	**magistrates**
consistory	sharia	coroner	complainants	prosecutors	prosecution
leet	criminology	appellant	winners	proceedings	prosecutors
magistrates	arbitration	defendant	plaintiffs	parliaments	prosecutor
prosecutor	llm	magistrate	**magistrates**	rulings	tribunal
contactfulhamba	regulation	complainant	appellant	law	consistory
appeal	courts	**magistrates**	senatus	prosecution	rulings
palace	penal	appeal	chairmen	leagues	judicature

Figure 1: Example of lists of 14 most similar words for the 5 cues "court law judge judges courts" and their sum vector

Figure 1 shows an example where the cues are "court law judge judges courts" and the target was magistrates. We present for each cue as well as for the sum of all cues the lists of 14 most similar terms. In gray the words that were cues or plural of a cue were ignored. In bold we show how "sheriff" would have been picked if we considered the sum only, while when considering the individual sets of similar terms in addition to the sum we could find that magistrates was a more likely target.

2.3 Training corpus

The corpus we used for learning the word representations is the UKWaC corpus (M. Baroni and Zanchetta, 2009). This is the corpus suggested by the organisers of the CogALex-IV 2014 Shared task, and contains web pages from the UK domain. We pre-processed the corpus by a) lower-casing all terms, b) replacing contractions with their expansion, eg. "it's" becomes "it is", c) removing all punctuation and d) replacing all digits with the single character '7'. The Skip-gram model that we used is able to scale to the whole UKWaC corpus (approximately 2 billion terms) but because of time constraints we selected only the first 20% of the corpus, and then processed the remainder of the corpus, adding to our corpus subset all sentences containing words that were present in the training set but not in the initial 20% subset. This was to ensure that representations for all the words in the training set could be learned.

3 Results

3.1 Shared task evaluation

The evaluation proposed in the shared task is the exact accuracy of a single proposed target for each query composed of 5 words. There were 2,000 queries in each of the training and test set, and the results are expressed in total number. All our results according to this metric are situated between 4% and 5%. We have included in table 1 the results according to the task metric, on the training and on the test set, for both the sum vectors and the combination of results from a sum and the individual words. The latter is the one that was submitted to the shared task.

Method	Train	Test
Sum	81	75
Combination	84	85

Table 1: Accuracy of the methods on the training and on the test corpus

3.2 Retrieval evaluation

We now consider a task where a system would support a user in finding a word that they describe using the 5 associations. In such a tip-of-the-tongue context, users would immediately recognise the word they are looking for when presented in a list and also if it is presented with a different inflection (ie. "run" instead of "running"). Therefore, if presented a list of words containing the target word or variation of the target word, the outcome of such a system would be considered successful. While it would be impractical to consider very long lists in a usability context, we have measured the accuracy for lists of 2, 3, 4 and 5 words, with a measure of 1 where the word (or at least one of its inflections) is in the list and 0 otherwise. In other words, the accuracy is the number of target words that appear as is or as an inflection in suggestion lists of varying sizes.

The results presented on Figure 2 show that taking inflections into account leads to only marginal improvements, but more importantly considering additional targets (as a list) can really improve outcomes for the users, with almost 13% of targets being retrieved in lists of 5 suggestions with the combined approach.

4 Discussion and conclusion

The accuracy of our approach, even when considering lists of 5 suggestions and inflections of words, show that results are still very low if one would consider a usable assistance system for users with lexical access issues. This is consistent with previous findings on a similar task in French (Sitbon et al., 2008).

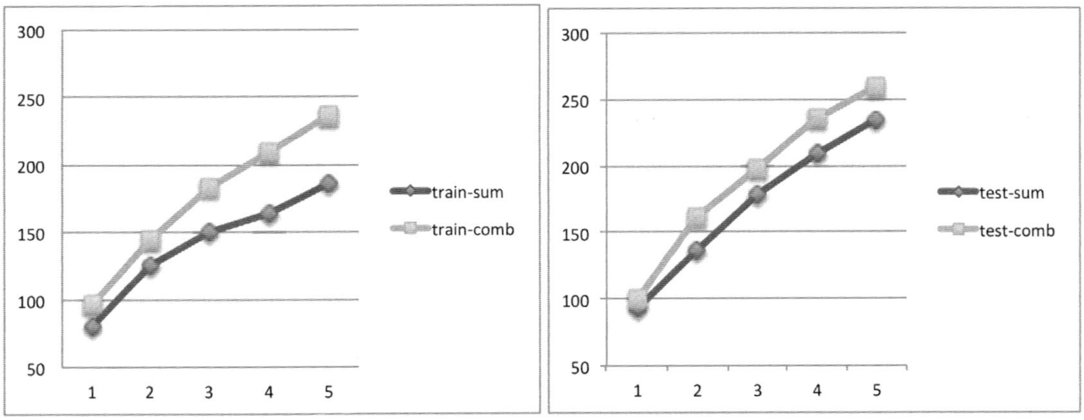

Figure 2: Total number of targets on the left, or inflections of target on the right, out of 2,000, found in lists of 1 to 5 results, in the training set and in the test set

This work suggested that a combination of resources encoding various types of semantic relations would be best, along with user models. CogALex-IV task was not based on associations drawn by a single user, but rather by majority associations drawn by many users, so this would not apply to the task specifically. However we believe that including definitional associations such as that drawn from an ESA model on the Wikipedia would be a way to dramatically improve the accuracy, at least when considering lists of results. Additionally it would be interesting to inspect a number of variables to weigh the contribution of each cue (depending on their specificity for example). In this paper we found that adding the vectors representing each word let to better results than only considering the words individually. This mode of combination is one of many proposed by (Mitchell and Lapata, 2010) and in future work we will experiment with alternative combination models. Finally, an area for future work would be to consider cleaning up the dataset so as to avoid effects such as several cues being inflections of one another (i.e.. "courts" and "court") or even the target being an inflection of one of the cues, as we have observed in the CogALex-IV dataset.

References

Marco Baroni and Alessandro Lenci. 2013. Distributional memory: A general framework for corpus-based semantics. *Computational Linguistics*, 36(4):673–721.

Y. Bengio, R. Ducharme, P. Vincent, and C. Jauvin. 2003. A neural probabilistic language model. *Journal of Machine Learning Research.*

Scott C. Deerwester, Susan T Dumais, Thomas K. Landauer, George W. Furnas, and Richard A. Harshman. 1990. Indexing by latent semantic analysis. *JASIS*, 41(6):391–407.

Gemma Bel Enguix, Reinhard Rapp, and Michael Zock. 2014. A graph-based approach for computing free word associations. In *Proceedings of LREC 2014.*

Mike Lewis and Mark Steedman. 2013. Combined distributional and logical semantics. *TACL*, 1:179–192.

A. Ferraresi M. Baroni, S. Bernardini and E. Zanchetta. 2009. The wacky wide web: A collection of very large linguistically processed web-crawled corpora. *Language Resources and Evaluation*, 43(3):209–226.

T. Mikolov, K. Chen, G. Corrado, and J. Dean. 2013. Efficient estimation of word representations in vector space. *Proceedings of Workshop at ICLR.*

J. Mitchell and M. Lapata. 2010. Composition in distributional models of semantics. *Cognitive Science*, (34):1388–1429.

L. Sitbon, P. Bellot, and P. Blache. 2008. Evaluation of lexical resources and semantic networks on a corpus of mental associations. In *Proceedings of the Language Ressources and Evaluation Conference.*

WordFinder

Catalin Mititelu
Stefanini / 6A Dimitrie Pompei Bd,
Bucharest, Romania
catalinmititelu@yahoo.com

Verginica Barbu Mititelu
RACAI / 13 Calea 13 Septembrie,
Bucharest, Romania
vergi@racai.ro

Abstract

This paper presents our relations-oriented approach to the shared task on lexical access in language production, as well as the results we obtained. We relied mainly on the semantic and lexical relations between words as they are recorded in the Princeton WordNet, although also considering co-occurrence in the Google n-gram corpus. After the end of the shared task we continued working on the system and the further adjustments (involving part of speech information and position of the candidate in the synset) and those results are presented as well.

1 Introduction

In this paper we present our experience in the shared task on lexical access in language production, organized as part of the CogALex workshop. Given a list of five words (let us call them seeds), the system should return a word (we will call it target) which is assumed to be the most closely associated to all the seeds. Two remarks are worth being made here: on the one hand, what we call word is in fact a word form, as inflected forms are both among the seeds and among the expected targets in the training and the test sets. On the other hand, the closeness of association remains understated by the organizers. It can be understood at several levels, given our analysis of the training data: the meaning and/or the form, the syntagmatic associations, i.e. associations of words in texts. However, our system dealt mainly with the semantic level. The form level is involved only to the extent to which lexical relations (usually derivational relations and antonymy) in Princeton WordNet (PWN) are used. The syntagmatic relations we use are the co-occurrences in the Google n-gram corpus

2 Our understanding of the lexical access task

Having already established what meaning we, as speakers, want to render, the lexical choice is influenced by several factors: the person we talk to, the circumstances (place, other participants) of our discussion, the social (or even other types of) relations between the participants to the discussion. The shared task focuses on the tip of the tongue (TOT) phenomenon, as rightly described in the shared task presentation: we do not remember the word "mocha", but we want to express the idea (i.e., the meaning) "superior dark coffee made of beans from Arabia". In a real life conversation, dealing with TOT is much simpler: the speaker (the one affected by TOT) has the ability of defining the word s/he is looking for or of enumerating some words AND specifying the relation(s) they establish with the looked for word. Thus, we consider that the task here, consisting of being able to find the target when receiving five seeds, does not mimic the real life situation. In fact, we deprive the system of vital information that, we, as speakers, possess, to our great advantage reflected in our success in dealing with the TOT problem, after all. Moreover, given the information provided by the organizers once the results were send, the seeds that we received are derived from the Edinburgh Associative Thesaurus, so they are, in fact, the associations introduced by the users to a seed. So, the organizers implicitly considered the association of two words is the same, irrespective of which of them is the seed and which is the target, which is definitely not the same, especially if the association is a syntagmatic one.

Zock/Rapp/Huang (eds.): Proceedings of the 4th Workshop on Cognitive Aspects of the Lexicon, pages 68–74,
Dublin, Ireland, August 23, 2014.

3 Related work

In a recent experiment (Zock and Shcwab, 2013), a set of seeds (called stimuli therein) is presented to a system and, relying on information available in the eXtended WordNet (Mihalcea, 2001) and in DBpedia, a list of words is returned. The authors explain the bad results by the small dimensions of the eXtended WordNet and by the small number of syntagmatic relations it contains. Although they emphasize the necessity of using big corpora, with heterogenous data, to help solve the TOT problem, the conclusions speculate about various elements that can lead to, but do not guarantee the success:

- the big size of the corpus, the heterogeneity of the texts it contains;
- high density of relations in a network;
- the quality of the search;
- all these together.

4 Our approach

4.1 The data

The training set contains a list of 2000 pairs of five seeds and the target. They look quite heterogeneous: there are content and functional words alike, lemmas and inflected forms (see "occurs ∼ happens happen often sometimes now"), capitalized (sometimes unnecessarily, for example "Nevertheless" in the pair "however ∼ but never Nevertheless when although") and uncapitalized words.
Interestingly, two different inflected forms are targets of (partially) different sets of seeds: compare:
occur ∼ happen event often perfume today
with
occurs ∼ happens happen often sometimes now.
This means that not only semantic relations are established between the seed and the target, but also grammatical ones.

4.2 Assumptions

In order to construct our system we made the assumption, supported by the manual analysis of the training set, that the seeds and the target are related to each other by different kinds of relations:

- semantic relations;
- co-occurrence, in either order;
- syntactic relations;
- gloss-like relations, i.e. the target may be defined using one or more seeds;
- domain relations, i.e. the target and at least some seeds may belong to the same domain;
- form relation, i.e. the target and one or more seeds may display a partial identity of form (and sometimes even of the acoustic form of words);
- inflection as a relation among forms of the same word;
- etc.

Given these, we were aware of the impossibility of dealing with cases involving inflected forms, some of them occurring as seeds, while one occurs as target, such as:
am ∼ I not is me are.
In this case, an inflectional relation can be found between "is" and "am" and between "are" and "am", whereas the relations between "am" and "I" and between "am" and "not" are syntagmatic (co-occurrences). No relation can we identify between "am" and "me".

4.3 Resources

As a consequence of the assumptions made, the language resources we used for the competition were the Princeton WordNet (PWN) (Fellbaum, 1998) and Google n-grams corpus (Brants and Franz, 2006). The implied limitations of our approach are:

- the impossibility of dealing with pairs involving only inflected words (as in the previous example) or only functional words (as in the case: "at $\sim$ home by here in on");
- no contribution made by some of the seeds in the process of finding the target;
- the partial dealing with inflected forms such as plurals, third person singular of verbs, gerunds, as they cannot be found in PWN; the only source of information about them is the n-grams corpus;
- some combinations (although quite frequent, according to our intuitions obout the language) cannot be found in the Google n-gram corpus.

For all (2000x5) pairs seed-target in the training set we extracted from PWN the shortest relations chains, as a kind of lexical chains (Moldovan and Novischi, 2002), existing between them, disregarding the part of speech of the words. These chains are made up of both semantic and lexical relations (as they are defined in the wordnet literature, i.e. lexical relations are established between word forms, while semantic relations are established between word meanings). The most frequent relations chains are presented in Table 1. Straightforwardly, the most frequent association between the seeds and the targets (occurring

Lexical chain	**Number of occurrences**
synonym	548
hypernym hyponym	332
hyponym	328
hypernym	182
antonym	143
similar_to	128
derivat	119
hypernym hyponym hyponym	115
hypernym hypernym hyponym	100
hyponym hyponym	81
hypernym hypernym hyponym hyponym	75
similar_to similar_to	59
derivat derivat	59
part_meronym	49
hyponym derivat	46
hypernym derivat	42
derivat hyponym	40
hypernym hyponym derivat	37
domain_TOPIC domain_member_TOPIC	36
derivat hypernym hyponym	35
also_see	35

Table 1: The most frequent relations chains between a seed and the target.

548 times) is of the kind synonymy. However, various combinations of hyponymy and hypernymy account for a significant number of pairs: 1213. Almost half of these cases (510) are solved by only one of the two relations (328 by hyponymy alone and 182 by hypernymy alone). Moreover, these relations contribute also in chains involving the derivat relation. So, we can consider them the most useful ones. (Our finding is similar to the weight associated to these relations by Moldovan and Novischi (Moldovan and

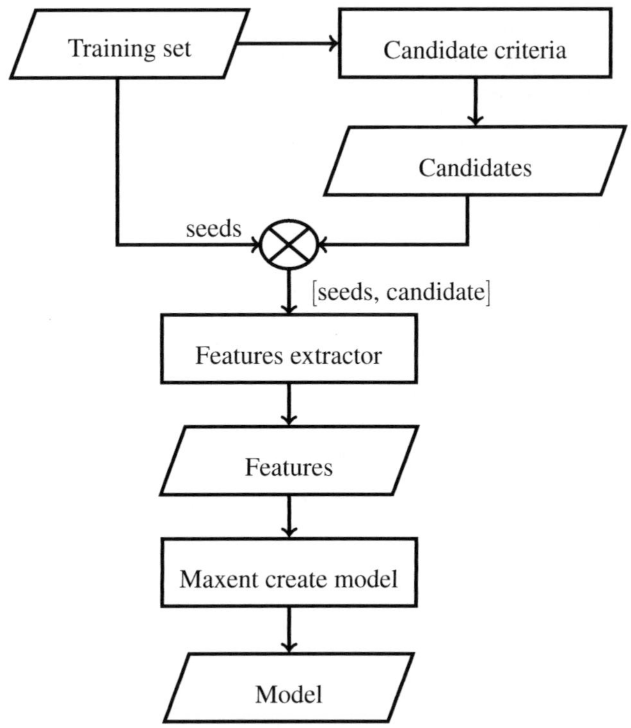

Figure 1: The training flowchart.

Novischi, 2002), who top rank them in finding paths between related concepts for a Question Answering system.) However, they introduce a lot of noise, too, especially when the last relation in the chain is hyponymy and the node from which it starts is one with very many hyponyms.

4.4 The system in the shared task competition

We reformulated this as a classification problem. Assuming that having a list of seeds and the list of their possible candidates, the problem will be solved by considering the most probable candidate as the closest to all seeds. We chose `valid` and `invalid` as classification categories.

The system uses the machine learning technique called Maximum Entropy Modeling (MaxEnt for short) and the features needed by MaxEnt are extracted from the kinds of relations presented above, in subsection 4.2. In other words, we mapped each kind of relation to a feature. The entire process has two distinct phases: training and prediction.

The training mechanism is presented in Figure 1. For each training set entry (i.e. the list of 5 seeds and the expected target) a list of possible candidates is generated using the PWN relations chains presented above. We called this process Candidate Criteria. Combining each set of seeds with their candidates we extracted the list of features needed to enter into the MaxEnt process to create the model. For instance, giving the sequence of seeds `away fonder illness leave presence` and two possible candidates `absence` and `being` we obtained the following lists of features ending with the corresponding classification category:

```
domain=s_factotum domain=t_factotum src=1 wn=an wn=he_he_ho_ho
wnshort=he_ho valid
```

```
domain=s_factotum domain=t_factotum src=1 wn=he_ho_d_d invalid
```

The following list of features were used:

- wn=*chain*: *chain* represents the relations chain found between any seed and the current candidate. We used short forms to label relations: for example, an stands for antonymy, he for hypernymy, ho for hyponymy, d for derivational relation;
- form=first_upper when at least one seed and the candidate begin with a capital letter; we did not allow for candidates with initial capital letter unless at least one seed had an initial capital letter;
- src=*n* marks the number *n* of seeds that reached the candidate using the PWN chains. In the case of the seed presence and candidate absence there are two chains linking the two words: an and he_he_ho_ho and only presence contributes to them;
- gloss=*n* marks the number *n* of seeds that occur in the target gloss;
- n2gram=high used when any seed occurs in any Google 2-grams with the candidate;
- domain=s_*domain* used to mark the seed domain(s);
- domain=t_*domain* used to mark the candidate domain(s);
- wnshort=*short_chain* here the *short_chain* represents a reduced version of the PWN chain. For example, the chain he_he_ho_ho can be reduced to he_ho (or to a co-hyponym relation, in an extended meaning). The reason is to create an invariant chain that can hold irrespectively of the number of similar consecutive relations. This is useful in hierarchies involving many scientific or artificial nodes which are not known or simply disregarded by common speakers. For example, the chain between hippopotamus and animal is 7 hyponyms long in PWN, whereas for a speaker they are in a direct relation.

The selection of candidates is done using exclusively the PWN relations chains with a maximun length of 5 relations in a chain and only the first literal from the target synset is taken into account (on the assumption that literals PWN synsets are in reverse order of their frequency of occurrence in corpora, with the first as the most frequent). To reduce the number of possible candidates some filtering criteria are applied before pairing them with their corresponding seeds to extract the features described above. These criteria are:

- the candidates that appear among seeds are eliminated;
- the compound terms (recognized by the use of underscore among elements) are excluded;
- the candidates should appear together with any seed among Google 5-grams with a minimum frequency of 5000 (occurrences).

The prediction phase takes the test set and, using the model created in the training phase, produces for each candidate a percent for each category (valid / invalid). The candidate selection and features extraction are done similarly to the training phase. The prediction phase is presented in Figure 2. The result of this phase is a list of candidates (sorted in reverse order) for each set of 5 seeds in the test set. The list of results presented to the shared task organizers contains, for each set of seeds, the best ranked candidate.

4.5 Modifications after the competition

After the end of the competition we tried several mechanisms that could improve our results. They were:

- adding two new features that dealt with the part of speech of the words:
  - pos= *s_pos*: the part-of-speech of the seed(s) corresponding to PWN chain that relates to the candidate;
  - pos= *t_pos*: similar for candidate/target;
- considering more literals from synsets when creating the list of candidates.

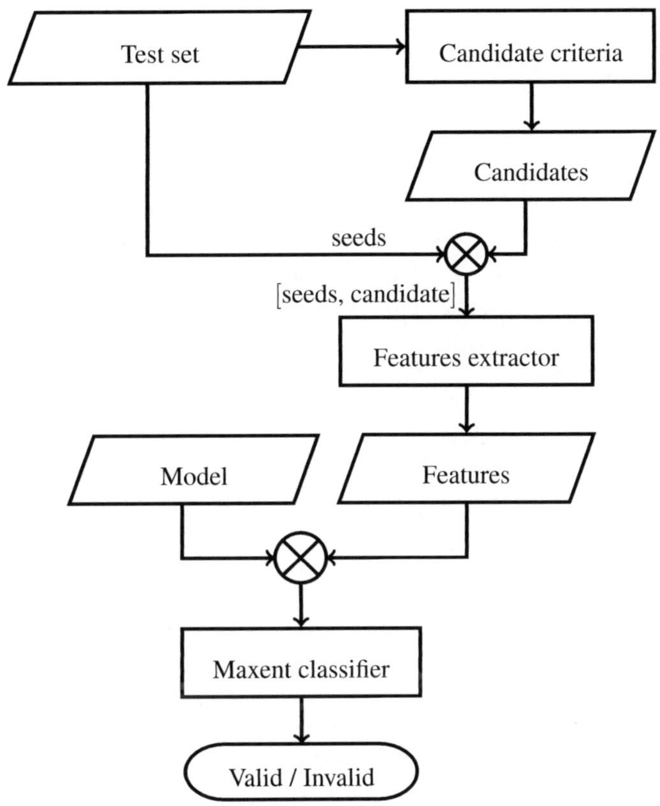

Figure 2: The prediction flowchart.

5 Results

5.1 Results within the competition

Out of the total number of items (2000) only 30 of our targets matched the ones expected by the organizers, so we obtained 1.50% accuracy.

5.2 Improved results after the competition

After considering the part of speech of the words, we were able to match 51 targets, thus increasing the accuracy to 2.55%.

After considering two literals from a synset in the candidates list, the number of matches was 59, so an accuracy of 2.95%.

Furthermore, if we consider the top five candidates in our list, we noticed that 140 targets could be found.

Considering three or even four literals in the synsets did not improve the results (either for the best ranked candidate or for the top 5 ones).

6 Conclusions

We presented here the way we dealt with the challenging task proposed by the organizers. Although initially we intended to consider using a large corpus (ukWAC) as well for finding candidates, we found ourselves in the technical impossibility of doing so, because of the costly (timewise especially) resources required by its processing. What is left to be checked is to what extent the lexical and syntactic patterns that can be extracted from a corpus help us improve the results.

We cannot boast good results of our approach mainly because we used only a dictionary (in the form of the PWN). Although it was created on psychological principles about the way words are structured in the speakers' mind, it cannot ensure satisfying results. At least within our approach, the contribution of the relations encoded in PWN is very low. An evaluation of the type n top-ranked candidates could have a higher accuracy for our type of approach. We could dare say that our approach was a further proof of the statement tested by (Zock and Shcwab, 2013): "Words storage does not guarantee their access".

References

Thorsten Brants, and Alex Franz. 2006. *Web 1T 5-gram Version 1 LDC2006T13.* Philadelphia: Linguistic Data Consortium.

Gemma Bel Enguix, Reinhard Rapp, and Michael Zock. 2014. *How Well Can a Corpus-Derived Co-Occurrence Network Simulate Human Associative Behavior?* Proceedings of the 5th workshop on Cognitive Aspects of Computational Language Learning (CogACLL 2014), pp. 43-48.

Christiane Fellbaum. 1998. *WordNet: An Electronic Lexical Database.* MIT Press.

Rada Mihalcea, and Dan Moldovan. 2001. *eXtended WordNet: Progress Report.* In Proceedings of NAACL Workshop on WordNet and Other Lexical Resources.

Dan Moldovan, and Adrian Novischi. 2002. *Lexical Chains for Question Answering.* Proceedings of COLING 2002.

Reinhard Rapp. 2008. *The Computation of Associative Responses to Multiword Stimuli.* Proceedings of the workshop on Cognitive Aspects of the Lexicon (CogALex 2008), pp. 102-109.

Michael Zock, and Didier Schwab. 2013. *L'index, une ressource vitale pour guider les auteurs à trouver le mot bloqué sur le bout de la langue.* In Ressources Lexicales : contenu, construction, utilisation, évaluation, N. Gala et M. Zock (eds.). John Benjamins.

(Digital) Goodies from the ERC Wishing Well: BabelNet, Babelfy, Video Games with a Purpose and the Wikipedia Bitaxonomy

Roberto Navigli
Dipartimento di Informatica
Sapienza Università di Roma
Viale Regina Elena, 295 – 00166 Roma Italy
navigli@di.uniroma1.it

Abstract

Multilinguality is a key feature of today's Web, and it is this feature that we leverage and exploit in our research work at the Sapienza University of Rome's Linguistic Computing Laboratory, which I am going to overview and showcase in this talk.

I will start by presenting **BabelNet 2.5** (Navigli and Ponzetto, 2012), available at http://babelnet.org, a very large multilingual encyclopedic dictionary and semantic network, which covers 50 languages and provides both lexicographic and encyclopedic knowledge for all the open-class parts of speech, thanks to the seamless integration of WordNet, Wikipedia, Wiktionary, OmegaWiki, Wikidata and the Open Multilingual WordNet. In order to construct the BabelNet network, we extract at different stages: from WordNet, all available word senses (as *concepts*) and all the lexical and semantic pointers between synsets (as *relations*); from Wikipedia, all the Wikipages (i.e., Wikipages, as *concepts*) and semantically unspecified *relations* from their hyperlinks. WordNet and Wikipedia overlap both in terms of concepts and relations: this overlap makes the merging between the two resources possible, enabling the creation of a *unified knowledge resource*. In order to enable multilinguality, we collect the lexical realizations of the available concepts in different languages. Finally, we connect the multilingual Babel synsets by establishing semantic relations between them.

Next, I will present **Babelfy** (Moro et al., 2014), available at http://babelfy.org, a unified approach that leverages BabelNet to perform Word Sense Disambiguation (WSD) and Entity Linking in arbitrary languages, with performance on both tasks on a par with, or surpassing, those of task-specific state-of-the-art supervised systems. Babelfy works in three steps: first, given a lexicalized semantic network, we associate with each vertex, i.e., either concept or named entity, a semantic signature, that is, a set of related vertices. This is a preliminary step which needs to be performed only once, independently of the input text. Second, given a text, we extract all the linkable fragments from this text and, for each of them, list the possible meanings according to the semantic network. Third, we create a graph-based semantic interpretation of the whole text by linking the candidate meanings of the extracted fragments using the previously-computed semantic signatures. We then extract a dense subgraph of this representation and select the best candidate meaning for each fragment. Our experiments show state-of-the-art performances on both WSD and EL on 6 different datasets, including a multilingual setting.

In the third part of the talk I will present two novel approaches to large-scale knowledge acquisition and validation developed in my lab. I will first introduce **video games with a purpose** (Vannella et al., 2014), a novel, powerful paradigm for the large scale acquisition and validation of knowledge and data (http://knowledgeforge.org). We demonstrate that converting games with a purpose into more traditional video games provides a fun component that motivates players to annotate for free, thereby significantly lowering annotation costs below that of crowdsourcing. Moreover, we show that video games with a purpose produce higher-quality annotations than crowdsourcing.

Zock/Rapp/Huang (eds.): Proceedings of the 4th Workshop on Cognitive Aspects of the Lexicon, pages 75–76, Dublin, Ireland, August 23, 2014.

Then I will introduce the **Wikipedia Bitaxonomy** (Flati et al., 2014, WiBi), available at `http://wibitaxonomy.org` and now integrated into BabelNet. WiBi is the largest and most accurate currently available taxonomy of Wikipedia pages and taxonomy of categories, aligned to each other. WiBi is created in three steps: we first create a taxonomy for the Wikipedia pages by parsing textual definitions, extracting the hypernym(s) and disambiguating them according to the page inventory; next, we leverage the hypernyms in the page taxonomy, together with their links to the corresponding categories, so as to induce a taxonomy over Wikipedia categories while at the same time improving the page taxonomy in an iterative way; finally we employ structural heuristics to overcome inherent problems affecting categories. The output of our three-phase approach is a bitaxonomy of millions of pages and hundreds of thousands of categories for the English Wikipedia.

Acknowledgements

The author gratefully acknowledges the support of the ERC Starting Grant MultiJEDI No. 259234.

References

Tiziano Flati, Daniele Vannella, Tommaso Pasini, and Roberto Navigli. 2014. Validating and Extending Semantic Knowledge Bases using Video Games with a Purpose. In *Proceedings of the 52nd Annual Meeting of the Association for Computational Linguistics (ACL 2014)*, pages 945–955, Baltimore, USA.

Andrea Moro, Alessandro Raganato, and Roberto Navigli. 2014. Entity linking meets word sense disambiguation: a unified approach. *Transactions of the Association for Computational Linguistics (TACL)*, 2:231–244.

Roberto Navigli and Simone Paolo Ponzetto. 2012. BabelNet: The automatic construction, evaluation and application of a wide-coverage multilingual semantic network. *Artificial Intelligence*, 193:217–250.

Daniele Vannella, David Jurgens, Daniele Scarfini, Domenico Toscani, and Roberto Navigli. 2014. Validating and Extending Semantic Knowledge Bases using Video Games with a Purpose. In *Proceedings of the 52nd Annual Meeting of the Association for Computational Linguistics (ACL 2014)*, pages 1294–1304, Baltimore, USA.

Measuring Similarity from Word Pair Matrices with Syntagmatic and Paradigmatic Associations

Jin Matsuoka
IPS, Waseda University
Fukuoka, Japan
jinmatsuoka@akane.waseda.jp

Yves Lepage
IPS, Waseda University
Fukuoka, Japan
yves.lepage@waseda.jp

Abstract

Two types of semantic similarity are usually distinguished: *attributional* and *relational* similarities. These similarities measure the degree between words or word pairs. Attributional similarities are bidrectional, while relational similarities are one-directional. It is possible to compute such similarities based on the occurrences of words in actual sentences. Inside sentences, syntagmatic associations and paradigmatic associations can be used to characterize the relations between words or word pairs. In this paper, we propose a vector space model built from syntagmatic and paradigmatic associations to measure relational similarity between word pairs from the sentences contained in a small corpus. We conduct two experiments with different datasets: SemEval-2012 task 2, and 400 word analogy quizzes. The experimental results show that our proposed method is effective when using a small corpus.

1 Introduction

Semantic similarity is a complex concept which has been widely discussed in many research domains (e.g., linguistics, philosophy, information theory communication, or artificial intelligence). In natural language processing (NLP), two types of semantic similarity are identified: *attributional* and *relational* similarities. Until now, many researchers reported for measuring these similarities.

Attributional similarity consists in comparing semantic attributes contained in each word. For example, the two words *car* and *automobile* share many attributes and, consequently, their attributional similarity is high , whereas the attributional similarity between *car* and *drive* is low. If the attributional similarity is high, this means that the words are structurally similar. Indeed, *car* and *automobile* are considered as synonyms because they share almost all of their structural attributes. Attributional similarity is not confined to synonymy but is also related to such relations as hypernymy/hyponymy.

Relational similarity compares the semantic relations between pairs of words. For example, *fish* : *fins* :: *bird* : *wings* asserts that *fish* is to *fins* as *bird* is to *wings*: i.e., the semantic relations between *fish* and *fins* are highly similar to the semantic relations between *bird* and *wings*. To find the relational similarity between two words, knowledge resources such as WordNet (Miller, 1995) or Ontology (Suchanek et al., 2007) are generally used. Lexical syntactic patterns between two words also help in identifying relational similarity. For instance, the lexical syntactic patten 'is a' helps to identify hypernyms (Hearst, 1992; Snow et al., 2004).

To measure the attributional similarity between words or the relational similarity between word pairs, Vector Space Models (VSM) are mainly used (Turney, 2005; Turney and Littman, 2005; Turney, 2006). The expressiveness of a vector space model differs in the way it is built the matrices. The different way to build the matrices is based on two types of associations. In this paper, we use two types of associations which are well-known in linguistics: syntagmatic associations and paradigmatic associations.

Syntagmatic associations originate from word co-occurrences in texts. Latent Semantic Analysis (LSA) relies on such syntagmatic associations. It has been successful at simulating a wide range of psychological and psycholinguistic phenomena, from judgments of semantic similarity (Landauer and

Zock/Rapp/Huang (eds.): Proceedings of the 4th Workshop on Cognitive Aspects of the Lexicon, pages 77–86, Dublin, Ireland, August 23, 2014.

Dumais, 1997). Paradigmatic associations, however, reflect more the semantic attributes of words. Hyperspace Analogue to Language (HAL) (Lund and Burgess, 1996) is related to LSA, but also makes use of paradigmatic associations by capitalizing on positional similarities between words across contexts. LSA and HAL consider simply different types of space built from texts, and the differences are reflected in the structural representations formed by each model (Jones and Mewhort, 2007).

In this paper, we propose a vector space model with both syntagmatic and paradigmatic associations to measure relational similarity between word pairs. The dimensions for each word pair in our proposed model show the distribution between words. To avoid data sparseness in the dimensions, we make use of a word clustering method in a preprocessing step. We then build our proposed model with syntagmatic and paradigmatic associations on the results of the clustering step. We conduct two experiments on SemEval-2012 task 2 and Scholastic Assessment Test (SAT) analogy quizzes to measure relational similarity to evaluate our model.

The rest of the paper is organized as follows. We describe similar research in Section 2. Our proposed vector space model to capture syntagmatic and paradigmatic associations is presented in Section 3. The experimental results and evaluations for relational similarity, and SAT analogy quizzes are shown in Section 4. We present our conclusions in Section 5.

2 Related work

A popular approach with vector space model for measuring similarities between words is to compute the similarities of their distribution in large text data. The underlying assumption is the *distributional hypothesis* (Harris, 1954): words with similar distribution in language should have similar meanings. The two main approaches, LSA and HAL, for producing word spaces differ in the way context vectors are produced. LSA with term-document matrices have a greater potential for measuring semantic similarity between words. LSA capitalizes on a word's contextual co-occurrence, but not on how a word is used in that context. HAL's co-occurrence matrix is a sparse word-word matrix. In HAL, words that appear in similar positions around the same words tend to develop similar vector representations. HAL is related to LSA, but HAL can be said to insist more on paradigmatic associations and LSA more on syntagmatic associations.

Bound Encoding of the AGgregate Language Environment (BEAGLE) (Jones and Mewhort, 2007) is a model that combines syntagmatic and paradigmatic associations. The BEAGLE model has two matrices for representing word meanings with syntagmatic and paradigmatic associations: one for order information and another one for contextual information. By combining the order information and contextual information, the BEAGLE model can express syntagmatic and paradigmatic associations. These models are built from word to word co-occurrences and word to document (context) co-occurrences, which measure only attributional similarity between words. We claim, however, that attributional similarity between words is of little value. For example, the attributional similarity between "*fish*" and "*fins*" is weak, and it is also the case between "*bird*" and "*wings*". However, in terms of relational similarity, there is a high similarity between "*fish*:*fins*" and "*bird*:*wings*". This shows that there may be more potentiality in comparing word pairs rather than simply words.

Turney (2005) and Turney and Littman (2005) used an approach called Latent Relational Analysis (LRA) in which a vector space of distributional features was derived from a large Web corpus and then reduced using singular value decomposition (SVD). For measuring relational similarity, the similarity between two pairs is calculated by the cosine of the angle between the vectors that represent the two pairs in their approach. The main difference between LSA and LRA is the way the semantic space is built. In LSA, the word-document matrices are built for measuring attributional similarity between words as above mentions. In LRA, the pair-pattern matrices are built for measuring relational similarity between word pairs. As an extension, Turney (2008) designed the Latent Relation Mapping Engine (LRME), by combining ideas from the Structure Mapping Engine (SME) (Gentner, 1983) and LRA, to remove the requirement for hand-coded representations in SME. Here, we consider that syntagmatic and paradigmatic associations can adapted to pair-pattern matrices for measuring relational similarity. The extension of pair-pattern matrices are *pair-feature* matrices in our proposed model.

3 Proposed model

In this section, we describe our proposed pair-feature matrices which capture syntagmatic and paradigmatic associations. To build the pair-feature matrices, we consider that syntagmatic associations between words are co-occurrences and paradigmatic associations are substitutions between words in the same contexts. The direct use of such features leads to a large number of dimensions, which may result in data sparseness. Section 3.1 will be dedicated to the solution we propose to avoid this problem. We show how to build our pair-feature matrices with syntagmatic and paradigmatic associations in Section 3.2.

3.1 Data sparseness

A critical problem in statistical natural language processing is *data sparseness.* One way to reduce this problem is to group words into equivalence classes. Typically, word classes are used in language modeling to reduce the problem of data sparseness.

The practical goal of our proposal is to achieve reasonable performance in measuring relational similarity and semantic proportional analogy from a small corpus. We will show that even small corpora have a great potential to measure similarity in actual tasks. Building a pair-feature matrices in such a setting obviously leads to sparseness since word pairs do not easily co-occur in the sentences of small corpora. We use clustering methods to cluster words into equivalence classes to reduce the problem. Here, we make use of monolingual word clustering (Och, 1999)[1]. This method is based on maximum-likelihood estimation with Markov model. We build our proposed pair-feature model described in Section 3.2 based on the results of word clustering.

3.2 Vector Space Model (VSM)

VSM (Salton et al., 1975) is an algebraic model for representing any object as a vector of identifiers. There are many ways to build a semantic space, like term-document, term-context, and pair-pattern matrices (Turney and Pantel, 2010). Turney (2006) showed that pair-pattern matrices are suited to measuring the similarity of semantic relations between pairs of words; that is, relational similarity. Conversely, word-context matrices are suited to measuring attributional similarity.

In this paper, we build a vector space of pair-feature after preprocessing the training corpus by a word clustering method. In a pair-feature matrix, row vectors correspond to pairs of words, such as "*fish*:*fins*" and "*bird*:*wings*", and column vectors correspond to the features grouped by the word clustering method. We set $3 \times N$ column vector size, N features annotated by the word clustering method described in previous section. The reason for setting the vector size to three times the number of features is to represent syntagmatic and paradigmatic associations in our proposed model. Our main original idea is to build a column vector of *affixes*. A sentence containing a word pair is divided into three parts:

- a prefix part, which consists in the word classes found around the first word of the word pair in the sentence in a window of a given size called the context window;
- an infix part, which consists in the word classes of the words found the words of between the word pair in the sentence;
- a suffix part, which consists in the word classes found around the second word of the word pair in the sentence in a window of a given size (context window);

We suppose that prefixes and suffixes are *paradigmatic* features and that infixes are *syntagmatic* features. The paradigmatic features indirectly capture similar words around the first and the second words. By opposition, the syntagmatic features directly capture the syntactical pattern between a word pair. These features also characterize the syntactic structure of sentences. This model will deliver similar features for word pairs appearing in sentences exhibiting similar syntactic patterns. By combining syntagmatic and paradigmatic features in our proposed model, we can express these associations in one vector space.

[1]The tool, mkcls, for 'make classes', is available at `http://www-i6.informatik.rwth-aachen.de/Colleagues/och/software/mkcls.html`.

We show below an example of how to build our pair-feature matrix representation. Let us consider the three following sentences.

diurnal bird of prey typically having short rounded wings and a long tail, (i)
tropical fish with huge fanlike pectoral fins for underwater gliding, (ii)
the occupation of catching fish for a living. (iii)

The words in the three sentences are clustered by the word clustering tool as indicated in Table 1. From

class	word	$p(c)$	$-\log p(c)$
c1	diurnal, tropical, huge, pectoral	0.17	1.79
c2	of, and, a, with, for	0.21	1.57
c3	bird, prey, wings, tail, fish, fins, underwater	0.29	1.23
c4	typically, rounded, fanlike	0.13	2.08
c5	having, short, long, gliding, catching	0.21	1.57

Table 1: An example annotated by the word clustering method.

the sentences annotated with the word classes, we add up weights for each class c for each feature part in the pair-feature matrix (see Table 5) according to the following formula.

$$weight(c) = \begin{cases} f(c) \times -\log p(c), & \text{if } w_1 \text{ and } w_2 \text{ co-occur in the sentence} \\ f(c), & \text{if only one of } w_1 \text{ or } w_2 \text{ occurs in the sentence} \\ 0, & \text{if neither } w_1 \text{ nor } w_2 \text{ occurs in the sentence} \end{cases} \quad (1)$$

Here, c is the class of a word (e.g., c1, c2, or c3) and f is the frequency of c, i.e., the number of times the class c appears in the sentence considered for each feature part (prefix, infix, suffix). The proportion $p(c)$ of a class is the relative proportion of occurrences of this class computed over the entire corpus. We show how to compute each feature in Table 2. If the word pair co-occur in some sentences, the $weight$

	Features		
	prefix (around w_1)	infix (between w_1 and w_2)	suffix (around w_2)
w_1 and w_2 co-occur	$f(c) \times -\log p(c)$	$f(c) \times -\log p(c)$	$f(c) \times -\log p(c)$
w_1 or w_2 occur	$f(c)$	0	$f(c)$
neither w_1 nor w_2 occur	0	0	0

Table 2: Computation of $weights$ for a given c and a given word pair "w_1:w_2" for a given sentence.

is modified by the self-information. If one word in the word pair occurs alone in some sentences, we compute only paradigmatic feature part (syntagmatic feature part, infix, is 0). All the weights coming from all the sentences are added up for each class for each feature part in the final vector corresponding to one word pair. In VSM, the weighting scheme is poring-wise information or TF-IDF.

For example, given the word pair "*fish:fins*", the feature parts are defined as follows:

bird of prey typically having short rounded wings and a long tail, (i)

tropical *fish* with huge fanlike pectoral *fins* for underwater gliding, (ii)

the occupation of catching *fish* for a living. (iii)

The boxes are the syntagmatic feature parts (only one here) and these underlined are paradigmatic features (in sentence (ii) prefix and suffix parts, in sentence (iii), prefix part only because '*fish*' is the first word in the word pair "*fish:fins*"). We show the computation of f in Table 3 for the same given word pair "*fish:fins*". The prefixes are the words around *fish*, the infixes are the words between *fish* and *fins*, and the suffixes are the words around *fins* from our main idea.

		c1	c2	c3	c4	c5
prefix	tropical, with, huge	2	1	0	0	0
infix	with, huge, fanlike, pectoral	2	1	0	1	0
suffix	fanlike, pectoral, for, underwater	1	1	1	1	0

Table 3: Computation of f for a given word pair "*fish:fins*" with Table 1.

		c1	c2	c3	c4	c5
prefix	of, catching, for, a	0	0	3	0	1
infix		0	0	0	0	0
suffix		0	0	0	0	0

Table 4: Computation of f for a given word pair "*fish:eat*" with Table 1.

Let us consider a word pair which is not found in any sentence, e.g., the word pair "*fish:eat*". The computation of f in this case is shown in Table 4. The word *fish* occurs in the sentence (iii). The word *eat* does not appear in any sentence. Consequently, the frequency of each class is 0 in the suffix feature part.

Table 5 shows the pair-feature matrix computed from the three above sentences for three word pairs. Each cell in Table 5 is computed using the results given in Tables 1-4. For example, for "*fish:fins*" the value for c1 in the prefix is 3.58 (computed according to Formula 1 using $-\log p(c1) = 1.79$ in Table 1 and $f(c1) = 2$ in Table 3). The infix cells corresponding to "*fish:eat*" are all 0.0 because of the null values for each class in Table 4.

	Features														
	prefix					infix					suffix				
	c1	c2	c3	c4	c5	c1	c2	c3	c4	c5	c1	c2	c3	c4	c5
bird:wings	1.79	1.57	1.23	0.0	0.0	0.0	1.57	2.46	2.08	1.57	0.0	3.14	0.0	2.08	1.57
fish:fins	3.58	1.57	0.0	0.0	0.0	3.58	1.57	0.0	2.08	0.0	1.79	1.57	1.23	2.08	0.0
fish:eat	0.0	4.71	0.0	0.0	1.57	0.0	0.0	0.0	0.0	0.0	0.0	0.0	0.0	0.0	0.0

Table 5: Pair-feature matrix computed using sentences (i)-(iii).

After building the pair-feature space, we make use of SVD to induce an approximation space. SVD is used to reduce the noise and compensate for the zero vectors in the model. We show that the formula is as follows:

$$M = U\Sigma V^T \tag{2}$$

Here, M is the pair-feature matrix (dimensions: $n \times m$), U is the pair matrix (dimensions: $n \times r$), Σ is a diagonal matrix of singular values (dimensions: $r \times r$) and V is feature matrix (dimensions: $m \times r$). n is the number of word pairs, m is the number of classes grouped by the word clustering method and r is rank of M. If M is of rank r, then Σ is also of rank r. We can redefine the value k using Formula 3 instead of r.

$$M \sim \hat{M} = U_k \Sigma_k V_k^T \tag{3}$$

Let Σ_k, where $k \leq r$, be the diagonal matrix formed from the top k singular values. And let U_k and V_k be the matrices produced by determining the corresponding columns from U and V. We determine the k (latent size) for our experiments empirically. This formula means that it is to remove the noise in the matrices M by using dimension reduction. Section 4 will show how we set the parameters in our experiments.

3.3 Relational and attributional similarity

In our proposed framework, relational similarity can be measured by using the distributions over two word pairs. After building the new space $\hat{M}$ according to Formula 3, we measure relational similarity between word pairs such as "A:B" and "C:D" in a classical way by computing their cosine:

$$\text{relsim}(\hat{M}_i, \hat{M}_j) = \frac{\hat{M}_i \cdot \hat{M}_j}{||\hat{M}_i|| \times ||\hat{M}_j||}, \quad \hat{M}_i = A : B, \quad \hat{M}_j = C : D. \tag{4}$$

Here, i and j are word pairs indexes and $||\hat{M}_i||$ is the norm. It is usually thought that attributional similarity can be deduced from relational similarity (i.e., this means two-sideness).

For instance, Bollegala et al. (2012) showed how to measure the degree of synonymy between words using relational similarity. Their formula for measuring attributional similarity between words using relational similarity between word pairs is as follows:

$$\text{attsim}(A, B) = \frac{1}{|T|} \times \sum_{(C,D) \in T} \text{relsim}(A : B, C : D) \tag{5}$$

Here T is a set of synonymy word pair collected from WordNet and $|T|$ is the cardinality of a set of T. If A and B are highly similar to that between synonymous words, this means that A and B themselves must also be synonymous.

To test measures of attributional similarity between words, the Miller-Charles dataset (Miller and Charles, 1991) is commonly used. The data consist of 30 word pairs such as "*gem:jewel*", all of them being nouns. The relatedness of each word pair has been rated by 38 human subjects, using a scale from 0 to 4. It should be said that the application of our proposed model to this task delivers results (0.28) which are far below the usually reported scores (around 0.87). This is explained by the fact that our model is not designed for attributional similarity, but aims directly at measuring relational similarity. The results indicate that the paradigmatic features are not useful to measure the attributional similarity between words in our proposed model. As a other method to measure the attributional similarity between words, point-wise mutual information is generally used.

4 Experiments and results

We perform two experiments on two datasets to prove the validity of our proposed model against the purpose it was designed for: the measure of relational similarity. In the two experiments, we make use of one corpus which contains about 150,000 sentences and about one million tokens. We set the latent size of Formula 3 to 40 to remove the noise in the matrices. The context window size is 2 for the paradigmatic features (prefixes and suffixes). The range of the syntagmatic feature (infixes) is from 1 to 5.

The first experiment shown in Section 4.1 directly outputs a measure of the relational similarity. The second experiment, on SAT analogy quizzes in Section 4.2 uses relational similarity to rank candidates. In both experiments, we do not preprocess with stemming and do not delete stop words.

4.1 Direct measure of relational similarity

To test our measure of relational similarity between word pairs, we make use of the SemEval-2012 task 2 (Jurgens et al., 2012). Jurgens et al. (2012) constructed a data set of prototypical ratings for 3,218 word pairs in 79 different relation categories with the help of Amazon Mechanical Turk[2].

There are two phases for measuring the degree of relational similarity in this task. The first phase is to generate pairs of a given relation. We do not perform this phase here. Another phase is used to rate word pairs from given word pairs. This task selects least and most illustrative word pairs in four word pairs ("oak:tree"; "vegetable:carrot"; "tree:oak"; "currency:dollar") based on several given word pairs ("flower:tulip", "emotion:rage", "poem:sonnet"). To rate word pairs, this task makes use of the MaxDiff technique (Louviere and Woodworth, 1991). The set with 79 word relations was randomly split into

[2]Task details and data are available at `https://sites.google.com/site/semeval2012task2/`

training and testing sets. The training set contains 10 relations and the test set contains 69 relations. For each relation, about one hundred questions were created.

We present how to determine the least and most illustrative word pairs in the four word pairs. The formula for rating a word pairs is as follows:

$$\text{score}(A:B) = \frac{\sum_{t \in T} \text{relsim}(A:B,t)}{|T|}. \quad (6)$$

Here, relsim is the same as shown in Section 3.3, T is a set of several given word pairs, and $|T|$ is the number of given word pairs. The score indicates that the higher is the most illustrative and the lower is the least illustrative for the four word pairs. This formula rates a word pair from several given word pairs by using relational similarity since the relation between the given word pairs is proportional to a targeted word pair.

The results of our experiments are given in Table 6 along with the score of other models. The maxDiff

Algorithm	Reference	MaxDiff
SuperSim	(Turney, 2013)	**47.2**
Com	(Zhila et al., 2013)	45.2
RNN-1600	(Mikolov et al., 2013b)	41.8
UTD-NB	(Rink and Harabagiu, 2012)	39.4
Ours		35.1
UTD-SVM	(Rink and Harabagiu, 2012)	34.5

Table 6: The top five results with SemEval-2012 task 2, from the ACL wiki. MaxDiff is a measure which ranges from 0 to 100%, the higher the better.

score is 35.1 by using our proposed model. Comparing with other methods on the ACL wiki[3] in Table 6, our method is lower, but is higher than UTD-SVM. We also detail the results for each category in Table 7. We obtained the highest maxDiff score for CLASS-INCLUSION category (the score is 43.8) and the

Category	Random	UTD-NB	UTD-SVM	Ours
CLASS-INCLUSION	31.0	37.6	31.6	**43.8**
PART-WHOLE	31.9	**40.9**	35.7	30.4
SIMILAR	31.5	**39.8**	34.7	34.6
CONTRAST	30.4	**40.9**	38.9	39.0
ATTRIBUTE	30.2	**36.5**	31.3	34.4
NON-ATTRIBUTE	28.9	**36.8**	34.5	34.0
CASE-RELATIONS	32.8	**40.6**	36.7	32.4
CAUSE-PURPOSE	30.8	**36.3**	33.3	30.5
SPACE-TIME	30.6	**43.2**	34.5	35.0
REFERENCE	35.1	**41.2**	34.2	35.1
Average	31.2	**39.4**	34.5	35.1

Table 7: The MaxDiff scores for each category.

lowest score for PART-WHOLE category (the score is 30.4), but all the other scores are lower than UTD-NB. We consider that it is easy to capture the syntagmatic and paradigmatic associations in our proposed model for CLASS-INCLUSION category than for PART-WHOLE category. Our pair-feature matrices are influenced by paradigmatic features when word pairs do not co-occur in any similar context. For measuring relational similarity, we consider that syntagmatic and paradigmatic associations are sufficient in our model from this results.

[3] http://wiki.aclweb.org/index.php?title=Main_Page

4.2 SAT analogy quizzes

We use 400 SAT analogy quizzes from a set of 501 (Dermott, 2002). 101 SAT analogy quizzes were discarded as they concern named entities (e.g., *Van Buren* : *8th* :: *Lincoln* : *16th*), symbolic or notational variants (e.g., $V : X :: L : C$), or the like, which are obviously out of the reach of our proposed model. The SAT analogy quizzes of *Van Buren* : *8th* :: *Lincoln* : *16th* and $V : X :: L : C$ are domain-specific cases in that domain-specific knowledge is needed to solve them. No specific domain knowledge is needed to solve *fish* : *fins* :: *bird* : *wings*. We show an example of the resolution of a proportional analogy quiz in Table 8 *pilfer* : *steal* :: *?* : *equip* randomly sampled from the 400 SAT analogy quizzes. Answering the quiz consists in selecting one solution among four candidates. To select one candidate

Stem :		*pilfer* : *steal* :: *?* : *equip*	relsim
Choice:	(a)	return	0.350
	(b)	damage	0.397
	(c)	exercise	0.400
	(d)	furnish	**0.541**
Solution:	(d)	furnish	0.541

Table 8: An example of a SAT analogy quiz.

out of the four, we rank them using the relational similarity of the candidate with the fourth word in the quiz. The rank is computed using Formula 4. As an example, in Table 8, we give the degree of relational similarity for the previous quiz. The selected answer is *furnish*, and the semantic relation between the word pairs is synonymy.

The results on 400 SAT analogy quizzes are given in Table 9 along with the accuracy of other methods. We obtain the highest score with our proposed model against another model, Word2vec (Mikolov et al., 2013a)[4], and a baseline model that draws a solution at random. It should be noticed that, here, word pairs do not involve only noun to noun pairs but also involve noun to verb pairs. Our model is effective in answering the proportional analogy quizzes by using syntagmatic and paradigmatic associations from a small corpus. It achieves this by using a training corpus of about 10 megabytes in size to build a pair-feature vector space. By contrast, Word2vec requires 100 megabytes of training corpus and fails at building a word space which is precise enough, to beat random selection. This clearly shows that clustering of words can make up for size of corpus and we can acquire the better accuracy.

Algorithm	Reference	Accuracy
Random		0.22
Word2vec	(Mikolov et al., 2013a)	0.20
Ours		**0.27**

Table 9: The evaluations comparing with other methods.

The SAT analogy quizzes and the SemEval-2012 task 2 are separate tasks. To assess the quality of proportional analogies two aspects are needed: vertical and horizontal dimensions. On the an example *fish* : *fins* :: *bird* : *wings*, the vertical dimension is between "*fish*:*bird*" and "*fins*:*wings*" and the horizontal dimension is between "*fish*:*fins*" and "*bird*:*wings*". In all generality, we should examine the score function of proportional analogies on both vertical and horizontal dimensions but practically the vertical dimension is not so important in SAT analogies quizzes.

5 Conclusion

Attributional similarity and relational similarity are usually distinguished in the study of semantic similarity. Many researchers proposed to build a various of vector space models to measure the attributional

[4]The tool is available at `https://code.google.com/p/word2vec/`.

similarity between words or the relational similarity between word pairs. Such similarities are commonly used to solve semantic problems on words, phrase or sentences in the NLP literature.

In this paper, we presented a pair-feature matrix model with syntagmatic and paradigmatic associations for measuring relational similarity. By using a sentence containing a word pair is divided into three parts, we represented the syntagmatic and paradigmatic associations for each word pair. We made use of a word clustering method to cope with data sparseness in a preprocessing step. We performed two experiments with different datasets: SemEval-2012 task 2, and SAT analogy quizzes. These experiments show that the pair-feature matrix model with syntagmatic and paradigmatic associations is effective to measure relational similarity. In future work, we propose to make use of stemming and to delete stop words to reduce even more the noise that affects decrease the performance of the word clustering step we introduced to deal with data sparseness.

References

Danushka Bollegala, Yutaka Matsuo, and Mitsuru Ishizuka. 2012. Measuring the degree of synonymy between words using relational similarity between word pairs as a proxy. *IEICE Transactions on Information and Systems*, 95(8):2116–2123.

Brigit Dermott. 2002. *501 Word Analogy Questions*. Learning Express.

Dedre Gentner. 1983. Structure-mapping: A theoretical framework for analogy. *Cognitive Science*, 7(2):155–170.

Zellig S. Harris. 1954. Distributional structure. *Word*, 10:146–162.

Marti A. Hearst. 1992. Automatic acquisition of hyponyms from large text corpora. In *Proceedings of COLING-92*, volume 2, pages 539–545. Association for Computational Linguistics.

Michael N. Jones and Douglas J.K. Mewhort. 2007. Representing word meaning and order information in a composite holographic lexicon. *Psychological Review*, 114(1):1–37.

David A. Jurgens, Peter D. Turney, Saif M. Mohammad, and Keith J. Holyoak. 2012. Semeval-2012 task 2: Measuring degrees of relational similarity. In *Proceedings of the First Joint Conference on Lexical and Computational Semantics-Volume 1: Proceedings of the main conference and the shared task, and Volume 2: Proceedings of the Sixth International Workshop on Semantic Evaluation*, pages 356–364. Association for Computational Linguistics.

Thomas K. Landauer and Susan T. Dumais. 1997. A solution to plato's problem: The latent semantic analysis theory of acquisition, induction, and representation of knowledge. *Psychological Review*, 104(2):211–240.

Jordan J. Louviere and G.G. Woodworth. 1991. Best-worst scaling: A model for the largest difference judgments. Technical report, Technical Report, University of Alberta.

Kevin Lund and Curt Burgess. 1996. Producing high-dimensional semantic spaces from lexical co-occurrence. *Behavior Research Methods, Instruments, & Computers*, 28(2):203–208.

Tomas Mikolov, Kai Chen, Greg Corrado, and Jeffrey Dean. 2013a. Efficient estimation of word representations in vector space. In *Proceedings of Workshop at International Conference on Learning Representations*.

Tomas Mikolov, Wen-tau Yih, and Geoffrey Zweig. 2013b. Linguistic regularities in continuous space word representations. In *Proceedings of NAACL/HLT*, pages 746–751. Citeseer.

George A. Miller and Walter G. Charles. 1991. Contextual correlates of semantic similarity. *Language and Cognitive Processes*, 6(1):1–28.

George A. Miller. 1995. Wordnet: a lexical database for english. *Communications of the Association for Computing Machinery*, 38(11):39–41.

Franz Josef Och. 1999. An efficient method for determining bilingual word classes. In *Proceedings of EACL*, pages 71–76. Association for Computational Linguistics.

Bryan Rink and Sanda Harabagiu. 2012. Utd: Determining relational similarity using lexical patterns. In *Proceedings of the First Joint Conference on Lexical and Computational Semantics*, pages 413–418, Montreal, Canada. Association for Computational Linguistics.

Gerard Salton, Anita Wong, and Chung-Shu Yang. 1975. A vector space model for automatic indexing. *Communications of the Association for Computing Machinery*, 18(11):613–620.

Rion Snow, Daniel Jurafsky, and Andrew Y. Ng. 2004. Learning syntactic patterns for automatic hypernym discovery. *Advances in Neural Information Processing Systems*.

Fabian M. Suchanek, Gjergji Kasneci, and Gerhard Weikum. 2007. Yago: a core of semantic knowledge. In *Proceedings of WWW*, pages 697–706. ACM.

Peter D. Turney and Michael L. Littman. 2005. Corpus-based learning of analogies and semantic relations. *Machine Learning*, 60(1-3):251–278.

Peter D. Turney and Patrick Pantel. 2010. From frequency to meaning: Vector space models of semantics. *Journal of Artificial Intelligence Research*, 37(1):141–188.

Peter D. Turney. 2005. Measuring semantic similarity by latent relational analysis. In *Proceedings of IJCAI*, pages 1136–1141.

Peter D. Turney. 2006. Similarity of semantic relations. *Computational Linguistics*, 32(3):379–416.

Peter D. Turney. 2008. The latent relation mapping engine: Algorithm and experiments. *Journal of Artificial Intelligence Research*, 33(1):615–655.

Peter D. Turney. 2013. Distributional semantics beyond words: Supervised learning of analogy and paraphrase. In *Transactions of the Association for Computational Linguistics*, volume 1, pages 353–366. Association for Computational Linguistics.

Alisa Zhila, Wen-tau Yih, Christopher Meek, Geoffrey Zweig, and Tomas Mikolov. 2013. Combining heterogeneous models for measuring relational similarity. In *Proceedings of NAACL/HLT*, pages 1000–1009.

Jibiki-LINKS: a Tool between Traditional Dictionaries and Lexical Networks for Modelling Lexical Resources

ZHANG Ying[1, 2] **Mathieu MANGEOT**[1] **Valérie BELLYNCK**[1] **Christian BOITET**[1]

1. GETALP-LIG, 41 rue des Mathématiques BP53, 38041 Grenoble Cedex

2. SAS Lingua et Machina, Domaine de Voluceau, Rocquencourt, 78153 Le Chesnay

{ying.zhang, mathieu.mangeot, valerie.bellynck, christian.boitet}@imag.fr

Abstract

Between simple electronic dictionaries such as the TLFi (computerized French Language Treasure)[1] and lexical networks like WordNet[2] (Diller et al., 1990; Vossen, 1998), the lexical databases are growing at high speed. Our work is about the addition of rich links to lexical databases, in the context of the parallel development of lexical networks. Current research on management tools for lexical databases is strongly influenced by the field of massive data ("big data") and by the Web of data ("linked data"). In lexical networks, one can build and use arbitrary links, but possible queries cannot model all the usual interactions with lexicographers-developers and users, that are needed, and derive from the paper world. Our work aims to find a solution that allows for the main advantages of lexical networks, while providing the equivalent of paper dictionaries by doing the lexicographic work in lexical DBs.

1 Introduction

The growing importance of IT in all human activities extends and expands the needs and usages of all key digital resources that include lexical resources. Thus, while applications valuing the linguistic processes rely on increasingly abstract representations, modelled for computer operations, it remains that models coming from the historical construction of resources foster human understanding, and therefore, the building of tools for studies centring on the humanities.

In this this section, we place the emergence of the concept of lexical database between electronic dictionaries and lexical networks. We show that this concept is still valid, that it is still necessary to enrich it, and that our work on improving tools for lexical databases helps solve real problems.

To do this, we analyse in the second section the evolution of lexical resources in 4 main steps (simple electronic dictionaries, simple lexical databases, multilevel and multiversion lexical databases, and lexical networks) and present the associated problems. In the third section, we present Jibiki-LINKS, a platform for building multilingual lexical databases that enriches the Jibiki generic platform by introducing the concept of *rich link* between the components it manages (dictionary entries and dictionary volumes). Finally, we show that it allows the construction of lexical databases such as Pivax-UNL, which support scaling up.

2 From computerized dictionaries to lexical databases with rich links

The first computerized lexical resources are electronic versions of printed dictionaries, mainly monolingual or bilingual. The use of computers has helped to overcome the constraints of the paper form. The impossibility to inverse bilingual dictionaries led to a model having a "pivot" consisting of axies[3]. Lexical pivot-based databases are invertible and transitive, but rooted on the form of the

[1] http://atilf.atilf.fr

[2] http://wordnet.princeton.edu

[3] "Axie" = "interlingual meaning," by analogy with "lexie".

Zock/Rapp/Huang (eds.): Proceedings of the 4th Workshop on Cognitive Aspects of the Lexicon, pages 87–98, Dublin, Ireland, August 23, 2014.

symbols, while the lexical networks allow a move towards the direct manipulation of semantic tokens, regardless of their surface form, and thus of the language.

In this section, we present the evolution of approaches, distinguishing four main types of lexical resources, the limitations that motivated this evolution, and the remaining hard problems.

2.1 Simple electronic dictionaries

A simple electronic dictionary is an electronic version of a printed dictionary, or the computer representation of a new kind of the same type of dictionary, for example, the TLFi[4], the morphological and bilingual dictionaries of Apertium[5], etc. A simple electronic dictionary contains either one volume or two volumes. The electronic version of a monolingual paper dictionary is (usually implicitly) based on its *microstructure*, that is to say, on the organization of its entries in the form of a small tree organizing the information it contains. In a paper dictionary, the presentation of an entry reflects the microstructure, but the microstructure is not always directly retrievable from it (for example, parts in italics can correspond to different types of information units, such as idiom or example of use).

In absolute terms, it is always possible to represent the information specified in each entry of a dictionary according to a common structure. In reality, the structures of paper dictionaries are less rigorous than what would be required for automatic processing, so that manual editing is required.

A bilingual paper dictionary is generally based on a structure in two volumes, one for each language pair, each volume conforming to the same microstructure. There are therefore generally one volume from language A (Lg A) to language B (Lg B) and a mirror volume from Lg B to Lg A. We define the *macrostructure* of a dictionary as the organization of the volumes that make up its structure. These macrostructures constitute the bulk of the printed dictionaries.

2.2 Lexical databases

A lexical database is a tool for unifying any set of dictionaries, where each dictionary can be monolingual, bilingual or multitarget. A multilingual lexical database is composed of volumes that are monolingual, direct multilingual, or indirect multilingual, i.e. connecting the entries of different languages via a pivot structure. It has an overall macrostructure, and a microstructure for each of its volumes. A link between 2 entries is realized by the software tool as a direct link, or as 2 links going through an intermediate language, or as a semantic link, etc.

The lack of symmetry of the correspondence between the entries of bilingual dictionaries (from word senses to words, not word senses) led to the concept of *interlingual pivot*. In the pivot macrostructure developed and used for the Papillon-NADIA multilingual lexical database (Sérasset and Mangeot, 2001), there is only one monolingual volume for each language. *Lexies* are word senses (of a lexeme or an idiom) and make up the entries of these volumes. To group the lexies of different languages together, there is a pivot volume of *axies* (interlingual acceptions). An axie connects synonymous lexies. The links are established only between lexies and axies. This is the simplest macrostructure for a pivot-based multilingual lexical resource that allows for the extraction of usage dictionaries for all pairs in all directions. The concept of axie-based pivot structure has been validated by the Papillon project and then included in the Lexical Markup Framework standard (Francopoulo et al. 2009).

2.3 Multilevel and multiversion databases

In this type of lexical database, several monolingual volumes are allowed for each *lexical space*[6], A volume of *axemes* (monolingual acceptions) is introduced to link synonymous lexies of the considered lexical space. Also, various levels are introduced to tag entries according to different points of view (sublanguage, version, type of link, reliability, preference). The simple links of previous versions are replaced by *rich links* that can be established not only between lexies, axemes and axies, but also between entries and subentries, monolingually (lexicosemantic functions) or bilingually (translations).

---

[4] Trésor de la Langue Française informatisé, http://atilf.atilf.fr/

[5] http://wiki.apertium.org/wiki/User:Alessiojr/Easy_dictionary_-_Application-GSOC2010

[6] A lexical space of a natural language contains various levels (wordform, lemma, lexie, prolexeme, proaxeme); it can also contain the lexical symbols of an artificial semantic representation language (e.g., the UWs of UNL).

For example, there is a 3-level macrostructure (lexie, axeme, axie) in PIVAX (Nguyen & al., 2007) and a 4-level macrostructure (lexie, prolexeme, proaxie, axie) in ProAxie (Zhang & Mangeot, 2013), described in more detail in section 4.1. Both allow us to manage one or more monolingual volumes for each lexical space. That has been quite useful in the ANR Traouiero GBDLex-UW++ subproject, during which we stored the UNL part of many UNL-Li dictionaries (the UW interlingual lexemes, built with slightly different conventions by different UNL groups for their languages), and tried then to unify them in a new monolingual UNL dictionary (using a set of "UW++" built from WordNet and from the previous UNL dictionaries).

2.4 Lexical network

A lexical network brings together the set of words that denote ideas or realities that refer to the same theme, as well as all the words that, because of the context and certain aspects of their meaning, also evoke this theme[7]. The theme may possibly be very broad. It is possible to represent the full vocabulary of a language in a lexical network, such as, for French, the JeuxDeMots network (Lafourcade and Joubert, 2010) or RFL (Lexical Network of French (Lux-Pogodalla, Polguère 2011)).

Lexical networks are traditionally represented as graphs. Nodes represent the lexemes of one or more languages, and links represent the relationships between these lexemes (translation, synonymy, etc.). A lexical network can be monolingual or multilingual. One can create syntactic, morphological and semantic relations between lexemes.

Although lexical networks have many advantages, they are not suitable for all usages. For example, lexical networks like WordNet (Diller & al., 1990; Vossen, 1998), HowNet (Dong et al., 2010) and MindNet (Dolan and Richardson, 1996) (Richardson et al., 1998) are not browsable in alphabetical order. But we need that possibility to have an idea of the content of a lexical repository, whatever its nature, or to play word games, or to find a word one has on the tip of the tongue[8]. On the other hand, in a lexical network, the concept of volume is missing, which prevents to create a resource in a simple way when studying a new language.

For example, the lexical network DBNary (Sérasset, 2012), which is based on the Lemon model (McCrae et al., 2011), contains millions of terms, but does not allow labelling the links. To navigate in this system, one must write SPARQL queries, which is not within the reach of everyone.

2.5 Conclusion: features, limitations and hard problems

Research efforts focus today mainly on lexical networks, but much remains to be done on the preceding types (pivot, multilevel). In particular, the import of lexical databases in lexical networks causes a loss of information, especially information born by the attributes of rich links. For example, what concerns the history, the etymology or the evolution of word senses is not systematically imported into lexical networks. They therefore cannot meet the needs of the humanities, nor allow the transition to "digital humanities."

A lexical network is actually the type of structure that enables the greatest freedom of representation. Indeed, we can create entries and links arbitrarily. But the possible queries cannot model all the usual interactions with lexicographers-developers and users, which come from the world of paper, and are felt necessary. They allow us to represent all categories of lexical resources, but the analogy with the real world is lost. Thus, the practical expertise of linguists-lexicographers is lost.

We must continue to equip lexical databases, because that is the right level to transfer the techniques used by lexicographers-linguists. Also, modelling by a volume-based macrostructure allows keeping a link to the original paper world. Moreover, there are already reusable resources of these types. That is why we focus on the management of resources having multiversion and multilevel macrostructures.

3 Reuse of rich links

In this section, we present an improvement that consists in introducing into lexical databases relational

[7] http://ddata.over-blog.com/xxxyyy/3/12/82/15/GRAMMAIRE/champs-et-reseaux-lexicaux.pdf

[8] For that kind of functionality, multiple sorting on subsets of inflected forms and on arbitray types of information seems to be a necessary first level of computer aid.

information in the form of *rich links* that will bring them closer to lexical networks. An important point is that these links may bear arbitrary labels.

3.1 Presentation of the Jibiki platform

Jibiki is a generic platform that enables the construction of contributive websites dedicated to the construction of multilingual lexical databases. That platform has been developed mainly by Mathieu Mangeot (Mangeot & Chalvin, 2006) and Gilles Sérasset (Sérasset & Mangeot, 2001). It has been used in various projects (EU LexALP project, Papillon project, GDEF project, etc.). The code is available in open source, and freely downloadable by SVN from ligforge.imag.fr. With this platform, one can perform import, export, edit and search operations in lexical databases. One can also manage the contributions. Jibiki allows handling almost all lexical resources of XML type, by using different microstructures and macrostructures.

In the Jibiki approach, resources are organized in *volumes*, which makes it easier to achieve the equivalent of paper dictionaries, keeping the mental image of the representation of the dictionary, while offering new interactions allowed in the digital world. Usages of dictionaries in Jibiki are also similar to those of paper dictionaries. For example, one can consult a database in alphabetical order, indicate a source and/or target language, group lexies in vocables, navigate in a volume, etc.

3.2 Classical Common Dictionary Markup

Version 1 of Jibiki uses "CDM pointers" (Common Dictionary Markup (Mangeot, 2002)) to import, view and edit any type of microstructure without modifying it. CDM pointers are also used to index specific parts of the information, and then allow a multi-criteria search.

Each CDM pointer indicates the path (XPath) to the corresponding element in the XML microstructure of the described resource (see Figure 1). Its description is stored in a XML metadata file. When the resource is imported in the Jibiki platform, the pointers are computed, and the result is stored in a table of the (postgresql) database, for each volume. This table is considered as an indexing table.

```
<cdm-elements>
 <cdm-volume xpath="/g:volume"/>
 <cdm-entry xpath="/g:volume/g:article"/>
 <cdm-entry-id xpath="/g:volume/g:article/@g:id" />
 <cdm-headword xpath="/g:volume/g:article/g:vedette/g:mot/text()" d:lang="fra" />
 <cdm-pronunciation xpath="//g:prononciation/text()" d:lang="fra" />
 <cdm-pos xpath="//g:cat-gram/text()" d:lang="fra" />
 <cdm-definition xpath="/g:volume/g:article/g:vedette/g:mot/text()"/>
</cdm-elements>
```

Figure 1: CDM pointers for the French volume of the GDEF[9] resource (Mangeot and Chalvin, 2006)

CDM tags	FeM[10] (Gut et al., 1996)	OHD[11]	JMdict[12] (Breen, 2004)
Volume	/volume	/volume	/JMdict
Entry	/volume/entry	/volume/se	/JMdict/entry
Entry ID	/volume/entry/@id		/JMdict/entry/ent_seq/text()
Headword	/volume/entry/headword/text()	/volume/se/hw/text()	/JMdict/entry/k_ele/keb/text()
Pron	/volume/entry/prnc/text()	/volume/se/pr/ph/text()	
PoS	//sense-list/sense/pos-list/text()	/volume/se/hg/ps/text()	/JMdict/entry/sense/pos/text()
Domain		//u/text()	
Example	//sense1/expl-list/expl/fra	//le/text()	/JMdict/entry/sense/gloss/text()

Table 1: Examples of Common Dictionary Markup

[9] GDEF is a large Estonian-French dictionary that is being created by the Franco-Estonian lexicography association (see http://estfra.ee/GDEF.po).

[10] FeM is a French-English-Malay dictionary (30000 entries, 50000 lexies, 8000 idioms, 10000 examples of use).

[11] OHD is abbreviation of Oxford-Hachette Dictionary, which is a French-English dictionary.

[12] JMdict is a Japanese-multilingual dictionary.

The translation links are treated at this stage with conventional CDM pointers, as classical information elements. It is not possible to index other information carried by the links, such as weights or labels.

Hence, multilevel macrostructures cannot be modelled in a generic manner with Jibiki-v1 and traditional CDM pointers. For example, it is not possible to link the same volume to several volumes at different levels. This has forced us initially to use palliatives that did not scale up. It became necessary to modify the conceptual model. We addressed these shortcomings in a new version, Jibiki-LINKS.

Table 1 above is an example of CDM for the different resources.

3.3 New version of Jibiki with CDM LINKS

To manage multilevel macrostructures, we enriched the CDM with a richer description of the links (see Figure 2). For each link, more information can be indexed:

- the identifier of the source entry.
- the identifier of the target entry.
- the identifier of the XML element of the source entry containing the link. For example, the sense number in a polysemous entry having a translation link for each translation direction. That allows us to precisely retrieve the origin of the link.
- the link name. It is used to distinguish between different types of links in a single entry, such as a translation link and a synonymy link.
- the target language (three-letter code ISO 639-2 / T).
- the target volume.
- the type of link. Some types are predefined, because they are used by the algorithms that compute the rich links (translation, axeme, axie), but it is possible to use other types of links.
- a label whose text is arbitrary.
- a weight whose value must be a real number.

These links can be established between two entries of the same volume or between two different volumes. The same volume may group entries connected to several volumes.

To realize the implementation of rich links, we separated the module processing the links from the module processing other CDM pointers. It means we have two CDM tables in the database associated to each volume. The first stores CDM traditional pointers, and the second CDM LINKS. All information of LINKS can be found in this table.

```
<cdm-elements>
  <cdm-volume    xpath="/p:volume"/>
  <cdm-entry    xpath="/p:volume/p:vocable"/>
  <cdm-entry-id    xpath="/p:volume/p:vocable/@p:id"/>
  <cdm-headword    xpath="/p:volume/p:vocable/p:lemma/text()"/>
  <cdm-headword-variant    xpath="/p:volume/p:vocable/p:altspelling/text()"    d:lang="eng"/>
  <cdm-pos xpath="/p:volume/p:vocable/p:pos/text()" />
  <cdm-sense-id    xpath="/p:volume/p:vocable/p:lexie/@p:id"/>
  <links>
     <link name="axeme" xpath="/p:volume/p:vocable/p:lexie/p:entryref">
          <type xpath="@type" />
          <volume xpath="@volume" />
          <value xpath="@p:idref" />
          <lang xpath="@lang" />
          <label xpath="@p:relation-mono" />
     </link>
  </links>
</cdm-elements>
```

Figure 2: CDM-LINKS for the English volume of the CommonUNLDict resource

3.4 Approach by rich links in searching in a complex lexical network

To explain how we create arbitrary links, let us give an example. A free label is available for each link. For example, in a lexical resource including SMS, in French "A+" has a link to "Over" with a "SMS" label, in English "L8R" corresponds to "later" with a "SMS" label, and the label of the link between "Over" and "later" is "translation."

A ProAxie macrostructure (Zhang & Mangeot, 2013) has been implemented on the Jibiki-Links platform. We present another example of rich links for semantic search in section 4.1.

3.5 Algorithms for computing rich links

The computer implementation is based on two algorithms. The first collects the links, and the second builds the result. More precisely, the first looks for all possible links in the set of all rich links of all volumes, for a desired entry. The second recursively performs the following steps: (1) selection of the start entry; (2) search of the links to other entries; (3) treatment of labels; (4) recursive call of the algorithm on the connected entry; (5) integration of the XML code of the entry connected to the start entry; (6) display.

4 Experimentation

4.1 Examples of multilevel macrostructures

We have already installed several multilevel macrostructures on Jibiki-LINKS. Here are 3 examples.

MotÀMot: trilingual lexical database with a pivot structure (Mangeot & Touche, 2010)

This project (2009-2012) has computerized a French-Khmer classical dictionary, initially in Word, into a Jibiki database (see http://jibiki.univ-savoie.fr/motamot/).

The macrostructure is composed of a monolingual volume for each language and a central pivot volume. However, in order not to confuse users, the contributing interface shows a classic view of a bilingual dictionary. Each bilingual link language A → language B added via this interface is actually translated into the background by creating two interlingual links as well as an axie link representing the original translation, to finally get: language A → pivot axie → language B (see Figure 3).

If a contributor wants to add a translation link between a vocable Va of language A and a vocable Vb of language B, s/he can establish this link at different levels. The ideal solution is to connect a word meaning (lexie) La of the vocable Va to another word meaning Lb of the vocable Vb. In this case, the link is bijective and Lb is also connected to La.

If the contributor cannot choose between word meanings, s/he can connect directly the word meaning La to the vocable Vb and the link is tagged for refinement.

With the pivot macrostructure, if two links language A → language B and language B → language C exist, then it will automatically create a link language A → language C tagged for refinement.

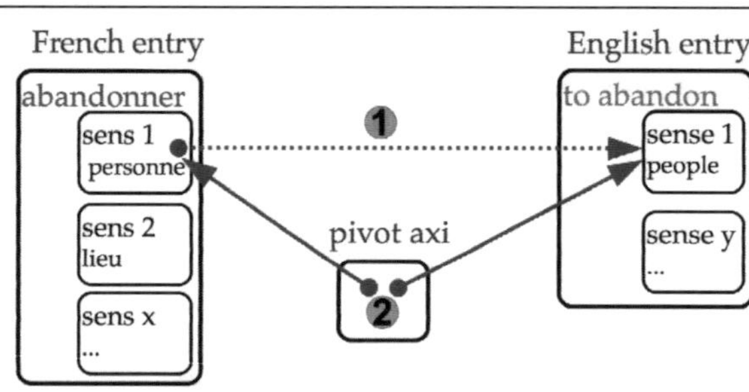

Figure 3: Example of MotÀMot

ProAxie: multilingual extension of ProxlexBase (Tran, 2006)

The ProAxie macrostructure aims at solving the problem of linking several terms that refer to one and the same referent, in particular for the management of acronyms (Zhang et Mangeot, 2013). In this macrostructure, there are two different layers. The base layer consists of two types of volume: volumes of lexies and volumes of axies. The axies are used to connect the lexies that match each other exactly. For example, one translates "ONU" by "UN" (see Figure 4) from French into English.

The "Pro" layer allows us to propose to users translations having the same referential meanings. This layer includes the volumes of *prolexemes* (Tran, 2006) and one volume of *proaxies*. A prolexeme entry links lexies having the same meaning with a label (aka, acronym, definition, etc.). A proaxie entry connects prolexemes of different languages. If one cannot find the translations directly using the lower layer, one will get the translations proposed by the "Pro" layer.

For example, for "Nations-Unies", translations by "United Nations" and "UN" will be proposed, with the "alias" label.

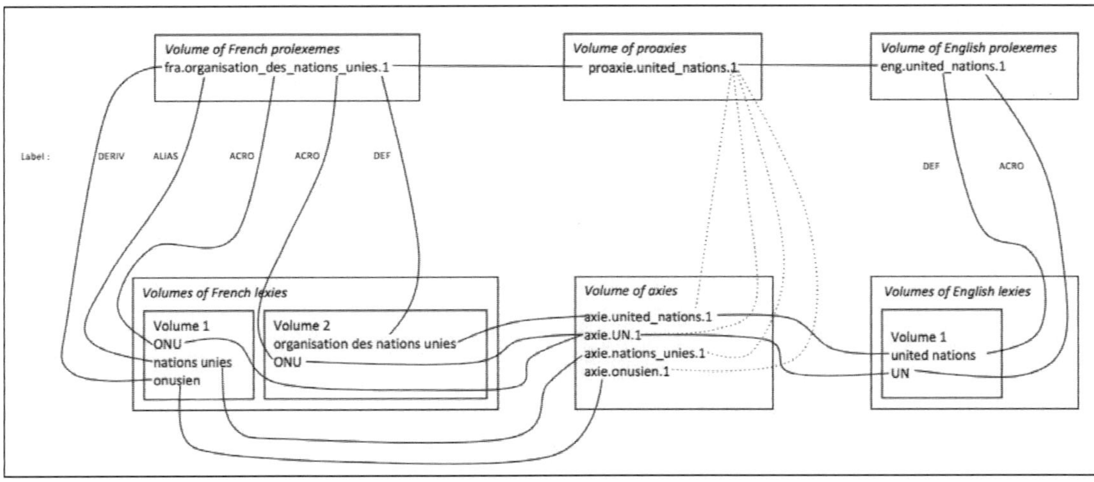

Figure 4: Example of ProAxie

For each natural language, there are one or more volumes of lexies, and a single volume of prolexemes. For each dictionary, there is a volume of axies and a volume of proaxies.

This gives three levels of translation, classified according to the precision obtained.

(1) The system finds a lexie directly, using the volume of axies. That is the first and most accurate level of translation.

(2) The system searches a link to the prolexemes volume of the source language with a certain label. When it finds the link in the proaxies volume, it follows the prolexeme link of the target language, and finally arrives at the volume of lexies in the target language, and finds a lexie that has the same label. That is the second, intermediate level.

(3) The system finds the lexies going through prolexemes and proaxies, without a corresponding label. These proposed lexies constitute the third and least accurate level.

Pivax: lexical multilingual multiversion database with 3 levels

The Pivax macrostructure has three levels: *lexie, axeme* and *axie* (Nguyen & al., 2007). Axemes are monolingual acceptions, and group monolingual lexies having the same meaning. Axies group synonymous axemes of different languages in a central "hub". In some situations, a lexical database has several volumes for a single language. For example, when there are several editions, or when the lexical resource is created for a machine translation system: one may have one volume coming from Systran, one from Ariane/Héloïse, one from IATE[13], etc. This macrostructure allows us to manage multiple volumes in the same language. Given a language, there are one or more volumes of lexies and a single volume of axemes. For any Pivax database, there is only one volume of axies. The links between the lexies and the axemes and between the axemes and the axies are rich links with attributes such as type, target volume, target language, free label, weight, etc.

4.2 CommonUNLDict: toward scaling up with a resource of Pivax type

In this section, we present the CommonUNLDict resource that uses the Pivax macrostructure. We have implemented this resource on the Pivax-UNL platform, which is an instance of Jibiki-Links. Users can easily use this resource via the link http://getalp.imag.fr/pivax/Home.po.

Resource created by linguists

Thanks to CDM-LINKS, all types of XML formats can be used in an instance of Jibiki-LINKS without modification. One needs only simple knowledge about XML to create a resource for Jibiki-LINKS. In addition, very useful available tools can be used to create an XML file, such as oXygen[14] that allows the creation of a DTD using a graphical interface.

---

[13] "A single database for all EU-related terminology (InterActive Terminology for Europe) in 23 languages opens to the public", 2007)

[14] http://www.oxygenxml.com

The CommonUNLDict resource has been created by the Russian lexicographer and linguist Viacheslav Dikonov (Dikonov & Boguslavsky, 2009). Figure 5 shows the graph of a monolingual volume structure using oXygen. In this example, each volume contains a large quantity of vocables, and each vocable includes one or more lexie. We will explain this structure in section 3.2.3.

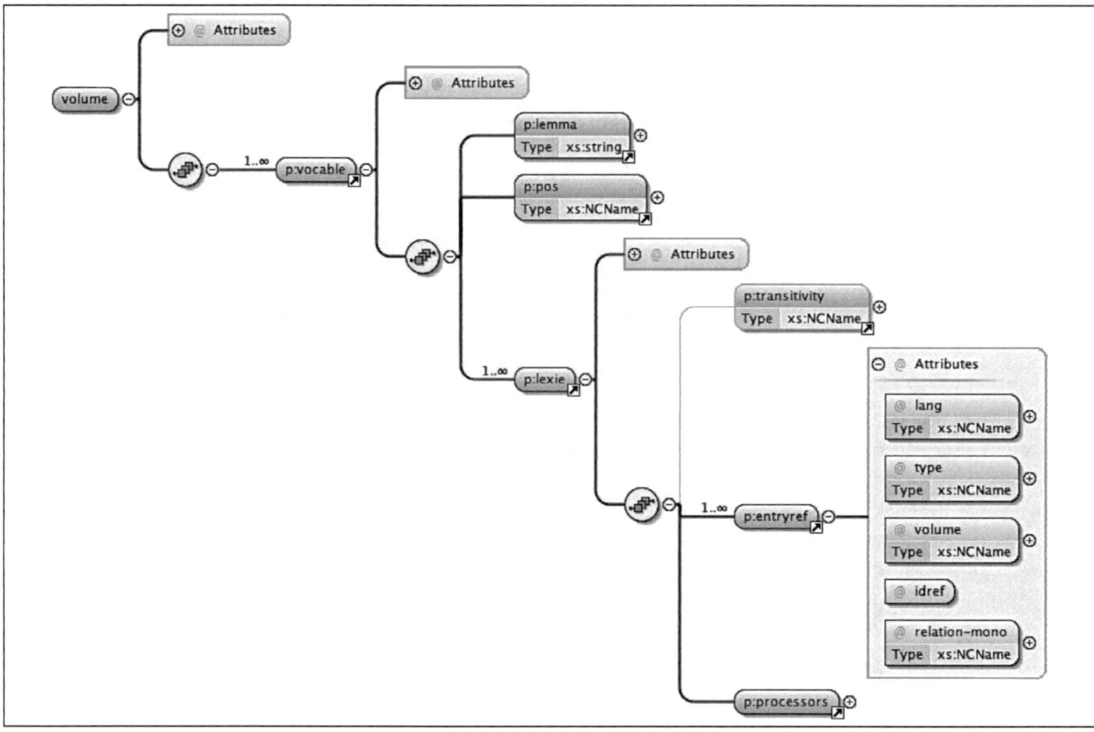

Figure 5: Structure of a monolingual volume

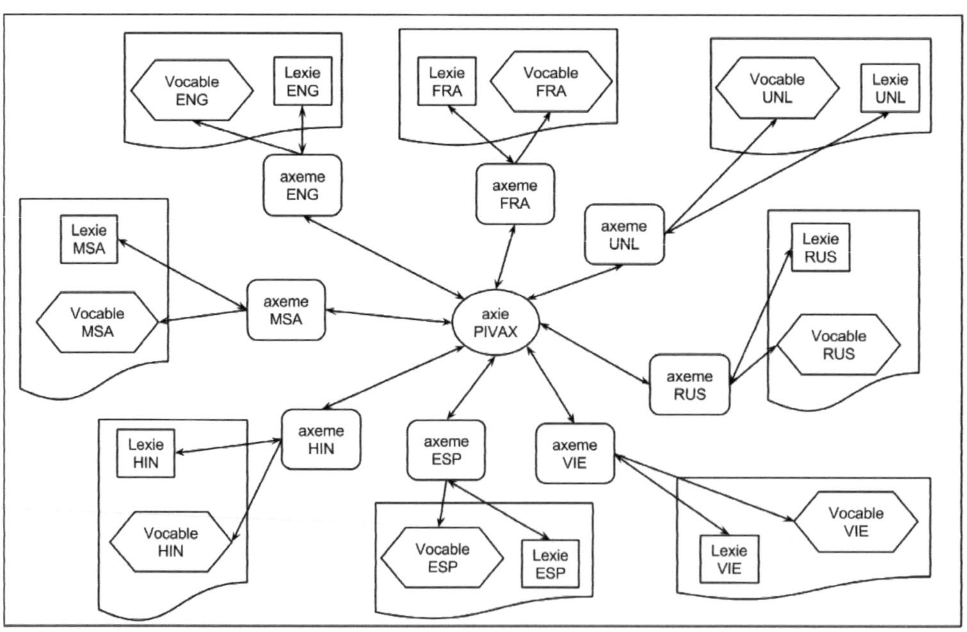

Figure 6: Macrostructure of CommonUNLDict

Macrostructure of CommonUNLDict

CommonUNLDict contains 8 languages (7 natural languages, French, English, Hindi, Malay, Russian, Spanish, Vietnamese, and the UNL language) and 17 volumes (8 volumes of monolingual data, 8 volumes of monolingual axemes, and 1 volume of axies ("interlingual meanings"). The macrostructure of CommonUNLDict is diagrammed in Figure 6. For each language, there is only one volume of monolingual data (vocables and lexical items) and a single volume of axemes. For the whole CommonUNLDict, there is only one volume of axies.

Microstructure of CommonUNLDict

The microstructure is the structure of the entries (Mangeot, 2001). In the CommonUNLDict resource, there are three types of entries (vocables, axemes and axies) and 720 K entries in total.

See Table 2.

Volume	*Language*	*Entries*
CommonUNLDict_axi	axi	82804
CommonUNLDict_eng	English	45471
CommonUNLDict_eng-axemes	English	82069
CommonUNLDict_esp	Spanish	7080
CommonUNLDict_esp-axemes	Spanish	22254
CommonUNLDict_fra	French	27537
CommonUNLDict_fra-axemes	French	48312
CommonUNLDict_hin	Hindi	31255
CommonUNLDict_hin-axemes	Hindi	50380
CommonUNLDict_msa	Malay	37342
CommonUNLDict_msa-axemes	Malay	31699
CommonUNLDict_rus	Russian	28475
CommonUNLDict_rus-axemes	Russian	45020
CommonUNLDict_unl	unl	82804
CommonUNLDict_unl-axemes	unl	82804
CommonUNLDict_vie	Vietnamese	6585
CommonUNLDict_vie-axemes	Vietnamese	8819

Table 2: Number of entries of CommonUNLDict

All volumes of the same type have the same microstructure. The example below (see Figure 7) shows the microstructure of a volume of *vocables*. Each entry of vocable type allows us to describe all detailed information, such as part of speech (POS), pronunciation, etc. Each vocable includes one or more lexies (word senses). Figure 2 shows an example. Therefore the number of axemes is greater than or equal to the number of vocables. In this microstructure, the "entryref" attribute allows us to manage the links between lexies and the entries of axeme type.

```
<p:vocable p:id="fra.ADN.n">
                <p:lemma>ADN</p:lemma>
                <p:pos>n</p:pos>
                <p:gender>m</p:gender>
                <p:lexie p:id="CommonUNLDict.lexie.fra.ADN.1">
                        <p:entryref type="axeme" volume="CommonUNLDict_fra-axemes" p:idref="CommonUNLDict
(icl&gt;polymer&gt;thing,equ&gt;deoxyribonucleic_acid)" lang="FRA" p:relation-mono="OTHER"/>
                        <p:processors>
                                <p:processor p:name="Ariane" p:access="Public">
                                <p:procref type="entry" id="ADN" var="CAT(CATN),GNR(MAS)" lang="FRA"/>
                                </p:processor>
                        </p:processors>
                </p:lexie>
</p:vocable>
```

Figure 7: Microstructure of a volume of lexies

- In this example, the value of "type" is the type of link, the value of "volume" is the target volume, the value of "idref" is the identifier of the axeme entry, the value of "lang" is the target language, and the value of "relationship-mono" is the label.

- The microstructure of the entries of axeme type allows us to describe the links with entries of lexie type and the links with entries of axie type. The microstructure of the axies allows us to describe the links with the entries of axeme type.

Response time and use case

The tests were performed with an instance of Jibiki-LINKS installed on a machine with an Intel Core i3 processor at 3.3 GHz with 8 GB of RAM.

The tool used to perform queries is wget. The command is run directly on the server to avoid the latency due to the network. We give three examples in Table 3, which show the number of links computed by the system, of entries displayed, of queries, of different languages, and the average response time. The response time, less than 1 second in these cases, is generally satisfactory. For better understanding, there is some details about the example "manger" (see Figure 8). We search "manger" in French, and find one entry with id "fra.manger.v" in the French vocable volume. The search direction is "up". This entry links to another entry of the volume of French axemes, whose id is CommonUNLDict.axeme.fra.eat(icl>consume>do, agt>living_thing, obj>concrete_thing, ins>thing)[15]. This axeme entry links with one axie entry and the vocable entry fra.manger.v. Because the search direction is "up", we just go to the axie entry. When we arrive in the volume of axies, the search direction is changed to "down". The axie entry links to 6 different axeme entries. We search each axeme entry and its links. Because the search direction is "down", we only take into account vocable entries links. For each axeme entry, we find at least one vocable entry. In other cases, one vocable entry has more than one lexie, so it links to one or several axeme entries, and there are more links.

Search argument	Links	Displayed entries	Number of requests	Different languages	Average time (ms)
French vocable "manger"	14	6	10	6	19.7
French vocable "recherche"	66	27	10	6	73.5
UNL "search(icl>action)"	51	20	10	6	56

Table 3: Response time on three examples

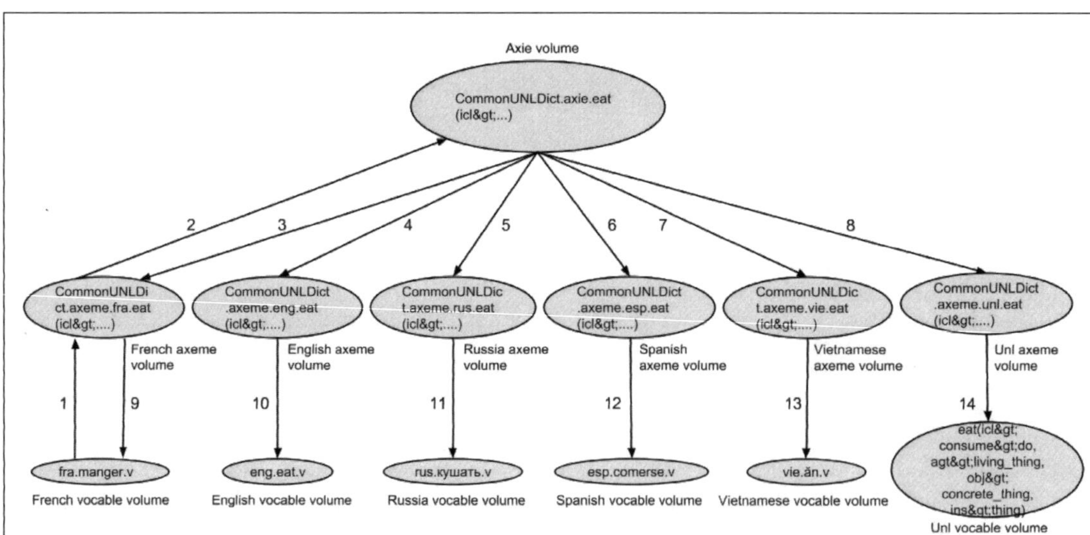

Figure 8: Links in the case of "manger"

Figure 9 shows the display of the interface for a classical search in a Web browser.

[15] In order to better display figure, we have simplified the id in figure 8.

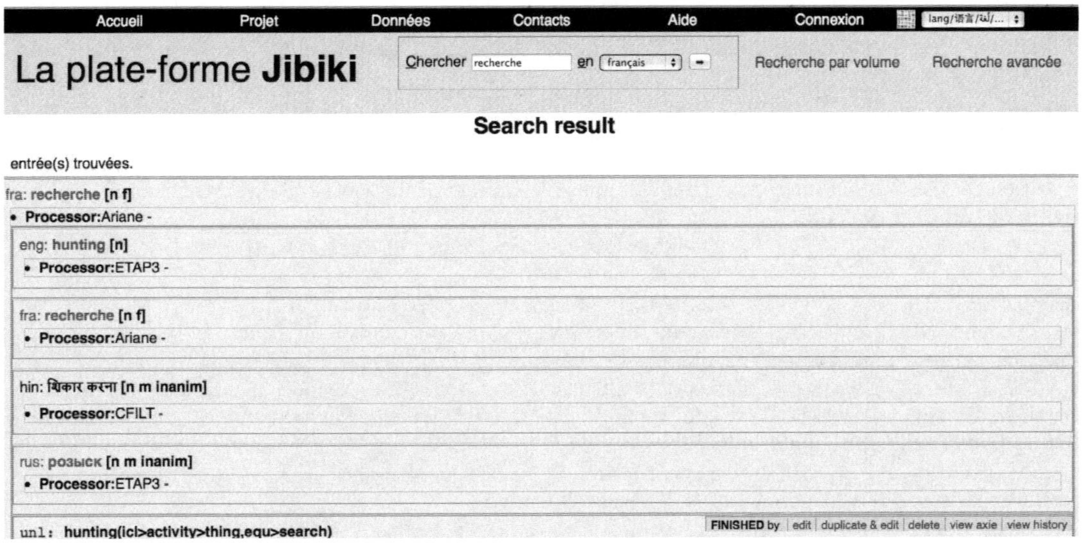

Figure 9: Display of the interface for a classical search

5 Conclusion and perspectives

In this article, we analysed the different types of lexical resource and presented a method of modelling lexical resources using *volumes*. This method allows us to manage complex resources while providing facilities for manipulation and treatment equivalent to those of a paper dictionary.

Jibiki-LINKS is a new version of the Jibiki platform, which can manage resources based on multilevel macrostructures using rich links, bearing attributes such as target volume, weight, type, language, open label, etc. To realize the implementation of rich links, we separated the module processing the links from the module processing other CDM pointers. Jibiki-LINKS has been used to implement the MotÀMot, ProAxie and Pivax macrostructures.

On the Pivax-UNL platform, another instance of the Jibiki-LINKS-based Pivax macrostructure, we have installed the volumes corresponding to the CommonUNLDict resource of V. Dikonov, and tested our platform with that resource.

There is also a UW (UNL interlingual lexemes) resource of 8G entries that was created from DBpedia by David Rouquet. In that resource, there are several volumes for the same language. As links were poorly structured, we are currently working on this resource in order to recompute them. We hope to be able to import this resource, and to make tests at that very large scale in the near future.

To sum up, lexical databases equipped with rich links allow for importing XML-based electronic dictionaries without loss of information, whether they have been elaborated from source or printable forms (such as Word, rtf, ps, pdf) or directly produced in XML from a relational database, or using a dedicated editor knowing their microstructures. They also allow us to automatically produce from them a pivot-based macrostructure organised in *volumes*, and after that to edit and improve them, using a mixed textual and graphical interface to merge or split lexies, axemes or axies, or to enrich the links with appropriate labels. The introduction of rich links to multilevel lexical databases enhances them with a very interesting aspect of the lexical networks while keeping the classical ways of using dictionaries and of performing lexicographic work.

References

EU-IATE (2007) A single database for all EU-related terminology (InterActiveTerminology for Europe) in 23 languages opens to the public. *Press release*. Brussels. 2007-06-28.

Breen, J. W., (2004) JMdict : a Japanese-Multilingual Dictionary. In Gilles Sérasset, Susan Armstrong, Christian Boitet, Andrei Pospescu-Belis, and Dan Tufis, editors, post COLING Workshop on Multilingual Linguistic Resources, Geneva, Switzerland, 28th August. International Committee on Computational Linguistics.

Dikonov V., Boguslavsky I., (2009) Semantic Network of the UNL Dictionary of Concepts. *Proceedings of the SENSE Workshop on conceptual Structures for Extracting Natural language SEmantics Moscow*, Russia, July 2009, 7 p.

Diller, G.A., Beckwith, R., Fellbaum, C., Gross, D., and Miller, K.J. (1990) Introduction to WordNet: an on-line lexical database, *International Journal of Lexicography 3(4)*, pp. 235-244.

Dolan, W.B. & Richardson, S.D., (1996) Interactive Lexical Priming for Disambiguation. Proc. *MIDDIM'96, Post-COLING seminar on Interactive Disambiguation*, C. Boitet ed. Le Col de Porte, Isère, France. 12-14 août 1996. vol. 1/1 : pp. 54-56.

Dong, Z.D., Dong, Q., Hao, C.L., (2010). HowNet and Its Computation of Meaning. In Actes de *COLING-2010*, Beijing, 4 p.

Francopoulo, G., Bel, N., George, M., Calzolari, N., Monachini, M., Pet, M. and Soria, C. (2009). Multilingual resources for NLP in the lexical markup framework (LMF). *In journal de Language Resources and Evaluation, March 2009, Volume 43,* pp. 55-57.

Gut, Y., Ramli, P. R. M., Yusoff, Z., Kim, Ch. Ch., Samat, S. A., Boitet, Ch., Nédobejkine, N., Lafourcade, M., Gaschler, J. and Levenbach, D. (1996). *Kamus Perancis-Melayu Dewan, dictionnaire français-malais.* Dewan Bahasa Dan Pustaka, Kuala Lumpur, 667 p.

Lafourcade, M., Joubert, A. (2010). Computing trees of named word usages from a crowdsourced lexical network. *Investigationes Linguisticae*, vol. XXI, pp. 39-56

Lux-Pogodalla, V., Polguère, A. (2011) Construction of a French Lexical Network: Methodological Issues. Proceedings of *the First International Workshop on Lexical Resources, WoLeR 2011. An ESSLLI-2011 Workshop*. Ljubljana, 2011, pp. 54-61.

Mangeot, M. (2002). An XML Markup Language Framework for Lexical Databases Environments: the Dictionary Markup Language. In Actes de *LREC-2002*, pp. 37-44.

Mangeot, M & Chalvin, A. (2006). Dictionary Building with the Jibiki Platform: the GDEF case. In Actes de *LREC-2006*, Genoa, pp. 1666-1669.

Mangeot, M. & Touch, S., (2010) MotÀMot project: building a multilingual lexical system via bilingual dictionaries. Proc. *SLTU 2010: Second International Workshop on Spoken Languages Technologies for Under-Resourced Languages*, Penang, Malaysia, 2010, 6 p.

McCrae, J., Spohr, D. and Cimiano, P., (2011) Linking lexical resources and ontologies on the semantic web with lemon. Proc. *ESWC'11*, Berlin, pp. 245-259.

Nguyen, H.T., Boitet, C. and Sérasset, G. (2007). PIVAX, an online contributive lexical data base for heterogeneous MT systems using a lexical pivot. In Actes de *SNLP-2007*, Bangkok, 6 p.

Richardson, S.D., Dolan, W.B. and Vanderwende, L. (1998) MindNet: acquiring and structuring semantic information from text, no. MSR-TR-98-23.

Sérasset, G. (2012) Dbnary: Wiktionary as a LMF-based Multilingual RDF network. In Actes de *LREC-2012*, Istanbul, 7 p.

Sérasset, G. & Mangeot, M. (2001). Papillon Lexical Database Project: Monolingual Dictionaries and Interlingual Links. In Proc. *NLPRS-2011*, Tokyo, pp. 119-125.

Tran, M. (2006). Prolexbase : Un dictionnaire relationnel multilingue de noms propres : conception, implémentation et gestion en ligne. *Thèse de doctorat*, Tours, pp. 54-57.

Vossen, P., (1998) EuroWordNet: A Multilingual Database with Lexical Semantic Networks, *Computers and the Humanities,* 32(2-3).

Zhang, Y. & Mangeot, M., (2013). Gestion des terminologies riches : l'exemple des acronymes. In Actes de *TALN-2013*, Les Sables d'Olonne, 8 p.

When Frequency Data Meet Dispersion Data in the Extraction of Multi-word Units from a Corpus: A Study of Trigrams in Chinese

Chan-Chia Hsu
Graduate Institute of Linguistics, National Taiwan University
No. 1, Sec. 4, Roosevelt Road, Taipei, 10617 Taiwan (R.O.C)
chanchiah@gmail.com

Abstract

One of the main approaches to extract multi-word units is the frequency threshold approach, but the way this approach considers dispersion data still leaves a lot to be desired. This study adopts Gries's (2008) dispersion measure to extract trigrams from a Chinese corpus, and the results are compared with those of the frequency threshold approach. It is found that the overlap between the two approaches is not very large. This demonstrates the necessity of taking dispersion data more seriously and the dynamic nature of lexical representations. Moreover, the trigrams extracted in the present study can be used in a wide range of language resources in Chinese.

1 Introduction

In the past decades, multi-word units have been of great interest not only to corpus linguists but also to cognitive linguists and psycholinguists. It has been empirically demonstrated that multi-word units are pervasive in our languages (cf. Wray and Perkins, 2000), and they are considered psychologically real when it is found that a language learner starts with formulaic phrases that serve specific functions (e.g., Ellis, 2003; Tomasello, 2003). One of the current approaches to extract multi-word units is the frequency threshold approach (cf. Wei and Li, 2013).

The frequency threshold approach reflects the argument that frequently used items are more entrenched in our mind. While many have recognized that frequency data are more useful when complemented with dispersion data (e.g., Juilland et al., 1970), the way the frequency threshold approach considers the dispersion of a multi-word unit still leaves a lot to be desired. For example, when automatically extracting multi-word units in English, Gray and Biber (2013) simply set a dispersion threshold, i.e., occurring in at least five corpus texts.

Therefore, the present study aims to probe more deeply into the interaction between the frequency data and the dispersion data of multi-word units. Both a frequency-based set of multi-word units and a dispersion-based set are automatically extracted from a Chinese corpus, and the two sets are compared. The present study adopts a more scientific method to compute the dispersion of a multi-word unit, i.e., the DP value (Gries, 2008). This method is argued to be more flexible, simple, extendable, and sensitive than previous methods (Gries, 2008:425-426). Note that given the limited resources, the present study focuses on three-word units (trigrams for short, hereafter).

The paper is organized as follows. Section 2 introduces the method of the present study. Section 3 presents the results. Section 4 is a general discussion of the findings and the implications. Section 5 highlights the contributions of the findings.

2 Method

The corpus for the present study is the Academia Sinica Balanced Corpus of Modern Chinese (the Sinica Corpus, hereafter).[1] The fourth edition contains 11,245,853 tokens.

Zock/Rapp/Huang (eds.): Proceedings of the 4th Workshop on Cognitive Aspects of the Lexicon, pages 99–104, Dublin, Ireland, August 23, 2014.

This study adopted a fully inductive approach to identify trigrams in Chinese. A computer program run in R automatically retrieved trigrams in the Sinica Corpus. Each trigram did not cross a punctuation boundary in a written text or a turn boundary in a spoken text. Then, the raw occurrence of each trigram was counted, and the raw occurrence was also normalized to the relative frequency in one million words. A frequency threshold was set to be 5 occurrences in one million words, and 1,279 trigrams passed the threshold. For each of them, the dispersion value was calculated.[2]

Regarding the dispersion value, the present study adopted Gries's (2008) measure. First, the corpus was roughly evenly divided into ten parts. Next, the raw occurrence of each trigram in each part was counted. Then, the dispersion value was calculated as shown in Table 1. Take the trigram *shi yi ge* 'be a CLASSIFIER', for example. Given that the first part of the corpus (1,081,955 tokens altogether) accounts for 9.6% of all the corpus data, the raw occurrences of *shi yi ge* in the first corpus part should also account for 9.6% of its overall occurrences. However, the observed frequency of *shi yi ge* in the first part (405/2,931 = 13.8%) was found to be slightly higher than its expected frequency. The absolute difference for each corpus part (shown in the third column) was summed up (shown in the fourth column), and the sum was divided by 2. The figure in the fifth column was the dispersion value for the trigram *shi yi ge*. The dispersion value always falls between 0 and 1: the lower the value is, the more evenly dispersed the trigram is in the corpus.

<table>
<tr><th>Expected Percentage

(A)</th><th>Observed Percentage

(B)</th><th>Absolute Difference

(C) = (A)-(B)</th><th>Sum of Absolute Differences
(D)</th><th>Divided by 2

(E) = (D)/2</th></tr>
<tr><td>1,081,955/11,245,853
= 0.096
(9.6%)</td><td>405/2,931
= 0.138
(13.8%)</td><td>|0.096 - 0.138|
= 0.042</td><td rowspan="10">0.257</td><td rowspan="10">0.1285</td></tr>
<tr><td>1,018,642/11,245,853
= 0.091</td><td>202/2,931
= 0.069</td><td>|0.091 - 0.069|
= 0.022</td></tr>
<tr><td>1,163,099/11,245,853
= 0.103</td><td>283/2,931
= 0.097</td><td>|0.103 - 0.097|
= 0.006</td></tr>
<tr><td>1,023,536/11,245,853
= 0.091</td><td>388/2,931
= 0.132</td><td>|0.091 - 0.132|
= 0.041</td></tr>
<tr><td>1,050,833/11,245,853
= 0.093</td><td>408/2,931
= 0.139</td><td>|0.093 - 0.139|
= 0.046</td></tr>
<tr><td>1,214,233/11,245,853
= 0.108</td><td>224/2,931
= 0.076</td><td>|0.108 - 0.076|
= 0.032</td></tr>
<tr><td>1,132,756/11,245,853
= 0.101</td><td>287/2,931
= 0.098</td><td>|0.101 - 0.098|
= 0.003</td></tr>
<tr><td>1,185,658/11,245,853
= 0.105</td><td>164/2,931
= 0.056</td><td>|0.105 - 0.056|
= 0.049</td></tr>
<tr><td>1,200,826/11,245,853
= 0.107</td><td>313/2,931
= 0.107</td><td>|0.107 - 0.107|
= 0</td></tr>
<tr><td>1,174,315/11,245,853
= 0.104</td><td>257/2,931
= 0.088</td><td>|0.104 - 0.088|
= 0.016</td></tr>
</table>

Table 1. Computation of the dispersion value of the trigram *shi yi ge* 'be a CLASSIFIER'.

After the dispersion value for each of the 1,279 trigrams was calculated, the top 300 trigrams in the frequency-based list and the top 300 trigrams in the dispersion-based list were further analyzed

[1] The fourth edition of the Sinica Corpus is currently available at http://asbc.iis.sinica.edu.tw/. For more information about the Sinica Corpus, refer to http://app.sinica.edu.tw/kiwi/mkiwi/98-04.pdf.

[2] The present study aims to compare frequency-based and dispersion-based trigrams, and the best way would be to compute the dispersion value for *all* the trigrams automatically extracted from the corpus. This, however, seems to be too difficult because this approach could be resource-intensive. Therefore, the present study set a frequency threshold to obtain a computationally reasonable number of trigrams, and computed the dispersion value for each trigram that passed that frequency threshold. Actually, the frequency threshold of the present study is relatively low.

manually.[3] Each of them were then manually coded based on the form. There are five categories, as shown in Table 2.

Category	Definition	Example
verb trigrams	trigrams that contain at least one verb	*you ren shuo* 'have person said'
finite trigrams	trigrams that contain a copula (e.g., *shi* 'be') and/or a modal verb (e.g., *hui* 'can'), but not a verb	*zhe ye shi* 'this is also'
content word trigrams	trigrams that contain at least one content word (i.e., a noun, an adjective, and an adverb), but not a verb or a finite	*shi nian qian* 'ten years ago'
function word trigrams	trigrams that contain only function words	*ling yi ge* 'another one CLASSIFIER'
incomprehensibly incomplete trigrams	trigrams that are structurally and/or semantically incomplete and incomprehensible	*bu yi bu* 'step one step'

Table 2. Categories for trigrams.

3 Results

The total numbers of trigram types at different frequency thresholds (per one million words) are presented in Table 3. The following discussions will center around trigrams that occur five or more times per one million words.

Table 3. The total numbers of trigram types at different frequency thresholds (per one million words).

Frequency Threshold	Trigram Types
> 1 time per one million words	15,655
> 5 times per one million words	**1,279**
> 10 times per one million words	422
> 40 times per one million words	35

Figure 1 presents the frequency distribution (per one million words) of the 1,279 trigrams, which occur five or more times. Among all the trigrams here, the most frequent one is *shi yi ge* 'be one CLASSIFIER' (260.62 times per one million words), and the least frequent one is *zhongyao de shi* 'important DE thing' (5.07 times).

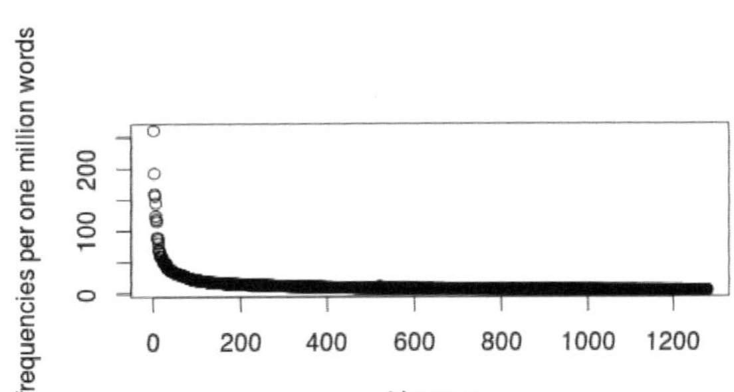

Figure 1. The frequency distribution (per one million words) of the 1,279 trigrams.

[3] The number of trigrams for further analysis was determined for convenience, with a view to yielding a manageable set of trigrams to be hand-coded.

Figure 2 presents the distribution of the dispersion values of the 1,279 trigrams, which occur five or more times. Among all the trigrams here, the best-dispersed one is *zhe ye shi* 'this also be' (0.0375), and the one with the highest dispersion value is *kaifang kongjian zhi* 'open space ZHI' (0.9085). As Figure 2 shows, the majority of trigrams are quite well-dispersed across the corpus (i.e., most of the dispersion values are lower than 0.4).

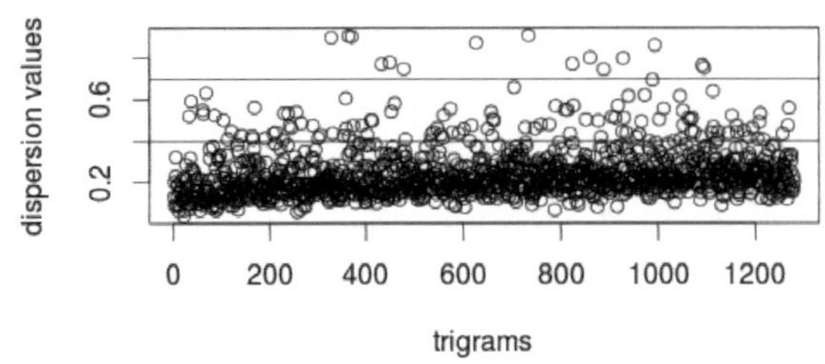

Figure 2. The distribution of the dispersion values of the 1,279 trigrams.

When zooming in to examine the top 300 trigrams in the frequency-based list and the top 300 trigrams in the dispersion-based list, we can find that there is an overlap of 126 trigrams (only 42%) between the two list. Table 4 summarizes the category distributions of the top 300 trigrams in the frequency-based list, the top 300 trigrams in the dispersion-based list, and the 126 trigrams in the overlap.

Category	Frequency-based		Dispersion-based		Overlapping	
content word trigrams	132	44.0%	125	41.7%	55	43.7%
finite trigrams	58	19.3%	62	20.7%	31	24.6%
verb trigrams	38	12.7%	42	14.0%	13	10.3%
function word trigrams	**42**	**14.0%**	**23**	**7.7%**	12	9.5%
incomprehensibly incomplete trigrams	**30**	**10.0%**	**48**	**16.0%**	15	11.9%
TOTAL	300	100%	300	100%	**126**	100%

Table 4. The category distributions of the top 300 trigrams in the frequency-based list, the top 300 trigrams in the dispersion-based list, and the 126 trigrams in the overlap.

4 Discussion

Overall, whether from the frequency-based perspective or from the dispersion-based perspective, content word trigrams are the most dominant. This is not too surprising, for this category covers a wide range of word classes (i.e., nouns, adjectives, and adverbs). In Chinese, finite trigrams are also frequent and well-dispersed, perhaps because the finite serves many interpersonal metafunctions (i.e., expressing the polarity of a sentence/utterance) (Thompson, 1996). In this category, *shi* 'be' is the most frequent. The main difference between the frequency-based approach and the dispersion-based approach is that the former extracts more function word trigrams, while the latter extracts more incomprehensibly incomplete trigrams.

Additionally, as shown in Table 4, the overlap between the two approaches is not very large (i.e., 126/300 = 42%). Now, consider Table 5.

Top *n* trigrams in the two lists	Overlap	
300	126/300 =	42%
500	262/500 =	52.4%
700	438/700 =	62.6%
1,000	798/1,000 =	79.8%
1,279	1,279/1,279 =	100%

Table 5. The overlap between the frequency-based approach and the dispersion-based approach.

Since the trigrams in the two lists are the same, the overlap should be getting larger as *n* is getting larger. However, even when *n* reaches 700, the overlap between the two approaches is only slightly more than half. This suggests that when a certain type number is set (e.g., 300, 500, or 700), the frequency-based approach and the dispersion-based approach can extract quite different sets of trigrams.

Some may argue that the frequency-based approach is more useful because it extracts fewer incomprehensibly incomplete trigrams (cf. Table 4). On the other hand, we can also see the dispersion value as an ancillary measure to the relative frequency, just as the standard deviation is usually presented whenever a mean is presented. Frequencies can be regarded as an important dimension of the sum of one's linguistic experience (cf. Bybee, 2006), and dispersion data should also be considered so. Items, whether single words or multi-word units, that achieve a high frequency *and* are well-dispersed across the corpus should be much more entrenched in the mental lexicon, for their frequent occurrences are ubiquitous, not just in certain text types. These items should deserve more attention from linguists and may be more useful in a language resource.

Moreover, the findings of the present study have demonstrated the dynamic nature of lexical representations. When different measures (e.g., the relative frequency, the dispersion value) are used, the ranking of a trigram may change dramatically. If the association measure is also taken into account or different measures are integrated in a certain way, another picture of trigrams in Chinese may emerge. This echoes Biber's (2009) suggestion that in the extraction of multi-word units, no methodology should be considered to be correct. That is to say, different sets of multi-word units extracted by different approaches can all be useful in one way or another and reflective of some aspects of our cognition. However, those ranking high in all the approaches may be at the core of our mental lexicon.

The implications of a list of trigrams (or other multi-word units) in Chinese can be pinpointed as follows. First, most dictionaries in Chinese compile words, but a dictionary of multi-word units in Chinese can also be of great use. For example, the trigram *you yi ge* 'have one CLASSIFER' is usually used to introduce a new topic in discourse, and this needs to be included in a dictionary in Chinese. Second, such useful sequences as *you yi ge* can also be included in teaching materials for language learners. Third, we can try to use automatically extracted sequences to build a language/lexical resource like WordNet (Miller et al., 1990). In such a resource (i.e., perhaps something like the Net of Multi-word Units), multi-word units in Chinese can be organized according to words or characters contained in them or even according to their discourse functions (and perhaps in some other creative ways), and lexical relations between multi-word units can be coded.

5 Conclusion

The contribution of the present study is twofold. Methodologically speaking, this study adopts a more sensitive dispersion measure (i.e., Gries, 2008) instead of setting an arbitrary dispersion threshold (e.g., occurring in at least five corpus files), and demonstrates that dispersion data are needed in the automatic extraction of multi-word units since those ranking high in a frequency-based list are not necessarily at the top of a dispersion-based list. It is argued that the dispersion of a multi-word unit, together with its frequency, can contribute to the entrenchment of the item in the mental lexicon because the dispersion measure reveals where a language user is confronted with the item. Practically speaking, trigrams in the overlap between the frequency-based approach and the dispersion-based approach may be at the core of the Chinese lexicon and can serve as a point of departure for future linguistic studies and resources in Chinese.

The present study can be extended in the following directions. First, some evaluations from psycholinguistic experiments are needed to further examine the role of frequency data and dispersion data in the mental lexicon. Second, the same method can be adopted to automatically extract multi-word units in different genres, and the results will be helpful for genre studies.

References

Alison Wray and Michael R. Perkins. 2000. The functions of formulaic language: An integrated model. *Language & Communication*, 20(1), 1-28.

Alphonse Juilland, Dorothy Brodin, and Catherine Davidovitch. *Frequency dictionary of French words*. The Hague: Mouton de Gruyter.

Bethany Gray and Douglas Biber. 2013. Lexical frames in academic prose and conversation. *International Journal of Corpus Linguistics*, 18(1):109-135.

Douglas Biber. 2009. A corpus-driven approach to formulaic language in English: Multi-word patterns in speech and writing. *International Journal of Corpus Linguistics*, 14(3):275-311.

Geoff Thompson. 1996. *Introducing Functional Grammar*. London; New York: Arnold.

George A. Miller, Richard Beckwith, Christiane Fellbuam, Derek Gross, and Katherine Miller. Introduction to WordNet: An on-line lexical database. *International Journal of Lexicography*, 3(4):235-244.

Joan Bybee. 2006. From usage to grammar: The mind's response to repetition. *Language*, 82(4):711-733.

Michael Tomasello. 2003. *Constructing a Language: A Usage-based Theory of Language Acquisition*. Cambridge, MA: Harvard University Press.

Naixing Wei and Jingjie Li. 2013. A new computing method for extracting contiguous phraseological sequences from academic text corpora. *International Journal of Corpus Linguistics*, 18(4):506-365.

Nick C. Ellis. 2003. Constructions, chunking, and connectionism: The emergence of second language structure. In C. Doughty and M. H. Long (Eds.), *Handbook of Second Language Acquisition*. Oxford: Blackwell. (pp. 33-68)

Stefan Th. Gries. 2008. Dispersions and adjusted frequencies in corpora. *International Journal of Corpus Linguistics*, 13(4):403-437.

Exploring Mental Lexicon in an Efficient and Economic Way: Crowdsourcing Method for Linguistic Experiments

Shichang Wang, Chu-Ren Huang, Yao Yao, Angel Chan
Department of Chinese and Bilingual Studies
The Hong Kong Polytechnic University
Hung Hom, Kowloon, Hong Kong
shi-chang.wang@connect.polyu.hk
{churen.huang, y.yao, angel.ws.chan}@polyu.edu.hk

Abstract

Mental lexicon plays a central role in human language competence and inspires the creation of new lexical resources. The traditional linguistic experiment method which is used to explore mental lexicon has some disadvantages. Crowdsourcing has become a promising method to conduct linguistic experiments which enables us to explore mental lexicon in an efficient and economic way. We focus on the feasibility and quality control issues of conducting Chinese linguistic experiments to collect Chinese word segmentation and semantic transparency data on the international crowdsourcing platforms Amazon Mechanical Turk and Crowdflower. Through this work, a framework for crowdsourcing linguistic experiments is proposed.

1 Introduction

Mental lexicon as a theoretical construct has two important implications. For an individual, it is where all the grammatical and world information is stored and organized to enable speech. For a group of speakers of the same language, however, the mental lexicon is a shared knowledge structure allowing speakers to process and understand what each other said. WordNets, for example the English WordNet (Miller, 1995) and the Chinese WordNet (CWN) (Huang et al., 2003), and ontologies, for example the Suggested Upper Merged Ontology (SUMO) (Niles and Pease, 2001) and the Sinica BOW (Huang et al., 2010), have been proposed as a representational framework for this shared mental lexicon; and psycho- and neuro-linguistic experiments have been designed to explore how individuals access their mental lexicon. However, the question of whether there is a shared principle or strategy of mental lexicon by all speakers of the same language was never seriously studied as the cognitive experimental paradigm does not allow manipulation of a large number of subjects simultaneously. In this paper, we explore the possibility of conducting lexical access related experiments through crowdsourcing. With the crowdsourcing experiments, we intend to ask specific question about the share strategy of determination of lexical units, as well as determination of semantic transparencies, two issues that would have direct implications of how individuals access their mental lexicon.

Many scholars discuss applying crowdsourcing method to language resource construction recent years (Snow et al., 2008; Callison-Burch and Dredze, 2010; Munro et al., 2010; Gurevych and Zesch, 2013). Crowdsourcing has been proved to be an efficient tool to build lexical resources, for example, Wiktionary, whose goal is to become the free online dictionary for all the words in all languages; Biemann (2013) presents another example which creates the Turk Bootstrap Word Sense Inventory for 397 frequent nouns from scratch using Amazon Mechanical Turk. And there is more and more literature focusing on conducting experiments on crowdsourcing platforms (Schnoebelen and Kuperman, 2010; Paolacci et al., 2010; Berinsky et al., 2011; Rand, 2012; Mason and Suri, 2012; Crump et al., 2013). Using crowdsourcing method, it is easier to access highly diverse and huge amount of participants, so it is possible to obtain more representative language behavioral data. The anonymous nature of crowdsourcing makes the participants more open to contribute sensitive data. And Crowdsourcing experiments are usually much faster and cheaper than laboratory experiments which enables " faster iteration between developing theory and

Zock/Rapp/Huang (eds.): Proceedings of the 4th Workshop on Cognitive Aspects of the Lexicon, pages 105–113, Dublin, Ireland, August 23, 2014.

executing experiments" (Mason and Suri, 2012). It can be a promising tool to explore mental lexicon in an efficient and economic way.

MTurk and Crowdflower are perhaps the two most important MTurk-like crowdsourcing platforms. MTurk is the platform appears most frequently in the literature, so popular that it represents a major genre of crowdsourcing and its name has become the name of that genre. Crowdflower is a rapid developing platform and is drawing more and more attention. Although they are both MTurk-like platforms, they differ from each other. On the MTurk platform, invalid responses submitted can be manually rejected which is a very convenient quality control method; however Crowdflower has a much larger worker pool than MTurk. Since MTurk is one channel of Crowdflower and Crowdflower can access the worker pool of MTurk[1], besides MTurk, Crowdflower has several dozens of other channels to which it can distribute tasks. More importantly, Crowdflower is more accessible to requesters outside the U.S. (MTurk does not support requesters outside the U.S. by now). Crowdflower basically doesn't support manual rejection of invalid responses but it integrates an effective quality control method named *Test Questions* which uses predefined gold standard questions to measure the quality of contributions of workers and screens low quality workers automatically in order to produce high quality data. Unfortunately, it is not suitable to our task, for it requires multiple submissions form a worker. Neither MTurk nor Crowdflower is a native Chinese crowdsourcing platform, so we can suppose that native Chinese speakers can only occupy a small proposition in their worker pools, in this case, a larger worker pool means higher possibility of successful data collection.

We have two objectives in this study: (1) to check if it is feasible to conduct Chinese language experiments to collect Chinese word segmentation and semantic transparency (Libben, 1998) data which can be used to explore the mental lexicon of Chinese speakers on international crowdsourcing platforms, such as Amazon Mechanical Turk (MTurk) and Crowdflower; (2) to identify and solve some quality control and experimental design issues in order to obtain high quality data and to establish a preliminary framework for crowdsourcing linguistic experiments.

2 Initial Calibration Tests

Before the experiment, we conducted initial calibration tests. The purpose is to lay a basic foundation (e.g., general experimental parameters, quality control methods, etc.) for the experiment. There are four tests. We employed a problem-driven bootstrapping strategy in the design and conduct of these tests in order to accumulate knowledge effectively. The repeated procedure is like this: one test is started and once a problem has been identified, the test will be paused or stopped; after a proper solution has been found, a modified version of that test will be resumed or a new test will be designed and started.

2.1 Parameters

Both MTurk and Crowdflower will be tested, however we cannot access MTurk directly as a requester since it doesn't support requesters outside the U.S. by now. Because MTurk is a channel of Crowdflower, Crowdflower can distribute jobs to it, we can access it indirectly through Crowdflower. So Crowdflower is selected as our job publishing platform. When we test MTurk, we will require Crowdflower to distribute our jobs to the MTurk channel only; and when we test Crowdflower, we will conduct Crowdflower to distribute our jobs to all of its channels.

The jobs published on Crowdflower can be divided into two types according to the existence or absence of data-sets to be processed. A job without a data-set to be processed is a survey. The survey type fits our objectives best since we want to collect data from different individuals and each person can only participate in any one of the tests/experiments once. In order to ensure this one-time participation, we use the following constrains: (1) each worker account can only submit one response, and (2) each IP address can only submit one response.

Crowdflower allows us to specify 'included countries' or 'excluded countries' as an access control method. We only use 'included countries' in our tests/experiments, only the countries and regions we

[1]However, this has become history, in December 2013, Crowdflower announced that Amazon Mechanical Turk would no longer be a partner channel, see http://www.crowdflower.com/blog/2014/01/crowdflower-drops-mechanical-turk-to-ensure-the-best-results-for-its-customers (Retrieved May 24, 2014).

selected are allowed to access our jobs. According to the distribution of Chinese people, we select the following countries and regions: Mainland China, Hong Kong, Macau, Taiwan, Singapore, Malaysia, Japan, Korea, Australia, Canada, the United States, the United Kingdom, France, Germany, Russia, and New Zealand.

2.2 Test 1

The objective is to evaluate the feasibility to collect Chinese language data from MTurk. We published a survey on Crowdflower and it was distributed to the MTurk channel only. The questionnaire contains 3 questions: (1) what place of China do you come from, (2) what country or region are you in now, (3) what dialect of Chinese do you speak; all the questions are in Chinese. There is a text-box for each question which allows the participants to input their answers. All the questions must be answered or the data are not allowed to be submitted. It only takes 10 to 15 seconds to fill up the questionnaire. The unit price of this survey is one cent. This test only collected 2 responses in 21 hours. Judged from the speed, we can preliminarily conclude that MTurk is not a feasible platform for Chinese language data collecting tasks. Because of the properties of crowdsourcing environment, this result can be accidental, so we will continue to open the MTurk channel to validate this result.

2.3 Test 2

We published a new test on Crowdflower in order to evaluate the feasibility of collecting Chinese language data from Crowdflower. It is mostly the same as Test 1, the only difference is that all the channels of Crowdflower are enabled so we can access a much larger worker pool. This time, we collected 23 responses in 2 hours. Nine of them (39.1%) are valid, 14 (60.9%) are invalid. The speed is good, but the data quality is not acceptable. In this test, we didn't use powerful quality control method, thus large number of invalid responses were submitted. Invalid responses deteriorated data quality. This demonstrates that quality control is essential to crowdsourcing practices.

2.4 Test 3

It's important to detect and identify invalid responses. "Checkpoint questions" (see section 5) can be used to distinguish valid responses from invalid responses. This test attempts to test the effectiveness of checkpoint questions. We added a Chinese character identification question to the questionnaire of Test 2. The participants are required to identify a Chinese character in a picture and then input this character into a text-box. The frequency of that character is very high, so it is easy for Chinese native speakers to identify. Because this an open-ended question, so it is robust enough. This question satisfies the conditions to be a checkpoint question (see section 5). Then the test was resumed. After 2 hours, 9 new responses were received (23 responses had been received since Test 2). Four of them (44.4%) are valid responses, 5 (55.6 %) are invalid. All of the responses with correct answers to the checkpoint question were checked to be valid responses.

Logically, correctly answering checkpoint questions doesn't definitely mean the other questions are also carefully answered. But human behaviors have certain consistency to some extent. If they carefully answered checkpoint questions, then they are likely to answer the other questions carefully. Although it is not 100% reliable to identify invalid/valid responses by checkpoint questions, it is acceptable if there is no better method.

2.5 Test 4

Checkpoint questions can identify invalid responses but they cannot block them. We can set some conditions for the submission of responses. Only the responses which satisfy these conditions can be submitted. We call these submission conditions "validations" (see section 5). Since checkpoint questions can be used to identify invalid responses, we can set validations on them in order to block the submission of invalid responses. We set a validation on the Chinese character identification checkpoint question: the response can be submitted only when the checkpoint question is correctly answered. Then the test was resumed and 28 new responses were received (a total of 60 responses had been received since Test 2). 26 of them (92.9%) are valid responses, 2 (7.1%) are invalid. Before the adoption of validation, the proportion of valid response is only 40.6%, after the adoption, it's 92.9%. This basically shows that it can effectively block invalid responses to set validation on checkpoint questions.

2.6 Summary

We collected 60 responses in Tests 1 to 4; among them, there are only two responses from MTurk. This verified the result of Test 1, i.e., it is not quite feasible to collect Chinese language data from MTurk at least by now. However Crowdflower is a feasible choice since it has a much larger worker pool. Because of the nature of Crowdsourcing, noise is everywhere. It is practically unacceptable to collect data without effective quality control methods; otherwise more invalid responses than valid ones will be received. Checkpoint questions can be used to identify valid and invalid responses. Validations are effective to block the submission of invalid responses. It is a good strategy to set validations on checkpoint questions in order to block invalid responses.

3 Experiment

The experiment was divided into two stages, and there was a time interval of about two months between them. Based on the initial calibration tests, the experiment was conducted to test the feasibility of collecting Chinese language data on international crowdsourcing platforms and to identify and solve some quality control and experimental design issues.

Our original plan was to conduct one experiment to collect a sample of 200 responses. But after we had collected 135 responses, we found a serious spammer problem which must be properly solved otherwise the data quality would be greatly threatened and the feasibility of our task would be questionable. Meanwhile, we found the amounts of responses from the region of mainland China and the channel "bitcoinget" were unexpectedly large, we doubted that it might result from the frequent media reports on bitcoin at that time in mainland China. When the media reports ebbed, would the experiment be replicable? Thus we thought it's necessary to pause the experiment to seek a solution for the spammer problem and to evade the strong external factor of media report. Thus the experiment was divided into two stages. We chose to pause the experiment instead of stopping it so that the participants who had already taken part in the experiment (Stage 1) could not take part again when the experiment was resumed (Stage 2). The experiment was resumed after two months, with a spammer monitor program based on the API of Crowdflower which could detect and combat spammers automatically. Other aspects of the experiment remained unchanged. The Stage 2 experiment could be used to check the experimental repeatability and to solve the spammer problem found in Stage 1.

3.1 Experimental Design

Questionnaire

The experiment we ran was a self-paced online questionnaire, consisting of 46 questions divided into three parts. The first part contained 10 screening questions designed to verify that the participants were (1) human and (2) native Chinese speakers. The second part of the experiment was a task of Chinese word segmentation. The participants were presented with 12 Chinese sentences and their task was to put a "/" sign at the word boundary that they perceived. The third part of the experiment was a semantic transparency data collection task. Semantic similarity rating tasks were used to obtain semantic transparency data. 12 di-morphemic Chinese compounds, (e.g., 帮助 *bangzhu*, help-assist, "help") were shown in 12 carrier sentences (one target compound per carrier sentence). The participant's task was to rate, on a 5-point scale, the degree of semantic similarity between the meaning of each character in the target compound and the meaning when it is used alone. In view of the different character systems used in different Chinese-speaking regions, we implemented two versions of the questionnaire: a simplified Chinese character version for participants from Mainland China and a traditional Chinese character version for participants from Hong Kong.

Experiment Control

Experiment control measures are used to ensure the validity of participants and their participations. Because we cannot access the real identities of the participants, we can only use some indirect methods which are not completely reliable but can satisfy our demands at large. Firstly, all the participants must be native Chinese speakers. The questionnaire was displayed in Chinese characters which can be a natural barrier to non-native Chinese speakers. Ten screening questions are designed in the questionnaire to test the language backgrounds of the participants. By the above measures, we can effectively discriminate native Chinese speakers from non-native ones. Chinese learners are not a major threat due to their small amount and low overall Chinese fluency. We invited two Chinese learners to test our questionnaire; neither of them could finish it. Secondly, one participant can only submit one response. We used the methods which are already explained in 2.1: one account can only submit one response; one IP address can only submit one response.

Quality Control

In addition to experiment control measures, quality control measures are used to further prevent invalid responses. We used checkpoint questions and other measures for data validation. Only those responses that fulfill the following conditions were considered as valid responses: (1) the screening questions in Part 1 were correctly answered, (2) the answers in Part 2 followed the correct format, and (3) the completion time was equal or greater than 5 minutes. Those that failed one or more conditions were considered as invalid. The effectiveness of the validation measures is discussed in 5. After the Stage 1 experiment, we found a serious spammer problem. After adopting the above quality control measures, spammers became the biggest threat to data quality. It can be exhausted to combat spammers manually due to their high speeds and randomness. Thus, based on the API of Crowdflower we wrote a spammer monitor program to detect and combat spammers automatically.

Parameters

The experiment uses the parameters described in 2.1. Besides that, the unit price of our task is set to US$0.25. Pricing strategy should be carefully chosen in crowdsourcing practices. High prices tend to attract cheating, but low prices may fail to attract enough participations, see (Mason and Watts, 2010).

4 Results and Evaluation

Stage 1 of the experiment lasted for about two days, with multiple manual pauses in between to resist spamming attempts. A total of 135 responses were received, out of which 88 (65.19%) were valid and 47 (34.81%) were invalid according to the criteria stated above. Among the valid responses, 81 (92.05%) were contributed by participants who claimed to be from Mainland China and only 7 (7.95%) by participants from Hong Kong. 38 out of the 47 invalid responses (80.85%) were probably produced by spammers because their completion times were very short and/or the validation measures were bypassed. The 3 largest source channels of valid responses were *bitcoinget* (n=52, 59.09%), *prodege* (n=11, 12.50%) and *getpaid* (n=7, 7.95%), while the 3 largest source regions (based on the IP addresses) were Mainland China (n=54, 61.36%), USA (n=14, 15.91%) and Canada (n=6, 6.82%).

Stage 2 of the experiment lasted for about 4 days also with several breaks. 65 responses were received in Stage 2, among which 54 (83.08%) were valid and 11 (11.92%) were invalid. 46 (85.19%) of the valid responses were contributed by participants from Mainland China and 8 (14.81%) by participants from Hong Kong. 6 (54.55%) of the invalid responses were probably produced by spammers. The main contributing source channels and regions of valid data in Stage 2 were slightly different from Stage 1. Top 3 source channels were *prodege* (n=25, 46.30%), *bitcoinget* (n=7, 12.96%) and *instagc* (n=5, 9.26 %); top 3 source regions were Canada (n=22, 40.74%), USA (n=15, 27.78%) and Mainland China (n=11, 20.37%). Despite the different distributions of source channels and regions, the data obtained from Stage 1 and Stage 2 were highly similar, suggesting that the experiment was highly replicable.

In total, we obtained 200 responses in this experiment, among which 142 (71%) were valid. The valid responses showed high consistency in their answers to the language tasks in Part 2 and Part 3. For example, among the 127 valid responses from Mainland China, the answers to the word segmentation questions in Part 2 had an average consistency[2] of 74.30% (SD=12.94%), while the semantic similarity ratings in

[2]Consistency here means the percentages of the majority-voted answers; if we consider the second most frequent answers,

Part 3 had an average consistency of 58.46% (SD=21.97%). Majority-voted answers and ratings were verified by a team of trained linguists as the most likely segmentations/ratings of the given linguistic materials, while the less popular answers were also verified as possible or reasonable alternatives. These results suggest that the language behavioral data acquired in this experiment, when pruned of invalid responses, were largely consistent with expectations for native language users' judgment.

4.1 Chinese Word Segmentation Data Example

In the experiment, the participants were required to segment 12 short Chinese sentences; because of space limitation, we will only present the results of one representative sentence here. The theoretical segmentation result of the target Chinese sentence "只有依靠群众才能做好工作" (*lit., character by character:* only-have-rely on-depend on-crowd-mass-only-can-do-well-job-work, "The job can only be done well by relying on the messes") is "只有/依靠/群众/才/能/做/好/工作" (*lit. word by word:* only/rely on/the messes/only/can/do/well/job) in which the symbol "/" indicates word boundaries. The segmentation results of this sentence obtained in the experiment are listed in Table 1. We can see that the consistency is high, however the majority-voted result "只有/依靠/群众/才能/做好/工作" is different from the theoretical segmentation result. Most participants treat the slice "才能" as one word instead of two words and the same thing happened to the slice "做好". Speakers' intuition can be different from theoretical analysis: this is an important clue to investigate the representation of Chinese words in the mental lexicon of Chinese speakers.

Segmentation Result	n	%
只有/依靠/群众/才能/做好/工作	100	78.74
只有/依靠/群众/才能/做/好/工作	11	8.66
只有/依靠/群众/才/能/做好/工作	5	3.94
只有/依靠/群众/才/能/做/好/工作	4	3.15
只有/依靠/群众/才/能做好/工作	2	1.57
只有/依靠/群众/才能做好工作	1	0.79
只有/依靠/群众/才能/做好工作	1	0.79
只有/依靠群众/才能/做好工作	1	0.79
只有/依靠群众/才能/做/好/工作	1	0.79
只/有/依靠/群众/才/能/做/好/工作	1	0.79
Total	127	100

Table 1: Chinese Word Segmentation Data Example

4.2 Semantic Similarity Rating Data Example

Semantic transparency affects the representation and processing of compounds (Libben, 1998; Han et al., 2014). In the experiment, we use semantic similarity rating tasks to collect semantic transparency data of 12 compounds which can be used in the studies of mental lexicon. Here we will only discuss two of them in detail. In Chinese, "东西" (*dongxi*, east-west, "thing") is a typical semantically opaque word, because its literal meaning is "east and west" but its actual meaning is "thing": we can hardly find any link between the two. In contrast, "帮助" (*bangzhu*, help-assist, "help") is a typical semantically transparent word, for its literal meaning equals its actual meaning. In our experiment, for each target word, we ask the participants to rate to what extent the meaning of each character when it is used alone is similar to its meaning in the target word. This kind of semantic similarity rating task enables us to estimate the semantic transparency of the target words. The semantic similarity rating data of the above two words are shown in Table 2, and for the results of all the words, see Table 3.

the consistency numbers can be much larger than the reported ones, especially the ones of semantic similarity rating results (see Table 3).

	东西 *dongxi*, east-west, "thing"		帮助 *bangzhu*, help-assist, "help"	
Rating Score	东 *dong*, "east"	西 *xi*, "west"	帮 *bang*, "help"	助 *zhu*, "assist"
1	115	121	6	4
2	2	2	2	13
3	1	1	8	7
4	0	1	23	38
5	8	1	88	63
?	1	1	0	2
Total	127	127	127	127

Table 2: Semantic Similarity Rating Data Example

In the tables, the rating scores 1 to 5 and "?" mean "not similar at all", "slightly similar", "moderately similar", "very similar", "identical", and "unable to rate" respectively. The consistency of the semantic similarity rating data is also very high. For example, most participants (115 out of 127) think the meaning of "东" (*dong*, "east") when it is used alone is not similar at all to its meaning in the word "东西" (*dongxi*, east-west, "thing"), and most participants (121 out of 127) think the meaning of "西" (*xi*, "west")when it is used alone is not similar at all to its meaning in the word "东西" (*dongxi*, east-west, "thing"). The consistency of the rating data of "帮助" (*bangzhu*, help-assist, "help") is not as high as "东西" (*dongxi*, east-west, "thing"), but most participants choose 5 which is our expectation and it is also normal that many participants choose 4, since it is next to 5. The semantic transparency estimation of the two words based on these data is quite consistent with our expectation.

5 The Quality Control Issues

In order to obtain high quality data in crowdsourcing environments, it is fundamental to identify invalid responses. Checkpoint questions can be used to identify them. Checkpoint questions should satisfy two conditions. Firstly, a checkpoint question should be super easy, since making wrong judgments to super easy questions is a clear signal of carelessness. Secondly, a checkpoint question should have a publicly recognized correct answer or it cannot act as a standard. Checkpoint questions can be open-ended or close-ended. Open-ended questions are usually more robust than close-ended ones, since their answers are difficult to guess.

There are at least 3 basic measures to deal with invalid responses: (1) blocking the submission of invalid responses; (2) rejecting the invalid responses that have been submitted; (3) refining the data-set received and filter out invalid responses before analysis. Adopting validations on checkpoint questions is a good strategy. A validation is a submission condition and the submission of responses will be blocked if the validations of them are failed. Since checkpoint questions can identify invalid responses, using validations on checkpoint questions can block the submissions of invalid responses. Crowdflower supports validation but it is implemented on the client end, so can be bypassed; but average participants usually don't have the required expertise to do that, so it is largely reliable.

After the adoption of the above quality control measures, spammers are the major threats to data quality. It can be exhausted to combat spammers manually, because of their high speed and randomness, so automatic monitor programs should be used to combat them. Monitor programs use patterns to detect spammers. Patterns may depend on the specifics of different crowdsourcing practices, but there are some general patterns which are based on the typical behaviors of spammers and can be applied to almost all crowdsourcing practices. One pattern is the "temporal pattern", abnormal high speed is an obvious feature of spammers and can be used as a general pattern. There are two cases. One case is that the completion time of a response is abnormally short. For instance, the normal completion time of a response is around 9 minutes, but the human spammers only needed an average of 138 seconds and the robot spammers only needed an average of 20 seconds. The other case is that the time interval between 2 responses is

Word	Character	Rating Score 1	2	3	4	5	?	Total
东西	东	115	2	1	0	8	1	127
	西	121	2	1	1	1	1	127
地步	地	94	12	8	3	9	1	127
	步	100	11	8	2	4	2	127
漂亮	漂	79	15	10	9	11	3	127
	亮	63	32	15	7	5	5	127
风度	风	109	8	3	0	7	0	127
	度	84	29	7	2	3	2	127
出息	出	97	13	4	3	8	2	127
	息	110	7	3	0	3	4	127
利索	利	80	15	15	3	9	5	127
	索	98	12	6	0	3	8	127
帮助	帮	6	2	8	23	88	0	127
	助	4	13	7	38	63	2	127
衣服	衣	2	8	12	27	78	0	127
	服	32	29	19	24	20	3	127
告诉	告	20	23	24	26	32	2	127
	诉	19	41	30	21	13	3	127
制作	制	4	22	20	43	36	2	127
	作	12	25	31	33	24	2	127
兑换	兑	3	13	13	44	54	0	127
	换	3	8	16	42	56	2	127
灾祸	灾	3	5	16	41	62	0	127
	祸	2	11	21	43	50	0	127

Table 3: The Complete List of Semantic Similarity Rating Data

abnormally short and several such events take place one after another. This temporal pattern can be used to detect concurrent attacks. The other pattern is the "violation of validations". If the validations of a response failed but it was still submitted, then the validations were bypassed and this is a typical behavior of spammers. Once a spammer is detected, we can block it and reject all the responses it submitted if the crowdsourcing platform supports these methods, otherwise we can just pause the task for a while in order to avoid or reduce its attack.

The effect of any single quality control measures is limited; multiple measures should be used at the same time to form a quality control system with much more control power. A reasonable quality control system should notice two key points: (1) maximally block the submission of invalid responses, and (2) maximally filter invalid responses out.

6 Conclusion

Our study showed that crowdsourcing is a very powerful experimental design for exploration cognitive access to the shared Mental Lexicon of the speakers of the same language. We showed that Mandarin speakers shared the same strategy in determination of lexical units. The strategy seems to be match more closely with distributional information. This suggests an empirical approach to lexical unit determination which is then subject to the influence of language use and can lead to changes in the mental lexicon. Although our study is far from conclusive as a proof for the shared lexical access strategy, it does point out to the great potential of pursuing this issue using crowdsourcing experiments.

Acknowledgements

The work described in this paper was supported by a grant from the Research Grants Council of the Hong Kong Special Administrative Region, China (Project No. 544011).

References

Adam J Berinsky, Gregory A Huber, and Gabriel S Lenz. 2011. Using mechanical turk as a subject recruitment tool for experimental research. *Submitted for review*.

Chris Biemann. 2013. Creating a system for lexical substitutions from scratch using crowdsourcing. *Language Resources and Evaluation*, 47(1):97–122.

Chris Callison-Burch and Mark Dredze. 2010. Creating speech and language data with amazon's mechanical turk. In *Proceedings of the NAACL HLT 2010 Workshop on Creating Speech and Language Data with Amazon's Mechanical Turk*, pages 1–12. Association for Computational Linguistics.

Matthew JC Crump, John V McDonnell, and Todd M Gureckis. 2013. Evaluating amazon's mechanical turk as a tool for experimental behavioral research. *PloS one*, 8(3):e57410.

Iryna Gurevych and Torsten Zesch. 2013. Collective intelligence and language resources: introduction to the special issue on collaboratively constructed language resources. *Language Resources and Evaluation*, 47(1):1–7.

Yi-Jhong Han, Shuo-chieh Huang, Chia-Ying Lee, Wen-Jui Kuo, and Shih-kuen Cheng. 2014. The modulation of semantic transparency on the recognition memory for two-character chinese words. *Memory & Cognition*, pages 1–10.

Chu-Ren Huang, Elanna I. J. Tseng, Dylan B. S. Tsai, and Brian Murphy. 2003. Cross-lingual Portability of Semantic relations: Bootstrapping Chinese WordNet with English WordNet Relations. *Language and Linguistics*, 4.3:509–532.

Chu-Ren Huang, Ru-Yng Chang, and Shiang bin Li, 2010. *Ontology and the Lexicon*, chapter Sinica BOW: Integration of Bilingual WordNet and SUMO, pages 201–211. Cambridge University Press, Cambridge.

Gary Libben. 1998. Semantic transparency in the processing of compounds: Consequences for representation, processing, and impairment. *Brain and Language*, 61(1):30 – 44.

Winter Mason and Siddharth Suri. 2012. Conducting behavioral research on amazon' s mechanical turk. *Behavior research methods*, 44(1):1–23.

Winter Mason and Duncan J Watts. 2010. Financial incentives and the performance of crowds. *ACM SigKDD Explorations Newsletter*, 11(2):100–108.

George A Miller. 1995. Wordnet: a lexical database for english. *Communications of the ACM*, 38(11):39–41.

Robert Munro, Steven Bethard, Victor Kuperman, Vicky Tzuyin Lai, Robin Melnick, Christopher Potts, Tyler Schnoebelen, and Harry Tily. 2010. Crowdsourcing and language studies: the new generation of linguistic data. In *Proceedings of the NAACL HLT 2010 Workshop on Creating Speech and Language Data with Amazon's Mechanical Turk*, pages 122–130. Association for Computational Linguistics.

Ian Niles and Adam Pease. 2001. Towards a standard upper ontology. In *Proceedings of the international conference on Formal Ontology in Information Systems-Volume 2001*, pages 2–9. ACM.

Gabriele Paolacci, Jesse Chandler, and Panagiotis G Ipeirotis. 2010. Running experiments on amazon mechanical turk. *Judgment and Decision making*, 5(5):411–419.

David G Rand. 2012. The promise of mechanical turk: How online labor markets can help theorists run behavioral experiments. *Journal of theoretical biology*, 299:172–179.

Tyler Schnoebelen and Victor Kuperman. 2010. Using amazon mechanical turk for linguistic research. *Psihologija*, 43(4):441–464.

Rion Snow, Brendan O'Connor, Daniel Jurafsky, and Andrew Y Ng. 2008. Cheap and fast—but is it good?: evaluating non-expert annotations for natural language tasks. In *Proceedings of the conference on empirical methods in natural language processing*, pages 254–263. Association for Computational Linguistics.

A Computational Approach to Generate a Sensorial Lexicon

Serra Sinem Tekiroğlu
FBK-Irst
Via Sommarive 18
Povo, I-38100 Trento
tekiroglu@fbk.eu

Gözde Özbal
Trento RISE
Via Sommarive 18
Povo, I-38100 Trento
gozbalde@gmail.com

Carlo Strapparava
FBK-Irst
Via Sommarive 18
Povo, I-38100 Trento
strappa@fbk.eu

Abstract

While humans are capable of building connections between words and sensorial modalities by using commonsense knowledge, it is not straightforward for machines to interpret sensorial information. To this end, a lexicon associating words with human senses, namely sight, hearing, taste, smell and touch, would be crucial. Nonetheless, to the best of our knowledge, there is no systematic attempt in the literature to build such a resource. In this paper, we propose a computational method based on bootstrapping and corpus statistics to automatically associate English words with senses. To evaluate the quality of the resulting lexicon, we create a gold standard via crowdsourcing and show that a simple classifier relying on the lexicon outperforms two baselines on a sensory classification task, both at word and sentence level. The results confirm the soundness of the proposed approach for the construction of the lexicon and the usefulness of the resource for computational applications.

1 Introduction

The connection between our senses and the way we perceive the world has been an important philosophical topic for centuries. According to a classification that dates back to Aristotle (Johansen, 1997), senses can be categorized as sight, hearing, taste, smell and touch. With the help of perception, we can process the data coming from our sensory receptors and become aware of our environment. While interpreting sensory data, we unconsciously use our existing knowledge, experience and understanding of the world to create a private experience (Bernstein, 2010).

Language has a significant role as our main communication device to convert our private experiences to shared representations of the environment that we perceive (Majid and Levinson, 2011). As a basic example, giving a name to a color, such as *red*, provides a tool to describe a visual feature of an object. In addition to the words which describe the direct sensorial features of objects, languages include many other lexical items that are connected to sense modalities in various semantic roles. For instance, while some words can be used to describe a perception activity (e.g., *to smell*, *to gaze*, *to listen*), others can simply be physical phenomenons that can be perceived by sensory receptors (e.g., *flower*, *fire*, *sugar*).

Common usage of language can be very dense in terms of sensorial words. As an example, the sentence "*I tasted a delicious soup.*" contains three sensorial words: *to taste* as a perception activity, *delicious* as a perceived sensorial feature and *soup* as a physical phenomenon. While we, as humans, have the ability to connect words with senses intuitively by using our commonsense knowledge, it is not straightforward for machines to interpret sensorial information.

From a computational point of view, a sensorial lexicon could be useful for many scenarios. Rodriguez-Esteban and Rzhetsky (2008) report that using words related to human senses in a piece of text could clarify the meaning of an abstract concept by facilitating a more concrete imagination. Based on this result, an existing text could be automatically modified with sensory words for various purposes such as attracting attention or biasing the audience towards a specific concept. In addition, sensory words can be utilized to affect private psychology by inducing a positive or negative sentiment (Majid and

Zock/Rapp/Huang (eds.): Proceedings of the 4th Workshop on Cognitive Aspects of the Lexicon, pages 114–125,
Dublin, Ireland, August 23, 2014.

Levinson, 2011). As an example, de Araujo et al. (2005) show that the pleasantness level of the same odor can be altered by labeling it as *body odor* or *cheddar cheese*. As another motivation, the readability and understandability of text could also be enhanced by using sensory words (Rodriguez-Esteban and Rzhetsky, 2008).

Yet another area which would benefit from such a resource is advertisement especially by using synaesthesia[1], as it reinforces creative thinking and it is commonly exploited as an imagination boosting tool in advertisement slogans (Pricken, 2008). As an example, we can consider the slogans "*Taste the rainbow*" where the sense of sight is combined with the sense of taste or "*Hear the big picture*" where sight and hearing are merged.

There are various studies both in computational linguistics and cognitive science that build resources associating words with several cognitive features such as abstractness-concreteness (Coltheart, 1981; Turney et al., 2011), emotions (Strapparava and Valitutti, 2004; Mohammad and Turney, 2010), colors (Özbal et al., 2011; Mohammad, 2011) and imageability (Coltheart, 1981). However, to the best of our knowledge, there is no attempt in the literature to build a resource that associates words with senses. In this paper, we propose a computational method to automatically generate a sensorial lexicon[2] that associates words in English with senses. Our method consists of two main steps. First, we generate the initial seed words for each sense category with the help of a bootstrapping approach. Then, we exploit a corpus based probabilistic technique to create the final lexicon. We evaluate this resource with the help of a gold standard that we obtain by using the crowdsourcing service provided by CrowdFlower[3].

The sensorial lexicon embodies 22,684 English lemmas together with their part-of-speech (POS) information that have been linked to one or more of the five senses. Each entry in this lexicon consists of a lemma-POS pair and a score for each sense that indicates the degree of association. For instance, the verb *stink* has the highest score for *smell* as expected while the scores for the other four senses are very low. The noun *tree*, which is a concrete object and might be perceived by multiple senses, has high scores for sight, touch and smell.

The rest of the paper is organized as follows. We first review previous work relevant to this task in Section 2. Then in Section 3, we describe the proposed approach in detail. In Section 4, we explain the annotation process that we conducted and the evaluation strategy that we adopted. Finally, in Section 4, we draw our conclusions and outline possible future directions.

2 Related Work

Since to the best of our knowledge there is no attempt in the literature to automatically associate words with human senses, in this section we will summarize the most relevant studies that focused on linking words with various other cognitive features.

There are several studies dealing with word-emotion associations. WordNet Affect Lexicon (Strapparava and Valitutti, 2004) maps WordNet (Fellbaum, 1998) synsets to various cognitive features (e.g., emotion, mood, behaviour). This resource is created by using a small set of synsets as seeds and expanding them with the help of semantic and lexical relations among these synsets. Yang et al. (2007) propose a collocation model with emoticons instead of seed words while creating an emotion lexicon from a corpus. Perrie et al. (2013) build a word-emotion association lexicon by using subsets of a human-annotated lexicon as seed sets. The authors use frequencies, counts, or unique seed words extracted from an n-gram corpus to create lexicons in different sizes. They propose that larger lexicons with less accurate generation method perform better than the smaller human annotated lexicons. While a major drawback of manually generated lexicons is that they require a great deal of human labor, crowdsourcing services provide an easier procedure for manual annotations. Mohammad and Turney (2010) generate an emotion lexicon by using the crowdsourcing service provided by Amazon Mechanical Turk[4] and it covers 14,200 term-emotion associations.

[1] American Heritage Dictionary (`http://ahdictionary.com/`) defines synaesthesia in linguistics as the description of one kind of sense impression by using words that normally describe another.

[2] The sensorial lexicon is publicly available, upon request to the authors.

[3] `http://www.crowdflower.com/`

[4] `http://www.mturk.com/mturk`

Regarding the sentiment orientations and subjectivity levels of words, Sentiwordnet (Esuli and Sebastiani, 2006) is constructed as an extension to WordNet and it provides sentiments in synset level. Positive, negative and neutral values are assigned to synsets by using ternary classifiers and synset glosses. Another study that has been inspirational for the design of our approach is Banea et al. (2008). The authors generate a subjectivity lexicon starting with a set of seed words and then using a similarity measure among the seeds and the candidate words.

Concerning the association between colors and words, Mohammad (2011) builds a color-word association lexicon by organizing a crowdsourcing task on Amazon Mechanical Turk. Instead, Özbal et al. (2011) aim to automate this process and propose three computational methods based on image analysis, language models and latent semantic analysis (LSA) (Landauer and Dumais, 1997). The authors compare these methods against a gold standard obtained by the crowdsourcing service of Amazon Mechanical Turk. The best performance is obtained by using image features while LSA performs slightly better than the baseline.

Finally, there have been efforts in the literature about the association of words with their abstractness-concreteness and imageability levels. MRC Psycholinguistic Database (Coltheart, 1981) includes abstractness-concreteness and imageability ratings of a small set of words determined according to psycholinguistic experiments. Turney et al. (2011) propose to use LSA similarities of words with a set of seed words to automatically calculate the abstractness and concreteness degrees of words.

3 Automatically Associating Senses with Words

We adopt a two phased computational approach to construct a large sensorial lexicon. First, we employ a bootstrapping strategy to generate a sufficient number of sensory seed words from a small set of manually selected seed words. In the second phase, we perform a corpus based probabilistic method to estimate the association scores to build a larger lexicon.

3.1 Selecting Seed Words

The first phase of the lexicon construction process aims to collect *sensorial seed words*, which are directly related to senses (e.g., *sound*, *tasty* and *sightedness*). To achieve that, we utilized a lexical database called FrameNet (Baker et al., 1998), which is built upon *semantic frame*s of concepts in English and lexical units (i.e., words) that evoke these frames. The basic idea behind this resource is that meanings of words can be understood on the basis of a semantic frame. A semantic frame consists of semantic roles called frame elements, which are manually annotated in more than 170,000 sentences. We have considered FrameNet to be especially suitable for the collection of sensorial seed words since it includes semantic roles and syntactic features of sensational and perceptional concepts.

In order to determine the seed lemma-POS pairs in FrameNet, we first manually determined 31 frames that we found to be highly connected to senses such as *Hear*, *Color*, *Temperature* and *Perception_experience*. Then, we conducted an annotation task and asked 3 annotators to determine which senses the lemma-POS pairs evoking the collected frames are associated with. At the end of this task, we collected all the pairs (i.e., 277) with 100% agreement to constitute our initial seed set. This set contains 277 lemma-POS pairs associated with a specific sense such as the verb *click* with *hearing*, the noun *glitter* with *sight* and *aromatic* with *smell*.

3.2 Seed Expansion via Bootstrapping

In this step, we aim to extend the seed list that we obtained from FrameNet with the help of a bootstrapping approach. To achieve that, we adopt a similar approach to Dias et al. (2014), who propose a repetitive semantic expansion model to automatically build temporal associations of synsets in WordNet. Figure 1 provides an overview of the bootstrapping process. At each iteration, we first expand the seed list by using semantic relations provided by WordNet. We then evaluate the accuracy of the new seed list for sense classification by means of cross-validation against WordNet glosses. For each sense, we continue iterating until the cross-validation accuracy becomes stable or starts to decrease. The following sections explain the whole process in detail.

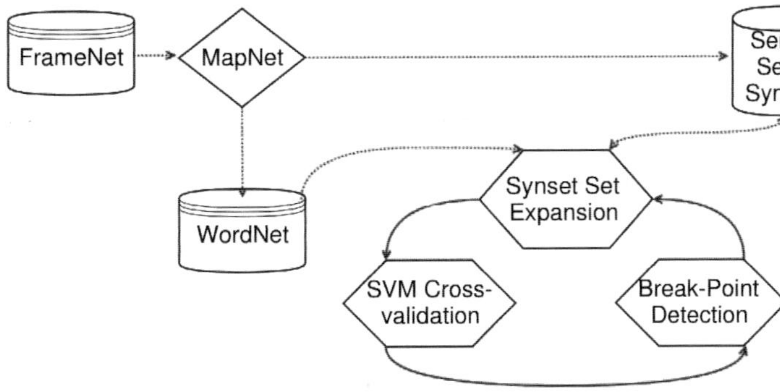

Figure 1: Bootstrapping procedure to expand the seed list.

Extending the Seed List with WordNet

While the initial sensory seed list obtained from FrameNet contains only 277 lemma-POS pairs, we extend this list by utilizing the semantic relations provided by WordNet. To achieve that, we first map each lemma-POS pair in the seed list to WordNet synsets with the help of MapNet (Tonelli and Pighin, 2009), which is a resource providing direct mapping between WordNet synsets and FrameNet lexical units. Then, we add to the list the synsets that are in WordNet relations *direct antonymy*, *similarity*, *derived-from*, *derivationally-related*, *pertains-to*, *attribute* and *also-see* with the already existing seeds. For instance, we add the synset containing the verb *laugh* for the synset of the verb *cry* with the relation *direct antonymy*, or the synset containing the adjective *chilly* for the synset of the adjective *cold* with the relation *similarity*. We prefer to use these relations as they might allow us to preserve the semantic information as much as possible during the extension process. It is worth mentioning that these relations were also found to be appropriate for preserving the affective connotation by Valitutti et al. (2004). Additionally, we use the relations *hyponym* and *hyponym-instance* to enrich the seed set with semantically more specific synsets. For instance, for the noun seed *smell*, we expand the list with the hyponyms of its synset such as the nouns *bouquet*, *fragrance*, *fragrancy*, *redolence* and *sweetness*.

Cross-validation for Sensorial Model

After obtaining new synsets with the help of WordNet relations in each bootstrapping cycle, we build a five-class sense classifier over the seed synsets defined by their glosses provided in WordNet. Similarly to Dias et al. (2014), we assume that the sense information of sensorial synsets is preserved in their definitions. Accordingly, we employ a support vector machine (SVM) (Boser et al., 1992; Vapnik, 1998) model with second degree polynomial kernel by representing the gloss of each synset as a vector of lemmas weighted by their counts. For each synset, its gloss is lemmatized by using Stanford Core NLP[5] and cleaned from the stop words. After each iteration cycle, we perform a 10-fold cross-validation in the updated seed list to detect the accuracy of the new sensorial model. For each sense class, we continue iterating and thereby expanding the seed list until the classifier accuracy steadily drops.

Table 1 lists the *precision* (*P*), *recall* (*R*) and *F1* values obtained for each sense after each iteration until the bootstrapping mechanism stops. While the iteration number is provided in the first column, the values under the last column group present the micro-average of the resulting multi-class classifier. The change in the performance values of each class in each iteration reveal that the number of iterations required to obtain the seed lists varies for each sense. For instance, the F1 value of *touch* continues to increase until the fourth cycle whereas *hearing* records a sharp decrease after the first iteration.

After the bootstrapping process, we create the final lexicon by repeating the expansion for each class until the optimal number of iterations is reached. The last row of Table 1, labeled as *Final*, demonstrates the accuracy of the classifier trained and tested on the final lexicon, i.e., using the seeds selected after iteration 2 for *Sight*, iteration 1 for *Hearing*, iteration 3 for *Taste* and *Smell* and iteration 4 for *Touch*.

[5] `http://nlp.stanford.edu/software/corenlp.shtml`

	Sight			Hearing			Taste			Smell			Touch			Micro-average		
It#	P	R	F1	P	R	F1	P	R	F1	P	R	F1	P	R	F1	P	R	F1
1	.873	.506	.640	.893	.607	**.723**	.716	.983	.828	.900	.273	.419	.759	.320	.451	.780	.754	.729
2	.666	.890	**.762**	.829	.414	.552	.869	.929	.898	.746	.473	.579	.714	.439	.543	.791	.787	.772
3	.643	.878	.742	.863	.390	.538	.891	.909	**.900**	.667	.525	**.588**	.720	.482	.578	.796	.786	**.776**
4	.641	.869	.738	.832	.400	.540	.866	.888	.877	.704	.500	.585	.736	.477	**.579**	.784	.774	.765
5	.640	.869	.737	.832	.400	.540	.866	.888	.877	.704	.500	.585	.738	.474	.578	.784	.774	.764
Final	.805	.827	.816	.840	.408	.549	.814	.942	.873	.685	.534	.600	.760	.582	.659	.800	.802	.790

Table 1: Bootstrapping cycles with validation results.

According to F1 measurements of each iteration, while *hearing* and *taste* have a lower value for the final model, *sight*, *smell* and *touch* have higher results. It should also be noted that the micro-average of the F1 values of the final model shows an increase when compared to the third iteration which has the highest avarage F1 value among the iterations. At the end of this step we have a seed synset list consisting of 2572 synsets yielding the highest performance when used to learn a sensorial model.

3.3 Sensorial Lexicon Construction Using Corpus Statistics

After generating the seed lists consisting of synsets for each sense category with the help of a set of WordNet relations and a bootstrapping process, we use corpus statistics to create our final sensorial lexicon. More specifically, we exploit a probabilistic approach based on the co-occurence of the seeds and the candidate lexical entries. Since working on the synset level would raise the data sparsity problem in synset tagged corpora such as SemCor (Miller et al., 1993) and we need a corpus that provides sufficient statistical information, we migrate from synset level to lexical level. Accordingly, we treat each POS role of the same lemmas as a distinct seed and extract 4287 lemma-POS pairs from 2572 synsets. In this section, we explain the steps to construct our final sensorial lexicon in detail.

Corpus and Candidate Words

As a corpus, we use a subset of English GigaWord 5th Edition released by Linguistic Data Consortium (LDC)[6]. This resource is a collection of almost 10 million English newswire documents collected in recent years, whose content sums up to nearly 5 billion words. The richly annotated GigaWord data comprises automatic parses obtained with the Stanford parser (Klein and Manning, 2003) so that we easily have access to the lemma and POS information of each word in the resource. For the scope of this study, we work on a randomly chosen subset that contains 79800 sentences and we define a co-occurrence event as the co-existence of a candidate word and a seed word within a window of 9 words (the candidate word, 4 words to its left and 4 words to its right). In this manner, we analyze the cooccurrence of each unique lemma-POS pair in the corpus with the sense seeds. We eliminate the candidates which have less than 5 cooccurences with the sense categories.

Normalized Pointwise Mutual Information

For the cooccurrence analysis of the candidate words and seeds, we use pointwise mutual information (PMI), which is simply a measure of association between the probability of the co-occurence of two events and their individual probabilities when they are assumed to be independent (Church and Hanks, 1990) and it is calculated as:

$$PMI(x,y) = \log\left[\frac{p(x,y)}{p(x)p(y)}\right] \tag{1}$$

To calculate the PMI value of a candidate word and a specific sense, we consider *p(x)* as the probability of the candidate word to occur in the corpus. Therefore, *p(x)* is calculated as $p(x) = c(x)/N$, where c(x) is the total count of the occurences of the candidate word *x* in the corpus and N is the total cooccurrence count of all words in the corpus. Similarly, we calculate *p(y)* as the total occurrence count of all the

[6] `http://www.ldc.upenn.edu/Catalog/catalogEntry.jsp?catalogId=LDC2011T07`

majority class	3	4	5	6	7	8	9	10
word	0	0.98	3.84	9.96	11.63	16.66	34.41	12.42
sentence	0.58	2.35	7.07	10.91	13.27	15.63	21.23	16.51

Table 2: Percentage of words and sentences in each majority class.

seeds for the sense considered (*y*). *p(y)* can thus be formulated as $c(y)/N$. *p(x,y)* is the probability of the cooccurence of a candidate word *x* with a sense event *y*.

A major shortcoming of PMI is its sensitivity for low frequency data (Bouma, 2009). As one possible solution, the author introduces Normalized Pointwise Mutual Information (NPMI), which normalizes the PMI values to the range (-1, +1) with the following formula:

$$NPMI(x,y) = \frac{PMI(x,y)}{-\log p(x,y)} \quad (2)$$

We calculated NPMI values for each candidate word and five sense events in the corpus. The sensorial lexicon covers 22,684 lemma-POS pairs and a score for each sense class that denotes their association degrees.

4 Evaluation

To evaluate the performance of the sensorial classification and the quality of the lexicon, we first created a gold standard with the help of a crowdsourcing task. Then, we compared the decisions coming from the lexicon against the gold standard. In this section, we explain the annotation process that we conducted and the evaluation technique that we adopted in detail. We also provide a brief discussion about the obtained results.

4.1 Crowdsourcing to Build a Gold Standard

The evaluation phase of the sensorial lexicon requires a gold standard data to be able to conduct a meaningful assessment. Since to our best knowledge there is no resource with sensory associations of words or sentences, we designed our own annotation task using the crowdsourcing service CrowdFlower. For the annotation task, we first compiled a collection of sentences to be annotated. Then, we designed two questions that the annotators were expected to answer for a given sentence. While the first question is related to the sense association of a whole sentence, the second asks the annotators the sense associations of the words in the same sentence to collect a fine-grained gold standard.

We collected a dataset of 340 sentences consisting of 300 advertisement slogans from 11 advertisement categories (e.g., fashion, food, electronics) and 40 story sentences from a story corpus. We collected the slogans from various online resources such as `http://slogans.wikia.com/wiki` and `http://www.adslogans.co.uk/`. The story corpus is generated as part of a dissertation research (Alm, 2008) and it provides stories as a collection of sentences.

In both resources, we first determined the candidate sentences which had at least five tokens and contained at least one adjective, verb or noun. In addition, we replaced the brand names in the advertisement slogans with *X* to prevent any bias. For instance, the name of a well-known restaurant in a slogan might cause a bias towards *taste*. Finally, the slogans used in the annotation task were chosen randomly among the candidate sentences by considering a balanced number of slogans from each category. Similarly, 40 story sentences were selected randomly among the candidate story sentences. To give a more concrete idea, for our dataset we obtained an advertisement slogan such as "*X's Sugar Frosted Flakes They're Great!*" or a story sentence such as "*The ground is frozen, and besides the snow has covered everything.*"

In the crowdsourcing task we designed, the annotators were required to answer 2 questions for a given sentence. In the first question, they were asked to detect the human senses conveyed or directly described by a given sentence. To exemplify these cases, we provided two examples such as "*I saw the cat*" that directly mentions the action of seeing and "*The sun was shining on the blue water.*" that conveys the sense of sight by using visual descriptions or elements like "*blue*" or "*shine*" which are notable for their visual

Category	Si	He	Ta	Sm	To
personal care	49.36	10.75	0.00	13.29	26.58
travel	58.18	0.00	29.09	0.00	12.72
fashion	43.47	0.00	0.00	26.08	30.43
beauty	84.56	0.00	0.00	0.00	15.43
computing	32.25	59.13	0.00	0.00	8.60
food	0.00	5.46	94.53	0.00	0.00
beverages	22.68	0.00	59.79	0.00	17.52
communications	25.00	67.50	0.00	0.00	0.075
electronics	45.94	54.05	0.00	0.00	0.00
education	28.57	42.85	0.00	0.00	28.57
transport	61.81	38.18	0.00	0.00	0.00
story	58.37	20.81	0.00	7.23	13.57

Table 3: The categories of the annotated data and their sense association percentages.

properties. The annotators were able to select more than one sense for each sentence and together with the five senses we provided another option as *None* which should be selected when an annotator could not associate a sentence with any sense. The second question was devoted do determining word-sense associations. Here, the annotators were expected to associate the words in each sentence with at least one sense. Again, annotators could choose *None* for every word that they could not confidently associate with a sense.

The reliability of the annotators was evaluated on the basis of 20 control sentences which were highly associated with a specific sense and which included at least one sensorial word. For instance, for the control sentence "*The skin you love to touch*", we only considered as reliable the annotators who associated the sentence with *touch* and the word *touch* with the sense *touch*[7]. Similarly, for the slogan "*The most colourful name in cosmetics.*", an annotator was expected to associate the sentence with at least the sense *sight* and the word *colorful* to at least the sense *sight*. The raters who scored at least 70% accuracy on average on the control questions for the two tasks were considered to be reliable. Each unit was annotated by at least 10 reliable raters.

Similarly to Mohammad (2011) and Özbal et al. (2011), we calculated the majority class of each annotated item to measure the agreement among the annotators. Table 2 demonstrates the observed agreement at both word and sentence level. Since 10 annotators participated in the task, the annotations with a majority class greater than 5 can be considered as reliable (Özbal et al., 2011). Indeed, for 85.10% of the word annotations the absolute majority agreed on the same decision, while 77.58% of the annotations in the sentence level have majority class greater than 5. The high agreement observed among the annotators in both cases confirms the quality of the resulting gold standard data.

In Table 3, we present the results of the annotation task by providing the association percentage of each category with each sense, namely sight (Si), hear (He), taste (Ta), smell (Sm) and touch (To). As demonstrated in the table, while the sense of *sight* can be observed in almost every advertisement category and in *story*, *smell* and *taste* are very rare. We observe that the story sentences invoke all sensorial modalities except *taste*, although the percentage of sentences annotated with *smell* is relatively low. Similarly, *personal care* category has an association with four of the senses while the other categories have either very low or no association with some of the sense classes. Indeed, the perceived sensorial effects in the sentences vary according to the category such that the slogans in the *travel* category are highly associated with *sight* whereas the *communication* category is highly associated with *hearing*. While the connection of the *food* and *beverages* categories with *taste* is very high as expected, they have no association with the sense of *smell*. This kind of analysis could be useful for copywriters to decide which sensory modalities to invoke while creating a slogan for a specific product category.

[7] If the annotators gave additional answers to the expected ones, we considered their answers as correct.

4.2 Evaluation Measures

Based on the annotation results of our crowdsourcing task, we propose an evaluation technique considering that a lemma-POS or a sentence might be associated with more than one sensory modalities. Similar to the evaluation framework defined by Özbal et al. (2011), we adapt the evaluation measures of SemEval-2007 English Lexical Substitution Task (McCarthy and Navigli, 2007), where a system generates one or more possible substitutions for a target word in a sentence preserving its meaning.

For a given lemma-POS or a sentence, which we will name as *item* in the rest of the section, we allow our system to provide as many sensorial associations as it determines using a specific lexicon. While evaluating a sense-item association of a method, a *best* and an *oot* score are calculated by considering the number of the annotators who associate that sense with the given item, the number of the annotators who associate any sense with the given item and the number of the senses the system gives as an answer for that item. More specifically, *best* scoring provides a credit for the best answer for a given item by dividing it to the number of the answers of the system. *oot* scoring, on the other hand, considers only a certain number of system answers for a given item and does not divide the credit to the total number of the answers. Unlike the lexical substitution task, a limited set of labels (i.e., 5 sense labels and *none*) are allowed for the sensorial annotation of sentences or lemma-POS pairs. For this reason, we reformulate *out-of-ten (oot)* scoring used by McCarthy and Navigli (2007) as out-of-two.

In Equation 3, *best* score for a given item *i* from the set of items I, which consists of the items annotated with a specific sense by a majority of 5 annotators, is formulated where H_i is the multiset of gold standard sense associations for item *i* and S_i is the set of sense associations provided by the system. *oot* scoring, as formulated in Equation 4, accepts up to 2 sense associations s from the answers of system S_i for a given item *i* and the credit is not divided by the number of the answers of the system.

$$best\,(i) = \frac{\sum_{s \in S_i} freq\,(s \in H_i)}{|H_i| \cdot |S_i|} \quad (3)$$

$$oot\,(i) = \frac{\sum_{s \in S_i} freq\,(s \in H_i)}{|H_i|} \quad (4)$$

As formulated in Equation 5, to calculate the precision of an item-sense association task with a specific method, the sum of the scores (i.e., *best* or *oot*) for each item is divided by the number of items A, for which the method can provide an answer. In recall, the denominator is the number of the items in the gold standard for which an answer is given by the annotators.

$$P = \frac{\sum_{i \in A} score_i}{|A|} \qquad R = \frac{\sum_{i \in I} score_i}{|I|} \quad (5)$$

4.3 Evaluation Method

For the evaluation, we compare the accuracy of a simple classifier based on the sensorial lexicon against two baselines on a sense classification task, both at word and sentence level. To achieve that, we use the gold standard that we obtain from the crowdsourcing task and the evaluation measures *best* and *oot*. The lexicon-based classifier simply assigns to each word in a sentence the sense values found in the lexicon. The first baseline simply assigns a random float value, which is in the range of (-1,1), to each sense association of each lemma-POS pair in the sensorial lexicon. The second baseline instead builds the associations by using a Latent Semantic Analysis space generated from the British National Corpus[8] (BNC), which is a very large (over 100 million words) corpus of modern English. More specifically, this baseline calculates the LSA similarities between each candidate lemma-POS pair and sense class by taking the cosine similarity between the vector of the target lemma-POS pair and the average of the vectors of the related sensory word (i.e., *see*, *hear*, *touch*, *taste*, and *smell*) for each possible POS tag. For instance, to get the association score of a lemma-POS pair with the sense sight, we first average the vectors of see (noun) and see (verb) before calculating its cosine similarity with the target lemma-POS pair.

[8] http://www.hcu.ox.ac.uk/bnc/

For the first experiment, i.e., word-sense association, we automatically associate the lemma-POS pairs obtained from the annotated dataset with senses by using i) the sensorial lexicon, ii) the random baseline, iii) the LSA baseline. To achieve that, we lemmatize and POS tag each sentence in the dataset by using Stanford Core NLP. In the end, for each method and target word, we obtain a list of senses sorted according to their sensorial association values in decreasing order. It is worth noting that we only consider the non-negative sensorial associations for the sensorial lexicon and the random baseline, and the associations above the value of 0.4 which we empirically set as the threshold for the LSA baseline. For instance, the sensorial lexicon associates the noun *wine* with [*smell, taste, sight*]. In this experiment, *best* scoring considers the associated senses as the best answer, *smell, taste, sight* according to the previous example, and calculates a score with respect to the best answer in the gold standard and the number of the senses in this answer. Instead, *oot* scoring takes the first two answers, *smell* and *taste* according to the previous example, and assigns the score accordingly.

To determine the senses associated with a sentence for the second experiment, we use a method similar to the one proposed by Turney (2002). For each sense, we simply calculate the average score of the lemma-POS pairs in a sentence. We set a threshold value of 0 to decide whether a sentence is associated with a given sense. In this manner, we obtain a sorted list of average sensory scores for each sentence according to the three methods. For instance, the classifier based on the sensorial lexicon associates the sentence *Smash it to pieces, love it to bits.* with [*touch*, *taste*]. For the *best* score, only *touch* would be considered, whereas *oot* would consider both *touch* and *taste*.

4.4 Evaluation Results

In Table 4, we list the F1 values that we obtained with the classifier using the sensorial lexicon and the two baselines (Random and LSA) according to both *best* and *oot* measures. In addition, we provide the performance of the sensorial lexicon in two preliminary steps, before bootstrapping (BB) and after bootstrapping (AB) to observe the incremental progress of the lexicon construction method. As can be observed from the table, the best performance for both experiments is achieved by the sensorial lexicon when compared against the baselines.

While in the first experiment the lexicon generated after the bootstrapping step (AB) provides a very similar performance to the final lexicon according to the *best* measure, it can only build sense associations for 69 lemmas out of 153 appearing in the gold standard. Instead, the final lexicon attempts to resolve 129 lemma-sense associations and results in a better recall value. Additionally, AB yields a very high precision as expected, since it is created by a controlled semantical expansion from manually annotated sensorial words. The LSA baseline slightly improves the random baseline according to both *best* and *oot* measures and it also outperforms BB for *oot*. BB lexicon includes only 573 lemmas which are collected from 277 synsets and we can not obtain 2 sense association scores for *oot* in this lexicon since each lemma is associated with only one sense with a value of 1.

Concerning the sentence classification experiment, the classifier using the sensorial lexicon yields the highest performance in both measures. The very high F1 value obtained with the *oot* scoring indicates that the right answer for a sentence is included in the first two decisions in many cases. The low performance of the LSA baseline might be arising due to its tendency to link the sentences with the sense of *touch* (i.e., 215 sentences out of 320 gold standard data). It would be interesting to see the impact of using another corpus to build the LSA space and constituting the sense vectors differently.

After the manual analysis of the sensorial lexicon and gold standard data, we observe that the sensorial classification task could be nontrivial. For instance, a story sentence "*He went to sleep again and snored until the windows shook.*" has been most frequently annotated as *hearing*. While the sensorial lexicon classifier associates this sentence with *touch* as the best answer, it can provide the correct association *hearing* as the second best answer. To find out the best sensorial association for a sentence, a classification method which exploits various aspects of sensorial elements in a sentence, such as the number of sensorial words or their dependencies, could be a better approach than using only the average sensorial values.

Based on our observations in the error cases, the advertisement slogan "*100% pure squeezed sunshine*" is associated with *touch* as the best answer by both the sensorial lexicon and LSA baseline while it is most frequently annotated as *sight* in the gold standard. This slogan is an example usage of synaesthesia and

Model	Lemma best	Lemma oot	Sentence best	Sentence oot
Random	21.10	37.59	21.10	37.59
LSA	26.35	37.60	31.01	37.63
Lexicon-BB	45.22	45.22	49.60	51.12
Lexicon-AB	55.85	55.85	59.89	63.21
Sensorial Lexicon	55.86	80.13	69.76	80.73

Table 4: Evaluation results.

metaphors in advertising language. To clarify, a product from the category of *beverages*, which might be assumed to have a *taste* association, is described by a metaphorical substitution of a *taste*-related noun, most probably the name of a fruit, with a *sight*-related noun; *sunshine*. This metaphorical substitution, then used as the object of a *touch*-related verb, *to squeeze*, produces a synaesthetic expression with *touch* and *sight*.

5 Conclusion

In this paper we have presented a computational method to build a lexicon that associates words with senses by employing a two-step strategy. First, we collected seed words by using a bootstrapping approach based on a set of WordNet relations. Then, we performed a corpus based statistical analysis to produce the final lexicon. The resulting sensorial lexicon consists of 22,684 lemma-POS pairs and their association degrees with five sensory modalities. To our best knowledge, this is the first systematic attempt to build a sensorial lexicon and we believe that our contribution constitutes a valid starting point for the community to consider sensorial information conveyed by text as a feature for various tasks and applications. The results that we obtain by comparing our lexicon against the gold standard are promising even though not conclusive. The results confirm the soundness of the proposed approach for the construction of the lexicon and the usefulness of the resource for text classification and possibly other computational applications.

As future work, we would like to explore the effect of using different kinds of WordNet relations during the bootstrapping phase. It would also be interesting to experiment with relations provided by other resources such as ConceptNet (Liu and Singh, 2004), which is a semantic network containing common sense, cultural and scientific knowledge. We would also like to use the sensorial lexicon for various applicative scenarios such as slanting existing text towards a specific sense with text modification. We believe that our resource could be extremely useful for automatic content personalization according to user profiles. As an example, one can imagine a system that automatically replaces hearing based expressions with sight based ones in pieces of texts for a hearing-impaired person. Finally, we plan to investigate the impact of using sensory information for metaphor detection and interpretation based on our observations during the evaluation.

Acknowledgments

We would like to thank Daniele Pighin for his insightful comments and valuable suggestions.
This work was partially supported by the PerTe project (Trento RISE).

References

Ebba Cecilia Ovesdotter Alm. 2008. *Affect in Text and Speech*. Ph.D. thesis, University of Illinois at Urbana-Champaign.

Collin F Baker, Charles J Fillmore, and John B Lowe. 1998. The berkeley framenet project. pages 86--90. Association for Computational Linguistics.

Carmen Banea, Rada Mihalcea, and Janyce Wiebe. 2008. A bootstrapping method for building subjectivity lexicons for languages with scarce resources. In *LREC*.

D. Bernstein. 2010. *Essentials of Psychology*. PSY 113 General Psychology Series. Cengage Learning.

Bernhard E. Boser, Isabelle Guyon, and Vladimir Vapnik. 1992. A Training Algorithm for Optimal Margin Classifiers. In *Proceedings of the 5th Annual Workshop on Computational learning theory*.

Gerlof Bouma. 2009. Normalized (pointwise) mutual information in collocation extraction. *Proceedings of GSCL*, pages 31--40.

Kenneth Ward Church and Patrick Hanks. 1990. Word association norms, mutual information, and lexicography. *Comput. Linguist.*, 16(1):22--29, March.

Max Coltheart. 1981. The mrc psycholinguistic database. *The Quarterly Journal of Experimental Psychology*, 33(4):497--505.

Ivan E de Araujo, Edmund T Rolls, Maria Inés Velazco, Christian Margot, and Isabelle Cayeux. 2005. Cognitive modulation of olfactory processing. *Neuron*, 46(4):671--679.

Gaël Harry Dias, Mohammed Hasanuzzaman, Stéphane Ferrari, and Yann Mathet. 2014. Tempowordnet for sentence time tagging. In *Proceedings of the Companion Publication of the 23rd International Conference on World Wide Web Companion*, WWW Companion '14, pages 833--838, Republic and Canton of Geneva, Switzerland. International World Wide Web Conferences Steering Committee.

Andrea Esuli and Fabrizio Sebastiani. 2006. Sentiwordnet: A publicly available lexical resource for opinion mining. In *Proceedings of LREC*, volume 6, pages 417--422.

Christiane Fellbaum, editor. 1998. *WordNet An Electronic Lexical Database*. The MIT Press, Cambridge, MA ; London.

Thomas Kjeller Johansen. 1997. *Aristotle on the Sense-organs*. Cambridge University Press.

Dan Klein and Christopher D. Manning. 2003. Accurate unlexicalized parsing. In *IN PROCEEDINGS OF THE 41ST ANNUAL MEETING OF THE ASSOCIATION FOR COMPUTATIONAL LINGUISTICS*, pages 423--430.

Thomas K Landauer and Susan T Dumais. 1997. A solution to plato's problem: The latent semantic analysis theory of acquisition, induction, and representation of knowledge. *Psychological review*, 104(2):211.

H. Liu and P. Singh. 2004. Conceptnet - a practical commonsense reasoning tool-kit. *BT Technology Journal*, 22(4):211--226, October.

Asifa Majid and Stephen C Levinson. 2011. The senses in language and culture. *The Senses and Society*, 6(1):5--18.

Diana McCarthy and Roberto Navigli. 2007. Semeval-2007 task 10: English lexical substitution task. In *Proceedings of the 4th International Workshop on Semantic Evaluations*, pages 48--53. Association for Computational Linguistics.

George A. Miller, Claudia Leacock, Randee Tengi, and Ross T. Bunker. 1993. A semantic concordance. In *Proceedings of the workshop on Human Language Technology*, HLT '93, pages 303--308, Stroudsburg, PA, USA. Association for Computational Linguistics.

Saif M Mohammad and Peter D Turney. 2010. Emotions evoked by common words and phrases: Using mechanical turk to create an emotion lexicon. In *Proceedings of the NAACL HLT 2010 Workshop on Computational Approaches to Analysis and Generation of Emotion in Text*, pages 26--34. Association for Computational Linguistics.

Saif Mohammad. 2011. Colourful language: Measuring word-colour associations. In *Proceedings of the 2nd Workshop on Cognitive Modeling and Computational Linguistics*, pages 97--106. Association for Computational Linguistics.

Gözde Özbal, Carlo Strapparava, Rada Mihalcea, and Daniele Pighin. 2011. A comparison of unsupervised methods to associate colors with words. In *Affective Computing and Intelligent Interaction*, pages 42--51. Springer.

Jessica Perrie, Aminul Islam, Evangelos Milios, and Vlado Keselj. 2013. Using google n-grams to expand word-emotion association lexicon. In *Computational Linguistics and Intelligent Text Processing*, pages 137--148. Springer.

Mario Pricken. 2008. *Creative Advertising Ideas and Techniques from the World's Best Campaigns*. Thames & Hudson, 2nd edition.

R. Rodriguez-Esteban and A. Rzhetsky. 2008. Six senses in the literature. The bleak sensory landscape of biomedical texts. *EMBO reports*, 9(3):212--215, March.

C. Strapparava and A. Valitutti. 2004. WordNet-Affect: an affective extension of WordNet. In *Proceedings of LREC*, volume 4, pages 1083--1086.

Sara Tonelli and Daniele Pighin. 2009. New features for framenet - wordnet mapping. In *Proceedings of the Thirteenth Conference on Computational Natural Language Learning (CoNLL'09)*, Boulder, CO, USA.

Peter D Turney, Yair Neuman, Dan Assaf, and Yohai Cohen. 2011. Literal and metaphorical sense identification through concrete and abstract context. In *Proceedings of the 2011 Conference on the Empirical Methods in Natural Language Processing*, pages 680--690.

Peter D Turney. 2002. Thumbs up or thumbs down?: semantic orientation applied to unsupervised classification of reviews. In *Proceedings of the 40th annual meeting on association for computational linguistics*, pages 417--424. Association for Computational Linguistics.

Alessandro Valitutti, Carlo Strapparava, and Oliviero Stock. 2004. Developing affective lexical resources. *PsychNology Journal*, 2(1):61--83.

Vladimir N. Vapnik. 1998. *Statistical Learning Theory*. Wiley-Interscience.

Changhua Yang, Kevin Hsin-Yih Lin, and Hsin-Hsi Chen. 2007. Building emotion lexicon from weblog corpora. In *Proceedings of the 45th Annual Meeting of the ACL on Interactive Poster and Demonstration Sessions*, pages 133--136. Association for Computational Linguistics.

Database Design of an Online E-Learning Tool of Chinese Classifiers

Helena Hong Gao
Nanyang Technological University
14 Nanyang Drive, HSS-03-05
Singapore 637332
helenagao@ntu.edu.sg

Abstract

Chinese noun classifiers are an indispensible part of the Chinese language, but are difficult for non-native speakers to use correctly. Chinese language teachers often face challenges in finding an effective way to teach classifiers, as the rules for defining which nouns can be associated with which classifiers are not straightforward. Many theoretical studies have explored the nature of Chinese classifiers, but few studies take an empirical approach to the investigation of effective teaching and learning methods of classifiers. Learners often find that existing dictionaries either do not have classifiers as lexical entries, or give very brief explanations that are hardly helpful. This paper presents the progress of an ongoing project on the construction of an e-dictionary of Chinese classifiers. The objective of the project is to provide a platform for Chinese language learners to explore and learn classifier uses in a bottom-up fashion. The current work is on the design of an e-learning tool database and its connection to the e-dictionary database. Descriptions of the design and the functions of the e-learning tool are provided in the paper.

1 Introduction

As a classifier language, Chinese does not provide a way for its speakers to avoid using classifiers. That is, they are a compulsory grammatical element in a phrase structure. The basic construction of a classifier phrase has a numeral (e.g., *yī* 'one', *shí* 'ten'), or a determiner (e.g., *zhè* 'this', *nà* 'that'), or a qualifier (e.g., *jǐ* 'several', *měi* 'each'), placed before a classifier and a noun after it. Thus, a simple English noun phrase such as 'a book' needs to be expressed in Chinese with the classifier *běn* in between the numeral *yī* and the noun, 'book' as *yīběn shū*. In brief, a classifier is a word or morpheme that is used to classify nouns based on their inherent semantic features. However, the semantics and the uses of Chinese classifiers have become far more complex than their syntactic structure looks. It is hard to define their lexical meanings and their uses seem to have rules to follow but violations are common. It is impossible for learners to make a correct choice of a classifier if they simply follow its grammatical rules. This is mainly because Chinese classifiers contain information about the features of the noun referents they can be associated with. However, most of the classifiers can be associated with a number of different types of nouns. Their noun-dependent meanings are inexplicit and ambigous. Conventional dictionaries give brief definitions of classifiers, which is a way to avoid complicated descriptions and lengthy listing of their associated nouns, but are of little help to language learners.

Classifiers can be divided into different types based on their semantic functions. Some of them carry the unique features of the Chinese language; others are representational of classifier languages, and yet all of them have the functions of measure words. Regarding the differences between classifiers and measure words, Tai & Wang (1990) stated that "A classifier categorizes a class of nouns by picking out some salient perceptual properties, either physically or functionally based, which are permanently associated with entities named by the class of nouns; a measure word does not categorize but denotes the quantity of the entity named by a noun". This definition makes a clear distinction between a classifier and a measure word from a multi-dimensional perspective. Measure words are language universal while classifiers are

Zock/Rapp/Huang (eds.): Proceedings of the 4th Workshop on Cognitive Aspects of the Lexicon, pages 126–137, Dublin, Ireland, August 23, 2014.

language specific. There is an ontological base on which classifiers and nouns are associated with (Sowa, 2000; Huang and Ahrens, 2003; Philpot et al., 2003; Nichols et al., 2005), while measure word associations with nouns could be simply based on the notion of quantification. Understanding the differences between the two concepts can help learners of Chinese increase their awareness of the semantic and cognitive bases of classifier associations with nouns (Gao, 2010; Gao, 2011; Quek and Gao, 2011).

Due to the complexity of classifiers' functions, different definitions and classifications have been found. Some researchers define Chinese classifiers based on their grammatical functions. For example, Chao (1968) divided classifiers into nine categories. They are 'classifiers or individual measures', 'classifiers associated with v-o', 'group measures', 'partitive measures', 'container measures', 'temporary measures', 'standard measures', 'quasi-measures or autonomous measures', and 'measures for verbs of action'. His classification shows that he did not distinguish between classifiers and measure words. The advantages of such a classification are that it includes all the types of classifiers mentioned above and that classifiers' measuring function is emphasized. But a big disadvantage is that the embedded meanings of the specific noun classifiers and the ontological nature of the noun referents that classifiers are associated with are largely ignored. This way of classification may help beginning learners to understand the basic functions of Chinese classifiers, but will not help more advanced learners.

Yue (2009) took a different approach. He treated classifiers and measure words as quantifiers and divided those collected from corpus data into eleven categories based on the kinds of nouns the quantifiers are associated with. They were defined as quantifiers 'representing a group of people', 'indicating groups of animals', 'representing types', 'representing individual thing or person', 'representing a pair', 'representing a set', 'representing a huge amount of things', 'representing a slight amount of things', 'representing capacity', 'representing weather', and 'representing emotions'. Regardless of the unnecessary new term he used to refer to classifiers, his classification is more cognitively based and closer to language learners' knowledge of noun referents and their categories.

Using computer technology to apply empirical research findings of classifier knowledge to natural language processing (NLP) has provided a new approach for the semantic analysis of classifiers (Nirenburg and Raskin, 2004; Hwang et al., 2008) and for computer-assisted language learning (Guo and Zhong, 2005). However, no e-learning systems developed so far have been found to be able to help language learners to use the semantic features of classifiers' associated nouns to learn classifiers systematically. Yet, the emergence of Computer-Assisted Language Learning (CALL) has made it possible for language learners to explore various kinds of user-friendly and flexible e-learning tools (Davies, 2011). CALL incorporates technology into the language learning process and also applies itself across a broad spectrum of teaching styles, textbooks, and courses (Donaldson and Haggstrom, 2006). Its bidirectional and individualized features make it possible for learners to use it effectively to improve different aspects of language skills (Mallon, 2006; Chang et al., 2008).

The idea of designing an e-dictionary of Chinese classifiers is similar to that of CALL. Findings from empirical studies on classifier learning provide a practical guideline in the process of the designing. In order to make the e-dictionary a useful learning tool for both beginning and advanced learners of Chinese, measure words and classifiers are both labelled as classifiers. However, in the feature descriptions learners can understand and identify the functions of the words categorically.

Currently the dictionary database includes 859 classifiers collected from dictionaries and other resources. The number of associated nouns classified is currently 6420. Different tables (as sub-databases) are set up according to the classifications of classifiers and the nouns included. In addition to the conventional functions of a dictionary built up for the e-dictionary of classifiers, an e-learning system is implemented to allow learners at different levels to have a self-paced exploration of the relationships between a classifier and a noun or many nouns from different categories. In this paper the focus will be on the descriptions of the designs of the e-learning database and its interface.

2 Classifier-based Classification of Noun Categories

Classifiers must be used together with nouns to form classifier phrases but their associations with nouns are not contextually based nor are they of a free choice. The mapping can be complicated. A classifier can be associated with a number of nouns from different categories and a noun can be mapped to more than one classifiers. For example, the classifier *tiáo* enters into nine noun categories and the noun *chē*'car' can be associated with *liàng* and *tái* as well. Learners may quickly feel intimidated when at a first trial to identify the possibilities of the multi associations. Therefore, in designing the database, instead of mapping classifiers to nouns directly, we make use of classifiers' noun-dependent features to first identify all the nouns that each classifier can be associated with and then classify the nouns into categories. So far eleven noun categories have been identified and classified as 'nature', 'humans & body parts', 'animals', 'vegetables & fruits', 'man-made objects', 'buildings', 'clothing', 'food','furniture', 'tools', and 'vehicles'. A hierarchy of noun classifiers is built up according to the number of noun categories each classifier is associated with. These noun categories are not word classes defined with the principles in lexicology. They are defined based on the ontological categories of the noun referents of real-world entities, which are supposedly directly linked to learners' understanding of nouns and their referents of the language. Grouping classifiers' associated nouns into categories based on the ontological categories of noun referents is one of the special features of the design of this dictionary.

The classifiers are set in a hierarchical order in the database according to the number of noun categories they enter into. The highest number of noun categories that a classifier has been identified as being associable with more than one noun categories is nine. Of all the classifiers in the database, about more than 50% of them are associated with more than three noun categories. The fewer noun categories a classifier is associated with, the easier it is assumed to be for learners to grasp. For example, the classifier *liàng* occurs only in the category of vehicles, (e.g., car, lorry, bicycle, etc.). Learners generally do not confuse or misuse it for other types of nouns. Due to the differences in the mult-categorical associations, some classifiers are more commonly used than others. The nineteen classifiers listed in Table 1 are the ones that are associated with at least three noun categories and they are the most commonly used ones as well.

In the analysis of linguistic categories, a cognitive approach defines categories by groups of features and relationships within certain linguistic domains. The occurrence of a noun with a particular classifier in a phrase structure is dependent upon the categorical features of both the noun and the classifier. However, the embedded semantic networks of the categories are not obviously well connected, which is mainly due to the diachronic and sociolinguistic changes of the Chinese language. As a result, native speakers' categorization dependent on not only noun referents' intrinsic properties but also their functional and human perceptual ones. In other words, classifier and noun associations encode as well human cognitive understandings of the real world entities. The use of classifiers has thus been found changed over time. More noun and classifier associations are found to be possible cross-categorically. That is, one single classifier can associate itself with a number of nouns from different noun categories and similarly, one single noun can also be associated with not one but two or three classifiers. This cross-categorization extension complicates the classification of classifiers to a great extent.

Theoretically, it does not seem to be possible for linguists to build a meta-theory for a systematic organization of logically transparent classifier-noun categories and thus hard for lexicographers to find an effective way to illustrate the semantic relationships between classifiers and nouns. The main obstacle in classifier acquisition seem to be due to the fact that the the nature of the semantic meanings of classifiers is opaque. The complex classifier associations with nouns have consequently caused noun categorizations to be linguistically unconventional.

Classifier in Chinese	Classifier in Pinyin	Number of noun categories the classifier is associated with	Examples of nouns the classifier is associated with
条	*tiáo*	9 (nature, humans & body parts, animals, vegetables & fruits, buildings, clothing, food, vehicles, other man-made objects)	rainbow, leg, snake, cucumber, road, scarf, potato chip, boat, necklace
根	*gēn*	7 (nature, humans & body parts, vegetables & fruits, buildings, food, tools, other man-made objects)	stick, bone, banana, pillar, sausage, needle, ribbon
块	*kuài*	6 (nature, humans & body parts, clothing, food, tools, other man-made objects)	stone, scar, handkerchief, candy, eraser, soap
层	*céng*	5 (nature, humans & body parts, building, clothing, other man-made objects)	wave/fog, skin, building storey, curtain, paper
张	*zhāng*	5 (humans & body parts, food, furniture, tool, other man-made objects)	mouth, pancake, bed, bow, map
只	*zhī*	5 (humans & body parts, animal, clothing, vehicle, other man-made objects)	ear, tiger, sock, sailing boat, watch
粒	*lì*	4 (nature, vegetables & fruits, food, other man-made objects)	sand, cherry, rice, sleeping tablet
段	*duàn*	4 (nature, vegetables & fruits, building, other man-made objects)	wood, lotus root, city wall, iron wire
口	*kǒu*	4 (humans & body parts, animal, tools, other man-made objects)	person (people), pig, sword, well
面	*miàn*	4 (buildings, tools, furniture, other man-made objects)	wall, drum, mirror, flag
节	*jié*	4 (building, food, tool, vehicle)	chimney, sugar cane, battery, railway carriage
道	*dào*	3 (nature, humans & body parts, building)	lightening, eyebow, dam
滴	*dī*	3 (nature, humans & body parts, other man-made objects)	water / rain, blood, ink
件	*jiàn*	3 (clothing, tools, other man-made objects)	shirt, (musical) instrument, toy
把	*bǎ*	3 (furniture, tools, other man-made objects)	chair, knife, cello
截	*jié*	3 (nature, tools, other man-made objects)	rope, pencil, pipe
颗	*kē*	3 (nature, humans & body parts, other man-made objects)	star, tooth, artillery shell
片	*piàn*	3 (nature, food, other man-made objects)	leaf, loaf, tablet
枝	*zhī*	3 (nature, tools, other man-made objects)	rose, pen, arrow / rifle

Table 1: Contents of the main database for the e-dictionary. Each role in the table is a sub-database in the system.

Studies show that native speakers of Chinese tend to take a cognitively-based bottom-up approach as a strategy to the learning of classifiers while second language learners of Chinese tend to take a top-down approach but often find their learning outcome inefficient (Soh and Gao, 2009; Gao, 2010; Quek and Gao, 2011). The cognitive approach taken for the design of the database is based on the findings of empirical studies on Chinese classifier learning by adults and children of both native and non-native speakers of Chinese. The classifier-based classifications of noun categories that reflect the ontological knowledge of this category of linguistic terms and its structure are assumed to be able to activate learners' cognitive processes when exploring the pragmatic use of classifiers.

3 Noun-based Semantic Features of Classifiers Decomposed

Table 1 is an illustration of the contents of the main database for the e-dictionary. Each role in the table is a sub-database in the system.

Table 1 is a demonstration of the semantic features of some most commonly used noun classifiers and their associated nouns. Through semantic decomposition of the noun-based classifier features, the cognitive mapping between a classifier and its associated nouns are revealed. Take the classifier *tiáo* for example (see Figure 1). It is associated with nouns such as rainbow, leg, snake, cucumber, road, scarf, potato chip, boat and necklace, which are from nine of the eleven noun categories listed in Section 2. Despite of the different categories they belong to, the nine nouns share one same property — the shape of the noun referents that is defined as 'longitudinal'. This shows that the classifier *tiáo* is inhabited with this semantic feature and it is possibly the cognitive basis on which native speakers of Chinese associate it with the related noun referents accordingly.

Similarly, the classifier *gēn* is used with the nouns such as stick, bone, banana, pillar, sausage, needle, and ribbon that belong to seven noun categories respectively. These nouns possess the same 'longitudinal' feature as *tiáo* does. This means that extracting one same feature from *gēn* and *tiáo* is not helpful enough for learners to understand the differences between the two classifiers though classifying nouns into ontological categories can constrain the interference to learners to a certain extent. What needs to be further specified is to define each noun with a unique feature of its own, no matter whether it is from its lexical semantic meanings, pragmatic functions, or human perceptions. For example, in addition to the feature labelled as 'longitudinal', 'for supporting walking' is added as a feature to 'stick', 'a piece of human skeleton' to 'bone', 'turning from green to yellow when ripe' to 'banana', 'one end stuck to the ground' to 'pillar'. More specifications are needed until finally each noun is distinguished from other nouns that are associated with one same classifier. These definitions are the core part of the database in the e-learning tool system linked to the e-dictionary.

4 Methodology

4.1 Application of Cognitive Strategies in Noun Classifier Acquisition

In this section we describe an approach that is used for extending the design of the e-dictionary to that of an e-learning tool as another part of the project. Developed first in the software environment of FileMaker Pro 8.5 (see Figure 2), the dictionary is established on a database system. Categorical records created as data files are used to store the associated nouns. The records created so far include eleven categories of nouns as are described in Section 2. Such a categorization appears explicit, but its top-down approach fails to reveal the feature-based mapping between a classifier and its associated nouns. The objective of the e-learning approach, on the other hand, is to guide users to search for correct classifier and noun pairs by looking for the defined features of the noun referents, firstly from those broadly defined as 'animacy', 'shape', 'size', 'thickness', 'length', and 'function' to those specific ones extracted from each particular noun referent.

With such a bottom-up approach, the e-dictionary allows users to learn to use the particularly interrelated features of a classifier and its associated noun referents in a case-by-case fashion. In this way learners can better understand the point that a classifier reflects the cognitive classification of its associated noun referents. Each individual record thus contains both general and specific information of a classifier and its associated nouns as data entries, The features decomposed from the noun referents are

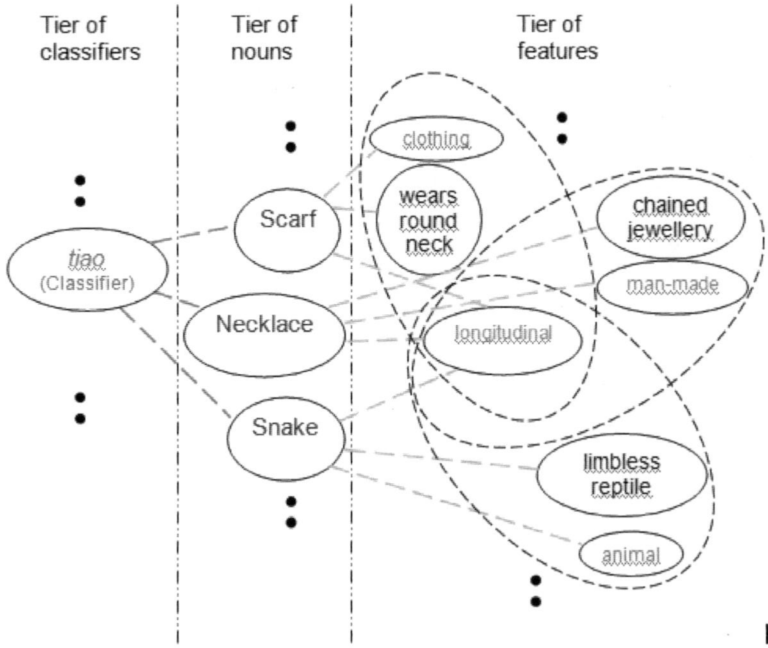

Figure 1: Mapping among the tiers of classifiers, nouns, and defined features.

defined and recorded as independent data entries linked to the e-learning tool. For example, if a learner wants to know which classifier is the correct one for 'boat', he or she can enter the word 'boat', find its category as 'vehicles', and choose its shape as 'longitudinal'. Then *tiáo* should automatically pop up in this case because 'boat' is the only noun referent from the 'vehicles' category (see Table 2). In other cases where there are two or more noun referents that are featured as 'longitudinal', the user will be guided to look for a more specific or unique feature with a few more clicks on the users' interface.

The e-learning environment in the dictionary also provides users the classifier phrases that are commonly used but they may not be easy for learners to acquire. Take the classifier *zhī* for example. It is associated with noun referents that belong to 'animals and body-parts', and 'man-made objects', such as 'bird', 'hand', and 'pen'. The unique perceptual features of these noun referents are identified and built into the e-learning system so that users can click different categories on the interface to make particular associations as long as they have some general knowledge of the noun referents in terms of functions and perceptual features.

CL in Character	**CL in Pinyin**	**Associated nouns in Chinese**	**Associated nouns in English**	**Associated noun categories**	**Shape**
根	*gēn*	电线杆	telegraph pole	buildings	longitudinal
根	*gēn*	骨头	bone	humans & body parts	longitudinal
根	*gēn*	棍	stick	tools	longitudinal
根	*gēn*	黄瓜	cucumber	vegetables & fruits	longitudinal
根	*gēn*	面条	noodle	food	longitudinal
根	*gēn*	绳子	rope	tools	longitudinal
根	*gēn*	丝带	ribbon	other man-made objects	longitudinal

Table 2: An example of how nouns are grouped in the database.

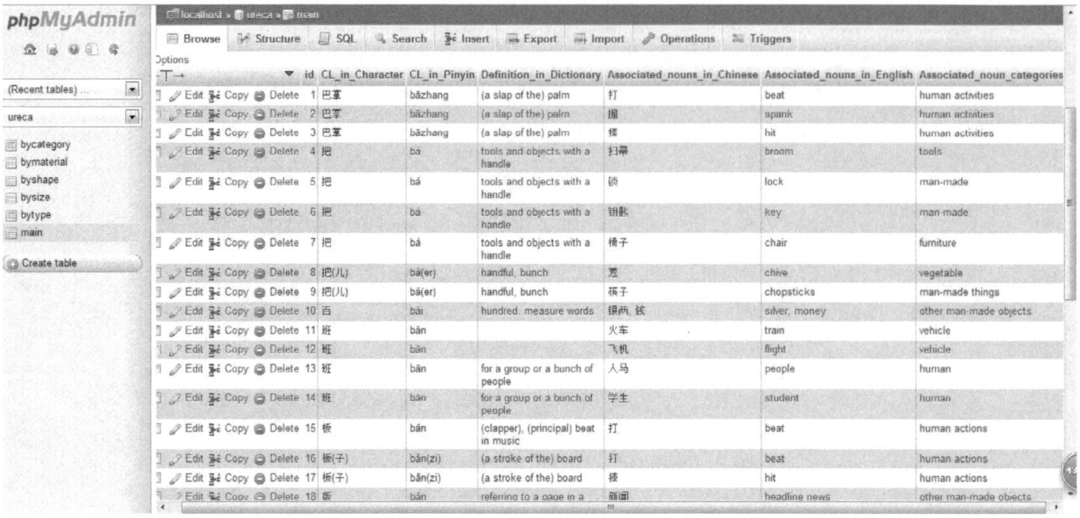

Figure 2: A view of the database interface.

4.2 Database Construction Using MySQL

In a Windows web development environment WAMPSEVER, this database is created under a database management system MySQL. Compared with other database systems, MySQL is relatively more reliable and easier to use, especially for the design of web applications. MySQL database can also be handled and managed using tools like phpMyAdmin. Figure 2 is a display of the database in the web environment.

Data in MySQL are stored in different tables and every unit in each table can be referred to by its row and column index. This feature makes online search convenient and applicable to the design of web application.

As shown in Figure 2, there are six tables that have been created in the database. In table ‘main’, data are sorted by classifiers. Basically, this table contains all of the information in a conventional dictionary that takes classifiers as lexical entries. This table is mainly used for searching classifiers for a noun or searching nouns for a classifier. Users can conduct their search for nouns using both Chinese and English. Search in Chinese has been designed to allow input either in Chinese characters or in Pinyin for both classifiers and nouns. The definition of a classifier, its associated nouns in Chinese and English, and the categories that its associated nouns belong to can all be searched categorically. The search outcome is then presented in a result page.

In table ‘byshape’, data are sorted by the shapes of noun referents such as ‘longitudinal’, ‘rectangular’, and ‘round’. In the other tables specific features of noun referents that have been so far defined are sorted respectively by size, quality of material, and ontological categories. In these tables, not every noun in table ‘main’ is included, as some nouns cannot be described using these features. For example, the word ‘customer’ cannot be described under the feature of shape, but it is classified into the category of human. Hence, it exists in table‘bycategory’ but not in the‘byshape’ one.

The database is designed in such a way so as to increase the efficiency of the search function in the web application. The idea of implementing this searching function is to add in the conditions one by one so as to narrow down the search field. For example, ‘hair’ is in the category of ‘human & body parts’ with features ‘longitudinal’, ‘thin’ and ‘soft’. Users can conduct the following step-by-step search:

1. Search in table ‘bycategory’ to find all the nouns in the category of ‘human & body parts’. Call them Group 1.

2. Search nouns with shape ‘longitudinal’ and in Group 1 in table ‘byshape’. Call them Group 2.

3. Search in table ‘bysize’ for the nouns with the condition ‘thin’ and in Group 2. Call them Group 3.

(a) Input page.

(b) Drop-down list search page.

Figure 3: The web application user interface.

4. Search in table'bymaterial', for the nouns with the condition 'soft'.

At Step 4 when the condition 'soft' is chosen, users should be left with the only noun 'hair'. As the sizes of Groups 1, 2 and 3 become smaller, the search time is reduced. If more features are added, then the steps of search can be repeated until the target noun is found.

4.3 Design of the Web Application Interface

The web application interface is designed using PHP, a server-side scripting language. Basically, it is a dynamic web page connected to the MySQL database built up for this purpose. It means that the content of this web application depends on the database and what is submitted to the server. On the client side or the web application interface for users, as shown in Figure 3a and Figure 3b, HTML language is applied to build up the basic structure as well as the presentation of the website.

The method used in the design of the web application interface make the e-learning tool instructive and self-exploratory. Once a user clicks one of the three links on the side bar, he or she will be directed to a webpage shown in Figure 3a or Figure 3b, where the search function is contained in an HTML form. With HTML form attribute 'action', data will be submitted to a specific page, that is, the php script containing that search function.

Inside the respective php script, there will be several common command lines:

```
@ $db = new mysqli('localhost', 'root', '', 'ureca');
  $db->set_charset("utf8");
if (mysqli_connect_errno()) {
  echo 'Error: Could not connect to database.';
  echo 'Please try again later.';
  exit;  }
```

These commands are to connect to and set the character set of the database built up for this purpose. Here *utf8* is used as there are both English and Chinese characters in the database. On these three web pages, forms are submitted using the 'post' method. POST method sends form-data as HTTP (Hypertext Transfer Protocol) post transaction and has no limitations on the size of data. However, restrictions may exist due to the nature of the database. Search results will then be grouped and displayed, with searchable words hyperlinked. Here the method used is GET, which works better for non-secure data with a limited size.

This web application interface enables learners to discover a noun classifier in three types of search, 'searching a noun for its classifier(s)', 'searching a classifier for its associated noun(s)', and 'searching classifiers for a group of nouns by restricting one or more conditions'.

- Search type 1: *Searching a noun for its classifier(s).*
  This function is similar to any other online dictionaries. Learners insert a noun to do a simple and direct search. On the result page learners can see which classifier or classifiers can be applied to the noun and the definitions of the classifier(s). This is an early design for the e-dictionary. An example of the steps is given in Figure 3b.

- Search type 2: *searching a classifier for its associated noun(s).*
  This function is for learners to start their search with a classifier. It is assumed that learners had learnt a classifier but had not known yet what nouns could be used with the classifier. The search result is shown on a new page that includes the definition of the classifier and its associated nouns.

The difference between search types 1 and 2 is that with search type 1 the result is simple and direct. Learners can understand right away how to form a classifier phrase with the result given. The result of search type 2, however, can display all the nouns that a single classifier can be associated with. Learners of Chinese at the beginning stage may feel intimidated seeing the result showing more nouns than they expect as they may not have learned yet why these different nouns are all related to each other.

- Search type 3: *searching classifiers for a group of nouns by restricting one or more conditions.*
  Instead of keeping all the conditions as the default in search types 1 and 2, learners can choose one condition or more at a time from the drop-down lists. The chosen lists allow the system to fetch desired data directly from the databases. Learners can delete any of the chosen conditions to start a new search and to compare the results. This function is for more advanced learners who have learned the general principles of classifier-noun associations and who have a clear target in their search for a particular type of classifiers or nouns.

Further search is also designed in the primary result page. This function is currently shown as a hyperlink, which is dynamically generated and assigned with a value in advance. The varieties of search functions and illustrations are expected to eventually enhance learners' understanding of the multi-dimensional noun-classifier associations.

5 Discussion

What is presented in this paper is the progress of an on-going project on the building up of an e-learning tool for learning Chinese classifiers. The aim of this project is to clarify the embedded relationships between classifiers and their associated nouns so as to assist Chinese language learners in the acquisition of classifier phrases. At the first stage of the project, classifiers and their associated nouns were collected from dictionaries and other resources. A database for the e-dictionary part which contains the functions that are characteristic of conventional dictionaries was designed and set up. Learners can search for a classifier or a noun for their association as a classifier phrase. Then, a feature-based approach in designing the classifier e-dictionary was extended to an e-learning environment created for learners to explore. At the current stage, the task is on the design and setting up of an e-learning system attached to the e-dictionary. As an experiment, MySQL was used to build up the database shared by the conventional dictionary and the e-learning system.

The structure of this database is formed in the way in which classifiers and nouns are stored in different tables but can be linked together. All the information stored in different tables was connected through respective grouping criteria which allow the data to be extended to the e-learning environemnt. One table contains one type of information, such as classifiers in character, classifiers in pinyin, definitions of classifiers, types of classifiers, classifier associated nouns in Chinese and English, categories of the associated nouns, and semantic features of the nouns. Every two tables share at least one common parameter, which enables cross-table search as described in Section 4.2. Such a design is able to boost the efficiency of the search function. In addition, the database can be enriched easily through MySQL code or phpMyAdmin to import new data.

A web application for self-learning in the e-learning environment was designed using PHP language. It serves as an e-learning tool for learning Chinese classifiers. The various searching functions provide progressive search for specified features of classifiers' associated nouns and their classified categories.

The feasibility of the functions of the e-learning tool and its web application need to be further improved. Currently there are a few limitations. For example, subjectivity is a limitation of this database. In the process of decomposing nouns into respective semantic features, human cognition plays an important role. However, this parameter varies from person to person. Moreoever, speakers of Chinese in different regions may tend to use different cognitive strategies in their associations with the semantic meanings of classifiers. Therefore, data from experiments and empirical studies are needed for the future improvement of the semantic analysis and descriptions of the noun-classifier associations. Another aspect to improve is that regional featured uses of certain classifiers such as Singaporean Chinese speakers' use of *lì* with noun referents that are both big and small (e.g., 'watermelon' and 'bean') can be explained and included in separate tables so that learners can be aware of the regional differences in classifier use.

The advantages of the web application design are its multipurpose search functions and flexible links to the various parts of the database behind. With the various search functions, learners will be able to investigate classifiers from different aspects, which is ideal for self-learning. On the page of 'Searching a noun for its classifier(s)', both Chinese and English entries are acceptable, which makes it easier for learners to explore and make a flexible use of its learning functions. However, on the page of 'Searching a classifier for its associated noun(s)', only Chinese character entries are available. A future addition can be made to allow entries by Pinyin as well.

For the database development in the future, the web application is designed to be linked to the database in a dynamical fashion. Any changes made to the database can be reflected on the web page automatically. This will also allow us to make further development without much of a change in the current layout in the e-learning system.

6 Conclusion

Based on the Chinese classifier e-dictionary of (Gao, 2011), designed to help students learn the proper use of Chinese classifiers, this paper further explores the designs of the database and of an e-learning tool interface to better understand the association of classifiers and nouns. In this experimental version of the e-learning tool design, 859 classifiers and 6420 associated nouns were stored and classified in different tables according to the respective noun referents' semantic features and prominent cognitive features. The system built-up with MySQL has shown its convenient linkage to database management tool phpMyAdmin and web-design language PHP. As the base of the e-learning tool, the database with an interface built-in can be searched step by step with individual or combined functions. The results can be displayed on the users' webpage. Learners can examine the property of a classifier and the link between this classifier and its associated nouns from several perspectives via various search functions. The multi-functional feature of this webpage is the design of the drop-down list search, which allows users to discover classifiers' noun-dependent features case by case. To make use of the advantage of internet, further investigation of another feature within a search can be made possible through hyperlinked text.

The final goal is to make the outcome of this project available online as learning resources for the general public and as an e-learning tool for Chinese language learners. Further development of this project and explorations of other possible database designs are necessary as our end goal is to provide an effective learning tool. Experimental studies are also needed to discriminate the subjectivity of the descriptions of human congnition in the illustrations of classifier-noun associations.

Acknowledgements

I would like to thank my research students Ong Shi Lun for the data entry, and Chen Jiaxing for her work on the database trials.

References

Yu-Chia Chang, Jason S. Chang, Hao-Jan Chen, and Hsien-Chin Liou. 2008. An automatic collocation writing assistant for Taiwanese EFL learners: A case of corpus-based NLP technology. *Computer Assisted Language Learning*, 21(3):283–299.

Yuen Ren Chao. 1968. *A Grammar of Spoken Chinese*. University of California Press.

Graham Davies. 2011. Introduction to multimedia CALL. In Graham Davies, editor, *Information and Communications Technology for Language Teachers (ICT4LT)*. Thames Valley University, Slough. `www.ict4lt.org/en/en_mod2-2.htm`.

Randall P. Donaldson and Margaret A. Haggstrom. 2006. *Changing Language Education Through CALL*. Routledge.

Helena Hong Gao. 2010. A study of the Swedish speakers' learning of Chinese classifiers. *Nordic Journal of Linguistics*, 33:56–63.

Helena Hong Gao. 2011. E-learning design for Chinese classifiers: Reclassification of nouns for a novel approach. In R. Kwan, C. McNaught, P. Tsang, F. Lee Wang, and K. C. Li, editors, *Communications in Computer and Information Science (CCIS)*, number 177, pages 186–199. Springer-Verlag.

Hui Guo and Huayan Zhong. 2005. Chinese classifier assignment using SVMs. In *4th SIGHAN Workshop on Chinese Language Processing*, pages 25–31, Jeju, South Korea.

Chu-Ren Huang and Katherine Ahrens. 2003. Individuals, kinds and events: Classifier coercion of nouns. *Language Sciences*, 25:353–373.

Soonhee Hwang, Ae-Sun Yoon, and Hyuk-Chul Kwon. 2008. Semantic representation of Korean numeral classifier and its ontology building for HLT applications. *Language Resources and Evaluation*, 42:151–172.

Adrian Mallon. 2006. ELingua Latina: Designing a classical-language e-learning resource. *Computer Assisted Language Learning*, 19(4):373–387.

Eric Nichols, Francis Bond, and Daniel Flickinger. 2005. Robust ontology acquisition from machine-readable dictionaries. In *19th International Joint Conference on Artificial Intelligence (IJCAI)*, pages 1111–1116, Edinburgh, UK.

Sergei Nirenburg and Victor Raskin. 2004. *Ontological Semantics*. MIT Press.

Andrew G. Philpot, Michael Fleischman, and Eduard H. Hovy. 2003. Semi-automatic construction of a general purpose ontology. In *Proceedings of the International Lisp Conference*, pages 1–8, New York, NY, USA.

See Ling Quek and Helena Hong Gao. 2011. An experimental investigation of the cognitive basis of Malaysian Chinese speakers' association of one noun with multiple classifiers. In *12th Chinese Lexical Semantics Workshop*, pages 232–243, Taipei, Taiwan.

Ning En Christabelle Soh and Helena Hong Gao. 2009. Chinese noun classifier usage by Singaporean bilingual children. *Proceedings of the URECA@NTU*, pages 88–91.

John F. Sowa. 2000. *Knowledge Representation*. Brooks Cole Publishing Co.

James H.-Y. Tai and Lianqing Wang. 1990. A semantic study of the classifier Tiao. *Journal of the Chinese Language Teachers Association*, 25(1):35–56.

Weiwei Yue. 2009. Contrastive analysis of quantifiers in Chinese and English from a cognitive perspective. Master's thesis, Shandong Normal University.

Default Physical Measurements in SUMO

Francesca Quattri
The Hong Kong Polytechnic University
Hong Kong
francesca.quattri@connect.polyu.hk

Adam Pease*
adam.pease@articulatesoftware.com

John P. McCrae
Universität Bielefeld
Germany
jmccrae@cit-ec.uni-bielefeld.de

Abstract

The following paper presents a further extension of the Suggested Upper Merged Ontology (SUMO), i. e. the development of default physical measurements for most of its classes (`Artifacts`, `Devices`, `Objects`) and respective children. The extension represents an arbitrary, computable and reproducible approximation of defaults for upper and middle-level concepts. The paper illustrates advantages of such extension, challenges encountered during the compilation, related work and future research.

1 Introduction

Over the last fourteen years SUMO (Pease, 2011; Niles and Pease, 2001) has been developed into a large, general-domain ontology, which currently[1] includes 20,000 terms and 80,000 axioms stated in higher-order logic (Pease and Schulz, 2014). SUMO provides an open source environment for the development of logical theories called SIGMA (Pease, 2011; Pease, 2003b). This enables the manipulation of different formal languages (including TPTP and OWL), (Adam Pease and Sams, 2003; Pease, 2003a). Among them, the logical formal language SUO-KIF has been selected for the development of knowledge-based (or KB) terms, through which SUMO can be searched. Another possible search of terms in SUMO is via the Princeton WordNet ®, to which the ontology has been fully mapped(Pease and Niles, 2003; Pease and Li, 2003; Pease and Murray, 2003).

In the first part of this paper, after introducing SUMO in generic terms, we explain the motivation behind the undergone extension of 300+ physical default measurements (the term 'default' is hereby used as synonym for 'approximation' or 'estimation'). The second part deals with the advantages and issues encountered during the compilation of the defaults, and presents some practical examples of defaults and higher-order annotation. Related research and future work follow.

2 Default physical measurements in SUMO

The original intent behind the development of default physical measurements in SUMO is to provide factual peer-reviewed information about physical measurements of ontological classes. Almost all approximations of the default values have been established with reference to current ISO standards or norms set by governmental regulations. Only in the case that standard values are not provided or could not be retrieved, the compiler of the defaults has relied on personal judgment. In both cases, all defaults have been manually double-checked for validity by the compiler and the SUMO developer.

SUMO seems to be one of the first general-knowledge ontologies to provide extensive information on physical default measurements. Other data bases like DBpedia have (according to the authors' knowledge) just recently started to provide a similar kind of information.[2] The physical defaults represent a big repository of approximated values based on physical properties, such as length, volume, size, width and

*Same affiliation of the first author.

[1] As for the year 2014.

[2] `http://dbpedia.org/property/reference`

Zock/Rapp/Huang (eds.): Proceedings of the 4th Workshop on Cognitive Aspects of the Lexicon, pages 138–143, Dublin, Ireland, August 23, 2014.

height. The approximation, as the term itself says, is partly arbitrary, computable, and comprehensively conducted. The measurements are formalized in minimum and maximum default values. The wording 'maximum' and 'minimum' should not been treated as the highest and lowest values attached to the respective `Artifacts`, but as some high or low values these `Entitys` can own.

2.1 Advantages

We believe that the compilation of the defaults accomplishes three major advantages in the current format of the SUMO ontology:

1. Ontological formalization.
2. Objective adjustable values of physical properties.
3. Computable reproducible estimations of physical values.

Point (1) mirrors SUMO attempt as extensive ontology of general knowledge. Natural language fails in providing specificity for every single word and predicate, partly due to polysemy, synonymy as well as objective limitations of extensive precise formal description. We often refer to a term in vague sense and meaning, such as in the case of 'car' or 'truck'. For further specification of the same, we tend to create new lemmas, derivatives and compounds. SUMO underscores a lemma in its definitional and ontological extent and the defaults consider the lemma as prototypical. As for its definitional extent, SUMO provides the definition of the lemma as reported in the Princeton WordNet ®. As ontological and prototypical entity, the lemma is described in first-order and/or higher-order logic and thus transformed into a SUO-KIF KB term. In the case of `Truck`, the term is enlisted under `TransportationDevice` in SUMO. The following description in first-order logic (containing the quantifier 'exists') specifically states: "If a `TransportationDevice` is an *instance* of a `Truck`, then there exists *a kind of* `Object` such that *a kind of* `Object` is a *subclass* of `Object` and *kind of* `Object` is a `Cargo` type of `TransportationDevice`.

```
(=>
    (instance ?T Truck)
    (exists (?L)
        (and
            (subclass ?L Object)
            (cargoType ?T ?L))))
```

Figure 1.: Example of a first-order axiom in SUO-KIF

```
Entity 2
    Physical 5
        Object 11
            Artifact 58
                Device 112
                    TransportationDevice 9
                        Vehicle 12
                            LandVehicle 10
                                RoadVehicle 6
                                PoweredVehicle 12
                                    SelfPoweredRoadVehicle 4
                                    CargoVehicle 1
                                        Truck 3
                                            MilitarySupplyTruck
                                            LightTruck
                                            TruckTractor 1
                                                PeterbiltTruck
```

Figure 2.: Graphic documentation of the relation *subclass* for the term `Truck` with relative enumerated *direct-children*

Fig. 2 represents a graphic documentation of the same term as taxonomically listed (with the selected levels "above" and "below" `Truck` set to the value 10). The graph can be further extended to more levels, thus enabling a comprehensive look of all the branches that depart from the upper concept `Entity`. As for fig. 2., SUMO provides a specific taxonomy of the different kinds of `Truck`.

The default measurements in fig. 3 have been partly set by looking at standard measures for the same `Artifact`[3]:

```
;; Truck
(defaultMinimumLength Truck (MeasureFn 39 Foot))
(defaultMaximumLength Truck (MeasureFn Fn 49 Foot))
(defaultMinimumHeight Truck (MeasureFn 13 Foot))
(defaultMaximumHeight Truck (MeasureFn 15 Foot))
(defaultMinimumWidth Truck (MeasureFn 8.4 Foot))
(defaultMaximumWidth Truck (MeasureFn 9 Foot))

;;Vehicle
(defaultMinimumLength Vehicle (MeasureFn 13.5 Foot))
(defaultMaximumLength Vehicle (MeasureFn 14 Foot))
(defaultMinimumHeight Vehicle (MeasureFn 4.6 Foot))
(defaultMaximumHeight Vehicle (MeasureFn 4.8 Foot))
(defaultMinimumWeight Vehicle (MeasureFn 1 TonMass))
(defaultMaximumWeight Vehicle (MeasureFn 1.7 TonMass))
```

Figure 3.: Extensions of physical defaults for `Truck` and `Vehicle`

In fig. 4 the physical default values for `CreditCard` have been established according to the international standard ISO/IEC 7810:2003.

```
;;CreditCard
(defaultMinimumLength CreditCard (MeasureFn 3.4 Inch))
(defaultMaximumLength CreditCard (MeasureFn 3.4 Inch))
(defaultMinimumHeight CreditCard (MeasureFn 2.1 Inch))
(defaultMaximumHeight CreditCard (MeasureFn 2.1 Inch))
```

Figure 4.: Extensions of physical defaults for `CreditCard`

The (2) advantage in having physical default measurements is the objectivity of the properties they are calculated upon. The defaults are set on objectively comparable properties, such as height, volume, weight, length and width. These are all features of size and mass that can be counted and approximated, with different units of measures.

Finally, the (3) advantage that we reckon exists in having the defaults is their computability. Despite being relative and partially arbitrary measures[4], the defaults are adjustable and reproducible, which makes them adaptable to representation models, peer-review and further estimations. We believe that this way of calculating defaults of physical `Objects` is certainly more reliable than other attempted methods (e. g. (Bennett, 2001):117-118).[5]

2.2 Issues encountered during the research

Some challenges were encountered during the compilation of default measurements.

- The defaults cover classes of upper concepts in SUMO, and part of their children, but not the predicates that can possibly collocate with them. For example, concepts like `Aircraft` or `Helicopter` are covered in SUMO, but not expressions like 'light aircraft' or 'civilian helicopter'. Sometimes, SUMO already provides a logical description of these adjectives as incorporated in the concept itself, as in the case of `MilitaryAircraft`, `SelfPoweredRoadVehicle`, or `PrintedBook` (fig. 4), meaning that rather then specifying the predicate, a new term is created. SUMO users should bare in mind that the `Artifacts` in SUMO always aim at representing a

[3]As in the case of `Truck` the defaults have been established by looking at the standard sizes as set by the U.S. Department of Transportation and Federal Highway Administration, `http://www.ops.fhwa.dot.gov/freight/sw/index.htm`

[4]As previously discussed in the paper, the defaults have been assigned on a subjective basis in case standard defaults could not been retrieved/are not available. Also, the defaults sometimes apply to one country's regulations, and are therefore not internationally valid. Finally, the defaults have been given with selected units of measures (e. g. inches instead of centimeters, or pounds instead of kilograms. This specified, one should bear in mind the intention of the default extensions, namely to provide an approximation of prototypical, not universal `Artifacts`.

[5]Bennett, in his study on physical objects and geographic concepts, tries to delimit the boundaries of vague entities by providing answers to size-related questions (e. g. "How large an area must a forest occupy? Are there any constraints in its shape? Must it be maximal or could it share a border with another region of forest?"). In SUMO, we believe that the defaults, through which some of these questions can be answered, are more reliable, since anchored to standard values.

prototypical form of the same Object, i. e. a kind that is possibly shared in the collective thinking. The representation for Book as showed below aims therefore at representing the possibly most commonly form of Book known, namely a printed and not an electronic version of the same.

```
(=>
  (instance ?BOOK PrintedBook)
  (exists (?SHEET1 ?SHEET2)
      (and
          (component ?SHEET1 ?BOOK)
          (component ?SHEET2 ?BOOK)
          (instance ?SHEET1 PrintedSheet)
          (instance ?SHEET2 PrintedSheet)
            (not
                 (equal ?SHEET1 ?SHEET2)))))

(=>
```

```
(and
  (instance ?ARTICLE1 Article)
  (instance ?BOOK Book)
  (subsumesContentInstance ?BOOK ?
  ARTICLE1))
(exists (?ARTICLE2)
  (and
    (instance ?ARTICLE2 Article)
    (not
       (equal ?ARTICLE2 ?ARTICLE1))
    (subsumesContentInstance ?
    BOOK ?ARTICLE2))))
```

Figure 5.: Comparison between the logical annotation for Book in SUMO with the collocational unit printed + Book

It needs to be specified that the concept of Attribute in SUMO is differently interpreted from the concept of predicate or adjective in natural language. Attributes in the Upper Merged Ontology are instances of upper classes, but there also exists classes of Attributes. The Attribute class can contain subclasses (e. g. Female, Male, BiologicalAttribute), but these have not been assigned default physical values. The motivation is basically that we cannot numerically define *abstracta*, such as gender, color, or emotions and feelings. In the case of abstract concepts, such as StockMarket or InterestRate, we have tried to figure out these, where possible, as physical objects (e. g. the place where financial transactions take place, or the sheet where rates are printed on).

Other sort of literally definable attributes (including comparative forms) are included in SUMO in the form of relations, which express, *inter alia*, equations and inequalities (greaterThan, smallerThan, larger, earlier, interiorPart, temporalPart, (Pease, 2011):113). Finally, what is defined in SUMO as PhysicalAttribute should not be confused with the physical default values added to the ontology. Instances of this class include Compliance, Conductivity, Flammable, Inductance, MutualInductance, Resistivity, Stiffness.

Despite the lack of a comprehensive cover of linguistically definable collocational compounds in SUMO (as above mentioned), we estimate that it is not impossible to approximate values for them, given the existence of defaults for the concept that carries the predicate. For instance, it can be derived that BigHouse (not enlisted in SUMO) is something that can be 1.9 times bigger than a Studio, or 0.1 times smaller than a Mansion, once the standard values for House, Studio and Mansion are given.

Given a partial ordering of gradable adjectives[6] that apply to a particular noun, we could create axioms (thus inducing a productive process) which would then partition the physical space with respect to that particular adjective. The fact that we have axioms would eventually release us from defining defaults for each class. In other words, the most frequently an adjective collocates with a class or a subclass, the higher is the chance to develop an axiom(s) that enables us to calculate the defaults for these same classes automatically.

- SUMO provides ontological information regarding concepts in their a-contextual and unidiomatic form. SUMO terms are not polysemous, therefore there is no notion of reusing a term to mean something else. This also means that specific cases of use for a term in specific ontologies, or as applied to metaphorical/idiomatic expressions, are not taken into account (e.ġ. turning tables'; 'cleared table'). Instead, we specialize terms via subclassing and adding axioms on the subclasses term when a new term is needed for a specific domain.

[6]As interpreted by: (de Melo and Bansal, 2013; Schulam and Fellbaum, 2010; de Melo, 2014a; de Melo, 2014b).

- The defaults are based on arbitrary subjective approximations of prototypes. The provided information has been carefully peer-reviewed and the defaults can be used, re-used, or changed according to the user's needs. The intent is in fact to provide a basic estimation of the physical values for that concept. Furthermore, we have used specific units of measurements to carry on the approximations (e. g. inches versus centimeters, tons and pounds versus kilos). We acknowledge that this might hinder or slow down the reausability process.

3 Practical applications of defaults in linguistic disambiguation

Since the development of the first several hundreds physical default measurements, their applicability and usefulness has been tested in two research studies.[7] The defaults have proven helpful in linguistic analysis, particularly in the disambiguation of vague terms, such as vague predicates and concepts, as well as more complex linguistic forms, such as similes and metaphors. The advantage of having physical defaults based on standards and norms has given further validity to the disambiguation process.

3.1 Default measurements and adjectives (*lemon*OILS and SUMO

The use of first order logic seems to break in the case of adjectives. In a recent research, we therefore make an in-depth analysis of different kinds of attributes and how they can be represented in different ontology-lexicon interfaces (*lemon*OILS and SUMO), and discuss the implications of the modelling with application to ontology-based question answering.

3.2 Default measurements, metaphors and similes

In another current study (see previous footnote), we use default physical measurements to disambiguate similes from metaphors. Starting from the claim that the taught difference between metaphors and similes in terms of which has or does not have 'like' or 'as' in its form is not a linguistically and cognitively satisfactory statement, we design a computable model to test the validity of novel metaphors and similes and use the physical default measurements for our purpose.

4 Future work

The extension of physical default measurements in SUMO is not intended to be the last of its kind. In our future work, we plan for instance a better specification of dimensionality. During the compilation of the physical defaults, we have in fact sometimes encountered the challenge of defining first the geometrical property proper of the concept. For instance, taking a `Leaf`, do we usually refer to its length, or to its height? Google can help to a certain extent in cases like this. A better disambiguation of contextually dependent measurements (length versus height, or width versus length) is therefore needed. A further improvement includes the compilation of mostly all subclasses and their children in higher-order logic as KB terms, as well as the assignment to them of physical defaults. To enable an automatic productive process in the generation of automatic axioms (as mentioned in 2.2), both with respect to collocational forms and with regards to the similar physical defaults that may exist between parent and child, we still need to evaluate whether there should exist a mechanism for conflict resolution or overwrite. If we take for instance the example of `Snake`, we consider at the moment that this instance of `Reptile` most probably can inherit some of the properties of the parent, and viceversa. As showed in 2.1 (fig. 3) above though, this derivation does not seem so obvious or even applicable, since there might be prototypical properties that might appear for one concept, but not for the other, or given the too high discrepancy of measurements.

Finally, once this comprehensive framework of properties and intuitive specification of defaults has been created, we could conduct psycholinguistic empirical experiments to determine what are the defaults and prototypes and examples that different classes of human beings hold to be true. This could give us indication on how and if prototypicality overlayers with dimensionality.

[7]Submitted accepted papers for the CogALex Workshop, COLING 2014, Dublin, Ireland and the CCLCC Workshop at ESSLI 2014, Tuebingen, Germany.

5 Conclusion

In this paper we present a current extension of the general-domain ontology SUMO, i. e. the compilation of default physical measurements for 300+ classes and subclasses. The aim of this extension is to provide a peer-reviewed reliable, reusable and reproducible estimation of physical values for the ontology. The defaults have already proven to be helpful in the disambiguation of vague predicates and concepts, as well as similes and metaphors. As open-source application, constantly updated and improved, it is planned to apply further changes to the SUMO ontology, which include an even more comprehensive development of physical defaults, as well as the inclusion of other defaults for other properties. Despite their approximation, the defaults represent a computational ground for representation models and further calculations.

References

W.R. Murray Adam Pease and Michael Sams. 2003. Applying formal methods and representations in a natural language tutor to teach tactical reasoning. In *Proceedings of the 11th International Conference on Artificial Intelligence in Education (AIED) Conference*, pages 349–356. IOS Publications.

Brandon Bennett. 2001. Application of supervaluation semantics to vaguely defined concepts. In Daniel R. Montello, editor, *Proceedings of the 5th International Conference on Spatial Information Theory (COSIT'01)*, number 2205 in LNCS, pages 108–123, Morro Bay. Springer.

Gerard de Melo and Mohit Bansal. 2013. Good, great, excellent: Global inference of semantic intensities. *Transactions of the Association for Computational Linguistics*, 1:279–290.

Gerard de Melo. 2014a. From linked data to tighly integrated data. LREC 2014 Workshop on Linked Data in Linguistics (LDL-2014). Invited speaker.

Gerard de Melo. 2014b. Link prediction in semantic knowledge graphs. The Hong Kong Polytechnic University, March. Invited speaker.

Ian Niles and Adam Pease. 2001. Towards a standard upper ontology. In Christopher A. Welty and Barry Smith, editors, *Proceedings of the 2nd International Conference on Formal Ontology in Information Systems (FOIS 2001)*.

Adam Pease and John Li. 2003. Agent-mediated knowledge engineering collaboration. In *Proceedings of the AAAI 2003 Spring Symposium on Agent-Mediated Knowledge Management*.

Adam Pease and W.R. Murray. 2003. An english to logic translator for ontology-based knowledge representation languages. In *Proceedings of the 2003 IEEE International Conference on Natural Language Processing and Knowledge Engineering*, pages 777–783.

Adam Pease and Ian Niles. 2003. Linking lexicons and ontologies: Mapping wordnet to the suggested upper merged ontology. In *Proceedings of the IEEE International Conference on Information and Knowledge Engineering*, pages 412–416.

Adam Pease and Stephan Schulz. 2014. Knowledge engineering for large ontologies with sigmakee 3.0. Submitted accepted version for journal paper.

Adam Pease. 2003a. Mapping linguistic elements to logical expressions. In *Workshop on Ontological Knowledge and Linguistic Coding at the 25th Annual Meeting of the German Linguistics Society (Deutsche Gesellschaft f́ur Sprachwissenschaft)*.

Adam Pease. 2003b. The sigma ontology development environment. In *Working Notes of the IJCAI-2003 Workshop on Ontology and Distributed Systems*, volume 71.

Adam Pease. 2011. *Ontology: A Practical Guide*. Articulate Software Press, Angwin, CA.

Peter F. Schulam and Christiane Fellbaum. 2010. Automatically determining the semantic gradiation of german adjectives. In *Proceedings of KONVENS*.

*** Formatting Issue - Best Available Paper/Graphic ***

Lexical Access Preference and Constraint Strategies for Improving Multiword Expression Association within Semantic MT Evaluation

Dekai Wu **Lo Chi-kiu** **Markus Saers**
HKUST
Human Language Technology Center
Department of Computer Science and Engineering
Hong Kong University of Science and Technology
{dekai|jackielo|masaers|dekai}@cs.ust.hk

Abstract

We examine lexical access preferences and constraints in computing multiword expression associations from the standpoint of a high-impact extrinsic task-based performance measure, namely semantic machine translation evaluation. In automated MT evaluation metrics, machine translations are compared against human reference translations, which are almost never worded exactly the same way except in the most trivial of cases. Because of this, one of the most important factors in correctly predicting semantic translation adequacy is the accuracy of recognizing alternative lexical realizations of the same multiword expressions in semantic role fillers. Our results comparing bag-of-words, maximum alignment, and inversion transduction grammars indicate that cognitively motivated ITGs provide superior lexical access characteristics for multiword expression associations, leading to state-of-the-art improvements in correlation with human adequacy judgments.

1 Introduction

We investigate lexical access strategies in the context of computing multiword expression associations within automatic semantic MT evaluation metrics—a high-impact real-world extrinsic task-based performance measure. The inadequacy of lexical coverage of multiword expressions is one of the serious issues in machine translation and automatic MT evaluation; there are simply too many forms to enumerate explicitly within the lexicon. Automatic MT evaluation has driven machine translation research for a decade and a half, but until recently little has been done to use lexical semantics as the main foundation for MT metrics. Common surface-form oriented metrics like BLEU (Papineni *et al.*, 2002), NIST (Doddington, 2002), METEOR (Banerjee and Lavie, 2005), CDER (Leusch *et al.*, 2006), WER (Nießen *et al.*, 2000), and TER (Snover *et al.*, 2006) do not explicitly reflect semantic similarity between the reference and machine translations. Several large scale meta-evaluations (Callison-Burch *et al.*, 2006; Koehn and Monz, 2006) have in fact reported that BLEU significantly disagrees with human judgments of translation adequacy.

Recently, the MEANT semantic frame based MT evaluation metrics (Lo and Wu, 2011a, 2012; Lo *et al.*, 2012; Lo and Wu, 2013b), have instead directly couched MT evaluation in the more cognitive terms of semantic frames, by measuring the degree to which the basic event structure is preserved by translation—the "who did what to whom, for whom, when, where, how and why" (Pradhan *et al.*, 2004)—emphasizing that a good translation is one that can successfully be understood by a human. Across a variety of language pairs and genres, MEANT was shown to correlate better with human adequacy judgment than both n-gram based MT evaluation metrics such as BLEU (Papineni *et al.*, 2002), NIST (Doddington, 2002), and METEOR (Banerjee and Lavie, 2005), as well as edit-distance based metrics such as CDER (Leusch *et al.*, 2006), WER (Nießen *et al.*, 2000), and TER (Snover *et al.*, 2006) when evaluating MT output (Lo and Wu, 2011a, 2012; Lo *et al.*, 2012; Lo and Wu, 2013b; Macháček and Bojar, 2013). Furthermore, tuning the parameters of MT systems with MEANT instead of BLEU or TER robustly improves translation

Zock/Rapp/Huang (eds.): Proceedings of the 4th Workshop on Cognitive Aspects of the Lexicon, pages 144–153, Dublin, Ireland, August 23, 2014.

*** Formatting Issue - Best Available Paper/Graphic ***

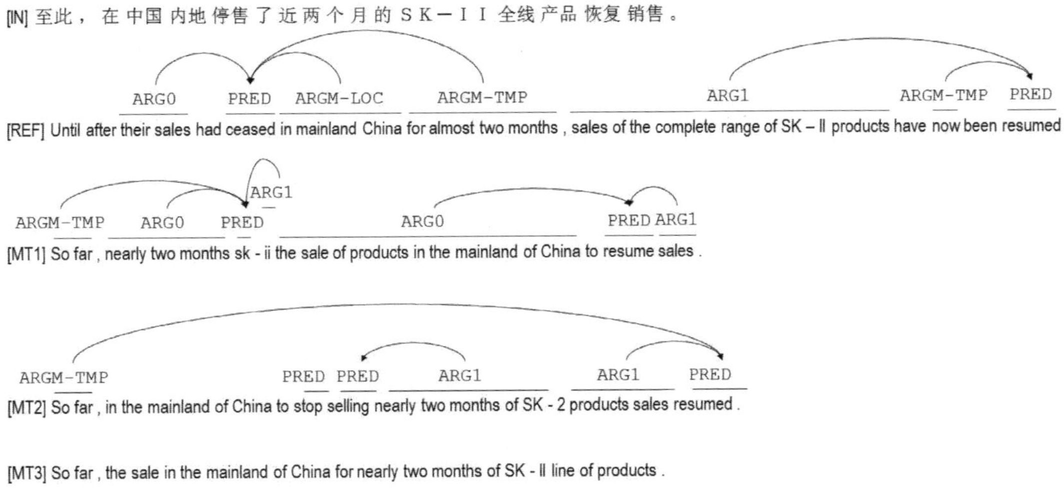

Figure 1: Examples of automatic shallow semantic parses. Both the reference and machine translations are parsed using automatic English SRL. There are no semantic frames for MT3 since automatic SRL decided to drop the predicate.

adequacy (Lo *et al.*, 2013a; Lo and Wu, 2013a; Lo *et al.*, 2013b) across different languages (English and Chinese) and different genres (formal newswire text, informal web forum text and informal public speech).

Because of this, we have chosen to run our lexical association experiments in the context of the necessity of recognizing matching semantic role fillers, approximately 85% of which are multiword expressions in our data, the overwhelming majority of which would not be enumerated within conventional lexicons. We compare four common lexical access approaches to aggregation, preferences, and constraints: bag-of-words, two different types of maximal alignment, and inversion transduction grammar based methods.

2 Background

The MEANT metric measures weighted f-scores over corresponding semantic frames and role fillers in the reference and machine translations. Whereas HMEANT uses human annotation, the automatic versions of MEANT instead replace humans with automatic SRL and alignment algorithms. MEANT typically outperforms BLEU, NIST, METEOR, WER, CDER and TER in correlation with human adequacy judgment, and is relatively easy to port to other languages, requiring only an automatic semantic parser and a monolingual corpus of the output language, which is used to gauge lexical similarity between the semantic role fillers of the reference and translation. More precisely, MEANT computes scores as follows:

1. Apply an automatic shallow semantic parser to both the references and MT output. (Figure 1 shows examples of automatic shallow semantic parses on both reference and MT.)

2. Apply the maximum weighted bipartite matching algorithm to align the semantic frames between the references and MT output according to the lexical similarities of the predicates.

3. For each pair of the aligned frames, apply the maximum weighted bipartite matching algorithm to align the arguments between the reference and MT output according to the lexical similarity of role fillers.

4. Compute the weighted f-score over the matching role labels of these aligned predicates and role fillers according to the following definitions:

***** Formatting Issue - Best Available Paper/Graphic *****

$$
\begin{aligned}
q^0_{i,j} &\equiv \text{ARG j of aligned frame i in MT} \\
q^1_{i,j} &\equiv \text{ARG j of aligned frame i in REF} \\
w^0_i &\equiv \frac{\text{\#tokens filled in aligned frame i of MT}}{\text{total \#tokens in MT}} \\
w^1_i &\equiv \frac{\text{\#tokens filled in aligned frame i of REF}}{\text{total \#tokens in REF}} \\
w_{\text{pred}} &\equiv \text{weight of similarity of predicates} \\
w_j &\equiv \text{weight of similarity of ARG j} \\
\mathbf{e}_{i,\text{pred}} &\equiv \text{the pred of the aligned frame } i \textit{ of the machine translation} \\
\mathbf{f}_{i,\text{pred}} &\equiv \text{the pred of the aligned frame } i \textit{ of the reference translation}
\end{aligned}
$$

$$
\begin{aligned}
\mathbf{e}_{i,j} &\equiv \text{the ARG } j \text{ of the aligned frame } i \textit{ of the machine translation} \\
\mathbf{f}_{i,j} &\equiv \text{the ARG } j \text{ of the aligned frame } i \textit{ of the reference translation} \\
s(e,f) &= \text{lexical similarity of token } e \text{ and } f \\
\text{prec}_{\mathbf{e},\mathbf{f}} &= \frac{\sum_{e\in\mathbf{e}} \max_{f\in\mathbf{f}} s(e,f)}{|\,\mathbf{e}\,|} \\
\text{rec}_{\mathbf{e},\mathbf{f}} &= \frac{\sum_{f\in\mathbf{f}} \max_{e\in\mathbf{e}} s(e,f)}{|\,\mathbf{f}\,|} \\
\text{precision} &= \frac{\sum_i w^0_i \frac{w_{\text{pred}} s_{i,\text{pred}} + \sum_j w_j s_{i,j}}{w_{\text{pred}} + \sum_j w_j |q^0_{i,j}|}}{\sum_i w^0_i} \\
\text{recall} &= \frac{\sum_i w^1_i \frac{w_{\text{pred}} s_{i,\text{pred}} + \sum_j w_j s_{i,j}}{w_{\text{pred}} + \sum_j w_j |q^1_{i,j}|}}{\sum_i w^1_i} \\
\text{MEANT} &= \frac{2 \cdot \text{precision} \cdot \text{recall}}{\text{precision} + \text{recall}}
\end{aligned}
$$

where the possible approaches to defining the lexical associations $s_{i,\text{pred}}$ and $s_{i,j}$ are discussed in the following section. $q^0_{i,j}$ and $q^1_{i,j}$ are the argument of type j in frame i in MT and REF, respectively. w^0_i and w^1_i are the weights for frame i in MT and REF, respectively. These weights estimate the degree of contribution of each frame to the overall meaning of the sentence. w_{pred} and w_j are the weights of the lexical similarities of the predicates and role fillers of the arguments of type j of all frame between the reference translations and the MT output. There is a total of 12 weights for the set of semantic role labels in MEANT as defined in Lo and Wu (2011b). For MEANT, they are determined using supervised estimation via a simple grid search to optimize the correlation with human adequacy judgments (Lo and Wu, 2011a). For UMEANT (Lo and Wu, 2012), they are estimated in an unsupervised manner using relative frequency of each semantic role label in the references and thus UMEANT is useful when human judgments on adequacy of the development set are unavailable.

3 Comparison of multiword expression association approaches

To assess alternative lexical access preferences and constraints for computing multiword expression associations, we now consider four alternative approaches to defining the lexical similarities $s_{i,\text{pred}}$ and $s_{i,j}$, all of which employ a standard context vector model of the individual words/tokens in the multiword expression arguments between the reference and machine translations, as descibed by Lo *et al.* (2012) and Tumuluru *et al.* (2012).

3.1 Bag of words (geometric mean)

The original MEANT approaches employed standard a bag-of-words strategy for lexical association. This baseline approach applies no alignment constraints on multiword expressions:

$$
\begin{aligned}
s_{i,\text{pred}} &= e^{\frac{\sum_{e\in\mathbf{e}_{i,\text{pred}}} \sum_{f\in\mathbf{f}_{i,\text{pred}}} \lg(s(e,f))}{|\mathbf{e}_{i,\text{pred}}|\cdot|\mathbf{f}_{i,\text{pred}}|}} \\
s_{i,j} &= e^{\frac{\sum_{e\in\mathbf{e}_{i,j}} \sum_{f\in\mathbf{f}_{i,j}} \lg(s(e,f))}{|\mathbf{e}_{i,j}|\cdot|\mathbf{f}_{i,j}|}}
\end{aligned}
$$

*** Formatting Issue - Best Available Paper/Graphic ***

3.2 Maximum alignment (precision-recall average)

In the first maximum alignment based approach we will consider, the definitions of $s_{i,\text{pred}}$ and $s_{i,j}$ are inspired by Mihalcea *et al.* (2006) who normalize phrasal similarities according to the phrase length.

$$\begin{aligned} s_{i,\text{pred}} &= \frac{1}{2}(\text{prec}_{\mathbf{e}_{i,\text{pred}},\mathbf{f}_{i,\text{pred}}} + \text{rec}_{\mathbf{e}_{i,\text{pred}},\mathbf{f}_{i,\text{pred}}}) \\ s_{i,j} &= \frac{1}{2}(\text{prec}_{\mathbf{e}_{i,j},\mathbf{f}_{i,j}} + \text{rec}_{\mathbf{e}_{i,j},\mathbf{f}_{i,j}}) \end{aligned}$$

3.3 Maximum alignment (f-score)

The second of the maximum alignment based approaches replaces the above linear averaging of precision and recall with a proper f-score. Although this is less consistent with the previous literature, such as Mihalcea *et al.* (2006), it seems more consistent with the overall f-score based approach of MEANT, and thus we include it in our comparison as a variant of the maximum alignment strategy.

$$\begin{aligned} s_{i,\text{pred}} &= \frac{2 \cdot \text{prec}_{\mathbf{e}_{i,\text{pred}},\mathbf{f}_{i,\text{pred}}} \cdot \text{rec}_{\mathbf{e}_{i,\text{pred}},\mathbf{f}_{i,\text{pred}}}}{\text{prec}_{\mathbf{e}_{i,\text{pred}},\mathbf{f}_{i,\text{pred}}} + \text{rec}_{\mathbf{e}_{i,\text{pred}},\mathbf{f}_{i,\text{pred}}}} \\ s_{i,j} &= \frac{2 \cdot \text{prec}_{\mathbf{e}_{i,j},\mathbf{f}_{i,j}} \cdot \text{rec}_{\mathbf{e}_{i,j},\mathbf{f}_{i,j}}}{\text{prec}_{\mathbf{e}_{i,j},\mathbf{f}_{i,j}} + \text{rec}_{\mathbf{e}_{i,j},\mathbf{f}_{i,j}}} \end{aligned}$$

3.4 Inversion transduction grammar based

There has been to date relatively little use of inversion transduction grammars (Wu, 1997) to improve the accuracy of MT evaluation metrics—despite (1) long empirical evidence the vast majority of translation patterns between human languages can be accommodated within ITG constraints, and (2) the observation that most current state-of-the-art SMT systems employ ITG decoders. Especially when considering *semantic* MT metrics, ITGs would seem to be a natural strategy for multiword expression association for several cognitively motivated reasons, having to do with language universal properties of cross-linguistic semantic frame structure.

To begin with, it is quite natural to think of sentences as having been generated from an abstract concept using a rewriting system: a stochastic grammar predicts how frequently any particular realization of the abstract concept will be generated. The bilingual analogy is a *transduction grammar* generating *a pair* of possible realizations of *the same* underlying concept. Stochastic transduction grammars predict how frequently a particular pair of realizations will be generated, and thus represent a good way to evaluate how well a pair of sentences correspond to each other.

The particular class of transduction grammars known as ITGs tackle the problem that the (bi)parsing complexity for general **syntax-directed transductions** (Aho and Ullman, 1972) is exponential. By constraining a syntax-directed transduction grammar to allow only monotonic **straight** and **inverted** reorderings, or equivalently permitting only binary or ternary rank rules, it is possible to isolate the low end of that hierarchy into a single equivalence class of **inversion transductions**. ITGs are guaranteed to have a two-normal form similar to context-free grammars, and can be biparsed in polynomial time and space ($O\left(n^6\right)$ time and $O\left(n^4\right)$ space). It is also possible to do approximate biparsing in $O\left(n^3\right)$ time (Saers *et al.*, 2009). These polynomial complexities makes it feasible to estimate the parameters of an ITG using standard machine learning techniques such as expectation maximization (Wu, 1995b) .

At the same time, inversion transductions have also been directly shown to be more than sufficient to account for the reordering that occur within semantic frame alternations (Addanki *et al.*, 2012). This language universal property has an evolutionary explanation in terms of computational efficiency and cognitive load for language learnability and interpretability (Wu, 2014).

ITGs are thus an appealing alternative for evaluating the possible links between both semantic role fillers in different languages as well as the predicates, and how these parts fit together to form entire semantic frames. We believe that ITGs are not only capable of generating the desired structural correspondences between the semantic structures of two languages, but also provide meaningful constraints to prevent alignments from wandering off in the wrong direction.

Following this reasoning, alternate definitions of $s_{i,\text{pred}}$ and $s_{i,j}$ can be constructed in terms of bracketing ITGs (also known as BITGs or BTGs) which are ITGs containing only a single non-differentiated nonterminal category (Wu, 1995a). The idea is to attack a potential weakness of the foregoing three lexical association strategies, namely that word/token alignments between the reference and machine translations are severely underconstrained. No bijectivity or permutation restrictions are applied, even between compositional segments where this should be natural. This can cause multiword expressions of semantic role fillers to be matched even when they should not be. In contrast, using a bracketing inversion transduction grammar can potentially better constrain permissible token alignment patterns between aligned role filler phrases. Figure 2 illustrates how the ITG constraints are consistent with the needed permutations between semantic role fillers across the reference and machine translations for a sample sentence from the evaluation data.

In this approach, both alignment and scoring are performed utilizing a length-normalized weighted BITG (Wu, 1997; Zens and Ney, 2003; Saers and Wu, 2009; Addanki *et al.*, 2012). We define $s_{i,\text{pred}}$ and $s_{i,j}$ as follows.

$$
\begin{aligned}
s_{i,\text{pred}} &= \lg^{-1}\left(\frac{\lg\left(P\left(\mathrm{A} \stackrel{*}{\Rightarrow} \mathbf{e}_{i,\text{pred}}/\mathbf{f}_{i,\text{pred}}|G\right)\right)}{\max(|\ \mathbf{e}_{i,\text{pred}}\ |, |\ \mathbf{f}_{i,\text{pred}}\ |)}\right) \\
s_{i,j} &= \lg^{-1}\left(\frac{\lg\left(P\left(\mathrm{A} \stackrel{*}{\Rightarrow} \mathbf{e}_{i,j}/\mathbf{f}_{i,j}|G\right)\right)}{\max(|\ \mathbf{e}_{i,j}\ |, |\ \mathbf{f}_{i,j}\ |)}\right)
\end{aligned}
$$

where

$$
\begin{aligned}
G &\equiv \langle \{\mathrm{A}\}, \mathcal{W}^0, \mathcal{W}^1, \mathcal{R}, \mathrm{A}\rangle \\
\mathcal{R} &\equiv \{\mathrm{A} \to [\mathrm{AA}], \mathrm{A} \to \langle \mathrm{AA}\rangle, \mathrm{A} \to e/f\}
\end{aligned}
$$

$$
\begin{aligned}
p([\mathrm{AA}]\,|\mathrm{A}) &= p(\langle \mathrm{AA}\rangle|\mathrm{A}) = 1 \\
p(e/f|\mathrm{A}) &= s(e,f)
\end{aligned}
$$

Here G is a bracketing ITG whose only nonterminal is A, and $\mathcal{R}$ is a set of transduction rules with $e \in \mathcal{W}^0 \cup \{\epsilon\}$ denoting a token in the MT output (or the *null* token) and $f \in \mathcal{W}^1 \cup \{\epsilon\}$ denoting a token in the reference translation (or the *null* token). The rule probability (or more accurately, rule weight) function p is set to be 1 for structural transduction rules, and for lexical transduction rules it is defined by MEANT's lexical similarity measure on English Gigaword context vectors. To calculate the inside probability (or more accurately, inside score) of a pair of segments, $P\left(\mathrm{A} \stackrel{*}{\Rightarrow} \mathbf{e}/\mathbf{f}|G\right)$, we use the algorithm described in Saers *et al.* (2009). Given this, $s_{i,\text{pred}}$ and $s_{i,j}$ now represent the length normalized BITG parse scores of the predicates and role fillers of the arguments of type j between the reference and machine translations.

4 Experiments

In this section we discuss experiments comparing the four alternative lexical access preference and constraint strategies.

4.1 Experimental setup

We compared using the DARPA GALE P2.5 Chinese-English translation test set, as used in Lo and Wu (2011a). The corpus includes the Chinese input sentences, each accompanied by an English reference translation and three participating state-of-the-art MT systems' output.

We computed sentence-level correlations following the benchmark assessment procedure used by WMT and NIST MetricsMaTr (Callison-Burch *et al.*, 2008, 2010, 2011, 2012; Macháček and Bojar, 2013), which use Kendall's τ correlation coefficient, to evaluate the correlation of evaluation metrics against human judgment on ranking the translation adequacy of the three systems' output. A higher value for Kendall's τ indicates more similarity to the human adequacy rankings by the evaluation metrics. The range of possible values of Kendall's τ correlation coefficient is [-1, 1], where 1 means the

*** Formatting Issue - Best Available Paper/Graphic ***

Table 1: Sentence-level correlation with human adequacy judgements on different partitions of GALE P2.5 data. For reference, the human HMEANT upper bound is 0.53—so the fully automatic ITG based MEANT approximation is not far from closing the gap.

	Kendall correlation
MEANT + ITG based	**0.51**
MEANT + maximum alignment (f-score)	0.48
MEANT + maximum alignment (average of precision & recall)	0.46
MEANT + bag of words (geometric mean)	0.38
NIST	0.29
METEOR	0.20
BLEU	0.20
TER	0.20
PER	0.20
CDER	0.12
WER	0.10

systems are ranked in the same order as the human judgment by the evaluation metric; and -1 means the systems are ranked in the reverse order as human judgment by the evaluation metric.

For both reference and machine translations, the ASSERT (Pradhan *et al.*, 2004) semantic role labeler was used to automatically predict semantic parses.

4.2 Results and discussion

The sentence-level correlations in Table 1 show that the ITG based strategy outperforms other automatic metrics in correlation with human adequacy judgment. Note that this was achieved with no tuning whatsoever of the rule weights (suggesting that the performance could be further improved in the future by slightly optimizing the ITG weights).

The ITG based strategy shows 3 points improvement over the next best strategy, which is maximal alignment under f-score aggregation. The ITG based approach produces much higher HAJ correlations than any of the other metrics.

In fact, the ITG based strategy even comes within a few points of the human upper bound benchmark HAJ correlations computed using the human labeled semantic frames and alignments used in the HMEANT.

Data analysis reveals two reasons that the ITG based strategy correlates with human adequacy judgement more closely than the other approaches. First, BITG constraints indeed provide more accurate phrasal similarity aggregation, compared to the naive bag-of-words based heuristics. Similar results have been observed while trying to estimate word alignment probabilities where BITG constraints outperformed alignments from GIZA++ (Saers and Wu, 2009). Secondly, the permutation and bijectivity constraints enforced by the ITG provide better leverage to reject token alignments when they are not appropriate, compared with the maximal alignment approach which tends to be rather promiscuous. The ITG tends whenever appropriate to accept clean, sparse alignments for role fillers, prefering to leave tokens unaligned instead of aligning them anyway as the other strategies tend to do. Note that it is not simply a matter of lowering thresholds for accepting token alignments: Tumuluru *et al.* (2012) showed that the competitive linking approach (Melamed, 1996) does not work as well as the strategies considered in this paper, whereas the ITG appears to be selective about the token alignments in a manner that better fits the semantic structure.

5 Conclusion

We have compared four alternative lexical access strategies for aggregation, preferences, and constraints in scoring multiword expression associations that are far too numerous to be explicitly enumerated in lexicons, within the context of semantic frame based machine translation evaluation: bag-of-words,

*** Formatting Issue - Best Available Paper/Graphic ***

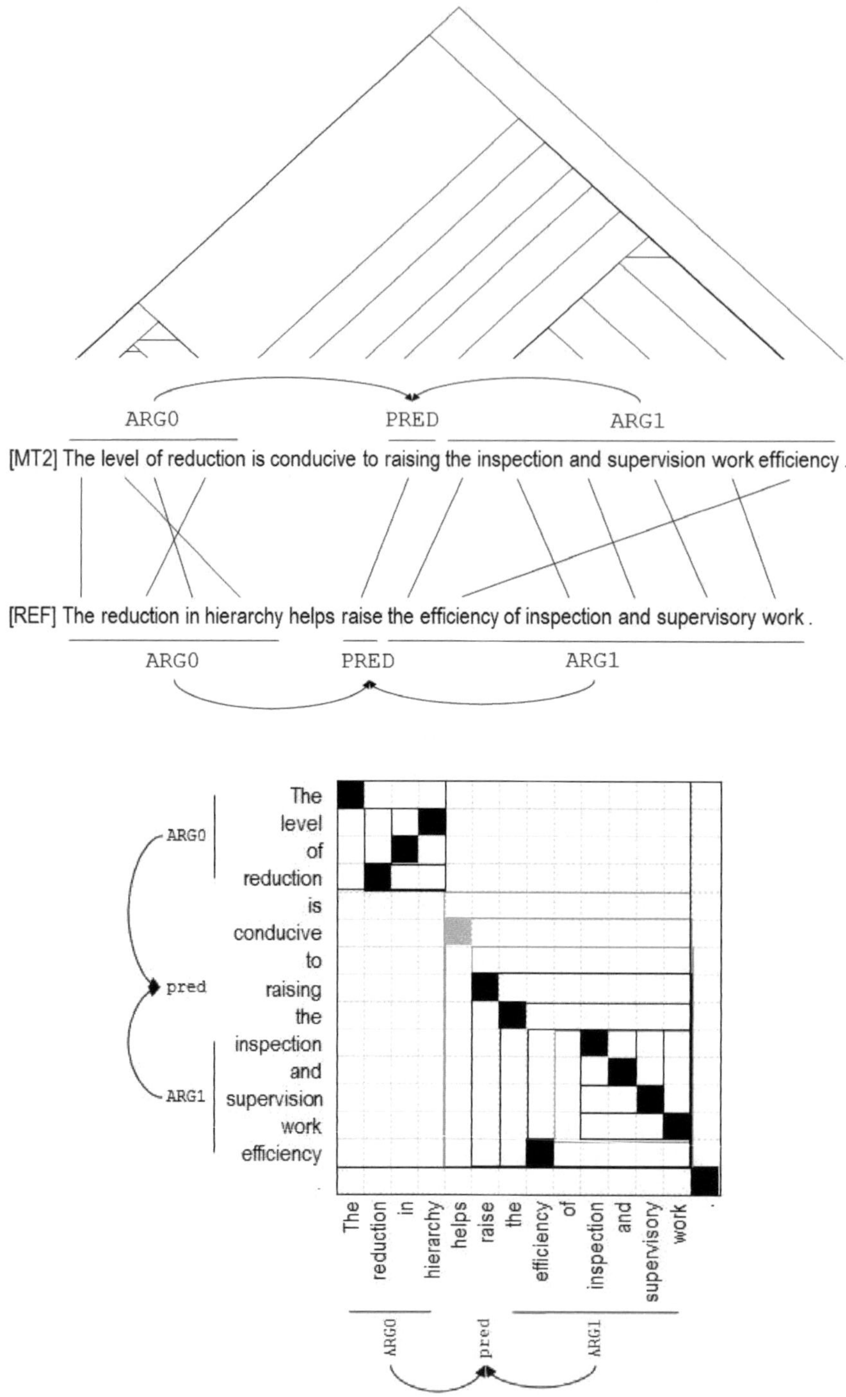

Figure 2: An example of aligning automatic shallow semantic parses under ITGs, visualized using both biparse tree and alignment matrix depictions, for the Chinese input sentence 汽玼滣珻緩蒨盹藴翣热珲沃珣潏煰蠣滣芢硃搓 Both the reference and machine translations are parsed using automatic English SRL. Compositional alignments between the semantic frames and the tokens within role filler phrases obey inversion transduction grammars.

***** Formatting Issue - Best Available Paper/Graphic *****

two maximum alignment based approaches, and an inversion transduction grammar based approach. Controlled experiments within the MEANT semantic MT evaluation framework shows that the cognitively motivated ITG based strategy achieves significantly higher correlation with human adequacy judgments of MT output quality than the more typically used lexical association approaches. The results show how to improve upon previous research showing that MEANT's explicit use of semantic frames leads to state-of-the-art automatic MT evaluation, by aligning and scoring semantic frames under a simple, consistent ITG that provides empirically informative permutation and bijectivity biases, instead of more naive maximal alignment or bag-of-words assumptions.

Cognitive studies of the lexicon are often described using intrinsic measures of quality. Our experiments complement this by situating the empirical comparisons within extrinsic real-world task-based performance measures. We believe that progress can be accelerated via a combination of intrinsic and extrinsic measures of lexicon acquisition and access models.

Acknowledgments

This material is based upon work supported in part by the Defense Advanced Research Projects Agency (DARPA) under BOLT contract nos. HR0011-12-C-0014 and HR0011-12-C-0016, and GALE contract nos. HR0011-06-C-0022 and HR0011-06-C-0023; by the European Union under the FP7 grant agreement no. 287658; and by the Hong Kong Research Grants Council (RGC) research grants GRF620811, GRF621008, and GRF612806. Any opinions, findings and conclusions or recommendations expressed in this material are those of the authors and do not necessarily reflect the views of DARPA, the EU, or RGC.

References

Karteek Addanki, Chi-kiu Lo, Markus Saers, and Dekai Wu. LTG vs. ITG coverage of cross-lingual verb frame alternations. In *16th Annual Conference of the European Association for Machine Translation (EAMT-2012)*, Trento, Italy, May 2012.

Alfred V. Aho and Jeffrey D. Ullman. *The Theory of Parsing, Translation, and Compiling*. Prentice-Halll, Englewood Cliffs, New Jersey, 1972.

Satanjeev Banerjee and Alon Lavie. METEOR: An automatic metric for MT evaluation with improved correlation with human judgments. In *Workshop on Intrinsic and Extrinsic Evaluation Measures for Machine Translation and/or Summarization*, Ann Arbor, Michigan, June 2005.

Chris Callison-Burch, Miles Osborne, and Philipp Koehn. Re-evaluating the role of BLEU in machine translation research. In *11th Conference of the European Chapter of the Association for Computational Linguistics (EACL-2006)*, 2006.

Chris Callison-Burch, Cameron Fordyce, Philipp Koehn, Christof Monz, and Josh Schroeder. Further meta-evaluation of machine translation. In *Third Workshop on Statistical Machine Translation (WMT-08)*, 2008.

Chris Callison-Burch, Philipp Koehn, Christof Monz, Kay Peterson, Mark Pryzbocki, and Omar Zaidan. Findings of the 2010 joint workshop on statistical machine translation and metrics for machine translation. In *Joint Fifth Workshop on Statistical Machine Translation and MetricsMATR (WMT10)*, pages 17–53, Uppsala, Sweden, 15-16 July 2010.

Chris Callison-Burch, Philipp Koehn, Christof Monz, and Omar F. Zaidan. Findings of the 2011 Workshop on Statistical Machine Translation. In *6th Workshop on Statistical Machine Translation (WMT 2011)*, 2011.

Chris Callison-Burch, Philipp Koehn, Christof Monz, Matt Post, Radu Soricut, and Lucia Specia. Findings of the 2012 workshop on statistical machine translation. In *7th Workshop on Statistical Machine Translation (WMT 2012)*, pages 10–51, 2012.

***** Formatting Issue - Best Available Paper/Graphic *****

George Doddington. Automatic evaluation of machine translation quality using n-gram co-occurrence statistics. In *The second international conference on Human Language Technology Research (HLT '02)*, San Diego, California, 2002.

Philipp Koehn and Christof Monz. Manual and automatic evaluation of machine translation between european languages. In *Workshop on Statistical Machine Translation (WMT-06)*, 2006.

Gregor Leusch, Nicola Ueffing, and Hermann Ney. CDer: Efficient MT evaluation using block movements. In *11th Conference of the European Chapter of the Association for Computational Linguistics (EACL-2006)*, 2006.

Chi-kiu Lo and Dekai Wu. MEANT: An inexpensive, high-accuracy, semi-automatic metric for evaluating translation utility based on semantic roles. In *49th Annual Meeting of the Association for Computational Linguistics: Human Language Technologies (ACL HLT 2011)*, 2011.

Chi-kiu Lo and Dekai Wu. SMT vs. AI redux: How semantic frames evaluate MT more accurately. In *Twenty-second International Joint Conference on Artificial Intelligence (IJCAI-11)*, 2011.

Chi-kiu Lo and Dekai Wu. Unsupervised vs. supervised weight estimation for semantic MT evaluation metrics. In *Sixth Workshop on Syntax, Semantics and Structure in Statistical Translation (SSST-6)*, 2012.

Chi-kiu Lo and Dekai Wu. Can informal genres be better translated by tuning on automatic semantic metrics? In *14th Machine Translation Summit (MT Summit XIV)*, 2013.

Chi-kiu Lo and Dekai Wu. MEANT at WMT 2013: A tunable, accurate yet inexpensive semantic frame based mt evaluation metric. In *8th Workshop on Statistical Machine Translation (WMT 2013)*, 2013.

Chi-kiu Lo, Anand Karthik Tumuluru, and Dekai Wu. Fully automatic semantic MT evaluation. In *7th Workshop on Statistical Machine Translation (WMT 2012)*, 2012.

Chi-kiu Lo, Karteek Addanki, Markus Saers, and Dekai Wu. Improving machine translation by training against an automatic semantic frame based evaluation metric. In *51st Annual Meeting of the Association for Computational Linguistics (ACL 2013)*, 2013.

Chi-kiu Lo, Meriem Beloucif, and Dekai Wu. Improving machine translation into Chinese by tuning against Chinese MEANT. In *International Workshop on Spoken Language Translation (IWSLT 2013)*, 2013.

Matouš Macháček and Ondřej Bojar. Results of the WMT13 metrics shared task. In *Eighth Workshop on Statistical Machine Translation (WMT 2013)*, Sofia, Bulgaria, August 2013.

I. Dan Melamed. Automatic construction of clean broad-coverage translation lexicons. In *2nd Conference of the Association for Machine Translation in the Americas (AMTA-1996)*, 1996.

Rada Mihalcea, Courtney Corley, and Carlo Strapparava. Corpus-based and knowledge-based measures of text semantic similarity. In *The Twenty-first National Conference on Artificial Intelligence (AAAI-06)*, volume 21. Menlo Park, CA; Cambridge, MA; London; AAAI Press; MIT Press; 1999, 2006.

Sonja Nießen, Franz Josef Och, Gregor Leusch, and Hermann Ney. A evaluation tool for machine translation: Fast evaluation for MT research. In *The Second International Conference on Language Resources and Evaluation (LREC 2000)*, 2000.

Kishore Papineni, Salim Roukos, Todd Ward, and Wei-Jing Zhu. BLEU: a method for automatic evaluation of machine translation. In *40th Annual Meeting of the Association for Computational Linguistics (ACL-02)*, pages 311–318, Philadelphia, Pennsylvania, July 2002.

Sameer Pradhan, Wayne Ward, Kadri Hacioglu, James H. Martin, and Dan Jurafsky. Shallow semantic parsing using support vector machines. In *Human Language Technology Conference of the North American Chapter of the Association for Computational Linguistics (HLT-NAACL 2004)*, 2004.

Markus Saers and Dekai Wu. Improving phrase-based translation via word alignments from stochastic inversion transduction grammars. In *Third Workshop on Syntax and Structure in Statistical Translation (SSST-3)*, pages 28–36, Boulder, Colorado, June 2009.

***** Formatting Issue - Best Available Paper/Graphic *****

Markus Saers, Joakim Nivre, and Dekai Wu. Learning stochastic bracketing inversion transduction grammars with a cubic time biparsing algorithm. In *11th International Conference on Parsing Technologies (IWPT'09)*, pages 29–32, Paris, France, October 2009.

Matthew Snover, Bonnie Dorr, Richard Schwartz, Linnea Micciulla, and John Makhoul. A study of translation edit rate with targeted human annotation. In *7th Biennial Conference Association for Machine Translation in the Americas (AMTA 2006)*, pages 223–231, Cambridge, Massachusetts, August 2006.

Anand Karthik Tumuluru, Chi-kiu Lo, and Dekai Wu. Accuracy and robustness in measuring the lexical similarity of semantic role fillers for automatic semantic MT evaluation. In *26th Pacific Asia Conference on Language, Information, and Computation (PACLIC 26)*, 2012.

Dekai Wu. An algorithm for simultaneously bracketing parallel texts by aligning words. In *33rd Annual Meeting of the Association for Computational Linguistics (ACL 95)*, pages 244–251, Cambridge, Massachusetts, June 1995.

Dekai Wu. Trainable coarse bilingual grammars for parallel text bracketing. In *Third Annual Workshop on Very Large Corpora (WVLC-3)*, pages 69–81, Cambridge, Massachusetts, June 1995.

Dekai Wu. Stochastic inversion transduction grammars and bilingual parsing of parallel corpora. *Computational Linguistics*, 23(3):377–403, 1997.

Dekai Wu. The magic number 4: Evolutionary pressures on semantic frame structure. In *10th International Conference on the Evolution of Language (Evolang X)*, Vienna, Apr 2014.

Richard Zens and Hermann Ney. A comparative study on reordering constraints in statistical machine translation. In *41st Annual Meeting of the Association for Computational Linguistics (ACL-2003)*, pages 144–151, Stroudsburg, Pennsylvania, 2003.

A Lexical Network with a Morphological Model in It

Nabil Gader
MVS Publishing Solutions
395, chemin de la Cartonnerie
88100 Sainte-Marguerite, France
nabil.gader@mvs.fr

Aurore Koehl
ATILF CNRS
44, avenue de la Libération, BP 30687
54063 Nancy Cedex, France
aurore.koehl@univ-lorraine.fr

Alain Polguère
Université de Lorraine & ATILF CNRS
44, avenue de la Libération, BP 30687
54063 Nancy Cedex, France
alain.polguere@univ-lorraine.fr

Abstract

The French Lexical Network (fr-LN) is a global model of the French lexicon presently under construction. The fr-LN accounts for lexical knowledge as a lexical network structured by paradigmatic and syntagmatic relations holding between lexical units. This paper describes how morphological knowledge is presently being introduced into the fr-LN through the implementation and lexicographic exploitation of a dynamic morphological model. Section 1 presents theoretical and practical justifications for the approach which we believe allows for a cognitively sound description of morphological data within semantically-oriented lexical databases. Section 2 gives an overview of the structure of the dynamic morphological model, which is constructed through two complementary processes: a Morphological Process—section 3—and a Lexicographic Process—section 4.

1 Introduction

We present a morphological model implemented in order to feed the French Lexical Network database—hereafter fr-LN—, presently under development at the ATILF CNRS lab. The fr-LN belongs to the broad family of lexical resources designed as networks of lexical units (Fellbaum, 1998; Baker *et al.*, 2003; Ruppenhofer *et al.*, 2010; Spohr, 2012). Its design, content and mode of construction has already been documented in various publications (Lux-Pogodalla and Polguère, 2011; Gader *et al.*, 2012; Polguère, 2014; Polguère, to appear) and we strictly focus here on its newly developed morphological component.

The morphological description of French lexemes discussed below possesses two main characteristics:

1. it is dynamically created from a full-fledged grammatical model of French inflectional morphology;

2. it is meant to be used in the context of a lexicographic project where morphological tables are individually associated to senses of (polysemic) vocables, thus accounting for potential morphological discrepancies between senses within a given vocable.

We believe that our approach allows for a cognitively sound implementation of morphology in lexical databases that are primarily oriented towards the description of senses (rather than forms). Indeed, we do not simply inject lists of lexical forms into the fr-LN database but describe *morphological knowledge* by means of a "true" model of French inflectional morphology.

Zock/Rapp/Huang (eds.): Proceedings of the 4th Workshop on Cognitive Aspects of the Lexicon, pages 154–165,
Dublin, Ireland, August 23, 2014.

1.1 Interconnection between lexical and morphological models

There are at least two main characteristics that a cognitively sound lexical model of a given language has to possess.

- First and foremost, it must account for the Speaker's knowledge of lexical rules (a lexical unit and all its properties being considered here as being a cluster of lexical rules).
- Second, it must be structured in a way that makes it possible to support the modeling of (i) "natural" processes of lexical knowledge evolution—acquisition, consolidation, relativization, loss of lexical knowledge—and (ii) linguistic processes of speech, understanding, paraphrase, translation, word association (Dunbar, 2012), etc.

Lexical knowledge, however, is intricately related to grammatical knowledge, to the point that it is not necessarily possible to radically separate lexical information from grammatical information in a cognitive lexicon. This is particularly true for language morphology, that can be said to belong simultaneously to both the lexical and grammatical modules of natural languages. Consequently, a lexical model that aims at cognitive relevance has to take the morphological bull by the horns and handle morphological properties and behavior of lexical units by modeling actual morphological knowledge.

Not all lexical resources link a lexical unit to its forms and morphology is often "externalized," using separate dedicated resources (see section 1.2 below). However, for a language that is rather rich in terms of inflectional morphology, such as French, it is particularly interesting to embed in lexical resources an explicit morphological model. The purpose of such model is to allow lexicographers to account for inflected forms of lexical units by associating each individual unit (= sense) to inflectional classes and dynamically obtain in the process morphological tables of all corresponding lexical forms.

Before we proceed, let us enumerate the basic terminology that will be used throughout the paper.

- *Lexical units* are of two kinds: (i) *lexemes*—CHEVAL **I.1a** 'horse' ~ CHEVAL **I.1b** 'horse riding'—are monolexemic lexical units; (ii) *idioms*—CULOTTE DE CHEVAL 'saddlebags'—are syntagmatic lexical units.
- *Vocables*—CHEVAL—are (potentially) polysemic words. They are modeled in the fr-LN as sets of lexical units connected by a relation of copolysemy.
- *Wordforms* are linguistic signs expressing lexemes—singular *cheval* **I.1a** and plural *chevaux* **I.1a** are the two wordforms for the CHEVAL **I.1a** lexeme. Because wordforms are linguistic signs, each individual wordform has to be described as a <signified, signifier, restricted combinatorics> triplet (Mel'čuk, 2012, Chapter 1).

1.2 Current approaches to morphology in sense-oriented lexical databases

In this section, we briefly summarize the treatment of morphological information in major sense-oriented lexical databases and explain why we decided to elaborate an approach of our own.

Our initial constraints were that we wanted to truly handle forms related to lexemes with respect to general rules of inflectional morphology. Additionally, we wanted to model in an elegant way phenomena such as spelling variation (*cuillère* 'spoon' ~ *cuiller*), euphony (*j'aime* 'I love' ~ *aimé-je*), alternative inflected forms (*je m'assois* ~ *je m'assieds*) or defectiveness (*je fris du lard* 'I fry bacon', but there is no corresponding 1st person plural; one has to say *nous faisons frire du lard* lit. 'We make bacon fry').

To our knowledge, no current general purpose lexical database—for French or other languages—currently meet these requirements. WordNet, for instance, only stores base forms of lexemes and has no embedded morphological model of English. An external lemmatizer, Morphy,[1] is used to access lexical senses via inflected forms. The situation is different in FrameNet. As indicated in (Ruppenhofer *et al.*, 2010, p. 93–94), lemmas are stored in the *Lexical Database* component of FrameNet, together with corresponding wordforms. However, no grammatical model of inflection is embedded in the database and made available for lexicographic purposes.

[1] `https://wordnet.princeton.edu/wordnet/man/morphy.7WN.html`

2 Dynamic approach to morphological description

This section is devoted to the presentation of the morphological model embedded in the fr-LN. We proceed in two steps. Firstly (section 2.1), we detail the limitations of existing morphological databases for French, which explain why we decided to not "inject" their content in the fr-LN. Secondly (section 2.2), we present the general design of our morphological model and detail its dynamic nature.

2.1 Limitations of existing morphological resources for French

In order to model "morphological knowledge" within a lexical database, one can either make use of an already existing morphological ressource (that will be connected to or embedded into the database), or develop a specific, tailor-made morphological database module—see (Issac, 2010) for a detailed discussion. There exist indeed several morphological resources for French that, in principle, could have been used as embedded morphological modules in the fr-LN. We will explain why limitations found in these resources have led us to choose the second option and design our own morphological model.

We have mainly examined six morphological resources for French, all developed during the past ten years: *Manulex*, *Morphalou*, *Lexique 3*, *Lefff*, *Flexique* and *Morfetik*.[2] Here is a brief recap of the observations we have made, based on our specific needs and expectations. For lack of space, we cannot make a detailed presentation of these resources and our evaluation will by necessity be rather sketchy.

Manulex was designed for psycholinguistic research (Lété *et al.*, 2004). It contains 48,886 French wordforms. The list of wordforms results from a "grade-based word frequency list extracted from a corpus of first to fifth grade readers used in French elementary schools" (Lété *et al.*, 2004, p. 159). *Manulex* has therefore a limited coverage, when compared to other existing resources that target the bulk of the French lexicon and can store up to 500,000 forms.

But coverage is not the only issue. The quality of data can vary greatly from database to database. In *Morphalou* (Romary *et al.*, 2004), for instance, one can find a lot of miscategorizations and misspellings. Reusing *Morphalou*'s data would thus raise many maintenance issues.

While having a larger coverage than *Manulex* and data of better quality than *Morphalou*, *Lexique 3* (New, 2006) poses several problems of its own. First, inflectional paradigms are not complete, because *Lexique 3*'s wordlist was extracted from the Frantext corpus (Montémont, 2008), that contains only part of the lexicon of contemporary French. Second, pairs like *chat* 'cat' ~ *chatte* 'female cat' have been encoded as one entry, which contradicts our theoretical and descriptive choices. Following (Mel'čuk, 2000; Delaite and Polguère, 2013), we consider that no inflectional mechanism is involved here. There are two distinct CHAT ~ CHATTE nominal lexemes in French; the feminine is morphologically **derived** (i.e. produced by morphological derivation) from the masculine and has to be accounted for separately. Both aspects—incompleteness and inapropriate descriptive postulates such as in the case of N_{masc} ~ N_{fem} pairs—disqualified *Lexique 3* in our quest for an already-existing resource.

Flexique (Bonami *et al.*, 2013) is derived from *Lexique 3*, but the problems we just mentioned are solved: paradigms are now complete and pairs like CHAT ~ CHATTE have been encoded as two separate entries. However, *Flexique*—just as the two remaining resources *Lefff*[3] (Sagot, 2010) and *Morfetik* (Mathieu-Colas, 2009)—lacks alternative forms for inflections[4] or orthographic variants, as reported by the authors themselves.

Last but not least, all resources cited above associate a morphological description to a lexical entry, **not to a specific sense**. However, not all senses of a given polysemic vocable necessarily possess the same morphological behavior, and this is valid for most of natural languages. For instance, the sense 'flag or other symbolic object' of the COLOR vocable is plural only (*to raise the colors*). In other words:

[2]These resources are all available for research. The dictionaries of the *Antidote* suite incorporate a powerful morphological model for French (Antidote, 2014). However, *Antidote* is a commercial product; we cannot examine its internal design and its morphological model is of course not available for embedding in a lexical database such as fr-LN, whose linguistic content will be freely available.

[3]*Lexique des Formes Fléchies du Français.*

[4]For instance, these resources do not indicate that Fr. AIL 'garlic' has two alternative plural forms *ails* ~ *aulx* (section 4.1 below) or that S'ASSEOIR 'to sit' has two alternative forms for most of its inflections—*je m'assoie* ~ *je m'assieds, tu t'assois* ~ *tu t'assieds, il s'assoit* ~ *il s'assied...*

A morphological model encapsulated in a lexical database should describe actual wordforms: linguistic signs made up of a signified, a signifier and combinatorial properties. Signifiers should not remain disconnected from the signified they express.

In this respect, and to our knowledge, there exists no sense-based morphological model available for French prior to our work. This left us with no choice but to design a model of our own, that would be specially designed to accompany our lexicographic project and be better suited for applications such as word sense identification backed by lexical knowledge (Leacock and Chodorow, 1998).

2.2 General design of the fr-LN dynamic morphological model

The core of our morphological model is a set of *Morphological Templates* that define corresponding inflection classes as *Prototypical Tables* of inflection. These latter tables are named after a lexeme that prototypically represents the corresponding morphological paradigm: Prototypical Table of nouns of the CHAT 'cat' family, of verbs of the DANSER 'dance' family, etc. The association of a Prototypical Table to a given lexeme automatically generates one or more *Lexeme Table(s)*, i.e. tables that contain the description of all wordforms expressing this lexeme. Wordforms themselves are defined as relations holding between three database elements: (i) a given Lexeme Table, (ii) a set of grammatical features (mainly, grammemes) associated to the wordform and (iii) a given signifier.

The integration of morphological knowledge into the fr-LN database is performed through two complementary processes, as visualized in Figure 1:

1. a *Morphological Process*—construction of Morphological Templates from which Prototypical Tables are generated;

2. a *Lexicographic Process*—creation of Lexeme↔Prototypical Table(s) associations, from which Lexeme Tables are automatically derived.

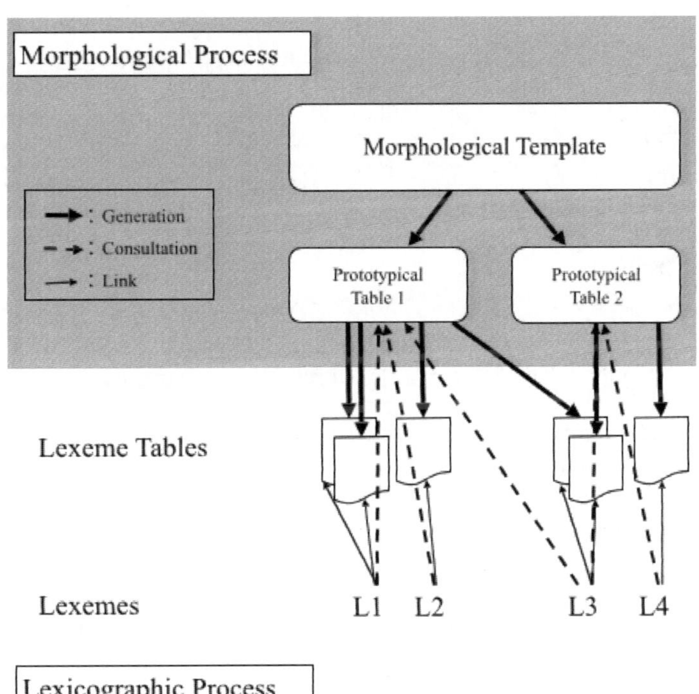

Figure 1: The fr-LN dynamic morphological model

Morphological Templates and Prototypical Tables are the core modules of our dynamic morphological model. In section 3 below, we describe the Morphological Process that leads to the creation of Morphological and Prototypical Tables. We then proceed, in section 4, with the Lexicographic Process that leads to the generation of individual Lexeme Tables. In both sections, we use examples to illustrate the descriptive power and flexibility of the approach in the context of our lexicographic enterprise.

3 Morphological Process → Morphological Templates and Prototypical Tables

The construction of the morphological model—Morphological and Lexicographic Processes—is performed with the *Dicet* editor (Gader *et al.*, 2012), the same lexicographic editor used to built the fr-LN lexical graph through weaving of lexical relations. Illustrative figures in this section and the next one are screen dumps of access to the morphological model by means of Dicet.

3.1 Morphological Templates

The role of Morphological Templates is to establish parameter and variable slots that are common to sets of related Prototypical Tables. For instance, the `Adjectifs` 'Adjectives' template, shown in Figure 2, is used to generate all adjectival Prototypical Tables.

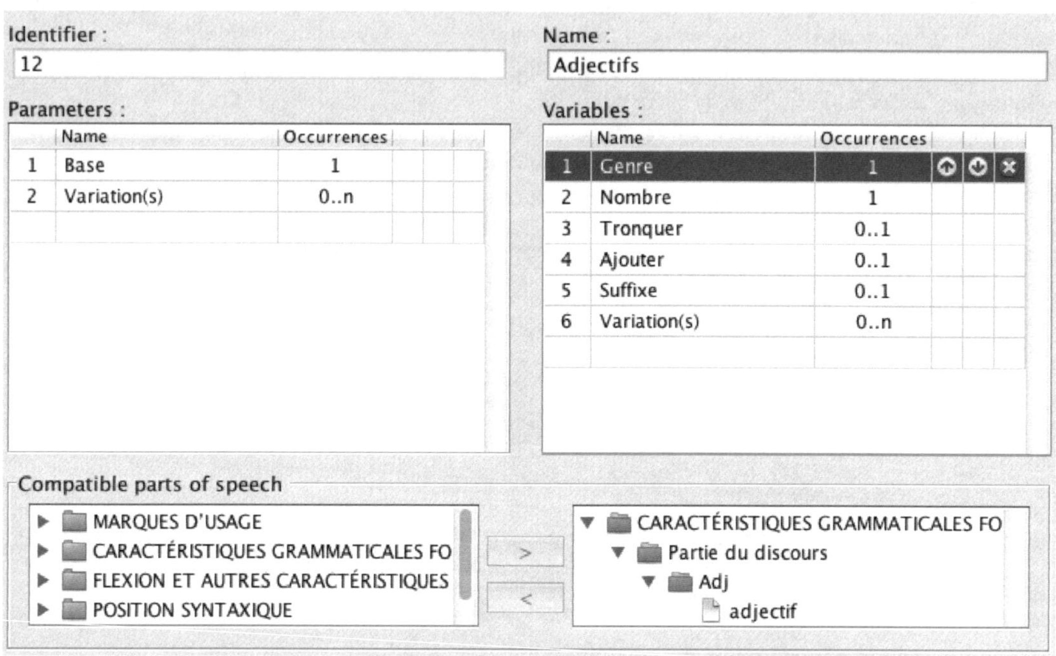

Figure 2: The `Adjectifs` Morphological Template

Figure 2 indicates that all Prototypical Tables that are created from the `Adjectifs` template will have the same set of columns, defined in the table called `Variables`: gender, number, truncation performed on the string of characters that corresponds to the stem, addition to it, suffixation and variation(s).

More generally, variables correspond to either:

- grammemes expressed by the wordforms;
- formal adjustments to be performed on the stem (truncation from/addition to the stem, suffixation);
- possible variations of given wordforms in the table.

Each wordform is related to a particular set of variables. For example, the wordform *actives*—which means 'active' $\oplus$ feminine $\oplus$ plural[5] and whose stem is *actif*—is associated to the following set of vari-

[5]The $\oplus$ operator represents the linguistic union of (components of) two linguistic signs (Mel'čuk, 2012, Chapter 1).

able instanciations: `Genre`=feminine, `Nombre`=plural, `Tronquer`=1, `Ajouter`=*-v-*, `Suffixe`=*-es*, `Variation(s)`=∅.

The `Parameters` table specifies the characteristics that are shared by all tables of a given template. For instance, all adjectival tables contain a `Base` 'stem' field and a `Variation(s)` field. This means that an adjectival table will force the lexicographer to declare the stem used to generate all the wordforms of the adjective and will allow her to declare possible variants for all wordforms of the table, which will condition the generation of more than one Lexeme Table.

Let us illustrate this with the lexeme ABÎMÉ 'damaged'. Declaring the morphology of this lexeme will trigger the generation of two morphological tables: one for the (default) "traditional" spelling (1.) and one for the "rectified" spelling (2.).[6]

1. ABÎMÉ {$abîmé_{\text{(masc, sing)}}$, $abîmés_{\text{(masc, plur)}}$, $abîmée_{\text{(fem, sing)}}$, $abîmées_{\text{(fem, plur)}}$};

2. ABÎMÉ {$abimé_{\text{(masc, sing)}}$, $abimés_{\text{(masc, plur)}}$, $abimée_{\text{(fem, sing)}}$, $abimées_{\text{(fem, plur)}}$}
   `Variation(s)`=rectified spelling.

Because of the rather rich morphology of French verbs, verbal templates require more parameters and variables than nominal or adjectival ones. For instance, verbal templates require two additional parameters in order to deal with (i) choice of auxiliary for compound tenses and (ii) possible use of the SE reflexive pronoun if the verb is pronominal (e.g. SE SUICIDER 'to commit suicide')—see section 4.3.

Notice that the rationale behind the use of Morphological Templates is the need to design a generic approach that will allow us to work on typologically unrelated languages—cf. final remarks in section 5. It is at the level of Morphological Templates that general principles of word construction are encoded, for each individual language.

3.2 Prototypical Tables

As mentioned earlier, Prototypical Tables are generated from Morphological Templates: they feature actualizations of all characteristics (parameters and variables) defined in their source template. **In other words, Prototypical Tables represent morphological classes.** At the time of writing, 15 Prototypical Tables have been created using the `Noms` 'Nouns' template, 34 using `Adjectifs` and almost a hundred Prototypical Tables have been created to account for French verbal morphology.

Figure 3 illustrates the approach with the `petit` 'small' Prototypical Table. This table instantiates the `Adjectifs` Morphological Template with `Base`=*petit* and `Variation(s)`=∅ as parameters.

Identifier : 16 | Name : petit | Template : Adjectifs

Parameters :

Base	Variation(s)
petit	

Rules :

	N...	Genre	Nombre	Tronquer	Ajouter	Suffixe	Variatio...	Form
2	☑	Masculin	Singulier					petit
3	☐	Masculin	Pluriel			s		petits
4	☐	Féminin	Singulier			e		petite
5	☐	Féminin	Pluriel			es		petites

Figure 3: The `petit` 'small' Prototypical Table

[6]The French language council of France—*Conseil de la langue française*—has officially introduced a new spelling system in 1990 (Conseil supérieur de la langue française, 1990), which concerns around 5,000 words and whose usage has been declared to be facultative. Some 25 years later, both the traditional and rectified systems are still cohabiting, even in official texts and at school, which pretty much disqualifies the spelling reform as being a stunning success. Based on current trends (or lack thereof), the approach of the fr-LN database is to maintain the two systems, using the traditional spelling as default one.

In Figure 3, the `Rules` table displays the result of the creation of the Prototypical Table, where each line corresponds to a given dynamically created wordform of PETIT. In each individual "rule" (i.e. grammatical characterization of the corresponding wordform) the gender and number features are instantiated with one grammeme of the pairs masculine ~ feminine and singular ~ plural, respectively. The rule corresponding to the wordform that functions as lexicographic name for the lexeme is checked on the left-hand side. (The lexicographic name of a lexeme is the default form that will be used to name this lexeme in dictionary wordlists, articles, etc.)

Remember that the `petit` Prototypical Table (Figure 3) is distinct from the Lexeme Table of PETIT: this latter is the model of an adjectival **inflectional class** identified as being, prototypically, that of PETIT. Actual Lexeme Table are produced in the context of a Lexicographic Process, that is our next topic.

4 Lexicographic Process → Lexeme Tables

The Lexicographic Process is operated through the creation of an association between given lexemes and given Prototypical Tables. Each association performed on a lexeme by the lexicographer produces the generation of one or more Lexeme Table(s) for this lexeme. We detail this process successively for nouns (4.1), adjectives (4.2) and verbs (4.3).

4.1 Nominal Lexeme Tables

French nouns carry grammatical number—singular or plural. The singular is expressed by a ∅-suffix (no addition to the stem). Canonical nominal plural in French is formed by suffixing the *-s* suffix to the nominal stem. As an example, the two wordforms of ACTEUR 'actor' are singular *acteur* and plural *acteurs*. All nominal lexemes inflecting in the canonical way are associated with the Prototypical Table `chat`. Figure 4 illustrates how this association is performed with the Dicet editor.

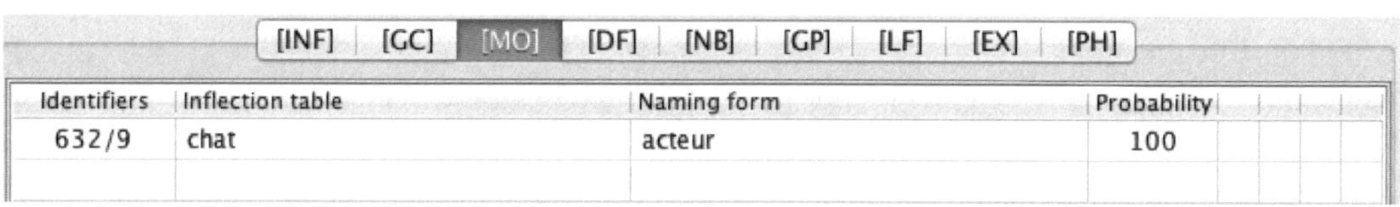

Identifiers	Inflection table	Naming form	Probability
632/9	chat	acteur	100

Figure 4: ACTEUR lexeme↔`chat` Prototypical Table association

There are however cases where the nominal plural is not formed by suffixing *-s*. Four cases can be mentioned.

1. There are unmarked nominal plurals. This concerns nouns ending with *-s*, *-z* or *-x*, like ABUS '[an] abuse', PRIX 'price' or RIZ 'rice', which are invariable. The Prototypical Table `nez` 'nose' has been created to handle such cases. The association of the Prototypical Table `nez` with a nominal stem generates two wordforms (one for singular and one for plural) which have an identical signifier (namely, that of the stem).

2. Some nouns are irregular: their inflected forms cannot be computed by means of general morphological rules. For instance, the plural form of AIL 'garlic' is *aulx*, though it can also be expressed by the regular form *ails*. To account for this, the lexeme AIL has been connected to the special Prototypical Table `ail` which generates a Lexeme Table containing both the regular and irregular plurals: $\{ail_{(\text{sing})}, ails_{(\text{plur})}, aulx_{(\text{plur})}\}$.

3. Lexemes can be defective: there is an "empty cell" (or more) in their table of wordforms (Baerman *et al.*, 2010). For nouns, the defective form is of course either the singular or the plural:

   - defective singular: COULEURS **III.1b** 'colors (= flag or other symbolic object)';
   - defective plural: CIGARETTE **II** 'habit of smoking' (*Je devrais arrêter la cigarette* 'I should quit smoking cigarette').

4. Some nouns can have spelling variants for their stem. (Catach, 1995) and (Sebba, 2003) studied spelling variations concerning the use of accents, the hyphen, archaic forms, the plural of compound words and double consonants. These possible orthographic variants are recorded as spelling variants in our resource. For example, the noun CUILLÈRE 'spoon' has two spellings, *cuillère* and *cuiller*. Consequently, the lexeme CUILLÈRE has been coupled with two tables, generating respectively the wordforms {*cuillère*$_{(\text{sing})}$, *cuillères*$_{(\text{plur})}$} and {*cuiller*$_{(\text{sing})}$, *cuillers*$_{(\text{plur})}$}. Most of the time, spelling variation of the stem follows the last orthographic reform of 1990 (footnote 6 above); in this case, the form recommended by the reform is labelled as "rectified spelling."

Unmarkedness (ABUS), irregularity (AIL), defectiveness (COULEURS **III.1b**) and spelling variation (CUILLÈRE) concern not only nouns but also lexemes of other parts of speech, as will be seen in the next sections.

4.2 Adjectival Lexeme Tables

As shown earlier in section 3.1, French adjectives carry both grammatical gender (masculine ~ feminine) and number (singular ~ plural). A few associations of Prototypical Tables with adjectival lexemes are used as illustrations in what follows.

Canonical inflection of French adjectives—namely, feminine formed by *-e* suffixation and plural by *-s* suffixation—is modeled in the `petit` 'small' Prototypical Table. The association of this table with an adjectival lexeme such as ABSENT$_{\text{Adj}}$ 'absent' dynamically generates the table of all corresponding wordforms: {*absent*$_{(\text{masc, sing})}$, *absents*$_{(\text{masc, plur})}$, *absente*$_{(\text{fem, sing})}$, *absentes*$_{(\text{fem, plur})}$}.

Additionally, a significant number of French adjectives are unmarked for gender—e.g. EFFICACE 'efficient' {*efficace*$_{(\text{masc, sing})}$, *efficaces*$_{(\text{masc, plur})}$, *efficace*$_{(\text{fem, sing})}$, *efficaces*$_{(\text{fem, plur})}$}. Their wordforms are generated using the `aimable` Prototypical Table.

Beside the two above-mentioned regular cases, many adjectives have rather idiosyncratic behavior. This includes invariability, allomorph stems or spelling variations.

1. Invariable adjectives are lexemes whose wordforms (inflected forms) are based on the same signifier. For example, the adjective DEBOUT 'standing up' possesses the formally identical wordforms {*debout*$_{(\text{masc, sing})}$, *debout*$_{(\text{masc, plur})}$, *debout*$_{(\text{fem, sing})}$, *debout*$_{(\text{fem, plur})}$}, that are generated using the `carmin` 'of carmine color' Prototypical Table.

2. Stem allomorphy can be exemplified with SEC$_{\text{Adj}}$ 'dry' {*sec*$_{(\text{masc, sing})}$, *secs*$_{(\text{masc, plur})}$, *sèche*$_{(\text{fem, sing})}$, *sèches*$_{(\text{fem, plur})}$} or BREF$_{\text{Adj}}$ 'brief' {*bref*$_{(\text{masc, sing})}$, *brefs*$_{(\text{masc, plur})}$, *brève*$_{(\text{fem, sing})}$, *brèves*$_{(\text{fem, plur})}$}. It is dealt with on a case-by-case basis, with the generation of specific Lexeme Tables.

3. As for nouns, we have to deal with spelling variation of adjectival stems—see the case of ABÎMÉ 'damaged' mentioned in section 3.1 above. This implies the creation of two (or more) Lexeme Tables for the same lexeme, one for each possible stem.

Another difficulty we had to deal with comes from the fact that adjectives may have a particular form when they are linearized before a vowel-initial noun (Bonami and Boyé, 2005). Such is the case of VIEUX 'old':

(1) a. *Ugo, c'était un* ***vieux copain*** *d'enfance.*
'Ugo was an old childhood friend'
[**Frantext**, IZZO Jean-Claude, *Total Khéops*, 1995, p. 41]

b. *Après tout, je suis ton plus* ***vieil ami****.*
'After all, I'm your oldest friend'
[**Frantext**, BEAUVOIR (de) Simone, *Les Mandarins*, 1954, p. 364]

In order to handle such cases, the lexeme VIEUX$_{\text{Adj}}$ is related to the **five** rather than four wordforms in its Lexeme Table, *vieil* being encoded as a variant wordform for masculine singular—see Figure 5.

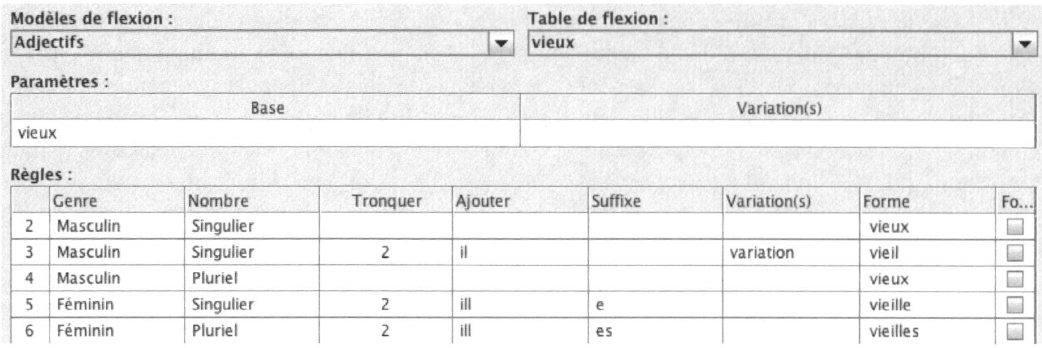

Modèles de flexion : Adjectifs

Table de flexion : vieux

Paramètres :

Base	Variation(s)
vieux	

Règles :

	Genre	Nombre	Tronquer	Ajouter	Suffixe	Variation(s)	Forme	Fo...
2	Masculin	Singulier					vieux	☐
3	Masculin	Singulier	2	il		variation	vieil	☐
4	Masculin	Pluriel					vieux	☐
5	Féminin	Singulier	2	ill	e		vieille	☐
6	Féminin	Pluriel	2	ill	es		vieilles	☐

Figure 5: Lexeme Table of VIEUX 'old'

Finally, we have included in adjectival Lexeme Tables wordforms that are **linguistically** possible and attested, though they may seem deviant for **conceptual** reasons. For instance, ENCEINTE$_{\text{Adj}}$ 'pregnant' is naturally related to two feminine wordforms: *enceinte*$_{\text{(fem, sing)}}$ $\sim$ *enceintes*$_{\text{(fem, plur)}}$; but in the eventuality that one does want to talk about a pregnant man (for instance, in order to state that this would be a challenging situation), two distinct pairs of masculine wordforms can be used *enceinte*$_{\text{(masc, sing)}}$ $\sim$ *enceintes*$_{\text{(masc, plur)}}$ or *enceint*$_{\text{(masc, sing)}}$ $\sim$ *enceints*$_{\text{(masc, plur)}}$. See the following examples found on the Internet:

(2) a. *Des jeunes* ***garçons enceintes****, c'est ce que voient les habitants de Chicago sur leurs panneaux publicitaires.*
'Young pregnant boys, that's what people in Chicago see on advertisement billboards'
[`http://www.grazia.fr/societe/news/etats-unis-des-hommes-enceintes-pour-promouvoir-la-contraception-551492`]

b. *À Chicago, les affiches publicitaires mettant en scène de jeunes* ***garçons enceints*** *ont remplacé celles, plus classiques, sur les préservatifs et la pilule.*
'In Chicago, advertisements showing pregnant teenage boys have replaced more traditional ones, about condoms and the birth control pill'
[`http://www.terrafemina.com/vie-privee/sexo/articles/27026-contraception-des-garcons-enceints-pour-sensibiliser-les-ados-de-chicago.html`]

These forms, that are amply attested, are labelled as `possible` in the Lexeme Table of ENCEINTE$_{\text{Adj}}$, where the feminine singular wordform is of course identified as naming form; cf. Figure 6.

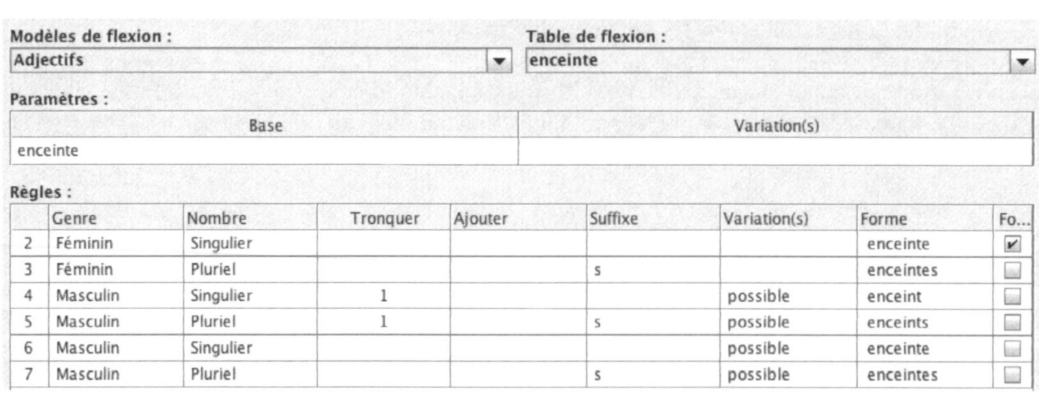

Modèles de flexion : Adjectifs

Table de flexion : enceinte

Paramètres :

Base	Variation(s)
enceinte	

Règles :

	Genre	Nombre	Tronquer	Ajouter	Suffixe	Variation(s)	Forme	Fo...
2	Féminin	Singulier					enceinte	☑
3	Féminin	Pluriel			s		enceintes	☐
4	Masculin	Singulier	1			possible	enceint	☐
5	Masculin	Pluriel	1		s	possible	enceints	☐
6	Masculin	Singulier				possible	enceinte	☐
7	Masculin	Pluriel			s	possible	enceintes	☐

Figure 6: Lexeme Table of ENCEINTE$_{\text{Adj}}$ 'pregnant'

This approach reflects actual usage and is more valid from a linguistic point of view than the alternative solution that consists in encoding ENCEINTE$_{\text{Adj}}$ as defective adjective.

4.3 Verbal Lexeme Tables

For lack of space, we provide only an outline of how the rich inflectional morphology of French verbs is being handled in our model. We focus on the most significant aspects of the question only.

The pairing of a Prototypical Table with a verbal lexeme implies that information is provided on (i) which auxiliary (*avoir* or *être*) is selected by the verb for compound tenses and (ii) whether the verb is pronominal (S'AMÉLIORER 'to become better') or not (AMÉLIORER 'to improve (something)'). This is illustrated in Figure 7, which shows a short sample of the Lexeme Table of the verb AGACER **I** 'to annoy'.

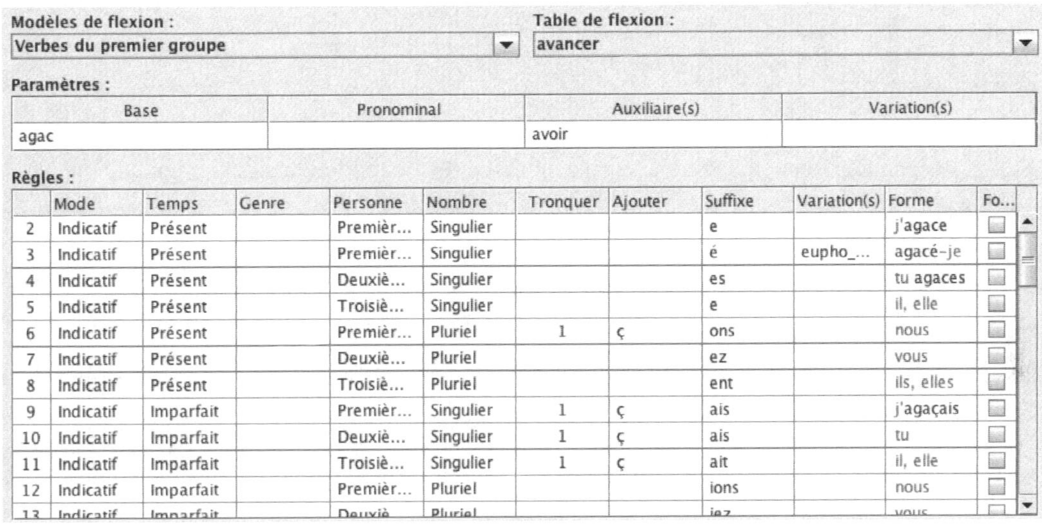

Modèles de flexion : Verbes du premier groupe

Table de flexion : avancer

Paramètres :

Base	Pronominal	Auxiliaire(s)	Variation(s)
agac		avoir	

Règles :

	Mode	Temps	Genre	Personne	Nombre	Tronquer	Ajouter	Suffixe	Variation(s)	Forme	Fo...
2	Indicatif	Présent		Premièr...	Singulier			e		j'agace	
3	Indicatif	Présent		Premièr...	Singulier			é	eupho_...	agacé-je	
4	Indicatif	Présent		Deuxiè...	Singulier			es		tu agaces	
5	Indicatif	Présent		Troisiè...	Singulier			e		il, elle	
6	Indicatif	Présent		Premièr...	Pluriel	1	ç	ons		nous	
7	Indicatif	Présent		Deuxiè...	Pluriel			ez		vous	
8	Indicatif	Présent		Troisiè...	Pluriel			ent		ils, elles	
9	Indicatif	Imparfait		Premièr...	Singulier	1	ç	ais		j'agaçais	
10	Indicatif	Imparfait		Deuxiè...	Singulier	1	ç	ais		tu	
11	Indicatif	Imparfait		Troisiè...	Singulier	1	ç	ait		il, elle	
12	Indicatif	Imparfait		Premièr...	Pluriel			ions		nous	
13	Indicatif	Imparfait		Deuxiè...	Pluriel			iez		vous	

Figure 7: Lexeme Table (sample) of AGACER **I** 'to annoy'

At present, 34 different Prototypical Tables—such as `danser` 'to dance'—have been constructed in order to generate Lexeme Tables for French verbs of the first conjugation class (*premier groupe*, in French grammatical terminology), i.e. verbs that take the *-er* infinitive suffix. Most of these tables were created in order to handle stem alternations, such as the alternation *agac-* ∼ *agaç-* for AGACER **I** in Figure 7.

The first conjugation class has the highest cardinality and it is basically the only productive one in contemporary French. (Neologisms normally belong to this class.) There are two other conjugaison classes. Verbs of the second conjugation class are dealt with using 3 Prototypical Tables, and 52 Prototypical Tables have been constructed for verbs of the third class.

As for nouns and adjectives, verbs can be defective—11 Prototypical Tables handle defective paradigms—and can have spelling variants. In addition, the morphological model has to deal with suppletive verbs—on suppletion, see (Mel'čuk, 1994; Bonami and Boyé, 2003; Corbett, 2007).

To conclude our description of the morphological Lexicographic Process, it is important to mention the fact that an inheritance mechanism has been implemented in the Dicet editor. Senses that are created inside an already existing vocable automatically inherit their morphological description from the basic lexical unit of the vocable (the sense controlling the vocable's polysemic structure). Inherited morphological data get a default measure of confidence of 50%. It has to later be either validated by lexicographers (measure of confidence pushed to 100%) or manually overwritten, if the sense in question has a specific morphological behavior.

5 Concluding remarks

The production of individual Lexeme Tables has started only four months ago, after the complex tasks of designing and implementing the dynamic morphological model had been completed. For the time being, approximatively 10% of the vocables (= entries) currently present in the database have been morphologically described.[7]

We expect to have finished the morphological work "on back order" in the fr-LN database within a few months. Future developments include:

- the treatment of compounds such as BOULANGER-PÂTISSIER lit. 'baker-pastry maker' {*boulanger-pâtissier*$_{\text{(sing)}}$, *boulangers-pâtissiers*$_{\text{(plur)}}$} (Mathieu-Colas, 2011);
- the computation of inflected forms of idioms using the encoding of their lexico-syntactic structure;
- the application of our dynamic approach to the modeling of morphology of languages other than French within their lexical networks, starting with the English Lexical Network (en-LN) presented in (Gader *et al.*, 2014).

Acknowledgments

Work on the fr-LN is supported by a grant from the Agence de Mobilisation Économique de Lorraine (AMEL) and Fonds Européen de Développement Régional (FEDER). We thank Cogalex 2014 anonymous reviewers for their comments on a first version of this paper.

References

Antidote. 2014. *Antidote 8* [software]. Druide informatique inc., Montreal, QC.

Matthews Baerman, Greville G. Corbett and Dunstan Brown. 2010. *Defective Paradigms: missing forms and what they tell us.* Oxford University Press, Oxford, UK.

Collin F. Baker, Charles J. Fillmore and Beau Cronin. 2003. The Structure of the FrameNet Database. *International Journal of Lexicography*, 16(3):281–296.

Olivier Bonami and Gilles Boyé. 2003. Supplétion et classes flexionnelles dans la conjugaison du français. *Langages*, 37(152):102–126.

Olivier Bonami and Gilles Boyé. 2005. Construire le paradigme d'un adjectif. *Recherches linguistiques de Vincennes*, 34:77–98.

Olivier Bonami, Gauthier Caron and Clément Plancq. 2013. Flexique: an inflectional lexicon for spoken French. Technical documentation [`http://www.llf.cnrs.fr/flexique/documentation.pdf`].

Nina Catach. 1995. Le problème des variantes graphiques: variantes du passé, du présent et de l'avenir. *Langue française*, 25–32.

Conseil supérieur de la langue française. 1990. *Les rectifications de l'orthographe.* Journal officiel de la République française N° 100. Édition des documents administratifs. Direction des journaux officiels, Paris.

Greville G. Corbett. 2007. Canonical Typolgy, Suppletion, and Possible Words. *Language*, 8–42.

Candice Delaite and Alain Polguère. 2013. Sex-Based Nominal Pairs in the French Lexical Network: It's Not What You Think. *Proceedings of the 6th International Conference on Meaning-Text Theory (MTT'13)*, Valentina Apresjan, Boris Iomdin, Ekaterina Ageeva (Eds.), Prague, 29–40.

George Dunbar. 2012. Adaptive Resonance Theory as a model of polysemy and vagueness in the cognitive lexicon. *Cognitive Linguistics*, 23(3):507–537.

Christiane Fellbaum (Ed.). 1998. *WordNet: An Electronic Lexical Database.* The MIT Press, Cambridge, MA.

Nabil Gader, Veronika Lux-Pogodalla and Alain Polguère. 2012. Hand-Crafting a Lexical Network With a Knowledge-Based Graph Editor. *Proceedings of the Third Workshop on Cognitive Aspects of the Lexicon (CogALex III)*, The COLING 2012 Organizing Committee, Mumbai, 109–125.

[7]More than 5% of these vocables required separate morphological characterization for their senses (cf. the case of COULEURS **III.1b** mentioned in section 4.1). This is a rather high proportion—considering the fact that many of the vocables we treated are monosemic and are thus not concerned by potential morphological discrepancies between senses—and it is a strong argument in favor fo the design of our sense- rather than vocable-based morphological model.

Nabil Gader, Sandrine Ollinger and Alain Polguère. 2014. One Lexicon, Two Structures: So What Gives?. *Proceedings of the Seventh Global Wordnet Conference (GWC2014)*, Heili Orav, Christiane Fellbaum, Piek Vossen (Eds.), Global WordNet Association, Tartu, 163–171.

Fabrice Issac. 2010. A framework for representing lexical resources. *Proceedings of the 23rd International Conference on Computational Linguistics*, Chu-Ren Huang, Dan Jurafsky (Eds.), Beijing, China, 490–497.

Claudia Leacock and Martin Chodorow. 1998. Combining Local Context with WordNet Similarity for Word Sense Identification. *WordNet: An Electronic Database*, Christiane Fellbaum (Ed.), The MIT Press, Cambridge, MA, 265–283.

Bernard Lété, Liliane Sprenger-Charolles and Pascale Colé. 2004. MANULEX: A grade-level lexical database from French elementary school readers. *Behavior Research Methods, Instruments and Computers*, 36(1):156–166.

Veronika Lux-Pogodalla and Alain Polguère. 2011. Construction of a French Lexical Network: Methodological Issues. *Proceedings of the First International Workshop on Lexical Resources, WoLeR 2011. An ESSLLI 2011 Workshop*, Ljubljana, 2011, 54–61.

Michel Mathieu-Colas. 2009. Morfetik: une ressource lexicale pour le TAL. *Cahiers de Lexicologie*, 94:137–146.

Michel Mathieu-Colas. 2011. Flexion des noms et des adjectifs composés: Principes de codage. Technical documentation [http://halshs.archives-ouvertes.fr/halshs-00635018/].

Igor Mel'čuk. 1994. Suppletion: toward a logical analysis of the concept. *Studies in Language*, 18(2):339–410.

Igor Mel'čuk. 2000. Un FOU/une FOLLE: un lexème ou deux? *Bulag*, hors-série:95–106.

Igor Mel'čuk. 2012. *Semantics: From meaning to text* (vol. 1). Studies in Language Companion Series 129, John Benjamins, Amsterdam/Philadelphia.

Véronique Montémont. 2008. Discovering Frantext. *New Beginnings in Literary Studies*, Jan Auracher, Willie van Peer (Eds.), Cambridge Scholars Publishing, Newcastle, UK, 89–107.

Boris New. 2006. Lexique 3: Une nouvelle base de données lexicales. *Proceedings of TALN 2006*, Chu-Ren Huang, Dan Jurafsky (Eds.), Leuven, Belgium, 490–497.

Alain Polguère. 2014. Principes de modélisation systémique des réseaux lexicaux. *Proceedings of TALN 2014*, Brigitte Bigi (Ed.), Marseille, France, 79–90.

Alain Polguère. To appear. From Writing Dictionaries to Weaving Lexical Networks. *International Journal of Lexicography*.

Laurent Romary, Susanne Salmon-Alt and Gil Francopoulo. 2004. Standards going concrete: from LMF to Morphalou. *Workshop on Electronic Dictionaries, Coling 2004*, Geneva [http://hal.inria.fr/docs/00/12/14/89/PDF/LRSSAGFFinal.pdf].

Josef Ruppenhofer, Michael Ellsworth, Miriam R. L. Petruck, Christopher R. Johnson and Jan Scheffczyk. 2010. *FrameNet II: Extended Theory and Practice*. International Computer Science Institute, Berkeley, CA.

Benoît Sagot. 2010. The Lefff, a freely available and large-coverage morphological and syntactic lexicon for French. *Proceedings of the 7th International Conference on Language Resources and Evaluation (LREC'10)*, Istanbul.

Mark Sebba. 2003. Spelling rebellion. *Pragmatics and beyond*, 151–172.

Dennis Spohr. 2012. *Towards a Multifunctional Lexical Resource. Design and Implementation of a Graph-based Lexicon Model*. Walter de Gruyter, Berlin & Boston, MA.

Dimensions of Metaphorical Meaning

Andrew Gargett[*], **Josef Ruppenhofer**[†] and **John Barnden**[*]
[*]University of Birmingham
United Kingdom
{a.d.gargett|j.a.barnden}@cs.bham.ac.uk
[†]Hildesheim University
Germany
ruppenho@uni-hildesheim.de

Abstract

Recent work suggests that *concreteness* and *imageability* play an important role in the meanings of figurative expressions. We investigate this idea in several ways. First, we try to define more precisely the context within which a figurative *expression* may occur, by parsing a corpus annotated for metaphor. Next, we add both concreteness and imageability as "features" to the parsed metaphor corpus, by marking up words in this corpus using a psycholinguistic database of scores for concreteness and imageability. Finally, we carry out detailed statistical analyses of the augmented version of the original metaphor corpus, cross-matching the features of concreteness and imageability with others in the corpus such as parts of speech and dependency relations, in order to investigate in detail the use of such features in predicting whether a given expression is metaphorical or not.

1 Introduction

Figurative language plays an important role in "grounding" our communication in the world around us. Being able to talk metaphorically about "the journey of life", "getting into a relationship", whether there are "strings attached" to a contract, or even just "surfing the internet", are important and useful aspects of everyday discourse. Recent work on such phenomena has pursued this kind of grounding in interesting directions, in particular, treating it as a way of injecting meanings that are somehow more "concrete" into daily discourse (Neuman et al., 2013; Turney et al., 2011; Tsvetkov et al., 2013), or else as a way of expressing abstract ideas in terms of concepts that are more "imageable", where imageability can be defined as *how easily a word can evoke mental imagery*, (Cacciari and Glucksberg, 1995; Gibbs, 2006; Urena and Faber, 2010). It should be noted that while it is generally accepted that imageability and concreteness are highly correlated, recent work has shown they are contrastive, in particular, in their interaction with additional cognitive dimensions such as affective states, so that they "can no longer be considered interchangeable constructs" (Dellantonio et al., 2014).

When someone describes love as a journey, or life as a test, one possible way of thinking about what they are doing is that they are trying to cast a fairly abstract idea or concept, such as love or life, in terms of more concrete or imageable experiences or concepts, such as a journey or a test. More formally, metaphor can be characterized as the mapping of properties from a "source" domain concept (typically more concrete) on to a "target" domain concept (typically more abstract). However, despite the ease with which people understand both established metaphors such as these, or even more novel ones[1], and despite well-established findings about the ubiquity of metaphor in everyday discourse (Lakoff and Johnson, 1980), explicit and testable proposals for the mechanisms underlying such forms of expression remain elusive.

When looking for such mechanisms, it seems natural to start with the patterns of language that so effectively convey metaphorical meanings. Along these lines, Deignan (2006) argues that:

[1]Consider how readily one can make sense of a novel, yet metaphorical utterance, such as "life is a box of chocolates" (from a recent film), despite never having heard it before.

Zock/Rapp/Huang (eds.): Proceedings of the 4th Workshop on Cognitive Aspects of the Lexicon, pages 166–173,
Dublin, Ireland, August 23, 2014.

> [M]etaphorical uses of words show differences in their grammatical behavior, or even their word class, when compared to their literal use. In addition, it shows that metaphorical uses of a word commonly appear in distinctive and relatively fixed syntactic patterns.

Focusing on word class of figurative expressions, so-called content words, such as nouns, adjectives and verbs, have long been considered to more strongly convey figurative meanings than so-called function words, such as prepositions (Neuman et al., 2013; Tsvetkov et al., 2013). Yet, Steen et al. (2010) find prepositions within figurative expressions to be as prevalent as content words such as nouns and verbs, and indeed, for particular genres (such as academic texts) prepositions are the most frequently attested part of speech for figurative expressions.

Further, there has been work on the interaction between metaphorical expressions and syntactically defined contexts (e.g. phrase, clause, sentence). For example, Neuman et al. (2013) investigate how metaphorical expressions apparently pattern by syntactically definable types, specifically: Type I, where "a subject noun is associated with an object noun via a form of the copula verb *to be*" (e.g. "God is a king"), Type II having the verb as "the focus of the metaphorical use representing the act of a subject noun on an object noun" (e.g. "The war absorbed his energy"), and Type III "involve an adjective-noun phrase" (e.g. "sweet girl"). While such work yields a useful typology of figurative expressions, such investigations into the syntactic patterns of figurative forms of expression is far from exhaustive. It would be useful to take this further somewhat, with a more rigorous, syntactically precise definition of the context of occurrence of figurative language.

Motivated by the above considerations, we have begun investigating the interaction of *concreteness* and *imageability* with figurative meanings in several ways. This paper reports the initial stages of this ongoing work into the dimensions of meaning of figurative language such as metaphor. As part of this work, we have attempted to define more precisely the context within which a figurative *expression* may occur, by parsing a corpus annotated for metaphor, the Vrije University Amsterdam Metaphor Corpus (VUAMC) (Steen et al., 2010), using an off the shelf dependency parser, the Mate parser (Bohnet, 2010). In addition, we add both concreteness and imageability as "features" to the dependency parsed metaphor corpus, by marking up words in this corpus using a psycholinguistic database of scores for concreteness and imageability, the MRC Psycholinguistic Database (Wilson, 1988). In this paper, we report detailed statistical analyses we have carried out of the resulting data set, cross-matching the features of concreteness and imageability with others in the corpus such as parts of speech (PsOS) and dependency relations, in order to investigate in detail the use of such features in determining whether a given expression is metaphorical or not.

2 Method

2.1 Data

Our data comes from the Vrije University Amsterdam Metaphor Corpus (VUAMC), consisting of approximately 188,000 words selected from the British National Corpus-Baby (BNC-Baby), and annotated for metaphor using the Metaphor Identification Procedure (MIP) (Steen et al., 2010). The corpus has four registers, of between 44,000 and 50,000 words each: academic texts, news texts, fiction, and conversations. We have chosen this corpus because of its broad coverage and its rich metaphorical annotation.

2.2 Procedure

PRE-PROCESSING. We have enriched the VUAMC in several ways. First, we have parsed the corpus using the graph-based version of the Mate tools dependency parser (Bohnet, 2010), adding rich syntactic information.[2] Second, we have incorporated the MRC Psycholinguistic Database[3] (Wilson, 1988), a dictionary of 150,837 words, with different subsets of these words having been rated by human subjects in psycholinguistic experiments. Of special note, the database includes 4,295 words rated with degrees of abstractness, these ratings ranging from 158 (meaning *highly abstract*) to 670 (meaning *highly concrete*),

[2] `https://code.google.com/p/mate-tools/`

[3] `http://ota.oucs.ox.ac.uk/headers/1054.xml`

and also 9,240 words rated for degrees of imageability, which can be defined as *how easily a word can evoke mental imagery*, these ratings also ranging between 100 and 700 (a higher score indicating greater imageability). It should be noted that it has long been known that the concreteness and imageability scores are highly correlated (Paivio et al., 1968), however, there are interesting differences between these sets of scores (Dellantonio et al., 2014), and we are currently investigating these differences in further studies (see Section (4) below). These scores have been used extensively for work that is similar to ours, e.g. (Neuman et al., 2013; Turney et al., 2011; Tsvetkov et al., 2013), and while our work is also largely computational in approach, a significant component of our research is devoted to investigating in some detail the cognitive aspects of figurative meanings.

EXPERIMENTAL DESIGN. We carried out five studies, all beginning with pre-processing tasks to prepare the data (additional to those listed immediately above, undertaken to prepare the entire corpus for these studies). We list the aims, details of pre-processing, and hypotheses below.

Study 1. This study initiated the investigation, and guided the setting up of the computational framework for our broader research activities. The VUAMC was extended with dependency information from the Mate dependency parser, enabling extraction of both dependency information and metaphorical annotation for each VUAMC word.[4] Hypotheses: H_1 = nouns are more prevalent in metaphorical expressions than verbs, verbs more than adjectives, adjectives more than prepositions; H_2 = metaphorical expressions are more likely to occur in sentences in which other metaphorical expressions occur.

Study 2. This study aimed to evaluate claims about syntactically-defined metaphor types (Neuman et al., 2013), and search for other types. The structure of a sentence revealed by a dependency parse is based on the relation between a word, known as a *head*, and its *dependents*. This extended VUAMC data provided variables for metaphor types I, II and III, respectively, *Noun-BE-Noun*, *Noun-ActiveVerb-Noun*, and *Adjective-Noun*, as well as the discovery of additional metaphor types.

Study 3. Going further than Studies 1 and 2, this study extended the VUAMC data with MRC concreteness and imageability scores, plus further processing of the VUAMC corpus, assigning MRC scores to each item in this corpus. Note here that the VUAMC data was examined word-by-word (rather than sentence-by-sentence, as for Study 2). However, the VUAMC data set is much larger than the MRC data set, so that many VUAMC words have no MRC scores. To smooth this discrepancy, for this initial stage of our investigations, we have implemented the fairly rudimentary approach of calculating global MRC scores by: first, from VUAMC words with MRC scores, a global average MRC score for each part of speech of the VUAMC data was calculated, and second, those VUAMC words without MRC scores (i.e. missing from the MRC database) were assigned a global score based on their part of speech. Of course, a range of possible smoothing strategies are available, and while at this stage we are employing a rather crude averaging of the score, this is an area we intend to investigate further in follow-up studies, inspired by the more sophisticated methods that have been implemented by others, e.g. (Feng et al., 2011; Tsvetkov et al., 2013).[5] For this study, we sought to answer the following two questions: Do concreteness and imageability scores correlate with metaphoricity of expressions? Do concreteness and imageability scores correlate with parts of speech of metaphorical expressions?

Study 4. This study replicated Study 3, but also considered the data sentence-by-sentence (cf. Study 2), to integrate syntactic information and MRC score. Examining MRC scores across syntactically fine-grained contexts, enabled collecting information about heads, their dependent/s, as well as the dependency relation/s, and this information could then be examined to see if it helped to distinguish between literal and nonliteral items. This approach enables us to investigate in detail the contexts in which *concreteness* and *imageability* with figurative meanings, a key aim of our work, as pointed out in Section (1). Hypotheses: H_3 = metaphorical expressions are more likely to occur in sentences where the head is more

[4]For more details on the VUAMC categories, see: `http://www.natcorp.ox.ac.uk/docs`.

[5]This work is part of a larger project, `http://www.cs.bham.ac.uk/~gargetad/genmeta-about.html`, which aims to annotate larger web-based corpora of discourse on illness and political conflict.

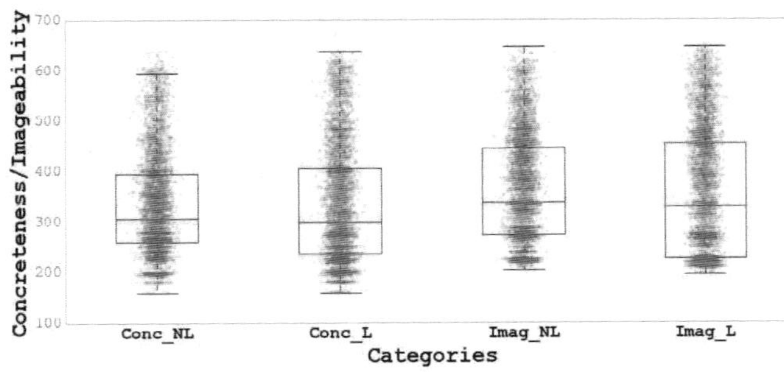

Figure 1: Plots of concreteness vs. imageability scores for literal vs. nonliteral words in the VUAMC (Conc=concreteness, Imag=imageability, NL=nonliteral, L=literal)

concrete than the dependent/s; H_4 = metaphorical expressions are more likely to occur in sentences where the head is more imageable than the dependent/s.

Study 5. Finally, this study finished by examining the relative importance of the variables identified so far, for predicting literal vs. nonliteral expressions, another key aim of our work (as mentioned in Section (1)). We implemented this study through building and evaluating a series of logistic regression models.

3 Results

3.1 Study 1

The first hypothesis listed for this study above has not been refuted, with the percentage of all nonliteral sentences in our collection having only one nonliteral item being 27%, while the percentage of all nonliteral sentences having more than one nonliteral item is 73%: so after finding one nonliteral item in a sentence, we can expect to find more. Regarding the second hypothesis, our data set had the following proportions of occurrence of nonliteral items according to parts of speech: Adjectives=10.8%, Prepositions=28%, Nouns=22.5%, Verbs=27%, Adverbs=5%, Pronouns=0.2%, Conjunctions=0.5%, Other=6%. Consistent with Steen et al. (2010), that function words can occur more frequently than content words in metaphorical expressions, we found prepositions to be far more prevalent than adjectives in such expressions, and occur about as frequently as verbs.

3.2 Study 2

We found the following percentages of metaphor types (across all metaphors): Type I = 3.06%, Type II = 33.53%, Type III = 7.56% (note the reversal for Type II vs. Type III, contrary to (Neuman et al., 2013)). Such differences may be due to differences in data sets, as well as different syntactic models.[6] Additionally, we found a pattern of expression we have dubbed "Type IV" metaphors, consisting of preposition as head, together with noun phrase dependents (e.g. "at the end of the decade", "after the break-up"): these account for 35.53% of the total occurrence of metaphors.

3.3 Study 3

The boxplots in Figure (1) compare concreteness and imageability scores for nonliteral vs. literal items, suggesting nonliteral and literal items are indistinguishable from one another with respect to their concreteness and imageability scores. Next, we further categorise our data according to parts of speech, the boxplots in Figure (2) showing results for concreteness, and the boxplots Figure (3) presenting results for imageability – these figures suggest literal and nonliteral items can be better distinguished, with respect to their concreteness and imageability scores, by increasing the granularity of annotation of the context (e.g. by including parts of speech). Note that imageability scores for prepositions seem to show the

[6]Neuman et al. (2013) used the Stanford Dependency Parser (De Marneffe and Manning, 2008).

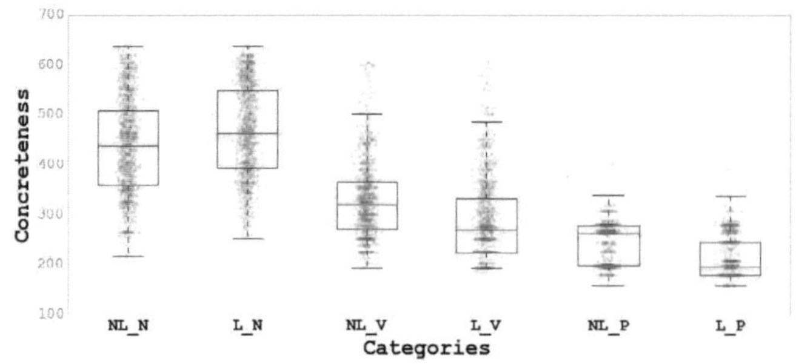

Figure 2: Plots of concreteness scores for literal vs. nonliteral/metaphorical words in the VUAMC, grouped by parts of speech (L=literal, NL=nonliteral, N=noun, V=verb, P=preposition)

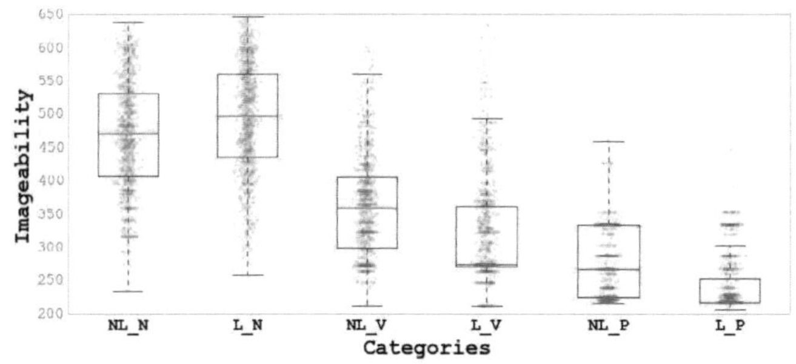

Figure 3: Plots of imageability scores for literal vs. nonliteral/metaphorical words in the VUAMC, grouped by parts of speech (L=literal, NL=nonliteral, N=noun, V=verb, P=preposition)

clearest distinction between literal vs. nonliteral items. But can we do better? What further categories in the data should we focus on in order to achieve even clearer distinctions between literal vs. nonliteral items?

3.4 Study 4

Figures (4) and (5) show the variation that can be achieved by making a more fine-grained distinction within our data set between heads and their dependents, plus MRC scores of each. Figure (4) shows that concreteness scores enable distinguishing between literal and nonliteral items for some parts of speech, such as nouns, where nonliteral heads have higher MRC scores than their dependents, distinct from literal head nouns (verbs appear to make no such a distinction). While literal and nonliteral head prepositions both seem indistinguishable from their dependents in terms of concreteness scores, nonliteral head prepositions seem to have imageability scores quite distinct from their dependents.

3.5 Study 5

Based on our previous studies, we here examine the following 5 independent variables: **POS** = part of speech of the head, **C_Head** = concreteness score of the head, **I_Head** = imageability score of the head, **C_Dep** = average concreteness score of the dependents, **I_Dep** = average imageability score of the dependents. Table (1) sets out the results for 7 logistic regression models we tested, and formulas representing these models **M1** to **M7** are as follows (**Nonliteral** of course being the dependent variable, its values being either "yes, this is nonliteral" or "no, this is not nonliteral"):

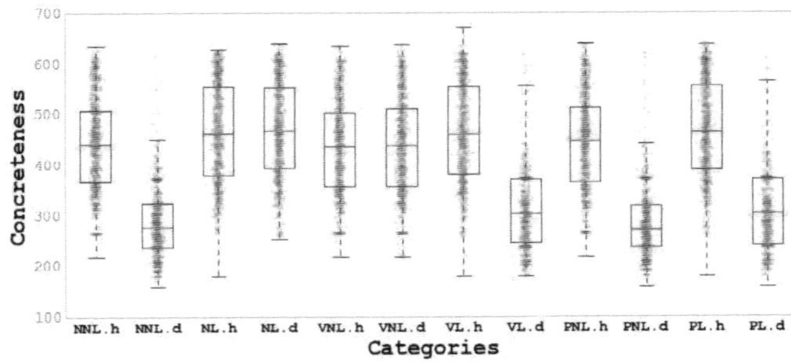

Figure 4: Plots of concreteness scores for literal vs. nonliteral/metaphorical heads vs. their dependents, in the VUAMC, grouped by parts of speech (L=literal, NL=nonliteral, N=noun, V=verb, P=preposition, h=head, d=dependents)

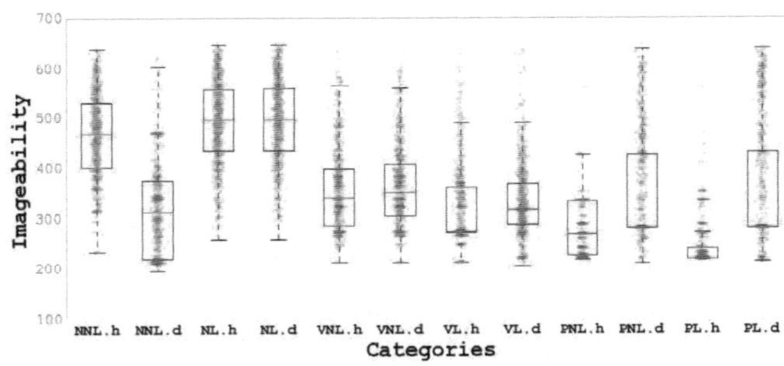

Figure 5: Plots of imageability scores for literal vs. nonliteral/metaphorical heads vs. their dependents, in the VUAMC, grouped by parts of speech (L=literal, NL=nonliteral, N=noun, V=verb, P=preposition, h=head, d=dependents)

M1: $Nonliteral \sim POS + C\_Head + I\_Head + C\_Dep + I\_Dep$
M2: $Nonliteral \sim C\_Head + I\_Head$
M3: $Nonliteral \sim POS + C\_Head + I\_Head$
M4: $Nonliteral \sim POS + C\_Head + C\_Dep + I\_Dep$
M5: $Nonliteral \sim POS + I\_Head + C\_Dep + I\_Dep$
M6: $Nonliteral \sim POS + C\_Head + C\_Dep$
M7: $Nonliteral \sim POS + I\_Head + I\_Dep$

In Table (1), p-values have three categories, $p < .0001$, $p < .001$, or $p < .01$: this value represents a test of the null hypothesis that the coefficient of the variable being considered is zero, i.e., the variable has no effect on the model (a lower p-value is stronger evidence for rejecting the null hypothesis). Where variables have significantly low p-values, Table (1) in effect presents optimal combinations of variables for specific models, with low p-values indicating variables likely to have a greater effect on the model and so more directly reflecting changes in the independent variable. For example, Table (1) shows that models selecting MRC scores for heads (e.g. **C_Head**) with the same kinds of scores for their dependents (e.g.**C_Dep**) seem most successful, which is perhaps to be expected, in light of studies 3 and 4.

It should be noted that no single variable models are reported here, since (1) while models such as $Nonliteral \sim I\_Head$ and $Nonliteral \sim C\_Head$ indeed achieve significant p-values, others such as $Nonliteral \sim I\_Dep$ and $Nonliteral \sim C\_Dep$ do not, (2) single variable models do not explain Figure (1), nor indeed the variation for multiple variable contexts as exhibited by Figures (4) and (5). We are currently comparing single vs. multiple variables, and early machine learning results suggest multiple variable models are superior compared to single variable models as predictive tools.

Variables	M1	M2	M3	M4	M5	M6	M7
Intercept	-7.534***	-2.609*	-9.088***	-7.836***	-7.522***	-7.816***	-7.614***
POS	9.265***		8.884***	9.330***	9.163***	9.316***	9.082***
C_Head	1.555	0.288	1.382	4.844***		4.876***	
I_Head	0.459	-1.312	0.513		4.611***		4.660***
C_Dep	-1.964			-1.982	-1.919	-3.799***	
I_Dep	0.682			0.699	0.660		-3.325**

Table 1: Results (t scores) of logistic regression model for predicting non/literal items from the VUAMC, n=1855 (nb. p-values are shown by asterisks, ***=p<.0001, **=p<.001, *=p<.01)

4 Discussion

This paper reports results from ongoing work we are carrying out toward building a tool for identifying metaphorical expressions in everyday discourse, through fine-grained analysis of the dimensions of meaning of such expressions. We have presented evidence that detecting metaphor can usefully be pursued as the problem of modeling how conceptual meanings such as concreteness and imageability, interact with syntactically definable linguistic contexts. We increase the granularity of our analyses by incorporating detailed syntactic information about the context in which metaphorical expressions occur. By increasing the granularity of context, we were able to distinguish between metaphorical expressions according to different parts of speech, and further, according to heads and their dependents.

We were able to show that for the purpose of determining whether a specific linguistic expression is metaphorical or not, the most successful approach seems to be to combine information about parts of speech with either concreteness scores for both heads and their dependents, or else with imageability scores for both heads and their dependents. Note that this result is in part a direct consequence of the high correlation between concreteness and imageability, whereby their combination will typically not result in an optimal regression model. Such high correlation between concreteness and imageability has been understood for some time (Paivio et al., 1968), yet, of course, there is good reason to think that concreteness and imageability do not in fact pattern identically, and that they are at some level distinct phenomena. Indeed, concreteness and imageability are likely related to distinct cognitive systems, and we are currently undertaking further investigations in this direction.

Finally, we should note that while our results are likely to be language-specific, it is reasonable to assume the general approach could be replicated across languages. We are currently planning such cross-linguistic research for future work.

Acknowledgements

We acknowledge financial support through a Marie Curie International Incoming Fellowship (project 330569) awarded to two of the authors (Gargett as fellow, Barnden as P.I.). We would also like to sincerely thank the reviewers for many very useful comments; of course, we assume full responsibility for the final version.

References

Bernd Bohnet. 2010. Very high accuracy and fast dependency parsing is not a contradiction. In *The 23rd International Conference on Computational Linguistics (COLING 2010), Beijing, China.*

Christina Cacciari and Sam Glucksberg. 1995. Imaging idiomatic expressions: literal or figurative meanings. In Martin Everaert, Erik-Jan van der Linden, Andr Schenk, and Rober Schreuder, editors, *Idioms: Structural and psychological perspectives*, pages 43–56. Lawrence Erlbaum.

Marie-Catherine De Marneffe and Christopher D Manning. 2008. The stanford typed dependencies representation. In *Coling 2008: Proceedings of the workshop on Cross-Framework and Cross-Domain Parser Evaluation*, pages 1–8. Association for Computational Linguistics.

Alice Deignan. 2006. The grammar of linguistic metaphors. In Anatol Stefanowitsch and Stefan Gries, editors, *Corpus-based approaches to metaphor and metonymy*, pages 106–122. Walter de Gruyter.

Sara Dellantonio, Claudio Mulatti, Luigi Pastore, and Remo Job. 2014. Measuring inconsistencies can lead you forward: The case of imageability and concreteness ratings. *Frontiers in Psychology*, 5(708).

Shi Feng, Zhiqiang Cai, Scott A Crossley, and Danielle S McNamara. 2011. Simulating human ratings on word concreteness. In *FLAIRS Conference*.

Raymond W Gibbs. 2006. Metaphor interpretation as embodied simulation. *Mind & Language*, 21(3):434–458.

George Lakoff and Mark Johnson. 1980. *Metaphors We Live By*. University of Chicago.

Yair Neuman, Dan Assaf, Yohai Cohen, Mark Last, Shlomo Argamon, Newton Howard, and Ophir Frieder. 2013. Metaphor identification in large texts corpora. *PloS one*, 8(4):e62343.

Allan Paivio, John C Yuille, and Stephen A Madigan. 1968. Concreteness, imagery, and meaningfulness values for 925 nouns. *Journal of experimental psychology*, 76(1, pt.2):1–25.

G.J. Steen, A.G. Dorst, J.B. Herrmann, A.A. Kaal, and T. Krennmayr. 2010. *A Method for Linguistic Metaphor Identification: From MIP to MIPVU*. Converging Evidence in Language and Communication Research. John Benjamins Publishing Company.

Yulia Tsvetkov, Elena Mukomel, and Anatole Gershman. 2013. Cross-lingual metaphor detection using common semantic features. In *Proceedings of the First Workshop on Metaphor in NLP*, pages 45–51, Atlanta, Georgia, June. Association for Computational Linguistics.

Peter D Turney, Yair Neuman, Dan Assaf, and Yohai Cohen. 2011. Literal and metaphorical sense identification through concrete and abstract context. In *Proceedings of the 2011 Conference on the Empirical Methods in Natural Language Processing*, pages 680–690.

Jose Manuel Urena and Pamela Faber. 2010. Reviewing imagery in resemblance and non-resemblance metaphors. *Cognitive Linguistics*, 21(1):123–149.

Michael Wilson. 1988. MRC psycholinguistic database: Machine-usable dictionary, version 2.00. *Behavior Research Methods, Instruments, & Computers*, 20(1):6–10.

Constructing an Ontology of Japanese Lexical Properties: Specifying its Property Structures and Lexical Entries

Terry Joyce
School of Global Studies,
Tama University,
Fujisawa, Japan
terry@tama.ac.jp

Bor Hodošček
School of Global Japanese Studies,
Meiji University,
Nakano, Japan
bor.hodoscek@gmail.com

Abstract

Regarding the construction of an ontology of Japanese lexical properties (JLP-O) as fundamental in terms of establishing a conceptual framework to guide and facilitate the construction of a large-scale lexical resource (LR) database of the Japanese lexicon, this paper primarily focuses on two major concerns for the construction of the JLP-O. The first is to map out and appropriately structure the numerous lexical and psycholinguistic properties, or variables, associated with the Japanese lexicon. The second concern is to specify an appropriate range of lexical entries classes within the JLP-O. Both concerns have far-reaching implications for effectively capturing the rich patterns of interconnections among lexical entries and lexical properties and thus for realizing a multifunctional LR. After discussing the solutions integrated into the current Resource Description Framework (RDF) representation of the JLP-O, the paper also briefly describes the extraction of a corpus-based lexicon from the recently released Balanced Corpus of Contemporary Written Japanese (BCCWJ; Maekawa et al., 2013), an authoritative sampling of the contemporary Japanese lexicon. Categorized according to the JLP-O's range of lexical entry classes, and supplemented with orthographic variant and decomposition information, the BCCWJ-based lexicon represents a key reference LR for constructing the large-scale LR.

1 Introduction

The overarching objective of our research project is to construct a large-scale lexical resource (LR) of Japanese lexical properties—interpreted inclusively as any characteristic or variable associated with words—which, as a comprehensive model of the Japanese lexicon, can potentially be beneficial for various researchers within the linguistic and cognitive sciences. Within that larger endeavor, we regard the task of constructing an ontology of Japanese lexical properties (JLP-O) as being absolutely foundational for two important reasons. The first is primarily pragmatic in nature. As reflected in the relatively recent trend towards merging LRs and ontologies (Huang et al., 2010; Oltramari et al., 2013), the formal specification of the ontology can unquestionably provide considerable advantages in terms of enhanced compatibility with natural language processing (NLP) and knowledge system tools for efficiently integrating data, checking for consistency, and realizing powerful query functionality. In contrast, however, the second reason is both more conceptual and more skeptical in nature. In many ways, ontology construction can be thought of as the very epitome of academic endeavor in seeking to clearly elucidate the phenomenon of interest, but it is also crucial to understand that natural systems, such as language, do not necessarily conform to the standards of ontological completeness. As outlined further in section 2, our approach to ontology construction particularly values the utility of the ontology as working conceptual framework. Reflecting this, our approach attempts to strike a reasonable balance between ontological rigor, on the one hand, and recognizing a number of other important cognitive criteria, on the other hand, such as theoretical description, consistencies, psychological reality, and preferences, in order to realize a core framework that can both guide the construction of the LR and, ultimately, facilitate multifunctional querying.

Against that larger background, this paper specifically focuses on two major concerns addressed in constructing the JLP-O. Given the extensive range of Japanese lexical properties that must be represented in a

Zock/Rapp/Huang (eds.): Proceedings of the 4th Workshop on Cognitive Aspects of the Lexicon, pages 174–185,
Dublin, Ireland, August 23, 2014.

satisfactory manner within a large-scale LR for the Japanese lexicon, the first concern has been to map out and appropriately structure the many and varied lexical and psycholinguistic properties, or variables, associated with the Japanese lexicon into domains, or modules. The second major concern has been to specify an appropriate range of lexical entries as core entities of the JLP-O for a highly agglutinative language like Japanese. As outlined in more detail in section 3, these concerns have direct implications for implementing effective links among lexical entries and lexical properties. In section 4, we explain how both concerns have been resolved within the JLP-O in ways that simultaneously help to represent the rich patterns of interconnectivity between various lexical properties and facilitate the realization of a multifunctional LR that both possesses powerful search capabilities and can be utilized by a wide range of users. Section 4 also outlines the extraction and formal encoding of a major corpus-based lexicon essential for constructing the LR. Section 5 recaps the main points and briefly discusses future work for the larger LR project.

2 Ontology as conceptual framework

After some general comments about defining ontologies, this section also briefly introduces the two models for LRs that we specifically draw inspiration from in constructing the JLP-O; namely, the lemon model (lexical model for ontologies; http://lemon-model.net/) and Spohr's (2012) model for multifunctional LRs.

2.1 General comments

Although Gruber's (1993; 199) immensely influential pronouncement that an "ontology is an explicit specification of a conceptualization" continues to provide the basic template, following Guarino (1998) and Guarino et al. (2009), many subsequent definitions of ontologies tend to also emphasize the shared nature of the conceptualization (Guarino et al., 2009; Prévot et al., 2010). The elements of this ontology definition require a little unpacking. First, conceptualization refers to both the explicit and implicit knowledge about a system or entity, such as its component entities and their relations. Next, explicit, or formal, specification refers to a commitment to encode the body of knowledge in the form of some representation language, usually in a machine-readable format. And, finally, shared conceptualization refers to the criterion that, to have value, there should be a general consensus among interested parties about the target conceptualization (Guarino et al., 2009; Prévot et al., 2010).

As already suggested, our approach towards ontology construction is admittedly somewhat nuanced in nature, reflecting a basic tension at the conceptual level. While we fully concur with the laudable drive towards clearer descriptions of phenomena that ontology construction entails, we are equally cautious of seeing ontologies alone as some magical panacea for all knowledge representation problems. The sentiment is particularly visceral in the case of natural systems like language which abounds in various forms of redundancy and biases that are not readily represented by ontologies. Thus, in our efforts to construct a comprehensive model of the Japanese lexicon, we are endeavoring to incorporate vital aspects of linguistic and cognitive knowledge that are embedded within its diverse lexical properties. However, at the pragmatic level, we acutely recognize the numerous benefits of adopting the ontology as a conceptual framework for effectively realizing the overall research objective of constructing a large-scale LR database of Japanese lexical properties. In some ways, our qualified position on ontology construction is rather aptly captured in the following comments from Franconi, Kerhet, and Ngo (2013):

> An ontology provides a conceptual view of the database and it is composed by constraints on a vocabulary extending the basic vocabulary of the data. Querying a database using the terms in such a richer ontology allows for more flexibility than using only the basic vocabulary of the relational database directly.

2.2 Models for linguistic resources

For the sake of clarity (albeit at some risk of possibly overstating what may already be sufficiently obvious), our primary objective in constructing the JLP-O is to have a conceptual view, or framework, to aid the development of a large-scale LR database with multifunctional querying capabilities, which we hope will come to serve as a comprehensive model of the Japanese lexicon. That is to say, we are seeking to apply linguistic, psycholinguistic and cognitive conceptualizations about Japanese words in order to realize a formal specification of the Japanese lexicon. This naturally brings into focus the next vital piece in the puzzle; namely, the need for an ontology model that is particularly suitable for linguistic resources, where linguistic and psycholinguistic conceptualizations (lexical properties) are linked to the lexical entries (words) of the database. Although a number of candidate models exist, such as LexInfo (Cimiano, Buitelaar, McCrae, & Sintek, 2011), LIR (Linguistic Information Repository; Peters, Montiel-Ponsoda, & Cea, 2007) and LMF (Lexical Markup Framework; Francopoulo, 2013), the present work draws inspiration most directly from the lemon model and Spohr's (2012) model for multifunctional LRs.

Building directly on the LexInfo, LIR and LMF models, lemon has been specifically developed to be a standard for the exchange of lexical information on the semantic web, and so it has a number of advantages that are particularly appealing for JLP-O. These include the facts that lemon is based on RDF, a semantic web standard that can greatly facilitate the representation of links between parts of the LR, and that, reflecting its policy not to prescribe over linguistics definitions, lemon effectively delegates the burdens of constraining domain-specific information to external sources, such as WordNet and ontologies of linguistic descriptions such as GOLD (General Ontology for Linguistic Description; http://linguistics-ontology.org/). Other advantages are that lemon is relatively concise, because it requires few classes and relies on external definitions, and that it is organized in terms of a number of separate modules, which can be constructed independently for greater flexibility. In contrast, reflecting its emergence from the intersection between semantic web technology and lexicography, Spohr's (2012) model for multifunctional LRs is particularly concerned with the informational needs of diverse users, encompassing both humans (from monolinguals, bilinguals, novices, to linguistic experts) and NLP applications, and with realizing suitable query and display interfaces. As the goal of achieving a high degree of multifunctionality, in Spohr's sense of the notion, is also central to our LR project, we particularly take to heart Spohr's suggestion that one vital key for realizing multifunctionality is the incorporation of an appropriate typology, or range, of lexical entries.

3 Construction concerns

This section briefly sketches out the two major issues for constructing the JLP-O; namely, appropriately structuring the wide range of lexical properties associated with the Japanese lexicon and determining a suitable range of lexical entries. The solutions incorporated into JLP-O's RDF representation are discussed further in section 4.

3.1 Range of Japanese lexical properties

For researchers within the language and cognitive sciences to be able conduct significant research on various aspects of the Japanese language, such as developing more robust models and simulations of linguistic and cognitive abilities, obviously, access to a wide range of information about the contemporary Japanese lexicon is absolutely essential. Traditionally, available LRs have been limited to various kinds of dictionaries, such as language dictionaries like Shinmura's (2008) *Kōjien* and Kindaiichi et al.'s (2011) *Shinmeikai Kokugojiten* and character dictionaries like Morohashi's (2000) *Daikanwajiten*. However, as dictionaries rarely provide much summary information beyond headword counts, researchers have also had to rely on scarce sources of data summaries. Hayashi's (1982) *Zūsetsu Nihongo* is a classic example that included a lexical section, with some frequency, word class and formation information, an orthographic section, with some counts, usage and readings information for kanji in particular, as well as sections on phonology and accent, grammar, and style.

Setting aside genuine issues for keeping such data up-to-date, however, a particularly serious problem is the tremendous expansion in the range of lexical properties that researchers require data about today. One helpful way to understand the variety of lexical properties is in terms of Nation's (2001/2013) aspects of knowing a word. Highly influential in the areas of vocabulary research and second language acquisition, his framework consists of nine broad types of word knowledge grouped under three main categories of form (spoken, written, and word parts), meaning (form and meaning, concept and referent, and associations) and use (grammatical functions, collocations, and constraints on use (such as register and frequency)). In addition to the breadth dimension, it is also useful to think about the considerable range of lexical properties in terms of the depths of analyses conducted within these various domains. For instance, taking just the domain of visual word recognition experiments to illustrate, Adelman (2012) recently notes 14 kinds of potentially confounding lexical variables that should be controlled for, including frequency and contextual diversity data, various forms of neighborhoods (orthographic, phonological, phonographic, and Levenshtein-distance), spelling-sound regularities and consistencies, length, morphological properties as well as rating-based measures. While granting that some of these form-related lexical properties will undoubtedly also be of interest to researchers in other areas, still, equally undeniably, they will also require information about many other lexical properties, such as semantic properties of denotation and semantic groups of thesauri, or usage information, such as valencies, collocations and associations, and educational levels.

In addition to facilitating the integration and ongoing maintenance of the large-scale LR, we see the construction of the JLP-O as being especially valuable for helping to elucidate divergent interpretations about lexical properties. For instance, regardless of the markedly different theoretical motivations underlying orthographic neighborhoods and morphological families, LRs of kanji compound neighborhoods and LRs of morphological families yield identical data, at least, with respect to the possible two-compound word combinations for a given set of kanji. Awareness of such data equivalencies despite contrasting ontological perspectives is vital both for realizing robust queries of the LR and, in turn, for developing more robust simulations and models.

3.2 UniDic's short-unit words

For a research project aiming to construct a large-scale LR that can serve as a comprehensive model of the Japanese lexicon, one of the thorniest issues that must be addressed is surely just what to treat as the core entities within the LR database in the case of a highly agglutinative language like Japanese where word boundaries are often ambiguous. While doubting that an ideal solution exists, given that any decision is certain to have broad implications for implementing a LR, the issue must be taken seriously.

In this context, it is illustrative to look at UniDic; the electronic morphological dictionary for the Japanese language that was developed as part of the BCCWJ project. Reflecting its objectives to be a high-performance dictionary for wide coverage of contemporary written Japanese, UniDic adopted as its prime entity the so-called short-unit word (SUW), which roughly corresponds to the shortest meaningful unit, the morpheme. However, although that decision is certainly not without some justification, as Joyce, Hodošček and Nishina (2012) discuss, it is also fair to say that the SUW is far from convenient for human users, unless additional information about higher-order groupings is also readily available. Although the BCCWJ project's provision of supplementary information in the form of annotations about so-called long-unit words (LUWs)—groupings of verb and adjective agglutinations and compound nouns as single units—probably originates from this issue, still, the distinction is somewhat artificial and requires a certain degree of familiarity. Figure 1 highlights the basic relationships between UniDic's SUWs and LUWs, with an example sentence of 報告書を読み始める /hōkokusho o yomihajimeru/ 'to begin reading a report (document)' consisting of three LUWs. The two content LUWs of 報告書/hōkokusho/ 'report (document)' and 読み始める /yomihajimeru/ 'to begin reading' are both combinations of two SUWs, while case-marking particles, like the object marker を/o/, are simultaneously both SUWs and LUWs.

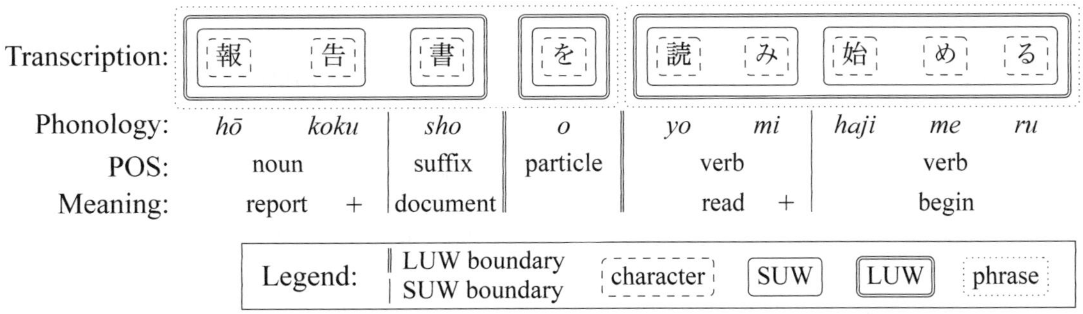

Figure 1: The relationships between characters, short-unit words, long-unit words and phrases in an example sentence of 報告書を読み始める /hōkokusho o yomihajimeru/ 'to begin reading a report (document)'.

While again acknowledging that any proposals about what to treat as core lexical entries within a LR of the Japanese lexicon are likely to involve some degree of compromise, still one obvious lesson to emerge from referring to the UniDic case is that a single lexical unit alone is insufficient in order to handle all items of the Japanese lexicon adequately for all kinds of users. As outlined further in section 4.2, our solution for JLP-O is to specify a wider range of lexical entries. However, despite the problems of SUWs and LUWs associated with the BCCWJ, it is an authoritative sampling of the contemporary Japanese lexicon, consisting of approximately 100 million words. Accordingly, it unquestionably remains the most valuable source from which to extract a corpus-based lexicon, with information about numerous core lexical properties, including lemma and orthographic specification, their respective frequencies, their phonological information and word classes, to establish a solid foundation to the construction of the large-scale LR project.

4 JLP-O construction

Having touched on the extensive range of Japanese lexical properties and the inherent tensions involved in selecting a range of lexical entry classes, this section turns to explain how these concerns have been handled in constructing the current version of the JLP-O. The section also outlines the extraction of the BCCWJ-based lexicon and the assignment of JLP-O's `LexicalEntry` subclasses as a foundation for the LR.

4.1 JLP-O modules

Although a number of separate Japanese LRs have already been created to address various lexical properties, given that they have been developed with different objectives and with diverging interpretations about the lexical properties themselves, their treatments of key properties, such as phonological, orthographic or semantic information, are not always consistent across resources, which can also vary greatly in terms of their levels of coverage. In order to help remedy this situation, the overall aim of our research project is to create a single comprehensive LR by constructing the JLP-O as its core framework to facilitate the integration of existing LRs.

Some of the initial groundwork for the LR project is outlined by Joyce, Masuda, and Ogawa (2014), within the context of discussing the revised jōyō kanji list as the core building block of the Japanese writing system. In addition to identifying and organizing a number of lexical properties at the jōyō kanji character level, they also describe a new analysis of the components of jōyō and JIS1 kanji, and apply an initial orthographic coding to the corpus word lists created in Joyce et al. (2012). Building directly from that, our continuing investigations of lexical properties have already identified 65 important properties; although, naturally, we fully expect the number to expand still further as additional LRs are consulted and examined for their particular merits. Reflecting both their natural mutual relationships and the need to structure their representations within the LR, these properties have also been organized under six modules of character, orthographic, phonological, morphological, semantic, and use. These are presented in Table 1 with a few examples of the relevant lexical properties.

Modules	Example properties
Character	type, configuration, internal structure, stroke counts, status, references, ...
Orthographic	representation, variations, length (in characters), neighborhood data, ...
Phonological	stress, length (in mora), CV structures, homophones, neighborhoods, consistency, ...
Morphological	word structure, family data (size/frequency), constituent analysis, transparency, ...
Semantic	denotation, connotations, sense range, lexical stratum, groups, concreteness, relations, ...
Use	frequency/familiarity data, collocations, grammatical patterns, genre/register/style, ...

Table 1: The six modules of the JLP-O with examples of relevant lexical properties.

This structuring of the lexical properties is highly consistent with lemon's modular design, which includes five modules in its core: linguistic description, variation, phrase structure, syntax and mapping, and morphology. We are, therefore, able to utilize a great deal of lemon's basic descriptive infrastructure pretty much intact, albeit with some relabeling of module names and some element reallocations to conform to JLP-O's modularization of lexical properties. For example, much of lemon's syntax and mapping module could be used with only minimal label changes in the integration of LRs such as Japanese versions of WordNet (Isahara et al., 2012) and FrameNet (Ohara et al., 2004) to JLP-O's semantic and use modules, respectively. In contrast, however, some basic characteristics of the Japanese lexicon, such as unit size issues and more extensive levels of orthographic variation, necessitate more expressive alternatives to both lemon's variation module and the decomposition property within the phrase structure module. Given these clear parallels, however, we believe that lemon's notion of modules is the most effective approach to structuring the lexical properties and to realizing their complex mappings to the range of lexical entries within our LR.

4.2 JLP-O's core range of lexical entries

As noted in subsection 3.2, one of the thorniest concerns to address in constructing a large-scale LR of the Japanese lexicon is to determine a suitable range of lexical entries to use as the core entities of the database. The issue is certainly far from straightforward, because it involves finding a workable compromise between a set of conflicting constraints. Naturally, these include the highly agglutinative nature of the Japanese language itself, which, understandably, encourages a focus towards the smallest components. However, these constraints also include the needs of diverse users of the LR, where, in contrast, as Spohr (2012) convincingly argues, a wider range is preferable for enhancing the search capabilities of an LR. At its heart, however, the issue is primarily about representation, or formal specification, given that the complex relationships between lexical entries themselves and between lexical entries and the modules of lexical properties must be efficiently captured within the JLP-O.

However, on consulting with our two reference models for LRs for guidance, we discover that they adopt radically different approaches to the specification of lexical entries. Consistent with its aspirations to be concise, lemon specifies just three classes of lexical entries; namely, `Part`, `Word` and `Phrase`. While this rather minimalist level of specification is, arguably, not so dissimilar to the de facto distinction that emerges with UniDic between SUWs and LUWs, comparisons quickly break down on closer inspection. For example, SUWs cover both bound morphemes (affixes and particles) and free morphemes (simple words), but these would correspond to lemon's part and word classes, respectively. The LUW concept also fails to fit nicely with lemon's tripartite division. Given that LUWs are either polymorphemic words or compound words formed by combining SUWs, the unit does not extend to phrases which are not marked by UniDic. In sharp contrast, but also consistent with his goal of multifunctionality, Spohr's MLR model incorporates a highly detailed typology of lexical entries (lexemes). Although the upper-level division into `BoundUnit`, `FreeUnit`, and `Clitic` may not, at first glance, appear so different, the subsequent divisions of `BoundUnit` into `BoundStem` and `Affix` (further divided into 9 kinds) and of `FreeUnit` into `Idiom`, `Syntactically-ComplexFreeUnit`, and `Syntactically-SimpleFreeUnit` (of which the final two are further divided eventually into 17 and 11 subclasses, respectively) clearly demonstrate very different theoretical motivations and objectives. That noted, however, the distinction between `Syntactically-SimpleFreeUnit` and `Syntactically-ComplexFreeUnit` parallels more closely to the contrast between SUWs and LUWs.

Aiming for a realistic balance between the constraints afforded by the characteristics of the Japanese lexicon, the LR's ambitions to realize a high degree of multifunctionality, and the need to achieve an acceptable degree of formal specification concerning the relationships among lexical entries and the six modules of lexical properties, the solution that we adopt for JLP-O is closer in spirit to the upper-levels of Spohr's (2012) typology of lexeme subclasses. More specifically, as illustrated in Table 2, we specify for JLP-O five classes of `LexicalEntry`, which are `Character`, `BoundUnit`, `SimpleWord`, `ComplexWord`, and `MultiWordExpression`. Thus, while the basic entities of the JLP-O draws inspiration more directly from Spohr's typology of lexeme classes, the range of JLP-O lexical entries has been increased in order to more faithfully represent the nature of the Japanese lexicon.

4.3 Extraction and RDF encoding of corpus lexicon

Having identified our practical solutions, this section briefly outlines their implementation in the RDF encoding. First, the current version of the JLP-O was specified by extending lemon's OWL specification using the Protégé ontology editor (http://protege.stanford.edu/). Second, a program was executed to simultaneously

Lexical entry type	Examples of units included
`Character`	kanji (仮), hiragana (か), katakana (カ), rōmaji (KA), ...
`BoundUnit`	prefixes (御—), suffixes (—的), auxiliary verbs (—れる), ...
`SimpleWord`	nouns (報告), verbs (読む), particles (を), adjectives (詳しい), ...
`ComplexWord`	nouns (報告書), verbs (読み始める), adjectives (詳しくない), ...
`MultiWordExpression`	collocations, idioms

Table 2: Examples of lexical entries.

extract the corpus lexicon from the BCCWJ corpus and assign the appropriate `LexicalEntry` subclasses.

In addition to replacing lemon's three classes of lexical entries with JLP-O's five `LexicalEntry` subclasses, two further minor extensions to the structure and facilities provided by the lemon model have also been necessary. The first minor extension relates to the high levels of orthographic variation that exists within the Japanese lexicon, as evidenced in Joyce et al. (2012), which is far beyond that envisioned by either lemon or Spohr's models. In seeking to be more consistent with UniDic's basic distinction between an abstract lemma form and all orthographic variations of a Japanese word, we have somewhat expanded upon lemon's distinction between `canonicalForm` and `otherForm`, by retaining the first label for the lemma form and changing the `otherForm` label to `orthographicForm` for each orthographic variant of a word. The second minor expansion is to more extensively utilize lemon's decomposition object property (which in lemon is limited to specifying the decomposition of phrases into parts). Thus, apart from the `Character` subclass within the current JLP-O (compositional analysis of radicals is not fully implemented at present), all lexical entry classes have a `decomposition` object property; such that both `BoundUnit` and `SimpleWord` entries are decomposed into one or more `Characters`, while the `orthographicForms` of `ComplexWord` and `MultiWordExpression` entries are decomposed into the relevant `orthographicForms` of `BoundUnits` and `SimpleWords`. By adopting this approach to linking structures, it is possible to search for complex lexical entries based on lower-level components, such as characters, by traversing the implemented hierarchical structure. Figure 2 shows a part of the lexical model with a focus on the lexical entries.

In order to extract the corpus lexicon, a program was written to convert the SUW and LUW information from the BCCWJ corpus into the JLP-O's RDF format, including the appropriate assignment of `LexicalEntry` subclasses. The M-XML format of the BCCWJ (version 1) includes basic structural encodings of LUWs in the form of lists of component SUWs. First, SUWs were assigned as either `BoundUnit` or `SimpleWord` lexical entries based on their unique identifier, which consists of the unique combination of the lemma and the POS category. Next, all orthographic variations of the lexical entry (based on their shared identifier) were recorded within the single entry specification using the `orthographicForm` object property, together with their decompositions into lists of characters. Finally, the frequency counts for orthographic variants were recorded using the `use` object property, allowing us to specify frequency counts together with their sources, which in the present case is a corpus identifier but could also specify a particular genre or style. The total frequency count, as sum of all `orthographicForm` variants, was also recorded under the `canonicalForm` property.

Figure 3 shows part of the RDF encoding in Turtle format for the `SimpleWord` lexical entry for the verb 読む /yomu/ 'to read'. For the sake of brevity, it is not possible to display all 12 orthographic variants, but the figure includes the three most frequent; the standard kanji-kana mixed orthography (of verbal stem and inflectional ending), the hiragana-orthography representation of よむ, and a kanji variation of 詠む with the nuances of 'to read or recite poetry; chant'.

Similarly, Figure 4 presents part of the RDF encoding in Turtle format for the `SimpleWord` lexical entry of the verb 始める /hajimeru/ 'to begin'. Interestingly, 始める is the verb2 element of many verb1-verb2 compounds that express senses of 'to begin V1'.

Finally, the extraction program also assigned LUWs to the `ComplexWord` subclass. The process essentially mirrored the extraction of `BoundUnit` or `SimpleWord` lexical entries, except that links under the decomposition object property link back to its constituent `BoundUnit` or `SimpleWord` lexical entries. Figure 5 presents part of the `ComplexWord` lexical entry for 読み始める /yomihajimeru/ 'to begin to read', which is

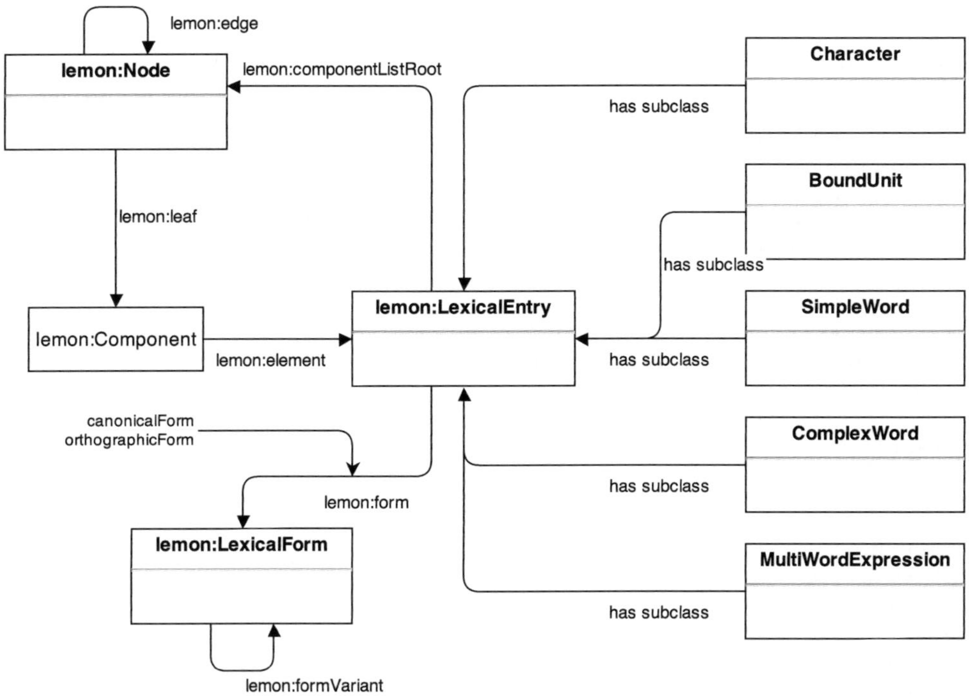

Figure 2: A subset of the JLP-O model.

```
jlpo:読む_動詞-一般
  a jlpo:SimpleWord ;
  lemon:canonicalForm [
    lemon:writtenRep "読む"@ja ;
    jlpo:decomposition (
      [ jlpo:Character jlpo:読_character ]
      [ jlpo:Character jlpo:む_character ] ) ;
    jlpo:use [ jlpo:frequency 23324 ; jlpo:corpus "BCCWJ" ] ] ;
  jlpo:orthographicForm [
    lemon:writtenRep "読む"@ja ;
    jlpo:decomposition (
      [ jlpo:Character jlpo:読_character ]
      [ jlpo:Character jlpo:む_character ] ) ;
    jlpo:use [ jlpo:frequency 20382 ; jlpo:corpus "BCCWJ" ] ] ;
  jlpo:orthographicForm [
    lemon:writtenRep "よむ"@ja ;
    jlpo:decomposition (
      [ jlpo:Character jlpo:よ_character ]
      [ jlpo:Character jlpo:む_character ] ) ;
    jlpo:use [ jlpo:frequency 322 ; jlpo:corpus "BCCWJ" ] ] ;
  jlpo:orthographicForm [
    lemon:writtenRep "詠む"@ja ;
    jlpo:decomposition (
      [ jlpo:Character jlpo:詠_character ]
      [ jlpo:Character jlpo:む_character ] ) ;
    jlpo:use [ jlpo:frequency 653 ; jlpo:corpus "BCCWJ" ] ] ;
  # [... 9 other orthographicForms ...]
  .
```

Figure 3: Part of the RDF representation for the `SimpleWord` lexical entry ‘読む’ in Turtle format.

```
jlpo:始める_動詞-非自立可能
  a jlpo:SimpleWord ;
  lemon:canonicalForm [
    lemon:writtenRep "始める"@ja ;
    jlpo:decomposition (
      [ jlpo:Character jlpo:始_character ]
      [ jlpo:Character jlpo:め_character ]
      [ jlpo:Character jlpo:る_character ] ) ;
    jlpo:use [ jlpo:frequency 30770 ; jlpo:corpus "BCCWJ" ] ] ;
  jlpo:orthographicForm [
    lemon:writtenRep "始める"@ja ;
    jlpo:decomposition (
      [ jlpo:Character jlpo:始_character ]
      [ jlpo:Character jlpo:め_character ]
      [ jlpo:Character jlpo:る_character ] ) ;
    jlpo:use [ jlpo:frequency 20591 ; jlpo:corpus "BCCWJ" ] ] ;
  jlpo:orthographicForm [
    lemon:writtenRep "はじめる"@ja ;
    jlpo:decomposition (
      [ jlpo:Character jlpo:は_character ]
      [ jlpo:Character jlpo:じ_character ]
      [ jlpo:Character jlpo:め_character ]
      [ jlpo:Character jlpo:る_character ] ) ;
    jlpo:use [ jlpo:frequency 10112 ; jlpo:corpus "BCCWJ" ] ] ;
  jlpo:orthographicForm [
    lemon:writtenRep "初める"@ja ;
    jlpo:decomposition (
      [ jlpo:Character jlpo:初_character ]
      [ jlpo:Character jlpo:め_character ]
      [ jlpo:Character jlpo:る_character ] ) ;
    jlpo:use [ jlpo:frequency 7 ; jlpo:corpus "BCCWJ" ] ] ;
  # [... 4 other orthographicForms ...]
  .
```

Figure 4: Part of the RDF representation for the `SimpleWord` lexical entry '始める' in Turtle format.

```
jlpo:読み始める_動詞-一般
  a jlpo:ComplexWord ;
  lemon:canonicalForm [
    lemon:writtenRep "読み始める"@ja ;
    jlpo:decomposition (
      [ jlpo:SimpleWord jlpo:読む_動詞-一般 ]
      [ jlpo:SimpleWord jlpo:始める_動詞-非自立可能 ] ) ;
    jlpo:use [ jlpo:frequency 228 ; jlpo:corpus "BCCWJ" ] ] ;
  jlpo:orthographicForm [
    lemon:writtenRep "読み始める"@ja ;
    jlpo:decomposition (
      [ jlpo:SimpleWord jlpo:読む_動詞-一般 ]
      [ jlpo:SimpleWord jlpo:始める_動詞-非自立可能 ] ) ;
    jlpo:use [ jlpo:frequency 139 ; jlpo:corpus "BCCWJ" ] ] ;
  jlpo:orthographicForm [
    lemon:writtenRep "読みはじめる"@ja ;
    jlpo:decomposition (
      [ jlpo:SimpleWord jlpo:読む_動詞-一般 ]
      [ jlpo:SimpleWord jlpo:はじめる_動詞-非自立可能 ] ) ;
    jlpo:use [ jlpo:frequency 82 ; jlpo:corpus "BCCWJ" ] ] ;
  # [... 4 other orthographicForms ...]
  .
```

Figure 5: Part of the RDF representation for the `ComplexWord` lexical entry '読み始める' in Turtle format.

a verb1-verb2 compound type consisting of 読み conjugation of 読む (verb1) together with 始める (verb2).

We executed the extraction and RDF encoding program to enumerate the BCCWJ-based corpus lexicon according to the JLP-O's core `LexicalEntry` classes. As summarized in Table 3, approximately 2.7 million lexical entries were assigned to the four core `LexicalEntry` classes.

Lexical entry	**Types**	**Tokens**
`Characters`	6,761	195,500,491
`BoundUnit`	433	11,327,729
`SimpleWord`	195,380	112,557,387
`ComplexWord`	2,438,506	101,684,786

Table 3: Type and token counts for the BCCWJ-based corpus lexicon.

The number of lexical entries assigned to the `Character` subclass is highly consistent with encoding specifications for Japanese characters. Similarly, the relatively smaller number of `BoundUnit` lexical entries is also consistent with the fact that this class consists of a small number of closed word classes, such as particles and the relatively limited sets of affixes. In contrast, the much higher counts for the `SimpleWord` and `ComplexWord` classes obviously reflect in large measure the fact that these cover the major open word classes, and, in particular, the noun class, which is extremely open. Another closely related factor is that these lexical entries also include vast numbers of proper nouns, which is a particular feature of large corpus data. The substantial difference between the `SimpleWord` and `ComplexWord` classes clearly illustrates the agglutinative nature of the Japanese language with rich verbal and adjectival conjugations and productive compounding. However, also a characteristic of large corpus data, it should also be noted that approximately 66% of the `ComplexWord` lexical entries occur only once within the BCCWJ corpus. And, a natural corollary is that while the `ComplexWord` lexical entries are on average decomposed into 3.1 `BoundUnit` and `SimpleWord` lexical entries, 94% of these have only one orthographic variant (because, for extremely low frequency words, one obviously requires even larger corpora to capture all possible orthographic variations). A final observation to make is that the corpus lexicon does not yield any lexical entries under the `MultiWordExpressions` subclass; although it would be feasible to extract collocational data from the BCCWJ, these will be identified for the large-scale LR in the future in the course of integrating other LRs.

5 Conclusion

As a principal component of a larger research project to construct a large-scale LR database concerned with the lexical and psycholinguistic properties associated with the Japanese lexicon, the paper has described the construction of the ontology of Japanese lexical properties (JLP-O) as its working conceptual framework. More specifically, the paper focused on two important issues. After outlining the first concern of mapping out and organizing the wide range of lexical and psycholinguistic properties that linguistic and cognitive science researchers require up-to-date information about in section 3.1, section 4.1 detailed how these are being structured under six modules, which mirrors the flexible approach towards construction employed by lemon. Similarly, after outlining the second difficult concern of what to treat as core entities of the LR database in section 3.2, section 4.2 explained the reason behind our solution to recognize five `LexicalEntry` classes, namely, that a wider range of classes is key to achieving the high degree of multifunctionality that our LR project aspires to (Spohr, 2012). Section 4.3 also outlined the extraction and RDF encoding of the BCCWJ-based corpus lexicon. Classified according to the JLP-O's range of lexical entries, and supplemented with information about orthographic variations, decompositions and frequencies, the corpus lexicon provides solid foundations for the large-scale project to construct the comprehensive LR of Japanese lexical properties.

Although we are fully aware that it will be necessary to further develop and refine the JLP-O as the larger LR project progresses, as the present working version has been constructed to specifically handle two fundamental aspects about the Japanese lexicon, we believe that it represents a sufficiently robust conceptual framework that can guide future work of integrating existing LRs. Thus, we approach the integration task not merely as a mechanical process of expanding the LR database by merging data, but as a dialectic one that requires ongoing consideration and investigation of the theoretical adequacies and psychological realities of candidate lexical properties; a reflective process that is exemplified by ontology construction. And, as a working conceptual framework for examining the LR database, the JLP-O represents the kind of architectural blueprint of the structural relationships within the LR database that is essential for realizing high degrees of multifunctionality in terms of developing various interfaces for search queries and data presentation. In this way, we hope to realize a comprehensive LR of Japanese lexical properties that will be beneficial as a systematic model of the Japanese lexicon that can be effectively mined in the pursuit of deeper insights into lexical knowledge.

Acknowledgments

This research was partially supported by a JSPS Grant-in-Aid for Foreign Postdoctoral Fellows (no. P13303).

References

Adelman, J. S. (2012). Methodological issues with words. In J. S. Adelman (Ed.), *Visual word recognition volume 1: Models and methods, orthography and phonology* (pp. 116–138). Current issues in the psychology of language. London: Psychology Press.

Cimiano, P., Buitelaar, P., McCrae, J., & Sintek, M. (2011). LexInfo: a declarative model for the lexicon-ontology interface. *Web Semantics: Science, Services and Agents on the World Wide Web*, *9*(1), 29–51. doi:http://dx.doi.org/10.1016/j.websem.2010.11.001

Franconi, E., Kerhet, V., & Ngo, N. (2013). Exact query reformulation over databases with first-order and description logics ontologies. *Journal of Artifical Intelligence*, *48*, 885–922. doi:10.1613/jair.4058

Francopoulo, G. (2013). *LMF Lexical Markup Framework* (G. Francopoulo & P. Paroubek, Eds.). Wiley Online Library.

Gruber, T. R. (1993). A translation approach to portable ontology specifications. *Knowledge acquisition*, *5*(2), 199–220.

Guarino, N. (1998). Formal ontology in information systems. In *Proceedings of the first international conference on Formal Ontology in Information Systems (FOIS'98)* (Vol. 46). IOS Press.

Guarino, N., Oberle, D., & Staab, S. (2009). What is an ontology? In *Handbook on ontologies* (pp. 1–17). International handbooks on information systems (E2). Springer.

Hayashi, O., Miyajima, T., Nomura, M., Egawa, K., Nakano, H., Sanada, S., & Satake, H. (Eds.). (1982). *Zūsetsu nihongo: Gurafu de miru kotoba no sugata [Graphic Japanese: State of vocabulary seen in graphs]*. Tokyo: Kadokawa Shojiten.

Huang, C.-R., Calzolari, N., Gangemi, A., Lenci, A., Oltramari, A., & Prévot, L. (2010). *Ontology and the lexicon: A natural language processing perspective* (C.-R. Huang, N. Calzolari, A. Gangemi, A. Lenci, A. Oltramari, & L. Prévot, Eds.). Studies in Natural Language Processing. Cambridge University Press.

Isahara, H., Bond, F., Kanzaki, K., Uchimoto, K., Kuroda, K., Kuribayashi, T., … Torisawa, K. (2012). Japanese WordNet. Retrieved May 30, 2013, from http://nlpwww.nict.go.jp/wn-ja/index.en.html

Joyce, T., Hodošček, B., & Nishina, K. (2012). Orthographic representation and variation within the Japanese writing system: Some corpus-based observations. *Written Language & Literacy*, *15*(2) Special Issue on Units of Language – Units of Writing, 254–278. doi:10.1075/wll.15.2.01rob

Joyce, T., Masuda, H., & Ogawa, T. (2014). Jōyō kanji as core building blocks of the Japanese writing system: Some observations from database construction. *Written Language & Literacy*, *17*(2), 173–194. doi:10.1075/wll.17.2.01joy

Kindaichi, K., Yamada, T., Shibata, T., Sakai, K., Kuramochi, Y., & Yamada, A. (2011). *Shinmeikai Kokugo Jiten (Shinmeikai Japanese-Japanese dictionary)* (7th edition). Tokyo: Sanseido.

Maekawa, K., Yamazaki, M., Ogiso, T., Maruyama, T., Ogura, H., Kashino, W., … Den, Y. (2013). Balanced Corpus of Contemporary Written Japanese. *Language Resources and Evaluation*, 1–27. doi:10.1007/s10579-013-9261-0

McCrae, J., Spohr, D., & Cimiano, P. (2011). Linking lexical resources and ontologies on the semantic web with lemon. In *The semantic web: research and applications* (pp. 245–259). Springer.

Morohashi, T. (2000). *Daikanwajiten [Comprehensive Chinese-Japanese dictionary]* (Vols. 13). Tokyo: Taishukan.

Nation, I. (2001). *Learning vocabulary in another language*. Cambridge Applied Linguistics. UK: Cambridge University Press.

Nation, I. (2013). *Learning vocabulary in another language* (2nd edition). Cambridge Applied Linguistics. UK: Cambridge University Press.

Ohara, K. H., Fujii, S., Ohori, T., Suzuki, R., Saito, H., & Ishizaki, S. (2004). The Japanese FrameNet project: An introduction. In *Proceedings of LREC-04 Satellite Workshop "Building Lexical Resources from Semantically Annotated Corpora" (LREC 2004)* (pp. 9–11).

Oltramari, A., Vossen, P., Qin, L., & Hovy, E. (2013). *New trends of research in ontologies and lexical resources: Ideas, projects, systems*. Springer.

Peters, W., Montiel-Ponsoda, E., & Cea, G. A. D. (2007). Localizing Ontologies in OWL. In *Proceedings of the OntoLex07 Workshop (held in conjunction with ISWC'07*.

Prévot, L., Huang, C.-R., Calzolari, N., Gangemi, A., Lenci, A., & Oltramari, A. (2010). Ontology and the lexicon: a multidisciplinary perspective. In C.-R. Huang, N. Calzolari, A. Gangemi, A. Lenci, A. Oltramari, & L. Prévot (Eds.), *Ontology and the lexicon: a natural language processing perspective* (pp. 3–24). Studies in Natural Language Processing. Cambridge University Press.

Shinmura, I. (2008). *Kōjien (Japanese dictionary)* (6th edition). Tokyo: Iwanami Shoten.

Spohr, D. (2012). *Towards a multifunctional lexical resource: Design and implementation of a graph-based lexicon model*. Walter de Gruyter.

Frames and Terminology:
Representing Predicative Terms in the Field of the Environment

Marie-Claude L'Homme **Benoît Robichaud**

Observatoire de linguistique Sens-Texte (OLST)
C.P. 6128, succ. Centre-ville
Montréal (Québec) H3C 3J7 CANADA

mc.lhomme@umontreal.ca benoit.robichaud@umontreal.ca

Abstract

Terminological resources have traditionally focused on terms referring to entities, thereby ignoring other important concepts (processes, events and properties) in specialized fields of knowledge. Consequently, large parts of the conceptual structure of these fields are not taken into consideration nor represented. In this article, we show how terms that refer to processes and events (and, to a lesser extent, properties) can be characterized using Frame Semantics (Fillmore, 1982) and the methodology developed within the FrameNet project (Ruppenhofer et al., 2010). More specifically, we applied the framework to a subset of terms in the field of the environment. Frames are unveiled first by comparing similarities between the argument structures of terms already recorded in a terminological database and the relationships they share with other terms. A comparison is also carried out with the lexical units recorded in FrameNet. Then, relations between frames are defined that allow us to build small conceptual scenarios that are specific to the field of the environment. These relations are determined on the basis of the set of relations listed in the FrameNet project. This article reports on the methodology, the frames defined up to now and two specific conceptual scenarios (**Risk_scenario** and **Managing_waste**).

1 Introduction

Traditionally, terminological resources have been designed as knowledge repositories and until recently the focus has been placed on finding ways to represent the knowledge conveyed by terms. In fact, in several terminological applications, terms are viewed as the linguistic components of knowledge structures (i.e. linguistic labels attached to nodes that represent concepts). This perspective has led to the design of domain ontologies (or less formal structures) in which concepts are linked via a network of relations (is-a, part-of, cause-effect, etc) and terms are disambiguated linguistic labels assigned to these concepts.

However, it has been pointed out that, although interesting, these knowledge structures have important drawbacks as far as linguistic aspects are concerned: 1. They tend to focus on terms that denote entities (expressed by nouns) and little consideration is given to processes and events; 2. Other types of units that could be relevant for terminology, such as predicative terms (that designate processes, events and properties) are not represented in a way that fully captures their meaning; 3. They either overlook the linguistic properties of terms altogether, or linguistic properties (such as variation) are taken into account in a peripheral component of the representation.

An increasing number of researchers proposed alternative methods to add linguistic components to terminological knowledge structures (Faber, 2006, 2012; Montiel et al., 2010, among others). Others have developed methods to describe terms as linguistic units with frameworks designed for the lexicon in general. An interesting aspect of this latter work is the consideration given to terms that have been overlooked in knowledge structures, i.e. predicative terms and more specifically verbs (Condamines 1993; Lerat 2002; L'Homme 1998; Lorente 2002).

It is generally recognized that both the relationship with knowledge and linguistic properties are important aspects of terminological description, and methods should be developed to merge them into resources. However, it seems that terminologists still struggle to find an adequate balance between conceptual and linguistic representations (L'Homme, 2014). One possible solution resides in frames or frame-like representations that attract the interest of an increasing number of researchers (Dolbey et al., 2006; Faber, 2006, 2012; Schmidt 2009, among others, see Section 3).

Zock/Rapp/Huang (eds.): Proceedings of the 4th Workshop on Cognitive Aspects of the Lexicon, pages 186–197,
Dublin, Ireland, August 23, 2014.

This is the solution we chose in this paper. More specifically, we applied principles based on Frame Semantics (Fillmore, 1982, 1985; Fillmore and Baker, 2010) and the methodology developed within the FrameNet project (Fillmore et al., 2003; Ruppenhofer et al., 2010) to linguistic data related to the field of the environment. A first part of this work was reported in L'Homme et al. (2014), in which frames were defined based on the contents of a resource containing environment terms (e.g., *change*, *impact*, *recycle*). In this paper, we summarize our methodology to discover frames, and report on what has been done to define relations between frames and build conceptual scenarios that represent processes and events in the field. We then describe two specific scenarios that apply to the field of the environment (**Risk_scenario** and **Managing_waste**).

2 Theoretical assumptions and motivations

Processes and events represent an important part of the set of concepts to be represented in many fields of knowledge. This is the case in environment where events (e.g., "storm", "melt", and "warming") and processes (e.g., "damage", "threaten") can be observed. However, traditional terminological models (and even less traditional ones, such as ontological representations) are not properly equipped to describe these concepts and account for their specific linguistic properties, namely the fact that they require arguments (*X changes Y*; *impact of X on Y*).

Frame Semantics (Fillmore, 1982; Fillmore and Baker, 2010) and its related application FrameNet (Ruppenhofer et al., 2010) are specifically adapted to account for these concepts and offer different means to represent their conceptual as well as their linguistic properties. Frame Semantics (FS) is based on the assumption that the meanings of lexical units (LUs) are constructed in relation to background knowledge, whose structure can be analyzed in terms of semantic frames. Frames are conceptual scenarios in which different participants (called *frame elements*, *FEs*) appear. For instance, the **Criminal_investigation** frame is defined as follows in FrameNet: This frame describes the process that involves the determination by an authority, the Investigator, of the circumstances surrounding an Incident by means of inquiry.

The frame states that there are three obligatory participants in this scenario (FEs): **Investigator**, **Incident**, and **Suspect** (other non-obligatory participants – *non-core FEs* – are also listed). Lexical units such as *clue.n, inquire.v, inquiry.n, investigate.v, investigation.n* evoke this frame. These lexical units and their participants are also annotated in selected sentences, thus linking the conceptual and linguistic representations levels of the description, as shown below for the verb *investigate*:

- NP police, sheriff, officer-T-(1)

  About 30 adults were arrested in raids on ten Children of God homes on Wednesday night by [$_{\text{Investigator}}$ police] **INVESTIGATING** ^{Target} [$_{\text{Incident}}$ claims of child abuse]. [$_{\text{Suspect}}$ INI]

  [$_{\text{Investigator}}$ Anti-terrorist officers] were quickly on the scene and **INVESTIGATING** ^{Target} [$_{\text{Incident}}$ the further reports of suspect devices]. [$_{\text{Suspect}}$ INI]

- T-NP allegation-(1)

  The Botswana government says that [$_{\text{Investigator}}$ it] will **INVESTIGATE** ^{Target} [$_{\text{Incident}}$ the torture allegations]. [$_{\text{Suspect}}$ INI]

- T-NP case-(1)

  [$_{\text{Investigator}}$ The union] is also **INVESTIGATING** ^{Target} [$_{\text{Incident}}$ a number of cases of child labour and the sexual abuse of children by employers]. [$_{\text{Suspect}}$ INI]

Frames can share relationships with other frames as shown in Figure 1. **Criminal_investigation** is a subframe of **Crime_scenario**, it is preceded by **Committing_crime** and precedes **Criminal_process**.

We believe that frames are well suited to represent the properties of predicative terms: annotations serve to capture their linguistic properties and link these properties to an abstract representation level, i.e. the frame. Furthermore, and this is what is explored in this paper, relations between frames, can help unveil larger conceptual scenarios in which these terms are involved. In FrameNet, some subject-specific frames can already be found, as shown below (Figure 1) with **Crime_scenario** and other related frames.

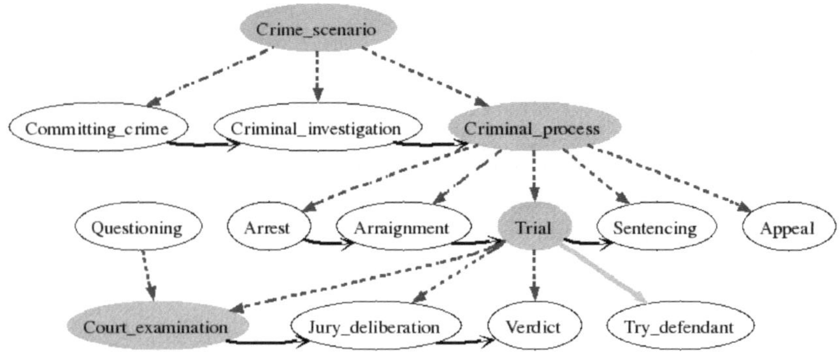

Figure 1. **Crime_scenario** and related frames in FrameNet (2014)

We assume that this can be applied to the frames of a specialized field such as the environment. However, we believe that the specialized lexicon will display some characteristics that will result in the necessity to define specific frames and perhaps specific scenarios. We explore this on a subset of data that is presented in Section 4.

3 Related work

In addition to projects aiming to describe the general lexicon in English (FrameNet, 2014), and in other languages, such as German, Japanese, and Spanish (Boas, 2009), an increasing number of researchers in terminology or related fields suggest that Frame Semantics (FS) or compatible frameworks are well suited to describe terms.

In Dolbey et al. (2006), Frame Semantics is adapted in order to develop frames in the field of biomedicine and link these frames to existing ontologies. Another application in medicine can be found in Wandji et al. (2013) where authors attempt to discover frames in the field with natural language processing techniques and an external resource (a medical terminology). Schmidt (2009) introduced some adaptations to the original framework of FS to account for multilingual data (English, French and German) in the field of soccer. Pimentel (2013) used the framework to establish equivalence relationships between English and Portuguese verbs in the field of law. L'Homme (2012) describes an annotation module added to two terminological resources (computing and environment) that is based on the annotation methodology developed within the FrameNet project. Finally, Faber (2012) refers to FS in order to account for concepts in the field of the environment and proposes a general frame (the environment event) to represent the interrelated processes and events observed in the field. The proposal has led to an approach in terminology called *Frame-based terminology*.

The work reported in this article bears some similarities with and differs from the work cited above in the following ways: 1. Contrary to some of this work, frames are discovered after terms are described rather than postulated prior to the descriptive work (we took a strictly bottom-up approach); 2. Frames are defined by observing similarities between terms (Sections 4.2 and 4.3); 3. Relations between frames are based on those already defined in FrameNet, but they must be valid from the point of view of the field of the environment. Hence, some differences are likely to be observed with similar frames appearing in FrameNet or with frames defined for other fields of knowledge.

4 Methodology

This section describes the data used in this work (extracted from a terminological database), and the different steps taken to unveil semantic frames and relations between them.

4.1 The terminological database

Our analysis is based on data recorded in an existing terminological database that contains terms in the field of the environment (it covers four subfields: climate change, residual material management, electric transportation, and renewable energy).[1] The database – compiled chiefly according to the principles of Explanatory Combinatorial Lexicology (Mel'čuk et al., 1995) – contains terms in English, French, Portuguese and Spanish. Entries provide a description of the lexico-semantic properties of terms (Figure 2): actantial (i.e. argument) structure, linguistic realizations of actants (i.e. arguments), and lexical relationships (including paradigmatic relationships and collocations).

threat $_1$, n

Status : 2

a threat: ~ of ***change*** $_{1a}$ ⊕ to ***ecosystem*** $_1$ ⊕

Contexts
Lexical relations

Explanation	Related term
Related Meanings	
≈	hazard # $_1$
≈	risk $_1$
Opposites	
Opposite	preservation protection $_1$
Other Parts of Speech and Derivatives	
Verb	threaten $_1$
An ***ecosystem*** that has undergone a t.	threatened $_1$
Combinations	
The ***change*** causes a t.	pose a ~
A ***change*** causes that a t. be more important	increase a ~
The ***ecosystem*** undergoes a t.	experience a ~
Someone or something causes that a t. be less important	reduce a ~

Figure 2. Entry *threat* in the environment database

Terms recorded in the database are nouns (Eng. *biodiversity*, *energy*; Fr. *bioénergie*, *environnement*), verbs (Eng. *erode*, *pollute*; Fr. *électrifier*, *incinérer*), adjectives (Eng. *anthropogenic*, *global*; Fr. *aride*, *vert*) or adverbs (Eng. *globally, locally*). In this work, we took into account verbs, nouns (that refer to events or processes) and a small set of adjectives (e.g., Eng. *absorb*, *concentration*, *threatened*; Fr. *menacé*, *réchauffer*, *tri*). A subset of 169 English terms and 205 French terms underwent the analysis described in the following subsections.

4.2 Annotated contexts

In the database, several predicative terms (and all those that were selected for this analysis) come with up to 20 annotated sentences. The annotation is based on the methodology developed within the FrameNet project (Ruppenhofer et al., 2010). The original objectives of the annotations were twofold: 1. Show how actants (i.e. arguments) stated in the actantial (i.e. argument) structure are realized linguistically; 2. Supply terminologists writing entries with linguistic evidence to support their intuitions.

In annotations (Figure 3), the predicative unit appears in capital letters and in bold. Participants are divided into two different types: actants (in bold) correspond to obligatory participants (roughly equivalent to FN's core frame elements); circumstants are non-obligatory participants (that correspond roughly to non-core FEs). Participants appear in different colors according to their role (Cause, Patient, etc.). A table summarizes the different patterns found in annotations.

> The major challenges for the environment today are climate change, the decline in biodiversity, the **THREAT to our health** from pollution, the way in which we use natural resources and the production of too much waste. [CHANG_1EUROPAENV 0 TK MCLH 19/07/2012]
>
> Changes in frequency and intensity of extreme weather and **climate events** could pose a serious **THREAT to human health**. [CHANG_VULNERABILITY 0 TK MCLH 19/07/2012]
>
> The specific **THREAT to some of these ecosystems** is discussed in detail elsewhere in this paper. [CHANG_2IPCCBIODIVERSITE 0 TK MCLH 19/07/2012]

[1] The database is enriched on an ongoing basis. Hence, some terms can be added to frames already defined. Other subfields will also be taken into account in the future.

Population growth and **degradation of water quality** are significant **THREATS to water security in many parts of Africa**, and the combination of continued population increases and global warming impacts is likely to accentuate water scarcity in subhumid regions of Africa. [CHANG_3IPCCCONSEQUENCE 0 TK MCLH 19/07/2012]

Actants		
Cause	Complement (PP-from) Indirect link	degradation event growth pollution
Patient	Complement (PP-to)	ecosystem health security
Others		
Degree	Modifier (AP)	serious significant
Descriptor	Modifier (AP)	Specific
Location	Complement (PP-in)	Part

Figure 3. Annotations for the term *threat*

4.3 Identification of frames

In a previous study (L'Homme et al. 2014), we analyzed data contained in an environment database to establish whether some lexical units could be associated with frames similar to those that are recorded in FrameNet or potentially lead to new ones. The methodology for discovering frames consists basically in: 1. Extracting relevant data from the environment database; and 2. Using FrameNet data (in English) as a reference to identify a first set of existing frames that the terms in our database could evoke. A set of tools were devised to help us carry out the analysis.

Identifying similarities between terms encoded in the environment database

The first tool we use is a script that extracts relevant data from the English and French versions of the environment database and presents it in two separate sortable tables (where the sort function was programmed to fit specific criteria). These tables are helpful as they bring together, flatten and sort information that is normally distributed in different entries of the database. Along with the terms and their part of speech, the following information is presented in additional columns (Figure 4).

Terme	Act 1	Act 2	Act 3	Act 4	Circ	Frames	Liens
alter.1.en alter: Cause or Agent ~ Patient	Cause	Agent	Patient	_	Degree Manner	Cause_change	Caus@Degrad : environment.1.en Caus@Degrad : habitat.1.en Degrad@ : seasonality.1.en
degrade.1.en degrade: Cause or Agent ~ Patient	Cause	Agent	Patient	_	Degree Location Manner	Damaging	Caus@Degrad : environment.1.en Caus@Degrad : watershed.1.en CausDegrad : ecosystem.1.en
effect.1.en an effect: ~ of Cause or Agent on Patient	Cause	Agent	Patient	_	Degree Duration	Objective_influence	_
influence.1.en an influence: ~ of Cause or Agent on Patient	Cause	Agent	Patient	_	Descriptor Duration Time	Objective_influence	_
influence.2.en influence: Cause or Agent ~ Patient	Cause	Agent	Patient	_	Degree Duration	Objective_influence	_

Figure 4. Data presenting frame-relevant information for English terms

- Semantic roles of actants placed in four consecutive columns and in the order in which they appear in the actantial structure of the term entries;
- Semantic roles of circumstants extracted from the annotated contexts associated with the terms, ordered and displayed in a fifth column;
- A frame name (taken from an extra file used aside the database entries). This name was added once it was defined by the terminologist that carried out the analysis (see Section 4.3.4);

- Verbs and nouns associated with the LUs through specific collocation relationships in a last column.[2]

Identifying similarities between terms encoded in the DiCoEnviro

In addition to the tables described in Section 4.3.1, another script was written to present a comparison page that contains information related to terms from the environment database along with LUs recorded in FrameNet. Each English entry of the environment database is first searched in the last release of the FrameNet data (Baker and Hung, 2010)[3], and presented side by side with the corresponding lexical units from FrameNet when matches are found (Figure 5). More specifically, the script retrieves the following information:

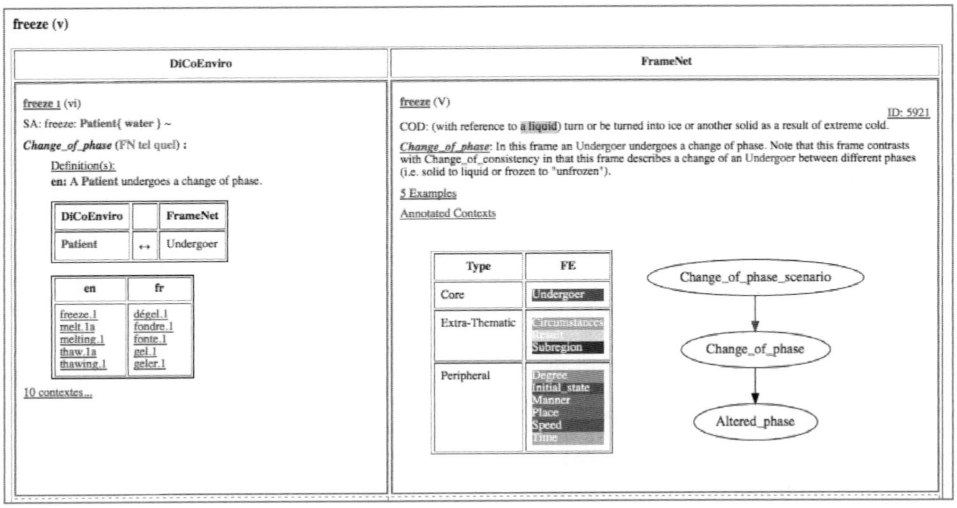

Figure 5. Comparison of environment terms with LUs in FrameNet

- From FrameNet: definitions of frames, their core and non-core FEs, relationships these frames have with other frames, and finally the annotated contexts accompanying the LUs themselves. A series of hyperlinks are also provided so that the terminologist analyzing the data can refer to FrameNet whenever necessary.
- From the environment database: actantial structures (i.e. showing the list of actants associated with the terms), the annotated contexts, and incidentally, for further stages of the analysis, the French and Spanish equivalents.

Differences between FrameNet and environment database

When comparing the data extracted from the environment database and FrameNet, we needed to take into consideration that the two resources bear some theoretical as well as methodological differences. We summarize them below:

- In FrameNet, FEs are defined at the level of frames while, in environment database, actants (and circumstants) are stated at the level of LUs. We established that terms in the environment database could evoke an existing frame if a relationship could be established between the set of core FEs and the actants, and if the FEs and actants were represented with comparable labels.

---

[2] Lexical relationships are represented in the database with lexical functions (LFs), a system developed in Explanatory Combinatorial Lexicology (Mel'čuk et al., 1995). In the online version, a natural language explanation is proposed (Figure 2): this explanation "translates" LFs' expressiveness in a way that is more accessible to users.

[3] For this, we used the XML files supplied by the FrameNet team. However, we noticed some differences with the online version of FrameNet: we needed to check whether the information had been updated.

- Secondly, due to the objectives of each resource, the number of core FEs in a frame could differ in comparison with the number of actants represented for a term in the environment database. Often, the number of core FEs was higher than the number of actants. In some cases, the environment database defines a participant as being a circumstant and a correspondence could be established with FrameNet. In other cases, the specificity of the specialized domain needed to be taken into consideration.
- Thirdly, labels used for most FEs are very specific since they are defined within a frame. In the environment database, labels are general and defined for the entire set of terms that are included in the database. In these cases, we generalized some of the labels. For example, labels such as Entity, Item, Theme, and Undergoer in FrameNet were assumed to correspond to Patient in the environment database.
- Fourthly, in FrameNet, different labels can account for an FE that would be realized in the same syntactic function. In the environment database, actants can be split (Agent or Cause for instance). In both cases, we considered these as being instantiations of the same argument position.

Assigning terms to frames

To make explicit the association of terms to frames (already recorded in FrameNet or especially created for the field of the environment), but also to facilitate the pairwise comparison of actants with FEs, we created an auxilary XML file aside from the files used to encode entries in the database (rather than adding this information in each terminological entry). Throughout the analysis, the file was enriched with additional information such as definitions and examples specific to the field of the environment, and relations frames have with other frames discovered or created (see Section 4.4).

Once created, the file can be loaded by the scripts mentioned earlier and used to help the analysis as it can be passed down to the comparison of terms and LUs. A comparison of actants and FEs is shown Figure 6.

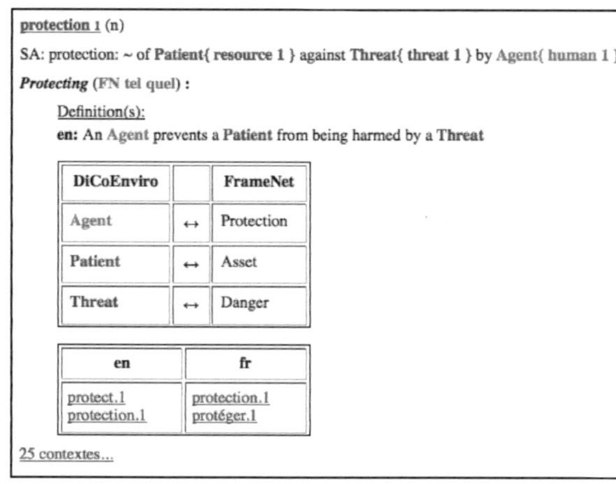
protection 1 (n)

SA: protection: ~ of Patient{ resource 1 } against Threat{ threat 1 } by Agent{ human 1 }

Protecting (FN tel quel) :

Definition(s):

en: An Agent prevents a **Patient** from being harmed by a **Threat**

DiCoEnviro		FrameNet
Agent	↔	Protection
Patient	↔	Asset
Threat	↔	Danger

en	fr
protect.1 protection.1	protection.1 protéger.1

25 contextes...

Figure 6. Comparison of FEs in FrameNet and actants in the environment database

4.4 Frames discovered for environment terms

In L'Homme et al. (2014), we had analyzed 105 English and 159 French terms. This first set of data allowed us to find that some LUs were equivalent to frames already recorded in FrameNet; but that new frames also needed to be defined.

Currently, the different frames defined and the terms that evoke them appear in Table 1. The difference between English and French simply reflect the fact that more terms have been analyzed in French and in English up to now.

- **Entirely compatible**: The description of the terms in the environment database and the frames in FrameNet are similar (the number of actants vs. FEs and their semantic type is basically the same). For instance, *threaten* (Agent or Cause ~ Patient) evokes the **Endangering** frame (An Agent or Cause is responsible for placing a Valued_entity at risk).[4]

[4] Even if these frames are entirely compatible with those described in FrameNet, some differences are worth mentioning (in addition to those already taken into consideration when comparing the data, see Section 4.3.3). First, frames described in the environment database are much more restricted that those appearing in FrameNet

- **Alternation**: This category was created for cases where the environment database distinguishes two separate entries for closely related LUs. For instance, *predict*$_{1a}$ (Method ~ Patient) and *Predict*$_{1b}$ (Agent ~ Patient with Method) evoke a single frame, i.e. **Predicting** (An Agent states or makes known a Patient based on a Method; FN. A Speaker states or makes known a future Eventuality on the basis of some Evidence).[5]

Category	Number of Frames	Number of English LUs	Number of French LUs
Entirely compatible	19	45	52
Partly compatible	21	68	70
Alternation	2	8	9
New	31	60	85
Pending	6	9	13
TOTAL	79	190	229

Table 1: Different frames defined and number of LUs

- **Partly compatible**: The description of the terms in the environment database and the frames described in FrameNet are not exactly the same (the numbers of actants vs. frame elements differ). For instance, *risk* has three actants (~ of Result on Patient from Cause) and evokes the **Run_risk** frame, but the original frame has four core frame elements (Action, Asset, Bad_outcome, and Protagonist).
- **New**: Sets of new frames were defined for cases in which no existing frame could be found or cases where an existing frame was not well adapted for the environment. For instance, a new frame was created to LUs such as *recycle* and *recycling*, i.e. **Preparing_for_reuse**.
- **Pending**: Some LUs have been assigned to frames only provisionally for a number of reasons (few occurrences in the corpus, only one LU in the frame, etc.).

4.5 Identification of relations between frames

It soon became obvious that some frames defined for the field of the environment were related conceptually. We determined these relations using as a starting point the set of relations defined in the FrameNet project: these relations were sought in our data. We assumed that they would be valid – at least in part – for the domain of the environment, since they had been defined on a substantial amount of data.

This allowed us to discover conceptual scenarios specific to the field. In Table 2, we first describe the list of FrameNet relations taken into account and relations that are defined for the purpose of this project.

Relations used to link frames

The list of relations based on FrameNet are listed in Table 2.[6]

---

and the terms that evoke these frames may correspond to subsenses or microsenses (as defined by Cruse, 2011). For instance, the **Being_at_risk** frame in the environment applies only to things such as *species*, *ecosystems*, *plants*, etc. In addition, the number of terms that evoke a frame is often much lower than those recorded in FrameNet. For instance, the terms evoking the **Being_at_risk** frame in the environment data are the following: *sensitivity*, *threatened*, *vulnerability*, *vulnerable* (whereas in FrameNet, the list comprises: *danger.n*, *insecure.a*, *risk.n*, *safe.a*, *safety.n*, *secure.a*, *security.n*, *unsafe.a*, *vulnerability.n*, *vulnerable.a*).

[5] The alternation can be illustrated with the following examples: *Even the most sophisticated models cannot* ***predict*** *the details of how the climate change will unfold; it is also possible that our models will better enable us to* ***predict*** *the consequences.*

[6] Here, some differences with the way relations are defined in FrameNet are probably present. This part of the analysis is based on our interpretation of the way relations are defined in Ruppenhofer et al. (2010), the ones that appear in FrameNet and our own data.

Is causative of	This relation was established between the **Endangering** (with terms such as *endanger*, *threaten*) and the **Being_at_risk** (with terms such as *threatened* and *vulnerable*) frames. *Loss of important habitats (wetlands, tundra, isolated habitats) would THREATEN some species, including rare/endemic species and migratory birds.* *Low-lying island states and atolls are especially VULNERABLE to climate change and associated sea-level rise.*
Is inchoative of	This relation was defined between the **Cause_temperature_change** (with terms such as $cool_{1b}$, $warm_{1b}$) and **Change_of_temperature** (with terms such as $cool_{1a}$, $warm_{1a}$, $warming_{1}$) frames. *... gases such as carbon dioxide (CO2) which WARM the Earth's surface.* *... the COOLING of the Northern Hemisphere may lead to increased warmth ...*
Inherits from	This relation was established between **Change_position_on_a_scale** (with terms such as *decline*, *decrease*, *grow*, *increase*, *rise*) and **Change_of_temperature** (with terms such as $cool_{1a}$, $warm_{1a}$, *warming*). *The global average surface temperature has INCREASED over the 20th century by about 0.6 °C* *... the Earth will WARM in the near future.* The inverse relation is **Is inherited by.**
Has subframe	This relation was established between **Managing_waste** (with the terms *manage* and *management*) and the **Recover** (with terms such as Eng. *recover*, Fr. *récupérer*, *récupération*), **Removing** (with terms such as Eng. *discard*, *disposal*, Fr. *éliminer*), **Separating** (with terms such as *segregate*, *separate* and *sort*), and **Collecting** (with terms such as Eng. *collect*, Fr. *collecte*, *ramassage*) frames. *The Guelph wet-dry recycling centre can MANAGE up to 44,000 tonnes of compostables ...* *... ensure that waste is RECOVERED or disposed of safely ...* The inverse relation is **Is subframe of.**
Is perspectivized in	This relation was established between the **Greenhouse effect** (with the terms Eng. *greenhouse effect* and Fr. *effet de serre*) and the **Accumulating** (with terms such as Eng. *accumulate*, Fr. *accumulation*, *concentration*) and **Trapping** (with terms such as Eng. *trap*, Fr. *emprisonner*, *piéger*) frames. *The Earth has a natural GREENHOUSE EFFECT which keeps it much warmer that it would be without an atmosphere.* *If injected into the atmosphere, these gases ACCUMULATE there.* *... the atmosphere is slowly TRAPPING more heat over the years and enhancing the Earth's natural greenhouse effect.* The inverse relation is **Perspective on.**
Precedes	This relation was defined between the **Separating** and the **Removing** and **Recover** frames. *SEPARATE unwanted impurities and inorganic material ...* *... all waste stabilization and DISPOSAL activities are preceded by some period of interim storage.* The inverse relation is **Is preceded by.**
Is used by	This relation was established between the **Protecting** (with Eng. *protect*, Fr. *protection*) and the **Run_risk** (with Eng. *risk* and Fr. *risque*) frames. *A greater number of people and those who are less indoctrinated seek to PROTECT humanity , even from itself ...* *... the RISK of aggregate net damage due to climate change ...* The inverse relation is **Uses**.

Table 2: Relations between frames of the field of environment

In addition to the relations based on those defined in the FrameNet project, we added new ones to capture some important conceptual perspective in the field of the environement:

- **Is opposed to**: This relation was established between the **Recover** and the **Removing** frames.
- Is a property of (has property): This relation was established between the **Judgment_of_intensity** (with LUs such as *intense*, *extreme*, *severe*) and the **Weather_event** frames (the latter one comprises LUs such as *event*, *activity*).

Up to now, among the 73 frames defined for the environment data, and about 70 are linked with one or two of the relations listed in this section. A small number of frames are linked provisionally with the **See also** relation. This simply indicates that a relation is present but its labelling is pending.

Displaying relations

After the creation of the auxiliary XML file recording the terms membership to frames described in Section 4.3.4, a search interface was designed and programmed to provide a more user-friendly access to its information.

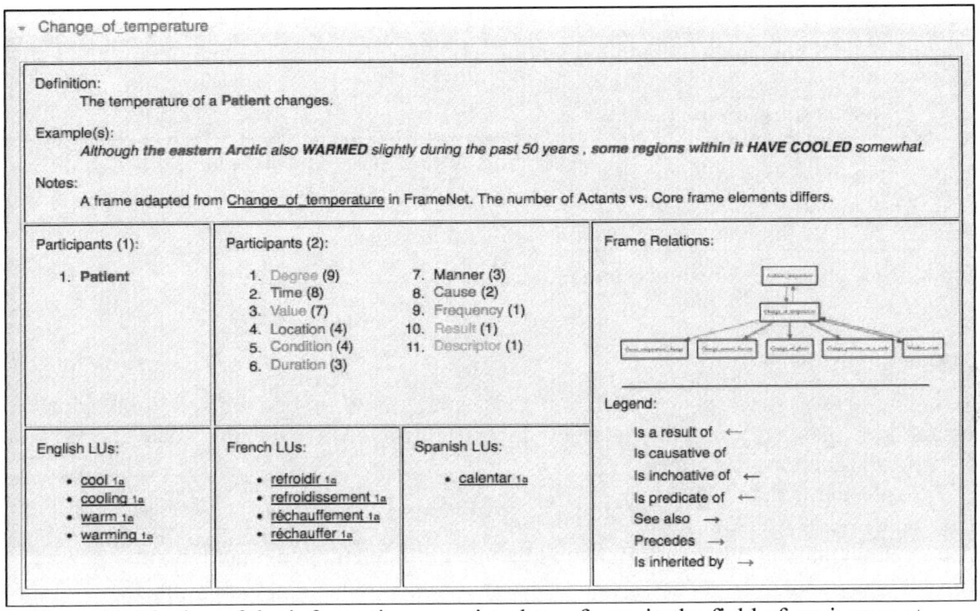

Figure 7: Display of the information associated to a frame in the field of environment

This interface allows us to select or search frames themselves, as well as terms or actantial roles. Search results display definitions, examples and notes associated to frames, their participants, together with lists of terms that evoke them. As in the FrameGrapher in FrameNet, rather than simply listing the relations that frames share with others frames, we present them as graphs (Figures 8 and 10). This provides a more comprehensive view of broader sets of frames and makes it easier to unveil some scenarios that we believe are specific to the field of the environment.

5 Two scenarios in the field of the environment

In this section, we describe two small conceptual scenarios that were discovered thanks to the establishment of relations described in Section 4. The first is the **Risk_scenario** that also appears in FrameNet. The second one is **Managing_waste** that has no direct counterpart in FrameNet (even though some frames appear to correspond to frames recorded in FrameNet). Other scenarios are in the process of being defined.

5.1 Risk_scenario

The **Risk_scenario** discovered on the basis of the data extracted from the environment database appears in Figure 8. We also reproduced the scenario proper to FrameNet in Figure 9 to highlight some of their differences.

The **Risk_scenario** in the field of the environment represents the potential threats to the ecosystem and some of its components. It also shows how the human (although responsible for most of these threats) takes measures to prevent some of them.

Interestingly, the **Risk_scenario** unveiled using data taken from an environment corpus and database shares some similarities, but also some differences with the one appearing in FrameNet. For instance, the **Wagering** frame (that comprises LUs such as *bet* and *wager*) was completely irrelevant for the environment. Conversely, a **Preserve_in_original_state** was defined for the environment data for terms such as Eng. *conserve*, and Fr. *conservation*, *préserver*.

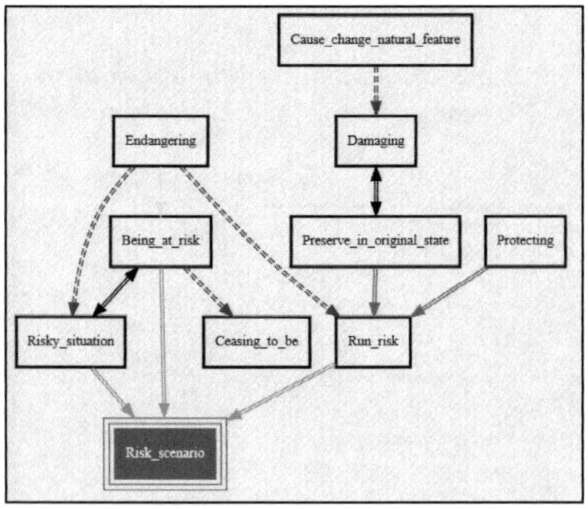

Figure 8. **Risk_scenario** in the environment

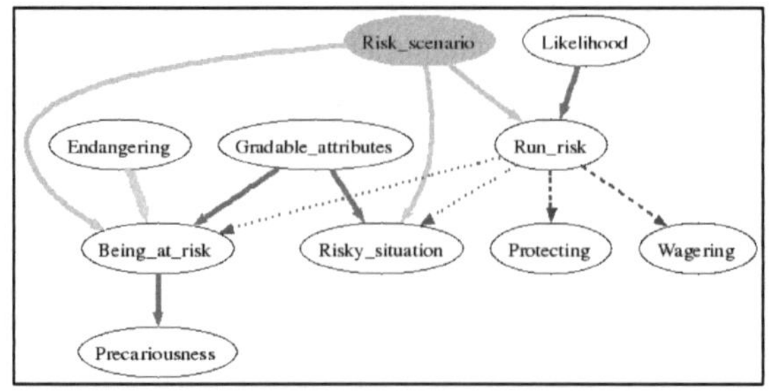

Figure 9. **Risk_scenario** in FrameNet (2014)

5.2 Managing_waste

The **Managing_waste** scenario was also defined based on the terms related to residual waste management. This scenario shows the different processes involved in managing waste and the order in which they are performed: first waste is collected, then it is separated; afterwards, it can be recovered or discarded. If waste is removed, it can then undergo incineration or landfilling. On the other hand, if waste is recovered, it is either recycled, composed or processed.

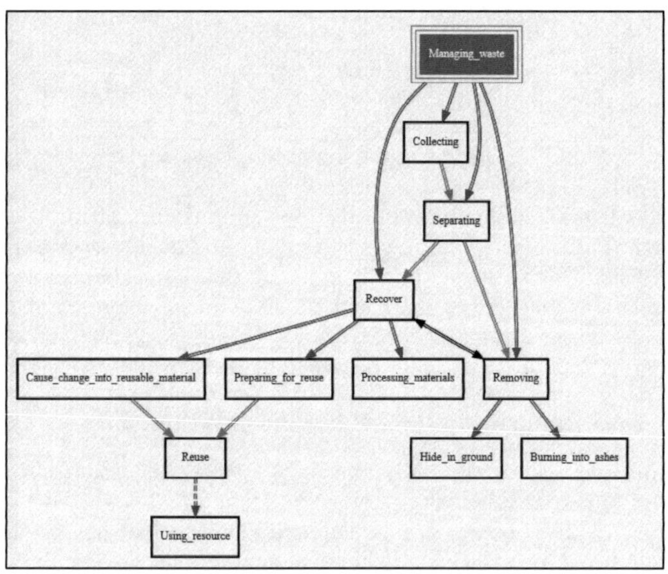

Figure 10. **Managing_waste** in the environment

6 Conclusion

In this paper, we presented a methodology to discover alternative conceptual structures for terminology. They complement structures often used to represent entity concepts (i.e. domain ontologies) and are well suited to account for terms denoting processes, events, and properties.

The methodology, based on principles borrowed from Frame Semantics and its implementation in FrameNet, was applied to English and French terms that are related to the field of the environment. It allowed us to unveil frames that are similar to those recorded in FrameNet, but also new ones that might be specific to the specialized field we chose to describe. It also allows us to represent small conceptual scenarios.

Acknowledgements

This work was supported by the Social Sciences and Humanities Research Council (SSHRC) of Canada. We would like to thank Carlos Subirats for his help during the first stages of this analysis and the three anonymous reviewers for their useful comments on a previous version of this paper.

References

Baker, C. & J. Hung. 2010. *Release 1.5 of the FrameNet data*. International Computer Science Institute. Berkeley.

Boas, H. C. (ed.) 2009. *Multilingual FrameNets in Computational Lexicography*. The Hague: Mouton.

Condamines, A. 1993. Un exemple d'utilisation de connaissances de sémantique lexicale : acquisition semi-automatique d'un vocabulaire de spécialité. *Cahiers de lexicologie* 62: 25-65.

Cruse, A. 2011. *Meaning in Language*. Oxford: Oxford University Press.

Dolbey, A., M. Ellsworh and J. Scheffczyk. 2006. BioFrameNet: A Domain-specific FrameNet Extension with Links to Biomedical Ontologies. *KR-MED 2006 Biomedical Ontology in Action*, Baltimore, Maryland.

Faber, P. et al. 2006. Process-oriented terminology management in the domain of Coastal Engineering. *Terminology* 12(2): 189-213.

Faber, P. (ed.). 2012. *A Cognitive Linguistics View of Terminology and Specialized Language*. Berlin/Boston: De Gruyter.

Fillmore, C. 1982. Frame Semantics. *Linguistics in the Morning Calm*, Seoul: Hanshin Publishing Co.: 111-137.

Fillmore, C.J. 1985. Frames and the semantics of understanding. *Quaderni di Semantica* 6(2): 222-254.

Fillmore, C.J. & C. Baker. 2010. A frames approach to semantic analysis. *The Oxford Handbook of Linguistic Analysis*, Bernd Heine and Haiko Narrog (eds): 313-339. Oxford: OUP.

Fillmore, C.J.. C.R. Johnson & M. Petruck. 2003. Background to FrameNet. *International Journal of Lexicography* 16(3): 235-250.

FrameNet [https://framenet.icsi.berkeley.edu/fndrupal/]. Accessed 16 May 2014.

L'Homme, M.C. 1998. Le statut du verbe en langue de spécialité et sa description lexicographique. *Cahiers de lexicologie* 73(2): 61-84

L'Homme, M.C. 2012. Adding syntactico-semantic information to specialized dictionaries: an application of the FrameNet methodology. Gouws, R. et al. (eds.). *Lexicographica* 28: 233-252.

L'Homme, M.C. 2014. Terminologies and taxonomies, Taylor, J. (ed.). *Handbook of the Word* Oxford: Oxford University Press.

L'Homme, M.C., B. Robichaud & C. Subirats. 2014. Discovering frames in specialized domains, In *Language Resources and Evaluation*. LREC 2014, Reykjavik, Iceland.

Lerat, P. 2002. Qu'est-ce que le verbe spécialisé ? Le cas du droit. *Cahiers de Lexicologie* 80: 201-211.

Lorente, M. 2002. Verbos y discurso especializado. *Estudios de lingüística española* (ELiEs) 16.

Mel'cuk, I., A. Clas & A. Polguère. 1995. *Introduction à la lexicologie explicative et combinatoire*, Bruxelles: Duculot.

Montiel-Ponsoda, E., G. Aguado de Cea, A. Gómez-Pérez, & W. Peters. 2010. Enriching Ontologies with Multilingual Information. *Journal of Natural Language Engineering* 17: 283-309.

Pimentel, J. 2013. Methodological bases for assigning terminological equivalents. A contribution. *Terminology* 19(2): 237-257.

Ruppenhofer, J., M. Ellsworth, M. Petruck, C. Johnson & J. Scheffczyk. 2010. FrameNet II: *Extended Theory and Practice.* 2010. [http://framenet.icsi.berkeley.edu]. Accessed 16 May 2014.

Schmidt, T. 2009. The Kicktionary – A Multilingual Lexical Resources of Football Language. Boas, H.C. (ed). *Multilingual FrameNets in Computational Lexicography. Methods and Applications*, Berlin/NewYork: Mouton de Gruyter: 101-134.

Wandji, O., N. Grabar & M.C. L'Homme. 2013. Discovery of semantic frames for a contrastive study of verbs in medical corpora. *Terminology and Artificial Intelligence*, TIA 2013, Paris.

Modelling the Semantics of Adjectives in the Ontology-Lexicon Interface

John P. M[c]Crae
Universität Bielefeld
Bielefeld
Germany
jmccrae@cit-ec.uni-bielefeld.de

Francesca Quattri
Hong Kong Polytechnic University
Hong Kong
francesca.quattri@connect.polyu.hk

Christina Unger
Universität Bielefeld
Bielefeld
Germany
cunger@cit-ec.uni-bielefeld.de

Philipp Cimiano
Universität Bielefeld
Bielefeld
Germany
cimiano@cit-ec.uni-bielefeld.de

Abstract

The modelling of the semantics of adjectives is notoriously challenging. We consider this problem in the context of the so called *ontology-lexicon interface*, which attempts to capture the semantics of words by reference to an ontology in description logics or some other, typically first-order, logical formalism. The use of first order logic (hence also description logics), while effective for nouns and verbs, breaks down in the case of adjectives. We argue that this is primarily due to a lack of logical expressivity in the underlying ontology languages. In particular, beyond the straightforward *intersective adjectives*, there exist *gradable adjectives*, requiring fuzzy or non-monotonic semantics, as well as *operator adjectives*, requiring second-order logic for modelling. We consider how we can extend the ontology-lexicon interface as realized by extant models such as *lemon* in the face of the issues mentioned above, in particular those arising in the context of modelling the ontological semantics of adjectives. We show how more complex logical formalisms that are required to capture the ontological semantics of adjectives can be backward engineered into OWL-based modelling by means of pseudo-classes. We discuss the implications of this modelling in the context of application to ontology-based question answering.

1 Introduction

Ontology-lexicon models, such as *lemon* (Lexicon Model for Ontologies) (M[c]Crae et al., 2012) model the semantics of open class words by capturing their semantics with respect to the semantic vocabulary defined in a given ontology. Such ontology-lexica are built around the separation of a *lexical layer*, describing how a word or phrase acts syntactically and morphologically, and a *semantic layer* describing how the meaning of a word is expressed in a formal logical model, such as OWL (Web Ontology Language) (Deborah L. M[c]Guinness and others, 2004). As such, the modelling is based around a lexical entry which describes the morphology and syntax of a word, and is linked by means of a lexical sense to an ontology entity defined in a given ontology described in formal logic. It has been shown that this principle known as *semantics by reference* (Buitelaar, 2010) is an effective model that can support the task of developing question answering systems (Unger and Cimiano, 2011) and natural language generation (Cimiano et al., 2013) over backends based on Semantic Web data models. The Pythia system, which builds on the *lemon* formalism to declaratively capture the lexicon-ontology interface, for example, has been instantiated to the case of answering questions from DBpedia (Unger and Cimiano, 2011). However, as has been shown by the Question Answering over Linked Data (Lopez et al., 2013, QALD) benchmarking campaigns, there are many questions that can be asked over this database that require a deeper representation of the semantics of words, adjectives in particular. For example, questions such

Zock/Rapp/Huang (eds.): Proceedings of the 4th Workshop on Cognitive Aspects of the Lexicon, pages 198–209, Dublin, Ireland, August 23, 2014.

as (1a) require understanding of the semantics of 'high' in a manner that goes beyond the expressivity of OWL. The formalization of this question as an executable query formulated with respect to the SPARQL query language is provided in (1b). In particular, the interpretation of this question involves the formal interpretation of the word 'high' as relating to the property `dbo:elevation`, including ordering and subset selection operations.

1. (a) What is the highest mountain in Australia?
   (b)
```
SELECT DISTINCT ?uri WHERE {
  ?uri rdf:type dbo:Mountain .
  ?uri dbo:locatedInArea res:Australia .
  ?uri dbo:elevation ?elevation .
} ORDER BY DESC(?elevation) LIMIT 1
```

In the above query, we select an entity denoted by the query variable `?uri` that has the properties that i) the entity's type is a mountain, ii) it is located in Australia, and iii) it has an elevation bound to the variable `?elevation`. We then sort the query in descending order by the value of the elevation and limit so the query returns only the first result, in effect choosing the largest value in the data set. It has been claimed that first-order logic and thus by extension description logics, such as OWL, "fail decidedly when it comes to adjectives" (Bankston, 2003). In fact, we largely agree that the semantics of many adjectives are difficult or impossible to describe in first-order logic. However, from the point of view of the ontology-lexicon interface, the logical expressivity of the ontology is not a limiting factor. In fact, due to the separation of the lexical and ontology layers in a model such as *lemon*, it is possible to express the meaning of words without worrying about the formalism used in the ontology. To this extent, we will first demonstrate that adjectives are in general a case where the use of description logics (DL) breaks down, and for which more sophisticated logical formalisms must be applied. We then consider to what extent this can be handled in the context of the ontology-lexicon, and introduce pseudo-classes, that is OWL classes with annotations, which we use to express the semantics of adjectives in a manner that would allow reasoning with fuzzy, high-order models. To this extent, we base our models on the previously introduced design patterns (McCrae and Unger, 2014) for modelling ontology-lexica. Finally, we show how these semantics can be helpful in practical applications of question answering over the DBpedia knowledge base.

2 Classification of adjectives

There are a number of classifications of adjectives. First we will start with the most fundamental distinction between *attributive* and *predicative* usage, that is the use of adjectives in noun phrases ("X is a A N") versus as objects of the copula ("X is A"). It should be noted that there are many adjectives for which only predicative or attributive usage is allowed, as shown in (3a) and (3).

2. (a) Clinton is a former president.
   (b) *Clinton is former.
3. (a) The baby is awake.
   (b) *The awake baby.

One of the principle classifications of the semantics of adjectives (for example (Partee, 2003; Bouillon and Viegas, 1999; Morzycki, 2013b)) is based on the meaning of adjective noun compounds relative to the meaning of the single words that form the compound. This classification is as follows (where $\Rightarrow$ denotes entailment).

Intersective (X is a A N $\Rightarrow$ X is $A \wedge X$ is a N) Such adjectives work as if they were another noun and indicate that the compound noun phrase is a member of class denoted by the noun and the class denoted by the adjective. For example, in the phrase "Belgian violinist" it refers to a person in the class intersection $Belgian \sqcap Violinist(X)$, and hence we can infer that a "Belgian violinist" is a subclass of a "Belgian". Furthermore, we could conclude that if the same person were a surgeon, he/she would also be a "Belgian Surgeon".

Subsective (X is a $A\ N \Rightarrow X$ is a N, but X is a $A\ N \not\Rightarrow X$ is A) Such adjectives acquire their specific meaning in combination with the noun the modify. For example, a "skilful violinist" is certainly in the class $Violinist(X)$ but the described person is 'skilful as a violinist', but not skilful in general, e.g. as a surgeon.

Privative (X is a $A\ N \not\Rightarrow X$ is a N) These adjectives modify the meaning of a noun phrase to create a noun phrase that is potentially incompatible with the original meaning. For example, a "fake gun" is not a member of the class of guns.

Another important distinction is whether adjectives are *gradable*, i.e. whether a comparative or superlative statement with these adjectives makes sense. For example, adjectives such as 'big' or 'tall' can express relationships such as 'X is bigger than Y'. However it is not possible to say that one individual is 'more former'. Most gradable adjectives are subsective (e. g.'a big mouse' is not 'a big animal' (Morzycki, 2013a)).

Finally, we consider *operator* or *property-modifying* adjectives. They can be understood along the lines of privative adjectives but differ in that they represent operators that modify some property in the qualia structure (Pustejovsky, 1991) of the class. For instance, we may express the adjective 'former' in lambda calculus as a function that takes a class C as input and returns the class of entities that were a member of C to some prior time point t (Partee, 2003):

$$\lambda C[\lambda x \exists t C(x,t) \cap t < \text{now}]$$

Such adjectives have not only a difference in semantic meaning but can also frequently have syntactic impact, for example in adjective ordering restrictions, as they may be reordered with only semantic impact (Teodorescu, 2006), e.g.,

4. (a) A big red car.
   (b) ?A red big car.
5. (a) A famous former actor.
   (b) A former famous actor.

Finally, we define *object-relational* adjectives as those adjectives which have a meaning that expresses a relationship between two individuals or events[1], for example:

6. He is related to her.
7. She is similar to her brother.
8. This is useful for something.

3 Representation of adjectives in the ontology-lexicon interface

In general it is assumed that adjectives form frames with exactly one argument except for extra arguments provided by adjuncts, typically prepositional phrases. Most adjectives are thus associated with a predicative frame, which much like the standard noun predicate frame (X is a N) is stereotyped in English as:

$$X \text{ is } A$$

The attributive usage of an adjective is associate to a stereotypical frame where the $N?$ argument is not semantically bound, but can instead be obtained by syntactic unification to a noun predicate frame:

$$X \text{ is } A\ N?$$

As such, when we encounter the attributive usage of an adjective such as in 9, we understand this as the realization of two frames, given in 10.

9. Juan is a Spanish researcher.
10. (a) Juan is a researcher.
    (b) Juan is a Spanish $N?$

Note that we do not provide modelling for adjectives where the meaning is unique for a particular noun phrase, such as 'polar bear', which we would capture as a normal noun phrase with meaning *ursus maritimus*.

[1]Our definition of relational here is borrowed from the idea of relational nouns (De Bruin and Scha, 1988) as a word that requires an argument. Our definition is also different from the one for 'relational adjectives' as proposed by (Morzycki, 2013a).

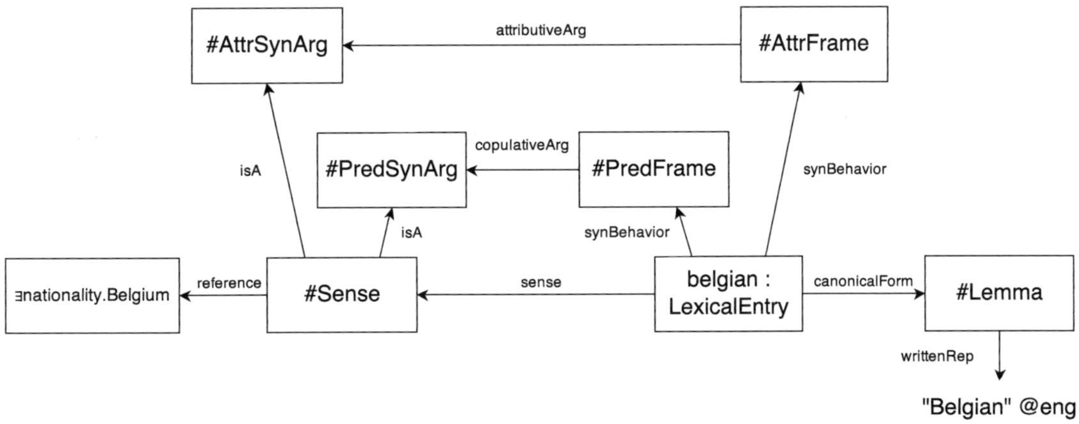

Figure 1: Modelling of an intersective adjective 'Belgian' in *lemon*

3.1 Intersective adjectives

Intersective adjectives are the most straightforward class, as in many cases they can be modelled essentially as a noun or verb (e.g. deverbal adjectives such as 'broken'). Intersective adjectives take one argument and can thus be modelled as unary predicates in first-order logic or classes in OWL, as described by McCrae and Unger (2014). For practical modelling examples, we will use the *lemon* model, since it is the most prominent implementation of the ontology-lexicon interface.

The primary mechanism of modelling the syntax-semantics interface in the context of *lemon* is by means of assigning a *frame* as a *syntactic behaviour* of an entry and giving it *syntactic arguments*, which can then be linked to the *lexical sense*, which stands proxy for a true semantic frame in the ontology. For example, the modelling of an adjective such as 'Belgian' can be achieved as follows (depicted in Figure 1)[2].

```
lexicon:belgian a lemon:LexicalEntry ;
  lemon:canonicalForm belgian:Lemma ;
  lemon:synBehavior   belgian:AttrFrame ,
                      belgian:PredFrame ;
  lemon:sense         belgian:Sense .

belgian:Lemma lemon:writtenRep "Belgian"@eng .

belgian:AttrFrame lexinfo:attributiveArg belgian:AttrSynArg .
belgian:PredFrame lexinfo:copulativeArg  belgian:PredSynArg .

belgian:sense lemon:reference [ a owl:Restriction ;
                                owl:onProperty dbpedia:nationality ;
                                owl:hasValue dbpedia:Belgium ] ;
              lemon:isA belgian:AttrSynArg , belgian:PredSynArg .
```

In this example, the word 'Belgian' is associated with a lemma with representation 'Belgian', two frame objects and a lexical sense. The frame objects describe the attributive and predicative usage, and are associated with an attributive and copulative argument respectively. The sense links the word to the anonymous ontological class for objects that have 'Belgium' as the value of their 'nationality' property and furthermore the arguments of each frame are linked to the sense in order to establish a correspondence between the ontology class and the syntactic frames. Note that here we use the external vocabulary defined in the LexInfo ontology (Cimiano et al., 2011) to define the meaning of the arguments of the frame as the *attributive argument*, corresponding to the frame stereotype 'X is A N?' and the *copulative argument* for the frame stereotype 'X is A'. Furthermore, the

[2]We assume that the namespaces are defined for the lexicon as `lexicon`, e.g., `http://www.example.org/lexicon` and for the entry, e.g., `belgian` is `http://www.example.org/lexicon/belgian#`. Other namespaces are assumed to be as usual.

class of Belgians is not named in our reference ontology DBpedia, so we introduce an anonymous class with the axiomatization, i.e. $\exists$ *nationality . Belgium.* It is in fact common that the referent of an adjective is not named in an ontology. An obvious choice is thus to model denominal adjectives as classes of the form $\exists$*prop.Value*, where *Value* is an individual that represents the semantics of the noun from which the adjective was derived. This modelling is so common that it has already been encoded as two design patterns, called `IntersectiveObjectPropertyAdjective` and `IntersectiveDatatypePropertyAdjective` (see (M^c^Crae and Unger, 2014)). Similarly, most deverbal adjectives refer to an event, and as such a common modelling is of the form $\exists\, theme^{-1}.\, EventClass$. For example, 'vandalized' may be $\exists\, theme^{-1}.VandalismEvent$.

3.2 Gradable adjectives and relevant observables

Gradable adjectives have a number of properties which differentiate them from intersective adjectives:

- They occur in comparative constructions, in English with either '-er' or 'more' (Kennedy and McNally, 1999), e.g. 'smaller' and 'more frequent', as opposed to intersectives such as '*less geological' and '*more wooden'.
- Gradable adjectives can be defined as 'scalar', since their value can ideally be measured on a scale of set degrees
- They have a context-dependent truth-conditional variability, meaning that their positive form is understood in relation to the class of the object modified by the adjective. For example, an 'expensive watch' has a different price scale to an 'expensive bottle of water'.
- They are frequently *fuzzy* (or *vague*) (Kennedy, 2007).
- There may be a minimum or maximum of the adjective's scale, which can be determined by, for example, whether they can modified by adverbs such as 'completely' or 'utterly'.

As such, we define gradable adjectives relative to a particular property. These adjectives are also called 'observable' (Bennett, 2006)[3] as they are related to some observable or measurable property, e.g. *size* in the case of *'big'*. However, a specification of the observable property is clearly not sufficient to differentiate between the meaning of antonyms such as *big* and *small.* Thus, we introduce the notions of *covariance* and *contravariance*, which specify whether the comparative form indicates a higher property value for the subject or the object. In this sense 'big' is covariant with size, as bigger things have a higher size value, and 'small' is contravariant with size.[4] We also introduce a third concept, i.e. the one of *absolute gradability*, which expresses the fact that the degree of membership in the denotation of the adjective is stronger the more it approaches a prototypical or ideal value. A common example of this is colours, where we may say that some object is redder than another if it is closer to some ideal value of red (e.g., RGB `0xff0000`).

While these notions can handle the comparative structure of the semantics of adjectives, the predicative and superlative usage of adjectives is complicated by three factors that we will outline below. We notice that gradable classes are not crisply defined like in the case of many intersective adjectives. In fact, while we can clearly define all people in the world as 'Belgian' or 'not Belgian', according to whom holds a Belgian passport or not, it is not easy to split the world's population into 'tall' and 'not tall' (This is known as *sorites* paradox (Bennett, 2006)). Furthermore, while it may be easy to say that someone with height 6'6" (198cm) is 'tall', it is not clear whether someone with height 6' (182cm) is 'tall', although compared to an average (different) height for a man, they are 'taller'. As such, one frequently used way to deal with this class of vague adjectives (and nouns) is via fuzzy logic (Goguen, 1969; Zadeh, 1975; Zadeh, 1965; Dubois and Prade, 1988; Bennett, 2006). Secondly, we notice that these class boundaries are non-monotonic, that is that with knowledge of more instances of the relative class we must revise our class boundaries. This is especially the case for superlatives, as the discovery of a new tallest person

[3]Note that in many cases the property is quite abstract such as in 'breakable'.

[4]The use of these terms is borrowed from type systems, and resembles the concept of 'converse observables' as introduced by ((Bennett, 2006):42). As stated by the author, adjectives often come in pairs of polar opposites (e. g. $conv(tall) = short$, and both refer to the same observable (in this case *size*). Some observables analogously hold converse relationships with other observables (e. g. $conv(flexibility) = rigidity$ or $conv(tallness) = shortness$).

in the world would remove the existing tallest person in the world from the class of tallest person in the world. This non-monotonicity also affects the class boundaries of the gradable class itself. For example, in the 18th century, the average height of a male was 5'5" (165cm)[5]; as such a male of 6' would have clearly been considered tall.

It follows from this that each instance added to our ontology might lead to a revision of the class boundaries of a gradable class, hence leading to the fact that gradable adjectives are fundamentally non-monotonic. We must also notice that gradability can only be understood relative to the class that we wish to grade. Thus, while it is a priori unclear whether 6' is tall for a male, it is clear that 6' is tall for a female given the current average height of a female being about 5'4" (162cm).

We can therefore conclude that gradable adjectives are *fuzzy*, *non-monotonic* and *context-sensitive*, all of which are incompatible with the description logic used in OWL.

Pseudo-classes in lemonOILS

Currently there are only limited models for representing fuzzy logic in the context of the Web (Zhao and Boley, 2008). In order to capture the properties of gradable adjectives, we introduce a new model which we name *lemonOILS* (The *lemon* Ontology for the Interpretation of Lexical Semantics)[6]. This ontology introduces three new classes:

- `CovariantScalar`, indicating that the adjective is covariant with its bound property
- `ContravariantScalar`, indicating that the adjective is contravariant with its bound property
- `AbsoluteScalar`, indicating that the property represents similarity to an absolute value

In addition, the following properties are introduced to enable the description of gradable adjectives. Note that all these properties are typed as *annotation properties* in the OWL ontology, so that they do not interfere with the standard OWL reasoning.

- `boundTo` indicates the property that a scalar refers to (e.g., 'size' for 'big')
- `threshold` specifies a sensible minimal value for which the adjective can be said to hold
- `absoluteValue` is the ideal value of an absolute scalar
- `degree` is specified as `weak`, `medium`, `strong` or `very strong`, corresponding to approximately 50%, 25%, 5% or 1% of all known individuals
- `comparator` indicates an object property that is equivalent to the comparison of the adjective (e.g., an object property `biggerThan` may be considered a comparator for the adjective class `big`)
- `measure` indicates a unit that can be used as a measure for this adjective, e.g., 'John is 175 *centimetres* tall'.

Using such classes we can capture the semantics of gradable adjectives syntactically but not formally within an OWL model. As such, we call these introduced classes *pseudo-classes*. An example of modelling an adjective such as 'high' is given below (and depicted in Figure 2).

```
lexicon:high a lemon:LexicalEntry ;
  lemon:canonicalForm high:Lemma ;
  lemon:synBehavior high:PredFrame ;
  lemon:sense high:Sense .

high:Lemma lemon:writtenRep "high"@eng .

high:PredFrame lexinfo:copulativeArg high:PredArg .

high:Sense lemon:reference [
    rdfs:subClassOf oils:CovariantScalar ;
    oils:boundTo dbpedia:elevation ;
    oils:degree oils:strong ] ;
  lemon:isA high:PredArg .
```

[5] `https://en.wikipedia.org/wiki/Human_height`
[6] `http://lemon-model.net/oils`

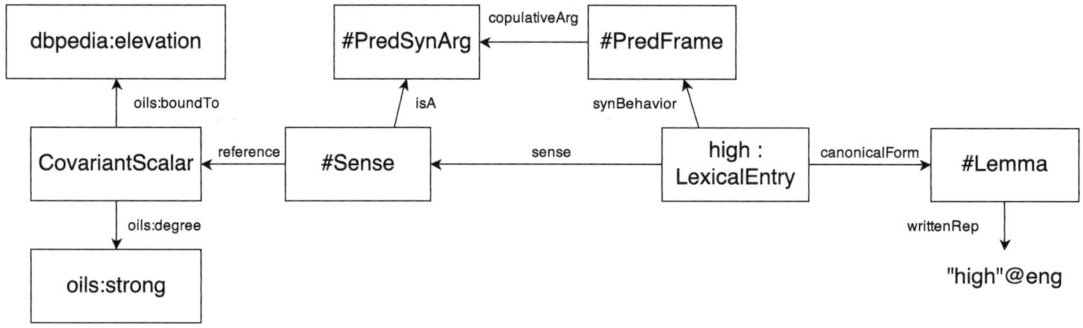

Figure 2: An example of the modelling of 'high' in *lemon*

As an example of a logic in which these annotations could be interpreted, we consider Markov Logic (Richardson and Domingos, 2006), which is an extension of first-order logic in which each clause is given a cost. The process of reasoning is thus transformed into an optimization problem of finding the extension which minimizes the summed weight of all violated clauses. As such, we can formulate a gradable adjective based on the number of known instances. For example, we can specify 'big' with respect to *size* for some class C as in (11).

11. $\forall x \in C, y \in C : size(x) > size(y) \rightarrow big_C(x) : \alpha$
    $\forall x \in C, y \in C : size(x) < size(y) \rightarrow \neg big_C(x) : \beta$

In this way, the classification of an object into 'big' or 'small' can be defined as follows. For an individual $x \in C$, the property $big_C(x)$ holds if and only if:

$$|\{y \in C, size(y) > size(x)\}|\alpha < |\{y \in C, size(y) < size(x)\}|\beta$$

where the values of α and β are related to the degree defined in the ontology.

We see that 'big' defined in this way has the three properties outlined above: it is non-monotonic (in that more individuals may change whether we consider an individual to be 'big' or not), it is fuzzy (given by the strength of the probability of the proposition $big_C(x)$), and it is context-sensitive (as whether an individual counts as big or not depends on the class C). Furthermore, our definition does not rely on defining 'big' for a given class, but instead is inferred from some known number of instances of this class. This eliminates the need to define a threshold for each individual class, or even to define the predicate big_C on a per-class basis.

The supervaluation theory and SUMO

Another way to capture the meaning of these vague terms can be achieved by *supervaluation semantics*. Through supervaluation theory, the modelling or positioning of *sorites* vague concepts is grounded in a judgement or meaning that lies on arbitrary thresholds, but these thresholds are based on a number of *relevant objective measures* (Bennett, 2006).

A recent extension of the SUMO ontology (Niles and Pease, 2001, Suggested Upper Merged Ontology)[7] includes default measurements (currently amounting to 300+) added to the `Artifacts`, `Devices` and `Objects` enlisted in the ontology (and marked with capitals). The compilation of `defaultMeasurements` in SUMO has been just conducted on observables, not on predicates. Given for instance an `Artifact` such as `Book`, the compilation of its default measurements would look like:

```
;;Book
(defaultMinimumHeight Book (MeasureFn 10 Inch))
(defaultMaximumHeight Book (MeasureFn 11 Inch))
(defaultMinimumLength Book (MeasureFn 5.5 Inch))
(defaultMaximumLength Book (MeasureFn 7 Inch))
(defaultMinimumWidth Book (MeasureFn 1.2 Inch))
(defaultMaximumWidth Book (MeasureFn 5.5 Inch))
```

[7] `www.ontologyportal.org`

The example for `Book` shows that the default measurements for the observable reflect a *standard* kind of book, i.e., one of the most commonly known kinds of the same artifact. As for this case, SUMO implies `Book` to be a physical object with a certain length, height and width (and possibly weight). A weakness here is that the there is no systematic connection between the `defaultMinimumHeight` and `Height` or `Width`, since these physical properties have been defined in SUMO just in terms of first-order logic, and have not been assigned default measurements yet. With *lemonOILS* we can add this information as follows:

```
sumo:Book oils:default [
    oils:defaultFor sumo:height ;
    oils:defaultMin "10in" ;
    oils:defaultMax "11in" ] .
```

Then, if we understand a lexical entry 'high' as referring to a scalar covariant pseudo-class for `sumo:height`, it is possible to understand that a 'high' object exceeds the default minimum set established for the same object and owns at the same time a value for 'high' which does not go beyond the established default maximum. A further weakness of this approach is captured by the following example:

12. Avery Johnson is a short basketball player.

Here, we see the difficulty in interpreting the sentence, as Avery Johnson is in fact of average height (5'10") but for the class of basketball players he is unusually short. While SUMO has some very specific listings of subsets for the same `Artifact`[8], SUMO does not provide a well-structured subset net for e. g. `Person`.As a way to address this bottleneck, we could introduce default values for every subclass of `Person`, as well as to introduce default values for the same Artifact in conjunction with a predicate or adjective (e. g. `BigPerson`, `BulkyPerson`). The creation of such *ad hoc* subclasses is not feasible in general, as we would have to introduce a new class into the ontology for every combination of an adjective and a noun. On the other side though, the SUMO default measurements serve the purpose they were originally conceived for, namely to be an arbitrary, yet computable approximation of physical measures.

3.3 Operator adjectives

Operator adjectives are those that combine with a noun to modify the meaning of the noun itself. There are two primary issues with the understanding of the adjective in this manner. Firstly, the reference of the lexical item does not generally refer to an existing item in the ontology, but rather is novel and productive, in the sense that it generates a new class. Secondly, the compositional nature of adjective-noun compounds is no longer simple, as in the cases of intersective and gradable adjectives. This means that, in order to understand a concept such as a 'fake gun', we must first derive a class of `FakeGuns` from the class of `Guns`. Thus the modified noun phrase must be an argument of the operator adjective.

To this extent we claim that it is not generally possibly to represent the meaning of an operator adjective within the context of an OWL ontology. Instead, following Bankston (Bankston, 2003), we claim that the reference of an operator adjective must be a higher order predicate. If we assume that there are operators of the form of a function, then the argument of an operator is the attributed noun phrase. As such, we introduce a frame *operator attributive*, that has one argument which is the noun. Thus we understand that the interpretation of 'fake gun' is by means of an operator $fake$, which is a function that takes a class and produces a new class, i.e., $[fake(Gun)](X)$. Capturing such an operator lies beyond the expressivity of first-order logic. To fully capture the semantics of such an operator adjective, formalisms beyond first-order logic are thus clearly needed.

3.4 Object-relational adjectives

Object-relational adjectives are those that require a second argument, such as 'known', which can only be understood as being 'known' to some person, in comparison to 'famous'. Thus, the modelling of the relational adjective *known* is quite similar to the semantics of the corresponding verb *know*. It can be modelled for instance via the frame 'X is known to Y' and reference `foaf:knows` as:

[8] For example, some of the subsets `Car` are: `CrewDormCar`, `GalleryCar`, `MotorRailcar`, `FreightCar`, `BoxCar`, `RefrigeratorCar`, `FiveWellStackCar`, and more.

```
lexicon:known a lemon:LexicalEntry ;
  lemon:canonicalForm known:Lemma ;
  lemon:sense known:Sense ;
  lemon:synBehavior known:Frame .

known:Lemma lemon:writtenRep "known"@eng .

known:Frame lexinfo:attributeArg known:Subject ;
  lexinfo:prepositionalObject known:Object .

known:Sense lemon:reference foaf:knows ;
  lemon:subjOfProp known:Subject ;
  lemon:objOfProp known:Object .

known:Object lemon:marker lexicon:to .
```

4 Adjectives in question answering

In this section we empirically analyze the adequacy of the modelling proposed in this paper with respect to the QALD-4[9] dataset, a shared dataset for Question Answering over Linked Data. The 250 training and test questions of the QALD-4 benchmark contain 76 adjectives in total (not counting adjectives in names such as 'Mean Hamster Software').

18 of the occurring adjectives do not have a semantic contribution w.r.t. the underlying DBpedia ontology, or at least none that is separable from the noun, as exemplified in the noun phrases in (13) and (14).[10]

13. (a) $[\![\text{official website}]\!]$ = `dbo:website`
    (b) $[\![\text{national anthem}]\!]$ = `dbo:anthem`
14. (a) $[\![\text{official languages}]\!]$ = `dbo:officialLanguages`
    (b) $[\![\text{military conflicts}]\!]$ = `dbo:battle`

Otherwise, the most common kinds of adjectives among them are gradable (27) and intersective (13) adjectives.

All intersective adjectives denote restriction classes that are not explicitely named in DBpedia, in correspondence with the modelling proposed in Section 3.1 above, for example:

15. (a) $[\![\text{Danish}]\!] = \exists$ `dbo:country.res:Denmark`
    (b) $[\![\text{female}]\!] = \exists$ `dbo:gender.res:Female`
    (c) $[\![\text{Methodist}]\!] = \exists$ `dbo:religion.res:Methodism`

In some cases these intersectives have a context-dependent and highly ontology-specific meaning, often tightly interwoven with the meaning of the noun, as in the following examples:

16. (a) $[\![\text{first president of the United States}]\!] = \exists$ `dbo:office.`'1st President of the United States'
    (b) $[\![\text{first season}]\!] = \exists$ `dbo:seasonNumber.1`

All gradable adjectives that occur in the QALD-4 question set can be captured in terms of *lemonOILS* as `CovariantScalar` (e.g. 'high') or `ContravariantScalar` (e.g. 'young') (cf. Section 3.2 above), bound to a DBpedia datatype property (e.g. `elevation` or `birthDate`). The positive form of those adjectives only occurs in 'how (much)' questions, denoting the property they are bound to, for example:

17. (a) $[\![\text{deep}]\!]$ = `dbo:depth` in 'How deep is Lake Placid?'
    (b) $[\![\text{tall}]\!]$ = `dbo:height` in 'How tall is Michael Jordan?'

[9] http://www.sc.cit-ec.uni-bielefeld.de/qald/

[10] $[\![\cdot]\!]$ stands for 'denotes' and the prefixes `dbo` and `res` abbreviate the DBpedia namespaces http://dbpedia.org/ontology/ and http://dbpedia.org/resource/, respectively.

The comparative form denotes the property they are bound to, together with an aggregation operation, usually a filter invoking a term of comparison that depends on whether the adjective is covariant or contravariant.

18. (a) ⟦Which mountains are higher than the Nanga Parbat?⟧ =

```
SELECT DISTINCT ?uri WHERE {
 res:Nanga_Parbat dbo:elevation ?x .
 ?uri rdf:type dbo:Mountain .
 ?uri dbo:elevation ?y .
 FILTER (?y > ?x)
}
```

Finally, the superlative form denotes the property they are bound to, together with an aggregation operation, usually an ordering with a cut-off of all results except the first one, as exemplified in (19). In some cases, the superlative property is already encoded in the ontology, e.g., in the case of the property `dbo:highestPlace`.

19. ⟦What is the longest river?⟧ =

```
SELECT DISTINCT ?uri WHERE {
 ?uri rdf:type dbo:River .
 ?uri dbo:length ?l .
} ORDER BY DESC(?l) OFFSET 0 LIMIT 1
```

There are three instances of operator adjectives. Examples are 'former', as in 20, which does not refer to an element in the DBpedia ontology but is instead a disambiguation clue in the given query, and 'professional', which refers to the property `dbo:occupation`, see 21.

20. ⟦the former Dutch queen Juliana⟧ = `res:Juliana`
21. ⟦professional surfer⟧ = ∃ `dbo:occupation.res:Surfing`

Finally, there were 8 remaining adjectives totalling 15 occurrences, which do not correspond to meaning in an ontology, but instead are part of the discourse structure, each 'same', 'other'.

5 Related work

The categorization of adjectives in terms of formal semantics goes back to Montague (1970) and Vendler (1968). However, one of the most significant attempts to assign a formal meaning was carried out in the Mikrokosmos project (Raskin and Nirenburg, 1995). The approach to adjective modelling in the Mikrokosmos provided one of the first computational implementations of a microtheory of adjective meaning. The modelling of adjectives presented in this paper is clearly inspired by the modelling of adjectives adopted in the Mikrokosmos project. In particular, scalar adjectives in the Microkosmos project are modeled by association with an attribute and a range, e.g., 'big' is described as being `>0.75` (i.e., 75% of all known instances) on the `size-attribute`. Still, these classifications do not clearly separate meaning and syntax and also require a separate modelling of comparatives and class-specific meanings for many adjectives.

Amoia and Gardent (2006) handled the problem of adjectives in the context of textual entailment. They analyzed 15 classes that show the subtle interaction between the semantic class (e.g., 'privative') and the issues of attributive/predicative use and gradability. Abdullah and Frost (2005) focused on the modelling of privative adjectives by arguing that these adjectives modify the underlying set itself in a manner that is naturally second-order. Similarly, Partee (2003) proposed a limited second-order model by means of the 'head primary principle' requiring that adjectives are interpreted within their context. Bankston's analysis (2003), however, shows that the fundamental nature of many adjectives is higher-order, and provides a very sophisticated formal representation framework for adjectives. A more thorough discussion of non-gradable, non-intersective adjectives is given by Morzycki (2013a). Bouillion and Viegas (1999) consider the case of the French adjective 'vieux' ('old'), which they interprete as selecting two different elements in the event structure of an attributed noun, that is whether the state, e.g., 'being a mayor' for 'mayor', is considered old or the individual itself. In this way, the introduction of two senses for 'vieux' is avoided, however it remains unclear if such reasoning introduces more complexity than the extra senses. In his analysis of adjectives, Larson (1998) suggests that many adjectives denote properties of *events*, rather than of simple heads or nouns (which does not fall very far from the statement, made above, that relational adjectives denote properties of kinds). Pustejovsky (1992; 1991) and Lenci (2000) state that lexical and semantic decomposition can be achieved generatively, assigning to each lexical item a specific qualia structure. For instance, in an expression like:

22. The round, heavy, wooden, inlaid magnifying glass
    - 'round' represents the *Formal* role (giving indications of shape and dimensionality)
    - 'heavy' and 'wooden' related to the *Constitutive* role and indicate the relation between the object and its parts (e. g. by specifying weight, material, parts and components)
    - 'inlaid' is the *Agentive* role of the lexical item, denoting the factors that have been involved in the generation of the objects, such as creator, artifact, natural kind, and causal chain
    - 'magnifying' describes the *Telic* role of 'glass', since it shows its purpose and function

Finally, Peters and Peters (2000) provide one of the few other practical reports on modelling adjectives with ontologies, in the context of the SIMPLE lexica. This work is primarily focussed on the categorization of by means of intensional and extensional properties, rather than due to their logical modelling.

6 Conclusion

In this paper we have proposed an approach to model the semantics of adjectives in the context of the lexicon-ontology interface with a focus on the ontology-lexicon model *lemon*. We have argued that the semantics of adjectives, in particular gradable and privative adjectives, is beyond what can be expressed in first-order logics, OWL in particular. Instead, capturing the semantics of such adjectives requires formalisms that are non-monotonic, second-order and can represent fuzzy concepts. We have proposed an extension of *lemon* by the *lemonOILS* vocabulary that adds 'syntactic sugar' that allows us to represent the semantics of adjectives in a way that abstracts from the actual representational formalism used. This work has been used in the construction of lexical resources to support a question answering system, and we found that this framework is sufficient to enable tractable computation of natural language to SPARQL mapping over at least a small but varied set of test questions used in the QALD evaluation task. Future work will show whether this model is scalable and applicable to most adjectives as well as domains and natural languages.

References

Nabil Abdullah and Richard A Frost. 2005. Adjectives: A uniform semantic approach. In *Advances in Artificial Intelligence*, pages 330–341. Springer.

Marilisa Amoia and Claire Gardent. 2006. Adjective based inference. In *Proceedings of the Workshop KRAQ'06 on Knowledge and Reasoning for Language Processing*, pages 20–27. Association for Computational Linguistics.

Paul Bankston. 2003. Modeling nonintersective adjectives using operator logics. *The Review of Modern Logic*, 9(1-2):9–28.

Brandon Bennett. 2006. A theory of vague adjectives grounded in relevant observables. In John Mylopoulos Patrick Doherty and Christopher A. Welty, editors, *Proceedings of the Tenth International Conference on Principles of Knowledge Representation and Reasoning*, pages 36–45. AAAI Press.

Pierrette Bouillon and Evelyne Viegas. 1999. The description of adjectives for natural language processing: Theoretical and applied perspectives. In *Proceedings of Description des Adjectifs pour les Traitements Informatiques. Traitement Automatique des Langues Naturelles*. Citeseer.

Pierrette Bouillon. 1999. The adjective "vieux": The point of view of "generative lexicon". In *Breadth and depth of semantic lexicons*, pages 147–166. Springer.

Paul Buitelaar, 2010. *Ontology-based Semantic Lexicons: Mapping between Terms and Object Descriptions*, pages 212–223. Cambridge University Press.

Philipp Cimiano, Paul Buitelaar, John McCrae, and Michael Sintek. 2011. Lexinfo: A declarative model for the lexicon-ontology interface. *Web Semantics: Science, Services and Agents on the World Wide Web*, 9(1):29–51.

Philipp Cimiano, Janna Lüker, David Nagel, and Christina Unger. 2013. Exploiting ontology lexica for generating natural language texts from rdf data. In *Proceedings of the 14th European Workshop on Natural Language Generation*, pages 10–19.

Jos De Bruin and Remko Scha. 1988. The interpretation of relational nouns. In *Proceedings of the 26th annual meeting on Association for Computational Linguistics*, pages 25–32. Association for Computational Linguistics.

Frank Van Harmelen Deborah L. McGuinness et al. 2004. Owl web ontology language overview. *W3C recommendation*, 10(2004-03):10.

Didier Dubois and Henri Prade. 1988. *Possibility theory*. Plenum Press, New York.

Joseph H. Goguen. 1969. The logic of inexact concepts. *Synthese*, 19:325–373.

Christopher Kennedy and Louise McNally. 1999. Deriving the scalar structure of deverbal adjectives. *Catalan Working Papers in Linguistics*, 7:125–139.

Christopher Kennedy. 2007. Vagueness and grammar: the semantics of relative and absolute gradable adjectives. *Linguistics and philosophy*, 30:1–45.

Richard K. Larson. 1998. Events and modification in nominals. In Devon Strolovitch and Aaron Lawson, editors, *Proceedings from Semantics and Linguistic Theory (SALT) VIII*, pages 145–168. CLC Publications, Itaca, New York.

Alessandro Lenci et al. 2000. Simple work package 2, linguistic specifications, deliverable d2.1.

Vanessa Lopez, Christina Unger, Philipp Cimiano, and Enrico Motta. 2013. Evaluating question answering over linked data. *Web Semantics: Science, Services and Agents on the World Wide Web*, 21:3–13.

Louise McNally and Gemma Boleda. 2004. Relational adjectives as properties of kinds. *Empirical issues in formal syntax and semantics*, 5:179–196.

Richard Montague. 1970. English as a formal language. In Bruno Visentini et al, editor, *Linguaggi nella societa e nella tecnica*, pages 189–224. Milan: Edizioni di Comunità.

Marcin Morzycki. 2013a. The lexical semantics of adjectives: More than just scales. Ms., Michigan State University. Draft of a chapter in *Modification*, a book in preparation for the Cambridge University Press series *Key Topics in Semantics and Pragmatics*.

Marcin Morzycki. 2013b. *Modification*. Cambridge University Press.

John P. McCrae and Christina Unger. 2014. Design patterns for the ontology-lexicon interface. In Paul Buitelaar and Philipp Cimiano, editors, *Towards the Multilingual Semantic Web: Principles, Methods and Applications*. Springer.

John McCrae, Guadalupe Aguado-de Cea, Paul Buitelaar, Philipp Cimiano, Thierry Declerck, Asunción Gómez-Pérez, Jorge Gracia, Laura Hollink, Elena Montiel-Ponsoda, Dennis Spohr, et al. 2012. Interchanging lexical resources on the semantic web. *Language Resources and Evaluation*, 46(4):701–719.

Ian Niles and Adam Pease. 2001. Towards a standard upper ontology.

Barbara H Partee. 2003. Are there privative adjectives. In *Conference on the Philosophy of Terry Parsons, University of Massachusetts, Amherst*.

Ivonne Peters and Wim Peters. 2000. The treatment of adjectives in simple: Theoretical observations. In *LREC*.

James Pustejovsky. 1991. The generative lexicon. *Computational linguistics*, 17(4):409–441.

James Pustejovsky. 1992. The syntax of event structure. In Bett Levin and Steven Pinker, editors, *Lexical & Conceptual Semantics*, pages 47–83. Oxford: Blackwell.

Victor Raskin and Sergei Nirenburg. 1995. Lexical semantics of adjectives. *New Mexico State University, Computing Research Laboratory Technical Report, MCCS-95-288*.

Matthew Richardson and Pedro Domingos. 2006. Markov logic networks. *Machine learning*, 62(1-2):107–136.

Alexandra Teodorescu. 2006. Adjective ordering restrictions revisited. In *Proceedings of the 25th West Coast Conference on Formal Linguistics*, pages 399–407. Citeseer.

Christina Unger and Philipp Cimiano. 2011. Pythia: Compositional meaning construction for ontology-based question answering on the semantic web. In Rafael Munoz, editor, *Natural Language Processing and Information Systems: 16th International Conference on Applications of Natural Language to Information Systems, NLDB 2011, Alicante, Spain, June 28-30, 2011. Proceedings*, volume 6716, pages 153–160. Springer.

Zeno Vendler. 1968. *Adjectives and nominalizations*. Number 5 in Papers on formal linguistics. Mouton.

Lofti A. Zadeh. 1965. Fuzzy sets. *Information and Control*, 8:338–353.

Lofti A. Zadeh. 1975. The concept of linguistic variable and its application to approximate reasoningi. *Information Sciences*, 8:199–249.

Jidi Zhao and Harold Boley. 2008. Uncertainty treatment in the rule interchange format: From encoding to extension. In *URSW*.

Discovering Conceptual Metaphors Using Source Domain Spaces

Samira Shaikh[1], Tomek Strzalkowski[1], Kit Cho[1], Ting Liu[1], George Aaron Broadwell[1], Laurie Feldman[1], Sarah Taylor[2], Boris Yamrom[1], Ching-Sheng Lin[1], Ning Sa[1], Ignacio Cases[1], Yuliya Peshkova[1] and Kyle Elliot[3]

[1]State University of New York – University at Albany

[2]Sarah M. Taylor Consulting LLC

[3]Plessas Experts Network

samirashaikh@gmail.com

Abstract

This article makes two contributions towards the use of lexical resources and corpora; specifically making use of them for gaining access to and using word associations. The direct application of our approach is for detecting linguistic and conceptual metaphors automatically in text. We describe our method of building *conceptual spaces*, that is, defining the vocabulary that characterizes a Source Domain (e.g., Disease) of a conceptual metaphor (e.g., Poverty is a Disease). We also describe how these conceptual spaces are used to group linguistic metaphors into conceptual metaphors. Our method works in multiple languages, including English, Spanish, Russian and Farsi. We provide details of how our method can be evaluated and evaluation results that show satisfactory performance across all languages.

1 Introduction

Metaphors are communicative devices that are pervasive in discourse. When understood in a cultural context, they provide insights into how a culture views certain salient concepts, typically broad, abstract concepts such as poverty or democracy. In our research, we are focusing on metaphors on targets of governance, economic inequality and democracy, although our approach works for metaphors on any target. Suppose it is found in a culture that its people use metaphors when speaking of poverty; for example, they may talk about "symptom of poverty" or that "poverty infects areas of the city". These expressions are linguistic metaphors that are instances of a broader conceptual metaphor: Poverty is a Disease. Similarly, if it is found that common linguistic metaphors about poverty for peoples of a culture include "deep hole of poverty" and "fall into poverty", it would lead to the conceptual metaphor: Poverty is an Abyss. A communicator wishing to speak of ways to deal with poverty would use metaphors such as "treat poverty" and "cure poverty" to make their framing consistent with the conceptual metaphor of Disease, whereas she would use metaphors such as "lift out of poverty" when speaking to people who are attuned to the Abyss conceptual metaphor. Here Disease and Abyss are source domains, and poverty is the target domain. Relations, like "symptom of", "infect" and "fall into" from the respective source domains are mapped onto the target domain of poverty.

In order to discover conceptual metaphors and group linguistic metaphors together, we make use of corpora to define the conceptual space that characterizes a source domain. We wish to discover the set of relations that are used literally for a given source domain, and would create metaphors if applied to some other target domain. That is, we wish to *automatically* discover that relations such as "symptom", "infect", "treat" and "cure" characterize the source domain of Disease, for example. To create the conceptual spaces, we employ a fully automated method in which we search a balanced corpus using specific search patterns. Search patterns are so created as to look for co-occurence of

Zock/Rapp/Huang (eds.): Proceedings of the 4th Workshop on Cognitive Aspects of the Lexicon, pages 210–220, Dublin, Ireland, August 23, 2014.

relations with members of a given source domain. Relations could be nouns, verbs, verb phrases and adjectives that are frequently used literally within a source domain. In addition, we calculate the frequency with which relations occur in a given source domain, or Relation Frequency. We then calculate the Inverse Domain Frequency (IDF), a variant of the inverse document frequency measure quite commonly used in field of information retrieval; the IDF captures the degree of distribution of relations across all source domains under consideration. Using these two measures, the relation frequency and inverse domain frequency, we are able to rank relations within a source domain. This ranked list of relations are then used to group linguistic metaphors belonging to the same source domain together. A group of linguistic metaphors so formed is a conceptual metaphor.

2 Related Research

Most current research on metaphor falls into three groups: (1) theoretical linguistic approaches (as defined by Lakoff & Johnson, 1980; and their followers) that generally look at metaphors as abstract language constructs with complex semantic properties; (2) quantitative linguistic approaches (e.g., Charteris-Black, 2002; O'Halloran, 2007) that attempt to correlate metaphor semantics with their usage in naturally occurring text but generally lack robust tools to do so; and (3) social science approaches, particularly in psychology and anthropology that seek to explain how people deploy and understand metaphors in interaction, but which lack the necessary computational tools to work with anything other than relatively isolated examples.

Metaphor study in yet other disciplines has included cognitive psychologists (e.g., Allbritton, McKoon & Gerrig, 1995) who have focused on the way metaphors may signify structures in human memory and human language processing. Cultural anthropologists, such as Malkki in her work on refugees (1992), see metaphor as a tool to help outsiders interpret the feelings and mindsets of the groups they study, an approach also reflective of available metaphor case studies, often with a Political Science underpinning (Musolff, 2008; Lakoff, 2001).

In computational investigations of metaphor, knowledge-based approaches include MetaBank (Martin, 1994), a large knowledge base of metaphors empirically collected. Krishnakumaran and Zhu (2007) use WordNet (Felbaum, 1998) knowledge to differentiate between metaphors and literal usage. Such approaches entail the existence of lexical resources that may not always be present or satisfactorily robust in different languages. Gedigan et al (2006) identify a system that can recognize metaphor. However their approach is only shown to work in a narrow domain (Wall Street Journal, for example).

Computational approaches to metaphor (largely AI research) to date have yielded only limited scale, often hand designed systems (Wilks, 1975; Fass, 1991; Martin, 1994; Carbonell, 1980; Feldman & Narayan, 2004; Shutova & Teufel, 2010; inter alia, also Shutova, 2010b for an overview). Baumer et al (2010) used semantic role labels and typed dependency parsing in an attempt towards computational metaphor identification. However, they self-report their work to be an initial exploration and hence, inconclusive. Shutova et al (2010a) employ an unsupervised method of metaphor identification using nouns and verb clustering to automatically impute metaphoricity in a large corpus using an annotated training corpus of metaphors as seeds. Their method relies on annotated training data, which is difficult to produce in large quantities and may not be easily generated in different languages.

More recently, several important approaches to metaphor extraction have emerged from the IARPA Metaphor program, including Broadwell et al (2013), Strzalkowski et al. (2014), Wilks et al (2013), Hovy et al (2013) inter alia. These papers concentrate on the algorithms for detection and classification of individual linguistic metaphors in text rather than formation of conceptual metaphors in a broader cultural context. Taylor et al (2014) outlines the rationale why conceptual level metaphors may provide important insights into cross-cultural contrasts. Our work described here is a first attempt at automatic discovery of conceptual metaphors operating within a culture directly from the linguistic evidence in language.

3 Our Approach

The process of discovering conceptual metaphors is necessarily divided into two phases: (1) collecting evidence about potential source domains that may be invoked when metaphorical expressions are used; and (2) building a conceptual space for each sufficiently evidenced source domain so that linguistic metaphors can be accurately classified as instances of appropriate conceptual metaphors. In this paper, we concentrate on the second phase only. Strzalkowski et al (2013) in their work have described a data-driven linguistic metaphor extraction method and our approach builds upon their work.

During the source domain evidencing phase, we established a set of 50 source domains that operate frequently with the target concepts we are focusing on (government, bureaucracy, poverty, wealth, taxation, democracy and elections). These domains were a joint effort of several teams participating in the Metaphor program and we are taking this set as a starting point. These are shown in Table 1.

A_GOD	CONFINEMENT	GAME	MONSTER	PLANT
A_RIGHT	CRIME	GAP	MORAL_DUTY	PORTAL
ABYSS	CROP	GEOGRAPHIC_FEATURE	MOVEMENT	POSITION AND CHANGE OF POSITION ON A SCALE
ADDICTION	DARKNESS	GREED	NATURAL_PHYSICAL_FORCE	RACE
ANIMAL	DESTROYER	HUMAN_BODY	OBESITY	RESOURCE
BATTLE	DISEASE	IMPURITY	PARASITE	STAGE
BLOOD_STREAM	ENERGY	LIGHT	PATHWAY	STRUGGLE
BODY_OF_WATER	ENSLAVEMENT	MACHINE	PHYSICAL_BURDEN	THEFT
BUILDING	FOOD	MAZE	PHYSICAL_HARM	VISION
COMPETITION	FORCEFUL_EXTRACTION	MEDICINE	PHYSICAL_LOCATION	WAR

Table 1. Set of 50 source domains that operate frequently with target concepts being investigated. Only English names are shown for ease of presentation, equivalent sets in Spanish, Russian and Farsi have been created.

Some of the domains are self explanatory, while others require a further specification since the labels are sometimes ambiguous. For example, PLANT represents things that grow in the soil, not factories; similarly, BUILDING represents artifacts such as houses or edifices, but not the act of constructing something; RACE refers to a running competition, not skin color, etc.

Consequently, each of these domains need to be seeded with the prototypical representative elements to make the meaning completely clear. This seeding occurs during the first phase of the process when a linguistic expression, such as "cure poverty" is classified as a linguistic metaphor. This process of classifying "cure poverty" as metaphorical is described in detail in Strzalkowski et al. (2013). Part of the seeding process is to establish that a source domain different than the target domain (here: poverty) is invoked by the relation (here: cure). To find the source domain where "cure" is typically used literally, we form a linguistic pattern [cure [OBJ: X/nn]] (derived automatically from the parsed metaphoric expression) which is subsequently run through a balanced language corpus. Arguments matching the variable X are then clustered into semantic categories, using lexical resources such as Wordnet (Felbaum, 1998) and the most frequent and concrete category is selected as a possible source domain (proto-source domain). From the balanced language corpus, it is possible to compute the frequency with which the arguments resulting from search appear with relation ("cure"). We determine concreteness by looking up concreteness score in MRC psycholinguistic database (Coltheart 1981, Wilson 1988). As may be expected, the initial elements of the proto-source obtained from the above patterns will include: *disease, cancer, plague*, etc. These become the seeds of the source domain DISEASE in our list. The same process was performed for each of the 50 domains listed here, for each of the 4 languages under consideration. Additional Source Domains are continously generated bottom-up fashion by this phase 1 process elaborated above. In Table 2, we show seeds so obtained for a few source domains.

DISEASE	disease, cancer, plague
ABYSS	abyss, chasm, crevasse
BODY_OF_WATER	ocean, lake river, pond, sea
PLANT	plant, tree, flower, weed, shrub, vegetable
GEOGRAPHIC_FEATURE	land, land form, earth, mountain, plateau, island, valley

Table 2. Example of seeds corresponding to a few source domains

Once such seeds are obtained, we perform another search through a balanced corpus in the corresponding language to discover relations that characterize the source domains. The purpose of source domain spaces in our research is two-fold: a) to provide a sufficiently complete characterization of a source domain via a list of relations ; and b) such a list of relations should sufficiently distinguish *between* different source domains. Creating these spaces is phase 2 of the conceptual metaphor discovery process.

We search for nouns, verbs and verb phrases, and adjectives that co-occur with seeds of given source domain with sufficiently high frequency and sufficiently high mutual information. Our goal with this process is to approximate normal usage patterns of relations within source domains. The results of balanced corpora search form our *conceptual spaces*. The balanced corpora we use are English: Corpus of Contemporary American English (Davies, 2008), Spanish: Corpus del Español Actual (Davies, 2002), Russian: Russian National Corpus[2] and Farsi: Bijankhan Corpus (Oroumchian et al., 2006). In addition to retrieving the relations, we retrieve the frequency with which these relations can be found to co-occur with seeds of a source domain, Relation Frequency (RF). We calculate Inverse Domain Frequency (IDF) of all relations across all 50 source domains using a variant of the inverse document frequency measure. The formula for IDF is as given below:

IDF = log (total number of source domains / total number of source domains a relation appears in)

For example, if a relation such as "dive into" is found to appear in two source domains, BODY_OF_WATER and GEOGRAPHIC_FEATURE, then the IDF for "dive into" would be log (50/2). The rank of a relation is computed as the product of RF and IDF. However, computing rank using RF without normalization results in inflated ranks for relations that are quite common across domains even when they do not sufficiently disambiguate between the domains. We assume a normal distribution of frequencies of relations within a source domain and normalize RF by taking its logarithm. We also normalize with respect to seeds within a source domain. If a relation frequency is disproportionately high with a specific seed, we disregard that frequency. For example, one of the seeds for the source domain of BUILDING is "house". A search through balanced corpus for nouns adjacent to "house" revealed a disproportionately large number for "white", which is meant to be the White House, and would be disregarded.

In Table 3, we show a few top ranked relations for the source domains DISEASE and BODY_OF_WATER. In columns 1 and 2, we show the source domain and the relation. Column 3 shows the relation frequency and column 4 shows the part of speech of relation (V=verb or verb phrase, N=noun, ADJ=adjective). An RF score of 800 for row 1 indicates that the relation "diagnose with" appears 800 times with one or more of the seeds we search for source domain DISEASE ("diagnose with cancer", "diagnose with disease" and so on. In column 5, we show the position where the relation is commonly found to co-occur with the source domain. For example, "afflict" in row 2 has a position "after" which means it appears after DISEASE: "DISEASE afflict(s)"; whereas row 3 would be read as "affict with DISEASE" since it appears "before". In column 6, we show the normalized RF*IDF score. The highest RF*IDF score for a relation across our spaces is 2.165. From Table 3, we can see that even if frequency for some relations may be relatively low, their rank would be high if they are strongly associated with a single source domain.

	1. Source Domain	2. Relation	3. RF	4. Type	5. Position	6. Norm RF*IDF
1	DISEASE	diagnose with	800	V	before	1.94
2	DISEASE	afflict	85	V	after	1.67
3	DISEASE	afflict with	33	V	before	1.52
4	DISEASE	cure of	29	N	before	1.46
5	BODY_OF_WATER	dive into	49	V	before	2.01
6	BODY_OF_WATER	wade through	44	V	before	1.88
7	BODY_OF_WATER	wade into	42	V	before	1.84
8	BODY_OF_WATER	rinse in	41	V	before	1.80

Table 3. A few top ranking relations for the source domains DISEASE and BODY_OF_WATER. Relations are ranked by their normalized RF*IDF score.

[2] http://ruscorpora.ru/en/

With the conceptual spaces defined in this manner, we can now use them to group linguistic metaphors together. Shaikh et al (2014) have created a repository of thousands of automatically extracted lingusitic metaphors in all four languages, which we are using to create conceptual metaphors. To discover which conceptual metaphors exist within such large sets of linguistic metaphors would be quite challenging, if not impossible, for a human expert. We automatically assign each linguistic metaphor to ranked list of source domains.

Consider the linguistic metaphor "plunge into poverty", where the relation is "plunge into". We search through our conceptual spaces and retrieve a list of source domains where the relation "plunge into" may appear. From this list, only the domains that have this relation RF*IDF score higher than a threshold are considered. This threshold is currently assigned to be 0.40, although it is subject to further experimentation. The source domain where the RF*IDF score of "plunge into" is the highest is chosen as the source domain, along with the next source domains only if the difference in scores is 5% or lower. Tables 4 and 5 depicts this part of algorithm for two relations, "plunge into" and "explorar" (from Spanish – "explore"). The relation "plunge into" is thus assigned to BODY_OF_WATER source domain. "explorar" is assigned to GEOGRAPHIC_FEATURE and BODY_OF_WATER since difference in RF*IDF scores is less than 5%.

Relation	Source Domains	RF*IDF
plunge into	BODY_OF_WATER	1.82
	DARKNESS	1.28
	ABYSS	0.68
	WAR	0.57
	GEOGRAPHIC_FEATURE	0.48

Relation	Source Domains	RF*IDF
explorar	GEOGRAPHIC_FEATURE	0.77
	BODY_OF_WATER	0.76
	PHYSICAL_LOCATION	0.56
	PATHWAY	0.56
	BUILDING	0.41

Table 4 and Table 5. Assigning relations of linguistic metaphor to source domains. "plunge into" is assigned to BODY_OF_WATER; "explorar" is assigned to GEOGRAPHIC_FEATURE and BODY_OF_WATER

Once this process of assigning linguistic metaphors to source domains is accomplished for all linguistic metaphors in our repository, we validate the resulting conceptual metaphors. A small percentage of metaphors cannot be assigned to any of the 50 Source Domains. We explain the validation process in Section 4. In Tables 6 and 7, we show sample conceptual metaphors in English and Spanish. Our validation process revealed an interesting insight regarding forming conceptual metaphor, wherein they should contain relations that are anchors for that given source domain that we shall describe next.

SD	Target	Source	Sentence	RF*IDF
BODY_OF_WATER	POVERTY	rise from	The United States has always had a culture with a high regard for those able to rise from poverty to riches .	1.78
		slide into	Government aid kept some Americans from sliding into poverty last year , some analysts say .	0.81
		shallow	By 2004 , the government was actually giving more , each month , to families in shallow poverty than to families in deep poverty .	1.13
		shallow	Those in what could be considered shallow poverty , between 50 and 100 percent of the poverty line , received $ 448 .	1.13
		tumble into	About 46 million more people are expected to tumble into poverty this year amid the largest decline in global trade in 80 years, according to the World Bank.	1.50
		slip into	Mountains of research tell us that children reared outside of intact marriages are much more likely than other kids to slip into poverty, become victims of child abuse, fail at school and drop out, use illegal drugs, launch into premature sexual activity, become unwed teen mothers, divorce, commit suicide and experience other signs of mental illness, become physically ill, and commit crimes and go to jail.	1.35
		deep	The Census Bureau uses a third measure , " deep poverty , " which it defines as living on less than half of the amount needed to escape poverty (for a family of three , that means living on less than $ 9,000 a year) .	0.40
		plunge into	With the economic crisis threatening to plunge more children into poverty	1.82

Table 6. A conceptual metaphor in English: POVERTY is a BODY_OF_WATER

SD	Target	Source	Sentence	RF*IDF
DISEASE	POVERTY	diagnosticar	Más Notas de este Especial Plantea PRD que Hacienda diagnostique deudas en estados y municipios...	2.04
		heredar	Afirmó que la comuna solventa deudas heredadas de la pasada administración que ascienden a 183 millones de pesos.	0.93
		erradicar	Viernes 29 de agosto de 2003 HACIA LA CUMBRE DE CANCUN Ese camino nunca ha erradicado la pobreza, dicen organizaciones católicas	0.91
		erradicar	Tweet EDUCACIÓN PARA ERRADICAR POBRE El magnate mexicano abogó en la ciudad colombiana de Cartagena de Indias, por erradicar la pobreza con educación y empleo para fortalecer las economías.	0.91
		combatir	Envía Banco Mundial expertos a Oaxaca para combatir pobreza Viernes, 25 de febrero de 20111 comentario Oaxaca.-	0.86

Table 7. A conceptual metaphor in Spanish: POVERTY is a DISEASE

3.1 Anchor relations in Conceptual Metaphors

When human assessors are presented with a set of linguistic metaphors and the task to assign them into a source domain, some relations will have stronger impact on their decision that others. For example, "cure" would almost invariably be assigned to DISEASE domain, while "dive in" would invoke BODY_OF_WATER domain. Other relations, such as "spread" or "fall into" are less specific, however, when paired with highly evocative relations above are likely to be classified the same way. Thus, there are two types of metaphorical relations in linguistic metaphors: (1) the highly evocative relations that unambigously point to a specific source domain – we shall call them anchors; and (2) the relations that are compatible with the anchor but are not anchors themselves. We can add another class: (3) the relations that are not compatible with a given anchor. Thus, a set of linguistic metaphors that provides evidence for a conceptual metaphor should contain at least some anchor relations and the balance of the set may be composed of anchor-compatible relations. Our current hypothesis is that there should be at least one anchor for each 7 anchor compatible relations for a group of linguistic metaphors to provide a sufficient evidence for a conceptual metaphor.

As part of our validation process, we conducted a series of experiments with human assessors. One of the tasks was to assign a single linguistic metaphor to one of 50 source domains. As an illustrative example, we show in Table 8, one linguistic metaphor. When presented with this example, a majority of assessors chose ENEMY source domain, while DISEASE was selected second. Additionally, there was greater variance among their selections, only 31% chose the top source domain of ENEMY.

Subsequently, human assessors were presented a set of linguistic metaphors where at least one anchor relation was present. In this case, the majority of assessors chose the DISEASE source domain. Even though the "fight against poverty" example was included in the set, the presence of anchors such as "cure poverty" and "treat poverty" lead assessors to choose DISEASE source domain. The variance in selection was also less, a 70% majority choosing DISEASE. We show the conceptual metaphor in Table 9.

The summit has proven that there is a renewed appetite for the fight against poverty.
ENEMY: 31%; DISEASE: 17%; ANIMAL, MONSTER,....<10%

Table 8. A single linguistic metaphor was assigned a varied number of source domains by human assessors.

Of course, many government programs aim to alleviate poverty.
We seek to stimulate true prosperity rather than simply treat poverty.
Unless the fight against poverty is honestly addressed by the West, there will be many more Afghanistans.
Above all, he knows that the only way to cure poverty is to grow the economy.
DISEASE: 70%; ENEMY: 30%

Table 9. A conceptual metaphor containing anchors. When sample metaphor from Table 8 is included in this set, human assessors still choose the source domain to be DISEASE.

4 Evaluation and Results

A group of human experts who are native speakers and have been substantively trained to achieve high levels of agreement (0.78 Krippendorf's alpha (1970) or higher) form our validation team. In addition, we aim to run crowd-sourced experiments on Amazon Mechanical Turk. In Figure 1, we show a web interface we built to present our human assessors. The task shown here is the assignment of a single linguistic metaphor to one of 50 source domains. Then, we present our validation team with conceptual metaphors we created. Each conceptual metaphor is validated by at least two language experts. This interface is shown in Figure 2. These interfaces are carefully created by our team of social scientists and psychologists, designed to elicit proper responses from native speakers of the language.

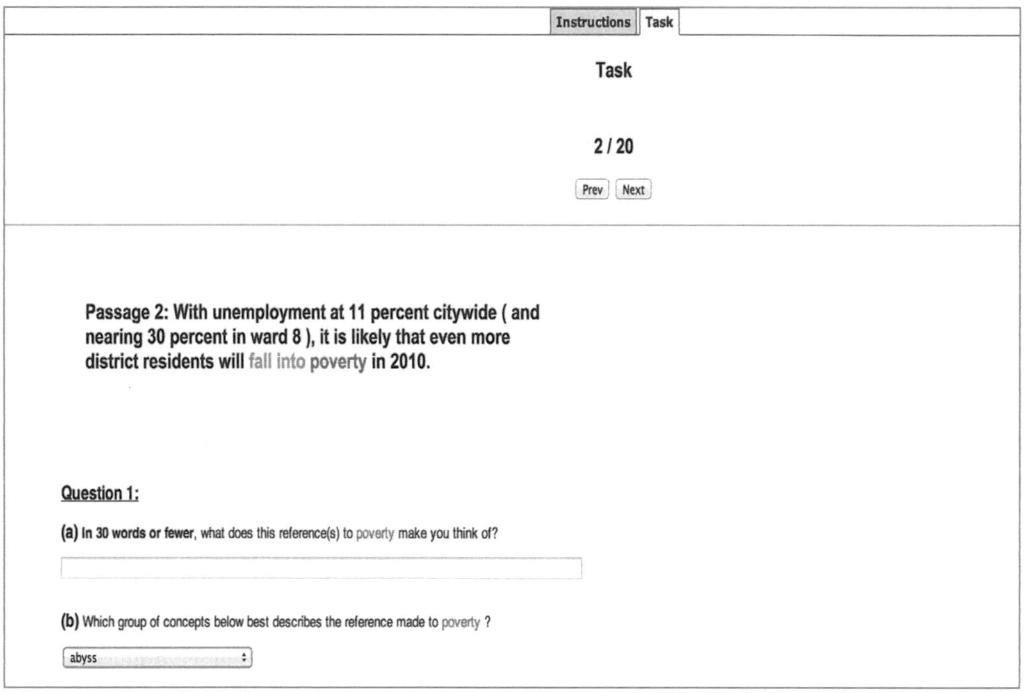

Figure 1. Interface of task where human assessors select source domain for a single linguistic metaphor.

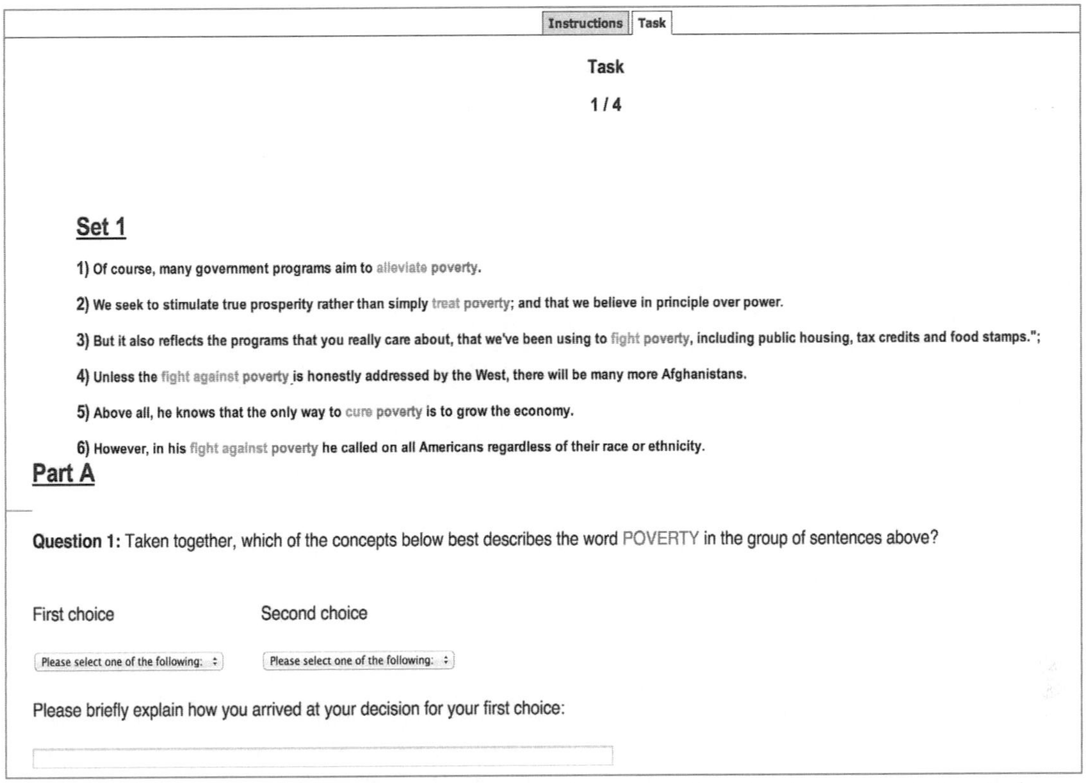

Figure 2. Interface of task where human assessors select source domains for a conceptual metaphor. Assessors provide their top two choices along with a description detailing how they made their decision.

In Table 10, we show the number of conceptual metaphors currently in the repository and the accuracy of our method across four languages, as computed by using validation data. We show the number of conceptual metaphors present in the Governance target domain (metaphors about government and bureaucracy), Economic Inequality (dealing with metaphors of poverty, wealth and taxation) and Democracy (democracy and elections metaphors). These conceptual metaphors on the three target domains of Governace, Economic Inequality and Democracy, when compared across cultures could provide deep insight about peoples' perceptions regarding salient concepts.

We note that Russian and Farsi performance is lower than that in English and Spanish. The size of balanced corpus and accuracy of lexical tools such as stemmers and morphological analyzers affect performance of our algorithm. The Farsi balanced corpus is relatively small when compared to English balanced corpus. The smaller size affects computation of statistics such as Relation Frequency and subsequently the thresholds of RF*IDF scores. One improvement we are currently investigating is that the thresholds may be set specifically for a language.

	ENGLISH	SPANISH	RUSSIAN	FARSI
# of Governance Conceptual Metaphors	27	7	8	7
# of Economic Inequality Conceptual Metaphors	32	26	57	7
# of Democracy Conceptual Metaphors	51	16	18	8
Total # of Conceptual Metaphors	110	49	83	22
Accuracy (%)	85%	76%	67%	62%

Table 10. Number of conceptual metaphors discovered thus far and performance of our approach across four languages.

5 Conclusion and Future Work

In this article, we presented our approach towards automatic discovery of conceptual metaphors directly from linguistic evidence in a given language. We make use of corpora in two unique ways: the first is to discover prototypical seeds that form the basis of source domains and second is to create conceptual spaces that allow us to characterize the relations that operate within source domains automatically. In addition, our approach also allows us to distinguish *between* source domains as necessary. The validation results show that this is indeed a promising first attempt of tackling a challenging research problem.

We note that the assignment of source domains is limited to the set of 50 in our current prototype. This assumes a closed set of 50 source domains, whereas in reality, there might be many others that operate in the realm of metaphors we are investigating. Although additional source domains are continually being discovered in a bottom-up fashion by the linguistic metaphor extraction process, we cannot account for every source domain that may be relevant. One way of overcoming this limitation would be to define a source domain "OTHER" that would be the all-encompassing domain accounting for any yet undiscovered domains. The details of how it would be represented are still under investigation.

Another potential improvement to our method is to experimentally refine the threshold score of RF*IDF. Through large scale validation experiments, we could learn the optimal thresholds automatically by using machine learning.

6 Acknowledgements

This paper is based on work supported by the Intelligence Advanced Research Projects Activity (IARPA) via Department of Defense US Army Research Laboratory contract number W911NF-12-C-0024. The U.S. Government is authorized to reproduce and distribute reprints for Governmental purposes notwithstanding any copyright annotation thereon. Disclaimer: The views and conclusions contained herein are those of the authors and should not be interpreted as necessarily representing the official policies or endorsements, either expressed or implied, of IARPA, DoD/ARL, or the U.S. Government.

References

David W. Allbritton, Gail McKoon, and Richard J. Gerrig. 1995. Metaphor-based schemas and text Representations: making connections through conceptual metaphors, *Journal of Experimental Psychology: Learning, Memory, and Cognition*, 21(3):612-625.

Jonathan, Charteris-Black. 2002. Second language figurative proficiency: A comparative study of Malay and English. *Applied Linguistics* 23(1):104–133.

George Aaron Broadwell, Umit Boz, Ignacio Cases, Tomek Strzalkowski, Laurie Feldman, Sarah Taylor, Samira Shaikh, Ting Liu and Kit Cho. 2013. *Using Imageability and Topic Chaining to Locate Metaphors in Linguistic Corpora*. In Proceedings of The 2013 International Conference on Social Computing, Behavioral-Cultural Modeling, & Prediction (SBP 2013), Washington D.C., USA.

Jaime Carbonell. 1980. Metaphor: A key to extensible semantic analysis. In *Proceedings of the 18th Annual Meeting on Association for Computational Linguistics*.

M. Coltheart. 1981. The MRC Psycholinguistic Database. *Quarterly Journal of Experimental Psychology*, 33A: 497-505.

Davies, Mark. 2008-. *The Corpus of Contemporary American English: 450 million words, 1990-present*. Available online at http://corpus.byu.edu/coca/.

Davies, Mark. 2002-. *Corpus del Español: 100 million words, 1200s-1900s*. Available online at http://www.corpusdelespanol.org.

Dan, Fass. 1991. met*: A Method for Discriminating Metonymy and Metaphor by Computer. *Computational Linguistics*, 17:49-90

Jerome Feldman, and Srinivas Narayanan. 2004. Embodied meaning in a neural theory of language. *Brain and Language*, 89(2):385–392.

Christiane D. Fellbaum. 1998. *WordNet: An electronic lexical database* (1st ed.). MIT Press.

Matt Gedigian, John Bryant, Srini Narayanan and Branimir Ciric. 2006. Catching Metaphors. In *Proceedings of the Third Workshop on Scalable Natural Language Understanding ScaNaLU 2006*, pages 41–48. New York City: NY.

Dirk Hovy, Shashank Shrivastava, Sujay Kumar Jauhar, Mrinmaya Sachan, Kartik Goyal, Huying Li, Whitney Sanders and Eduard Hovy. 2013. Identifying Metaphorical Word Use with Tree Kernels. In the *Proceedings of the First Workshop on Metaphor in NLP, (NAACL)*. Atlanta.

Krippendorff, Klaus. 1970. Estimating the reliability, systematic error, and random error of interval data. *Educational and Psychological Measurement, 30* (1),61-70.

Saisuresh Krishnakumaran and Xiaojin Zhu. 2007. Hunting elusive metaphors using lexical resources. In *Proceedings of the Workshop on Computational Approaches to Figurative Language*, pages 13–20. Rochester, NY.

George Lakoff, and Mark Johnson. 1980. *Metaphors we live by*. University Of Chicago Press, Chicago, Illinois.

George, Lakoff. 2001. *Moral politics: what conservatives know that liberals don't.* University of Chicago Press, Chicago, Illinois.

Liisa, Malkki. 1992. National geographic: The rooting of people and the territorialization of national identity among scholars and refugees. *Society for Cultural Anthropology*, 7(1):24–44.

James Martin. 1988. A computational theory of metaphor. *Ph.D. Dissertation.*

Musolff, Andreas. 2008. What can critical metaphor analysis add to the understanding of racist ideology? Recent studies of Hitler's anti-semitic metaphors, critical approaches to discourse analysis across disciplines. Critical *Approaches to Discourse Analysis Across Disciplines*, 2(2):1–10.

Kieran, O'Halloran. 2007. Critical discourse analysis and the corpus-informed interpretation of metaphor at the register level. *Oxford University Press*

Farhad Oroumchian, Samira Tasharofi, Hadi Amiri, Hossein Hojjat, Fahime Raja. 2006. Creating a Feasible Corpus for Persian POS Tagging.Technical Report, no. TR3/06, University of Wollongong in Dubai.

Samira Shaikh, Tomek Strzalkowski, Ting Liu, George Aaron Broadwell, Boris Yamrom, Sarah Taylor, Laurie Feldman, Kit Cho, Umit Boz, Ignacio Cases, Yuliya Peshkova and Ching-Sheng Lin. 2014. A Multi-Cultural Repository of Automatically Discovered Linguistic and Conceptual Metaphors. In *Proceedings of the The 9th edition of the Language Resources and Evaluation Conference* , Reykjavik, Iceland.

Ekaterina Shutova and Simone Teufel. 2010a. Metaphor corpus annotated for source - target domain mappings. *In Proceedings of Language Resources and Evaluation Conference 2010*. Malta.

Ekaterina Shutova. 2010b. Models of metaphor in nlp. In *Proceedings of the 48th Annual Meeting of the Association for Computational Linguistics*, ACL '10, pages 688–697.

Ekaterina Shutova, Tim Van de Cruys, and Anna Korhonen. 2012. *Unsupervised metaphor paraphrasing using a vector space model* In *Proceedings of COLING 2012*, Mumbai, India

Tomek Strzalkowski, George Aaron Broadwell, Sarah Taylor, Laurie Feldman, Boris Yamrom, Samira Shaikh, Ting Liu, Kit Cho, Umit Boz, Ignacio Cases and Kyle Elliott. 2013. Robust extraction of metaphor from novel data. In *Proceedings of Workshop on Metaphor in NLP, NAACL.* Atlanta.

Tomek Strzalkowski, Samira Shaikh, Kit Cho, George Aaron Broadwell, Laurie Feldman, Sarah Taylor, Boris Yamrom, Ting Liu, Ignacio Cases, Yuliya Peshkova and Kyle Elliot. 2014. Computing Affect in Metaphors. In *Proceedings of the Second Workshop on Metaphor in NLP,* Baltimore Maryland.

Sarah Taylor, Laurie Beth Feldman, Kit Cho, Samira Shaikh, Ignacio Cases,Yuliya Peshkiva, George Aaron Broadwell Ting Liu, Umit Boz, Kyle Elliott. Boris Yamrom, and Tomek Strzalkowski. 2014. Extracting Understanding from automated metaphor identification: Contrasting Concepts of Poverty across Cultures and Languages. *AHFE Conference*, Cracow, Poland.

Yorick, Wilks. 1975. Preference semantics. *Formal Semantics of Natural Language*, E. L. Keenan, Ed. Cambridge University Press, Cambridge, U.K., 329–348.

Yorick Wilks, Lucian Galescu, James Allen, Adam Dalton. 2013. Automatic Metaphor Detection using Large-Scale Lexical Resources and Conventional Metaphor Extraction. In the *Proceedings of the First Workshop on Metaphor in NLP, (NAACL)*. Atlanta.

Wilson, M. D. 1988. The MRC Psycholinguistic Database: Machine Readable Dictionary, Version 2. *Behavioural Research Methods, Instruments and Computers*, 20(1): 6-11.

Wordfinding Problems and How to Overcome them Ultimately With the Help of a Computer

Michael Zock
LIF-CNRS / TALEP
163, Avenue de Luminy
13288 Marseille / France
michael.zock@lif.univ-mrs.fr

Abstract

Our ultimate goal is to help authors to find an elusive word. Whenever we need a word, we look it up in the place where it is stored, the dictionary or the mental lexicon. The question is how do we manage to find the word, and how do we succeed to do this so quickly? While these are difficult questions, I believe to have some practical answers for them. Since it is unreasonable to perform search in the entire lexicon, I suggest to start by reducing this space (step-1) and to present then the remaining candidates in a clustered and labeled form, i.e. categorial tree (step-2). The goal of this second step is to support navigation.

Search space is determined by considering words directly related to the input, i.e. direct neighbors (associations/co-occurrences). To this end many resources could be used. For example, one may consider an associative network like the Edinburgh Association Thesaurus (E.A.T.). As this will still yield too many hits, I suggest to cluster and label the outputs. This labeling is crucial for navigation, as we want users to find the target quickly, rather than drown them under a huge, unstructured list of words. Note, that in order to determine properly the initial search space (step-1), we must have already well understood the input [$mouse_1$ / $mouse_2$ (rodent/device)], as otherwise our list will contain a lot of noise, presenting '*cat, cheese*' together with '*computer, mouse pad*', which is not quite what we want, since some of these candidates are irrelevant, i.e. beyond the scope of the user's goal.

1 Introduction

Whenever we read a book, write a letter, or launch a query on Google, we always use words, the shorthand labels for more or less well specified thoughts. No doubt, words are important, a fact nicely expressed by Wilkins (1972) when he writes: *without grammar very little can be conveyed, without vocabulary, nothing can be conveyed.* Still, ubiquitous as they may be, words have to be learned, that is, they have to be stored, remembered, and retrieved. Given the role words play in our daily lives, it is surprising to see how little we have to offer so far to help humans to memorize, find or retrieve them. Hoping to contribute to a change for this, I have started to work on one of these tasks: word access, also called *retrieval* or *wordfinding*.

Imagine the following situation: your goal is to express the following ideas: *superior dark coffee made of beans from Arabia*" by a single word, but you cannot access the corresponding form *mocha*, even though you know it, since you've used it not so long ago. This kind of problem, known as the *tip-of-the-tongue* (TOT)-problem, has received a lot of attention from psychologists (Schwartz, 2002; Brown, 1991). It has always been pointed out that people being in this state know quite a bit concerning the elusive word (Brown and McNeill, 1996). Hence, using it should allow us to reduce the search space. Put differently, it would be nice to have a system capable to use whatever you have, incomplete as it may be, to help you find what you cannot recall. For example, for the case at hand, one might think of *dark*, *coffee*, *beans*, and *Arabia*, to expect from system a set of reasonable candidates, like *arabica*, *espresso*, or *mocha*. In the remainder of this paper I will try to show how this might be achieved, but before doing

Zock/Rapp/Huang (eds.): Proceedings of the 4th Workshop on Cognitive Aspects of the Lexicon, pages 221–229,
Dublin, Ireland, August 23, 2014.

so, I would like to clarify what I mean by *computer-aided lexical access*, what characterizes the problem of word production, i.e. the process.

2 Computer-aided lexical access

Under normal circumstances, words are accessed on the fly, that is, the lexical access is immediate, involontary and autonomous. Also, it takes place without any external help. As we all know, things do not always work that smoothly, which is why we may ask for help. In this latter case, lexical access is deliberate, incremental (i.e., distributed over time), and may be mediated via some external resource (another person or a dictionary). This situation may well arise in writing, where we are much more demanding and where we have much more time. Hence words are chosen with much more care than during speaking, i.e., spontaneous discourse.

I view *computer-aided lexical access* as an interactive, cognitive process. It is *interactive* as it involves two cooperative agents, the user and the computer, and it is *cognitive* as it is largely knowledge-driven. The knowledge concerns words, i.e. meanings and forms, as well as their relations to other words. Since the knowledge of both agents is incomplete, they cooperate: neither of them alone can point to the target word (t_w), but by working together they can. It is as if one had the (semantic) *map* and the other the *compass*, i.e., the knowledge to decide where to go. Since both types of knowledge are necessary, they complete each other, helping utlimately the user to find the elusive word, which is the goal.

To be more concrete, consider some user input (one or several words), the system reacts by providing all directly associated words. Since all words are linked, they form a graph, which has two major consequences : the system knows *everyone*, the immediate neighbors, the neighbors' neighbors, etc. and the user can initiate search from anywhere, to continue it until he has reached the target word, t_w. Everything being connected, everything is reachable, at least in principle. Search may require several steps, but in most cases the number of steps is surprisingly small.

As mentioned already, the user definitely has some knowledge concerning words, their components and their organisation in the mental lexicon, but this knowledge is by no means complete. The user also has some knowledge (or, more precisely, meta-knowledge) concerning the topology of the graph,[1] but he certainly does not know as much as the system. The fact that an author does have this kind of knowledge is revealed via word associations (Cramer, 1968; Deese, 1965; Nelson et al., 1998; Kiss et al., 1972) and via the observed average path length (Vitevitch, 2008) needed in order to get from some starting point (s_w) to the goal (t_w). This path is generally quite short. It hardly ever exceeds three steps, and in many cases even less: search is launched via an item directly related to the t_w (direct neighbor).

If the user does not know too much concerning the topology of the network, he does know quite a bit concerning the t_w,[2] information the system has no clue of at this point. Eventhough it knows 'everyone' in the network, it cannot do mind-reading, i.e. guess the precise word a user has in mind (t_w) when providing a specific input (s_w). Yet the user can. Even if he cannot access the word at a given moment, he can recognize it when seeing it (alone or in a list). This fact is well established in the literature on the 'tip-of-the-tongue problem' (Aitchison, 2003).

3 From mind to mouth, or what characterizes the process of word production?

According to the father of modern linguistics (de Saussure, 1916), word forms (signifier) and their associated meaning (signified) are but one, called the sign. They are said to be an inseparable unit. This is in sharp contrast to what psychologists tell us about words synthesis. For example, one of the leading specialists of language production (Levelt, 1989; Levelt, 1999) has convincingly shown that, when speaking

[1] For example, he knows that for a given word form there are similar forms in terms of sound or meaning. There are also words that are more general/specific, or others meaning exactly the opposite than a given input. This kind of knowledge is so obvious and so frequent that it is encoded in many resources like WordNet, Roget's thesaurus or more traditional dictionaries (incuding synonym and rhyming dictionaries).

[2] For example, parts of the *form* (rhymes with x: health/wealth) or *meaning*, like the 'type' (animal), the 'function' (used for eating) or the 'relationship' (synonym, antonym, ...) with respect the source word (s_w). He may even be able to provide parts of the definition (say, 'very small' for 'liliput'). His main problem problem resides in the fact that he cannot access at this very moment the exact word form (he experiences the so called 'tip-of-the-tongue problem, TOT), which is why he tries to find it in a lexical resource (dictionary).

we go, step by step, from *meanings* (concepts), to the *lexical concept* (also called lemma) to the *sound* (written or spoken form). Depending on the theory, there may be retroaction or not, a lower level, say, phonology, influencing a higher level, the lexical concept.

Note that the notion of *lemma* has completely different meanings in psychology and in lexicography. While for linguists it is roughly speaking the word's base-form or dictionary-form, for psycholinguists it is a schema, i.e. an abstract form representing a specific meaning (a lexicalized concept) and a syntactic category (part of speech), but it lacks entirely specific values concerning the form (sounds/graphemes). This is being take care of at the next step (sound form encoding). In short, in contrast to Saussure's view, the information contributing to what we commonly call words (lemma or word forms) is distributed. This is a well established empirical fact observed by psychologists working on the time course of word production (Stemberger, 1985; Levelt and Schriefers, 1987; Dell et al., 1999), as by those who analyze and interpret speech errors (Fromkin, 1973; Fromkin, 1980; Fromkin, 1993).

Yet, what concerns us here in particular is the following: as noted, speakers go from meanings to sounds via lexical concepts (abstract word forms). More importantly, the conceptual input may lack information to determine a precise lexical form. Put differently, rather than starting from a full fledged definition or complete meaning representation, authors may well start from an underspecified input ('small bird' rather than 'sparrow'). Note that the specific requirements of a culture may help us to clarify our thoughts, as well as induce biases or imprecisions because of lexical gaps. Hence we end up using an existing words (eventhough it does not express excatly what we had in mind) rather than coining a new one fitting better our purpose (expressibility problem). For a psycholinguistic explanation concerning gradual refinement, see (Zock, 1996).

Let me briefly illustrate this here via an example, and comment then on the way how specific knowledge states may ask for different kind of information from the lexicon. Suppose you wanted to talk about a given reptile having certain features (dangerous, size, living space, ...). If you cannot come up immediately with the intended word, any of the following could be candidates: alligator, crocodile, cayman. At some point you need to make up your mind though, as the form synthesizer needs to know what items to activate so that it can produce the corresponding form (graphemes, sounds).

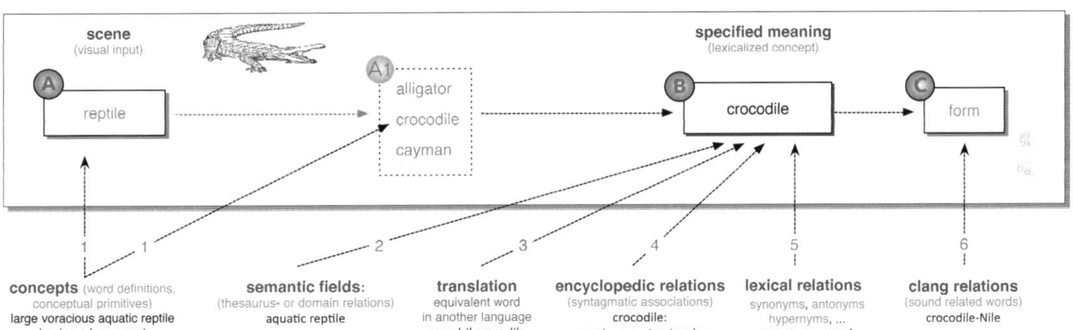

Figure 1: Underspecified input and progressive refinement

As we can see in the figure above, there are two critical moments in word production: meaning *specification* (A-B) and *sound-form encoding* (B-C). It is generally this latter part that poses problems. How to resolve it has been nicely illustrated in an experiment done by (James and Burke, 2000). They showed that phonologically similar words of the target could resolve the TOT state. To show this they put participants into the TOT state by presenting them low-frequency words: abdicate, amnesty, anagram,.... Those who failed were used for the experiment. Next the experimenters read a list of words containing parts of the syllables of the TOT word. For example, if the definition 'to renounce a throne' put a participant into a TOT state, he was asked to read aloud a list of ten words, like *ab*stract, in*di*gent, trun*cate*, each of which contains a syllable of the target. For the other half, participants were given a list of 10 phonologically unrelated words. After that participants were primed again to produce the elusive word (abdicate). As the results clearly showed those who were asked to read phonologically related words resolved more

TOT states than those who were presented with unrelated words.

This is a nice example. Alas, we cannot make use of it, as, not knowing the target word we cannot increase (directly) the activation level of the phonological form. Hence we have to resort to another method, namely, association networks (see section 3). Let us see how search strategies may depend on cognitive states.

4 Search strategies function of variable cognitive states

Search is always based on knowledge. Depending on the knowledge available at the onset one will perform a specific kind of search. Put differently, there are different information needs as there are different search strategies.

There are at least three things that authors typically know when looking for a specific word: its *meaning* (definition) or at least part of it (this is the most frequent situation), its *lexical relations* (hyponymy, synonymy, antonymy, etc.), and the collocational or encyclopedic relations it entertains with other words (Paris-city, Paris-French capital, etc.). Hence there are several ways to access a word (see Figure 1): via its meaning (concepts, meaning fragments), via syntagmatic links (thesaurus- or encyclopedic relations), via its form (rhymes), via lexical relations, via syntactic patterns (search in a corpus), and, of course, via another language (translation). Note that access by meaning is the golden route, i.e. the most normal way. We tend to use other means only if we fail to access straight away the desired word.

I will consider here only one of them, word associations (mostly, encyclopaedic relations). Note that, people being in the TOT-state clearly know more than that. Psychologists who have studied this phenomenon (Brown and McNeill, 1996; Vigliocco et al., 1997) have found that their subjects had access not only to meanings (the words definition), but also to information concerning grammar (gender) and lexical form: sound, morphology and part of speech. While all this information could be used to constrain the search space, the ideal dictionary being multiply indexed, I will deal here only with semantically related words (associations, collocations in the large sense of the word). Before discussing how such a dictionary could be built and used, let us consider a possible search scenario.

I start from the assumption that in our mind, all words are connected, the mental lexicon (brain) being a network. This being so, anything can be reached from anywhere. The user enters the graph by providing whatever comes to his mind (source-word), following the links until he has reached the target. As has been shown (Motter et al., 2002), our mental lexicon has small-world properties: very few steps are needed to get from the source-word to the target word. Another assumption I make is the following: when looking for a word, people tend to start from a close neighbour, which implies that users have some meta-knowledge containing the topology of the network (or the structure of their mental lexicon): what are the nodes, how are they linked to their neighbours, and what are more or less direct neighbours ? For example, we know that black is related to white, and that both words are fairly close, at least a lot closer than, say, black and flower.

Search can be viewed as a dialogue. The user provides as input the words that a concept he wishes to express evokes, and the system displays then all (directly) connected words. If this list contains the target search stops, otherwise it will continue. The user chooses a word of the list, or keys in an entirely different word. The first part described is the simplest case: the target is a direct neighbour. The second addresses the problem of indirect associations, the distance being bigger than 1.

Before presenting our method in section 3, let us say a few words about existing resources. Since the conversion of meaning to sounds is mediated via a lexicon, one may wonder to what extent existing resources can be of help.

5 Related work

While there are many kinds of dictionaries or lexical resources, very few of them can be said to meet truly the authors' needs. To be fair though, one must admit that great efforts have been made to improve the situation both with respect to lexical resources and electronic dictionaries. In fact, there are quite a few *onomasiological dictionaries* (van Sterkenburg, 2003). For example, Roget's Thesaurus (Roget, 1852), analogical dictionaries (Boissière, 1862; Robert et al., 1993), Longman's Language Activator

(Summers, 1993), various network-based dictionaries: WordNet (Fellbaum, 1998; Miller et al., 1990), MindNet (Richardson et al., 1998), HowNet (Dong and Dong, 2006), Pathfinder (Schvaneveldt, 1989), 'The active vocabulary for French' (Mel'čuk and Polguère, 2007) and Fontenelle (Fontenelle, 1997). Other proposals have been made by Sierra (Sierra, 2000) and Moerdijk (2008). There are also various collocation dictionaries (Benson et al., 2010), reverse dictionaries (Bernstein, 1975; Kahn, 1989; Edmonds, 1999) and OneLook,[3] which combines a dictionary (WordNet) and an encyclopedia (Wikipedia). Finally, there is MEDAL (Rundell and Fox, 2002), a thesaurus produced with the help of Kilgariff's Sketch Engine (Kilgarriff et al., 2004). There has also been quite a lot of work on the time-course of word production, i.e. the way how one gets progressively from a more or less precise idea to its expression, a word expressed in written or spoken form. See for example (Levelt et al., 1999; Dell et al., 1999). Clearly, a lot of progress has been made during the last two decades, yet more can be done especially with respect to indexing (the organization of the data) and navigation.

Two key idea underlying modern lexical resources are the notions of 'graphs' and 'association'. For a useful introduction to graph-based natural language processing, see (Mihalcea and Radev, 2011). Associations have a long history. The idea according to which the mental lexicon (or encyclopedia) is basically an associative network, composed of nodes (words or concepts) and links (associations) is not new at all. Actually the very notion of association goes back at least to Aristotle (350BC), but it is also inherent in work done by philosophers (Locke, Hume), physiologists (James & Stuart Mills), psychologists (Galton, 1880; Freud, 1901; Jung and Riklin, 1906) and psycholinguists (Deese, 1965; Jenkins, 1970; Schvaneveldt, 1989). For good introductions see (Hörmann, 1972; Cramer, 1968) and more recently (Spitzer, 1999). The notion of association is also implicit in work on semantic networks (Quillian, 1968), hypertext (Bush, 1945), the web (Nelson, 1967), connectionism (Dell et al., 1999) and, of course, in WordNet (Miller, 1990; Fellbaum, 1998).

6 The framework for building and using our resource

To understand the problems at stake, I describe the communicative setting (system, user), the existing and necessary components, as well as the information flow (see figure 2).

Imagine an author wishing to convey the name of a special beverage ('mocha') commonly found in coffee shops. Failing to do so, he tries to find it in a lexicon. Since dictionaries are too huge to be scanned from beginning to the end, I suggest another solution : reduce the search space based on some input (step-1) and presentation of the results (all directly related words) in a clustered form (step-2). More concretely speaking, I suggest to have a system that accepts whatever comes to an author's mind, say 'coffee' in our 'mocha' case, to present then all directly associated words. Put differently, given some cue, we want the system to guess the user's goal (the elusive word). If this list contains the target, search stops, otherwise the user will pick one of the associated terms or provide an entirely new word and the whole process is repeated again, that is, the system will come up with a new set of proposals.

What I've just described here corresponds to step-1 in figure 2 (see next page). While there are a number of resources that one could use to allow for this transition, I rely here on the E.A.T., i.e. the 'Edinburgh Association Thesaurus'. Note that the output produced by this resource is still too big to be really useful. Suppose that each input word yielded 50 outputs (the EAT often presents 100, and one could think of a lot more). Having provided three words the system will return 150 outputs. Actually, it will take an intersection of the associated words to avoid redundancies. Since this list is still too big to be scanned linearly (one by one), I suggest to structure it, by clustering words into categories (step-2).

This yields a tree whose leaves are words (our potential targets) and whose nodes are categories, that is, also words, but with a completely different status, namely to group words. Category names function like signposts, signalling the user the direction to go. Note that it is not the system that decides on the direction, but the user. Seeing the names of the categories he can make reasonable guesses concerning their content. Categories act somehow like signposts signaling the user the kind of words he is likely to find if he goes one way or another. Indeed, knowing the name of a category (fruit, animal), the user can guess the kind of words contained in each bag, a prediction which is all the more likely as each

[3]http://onelook.com/reverse-dictionary.shtml

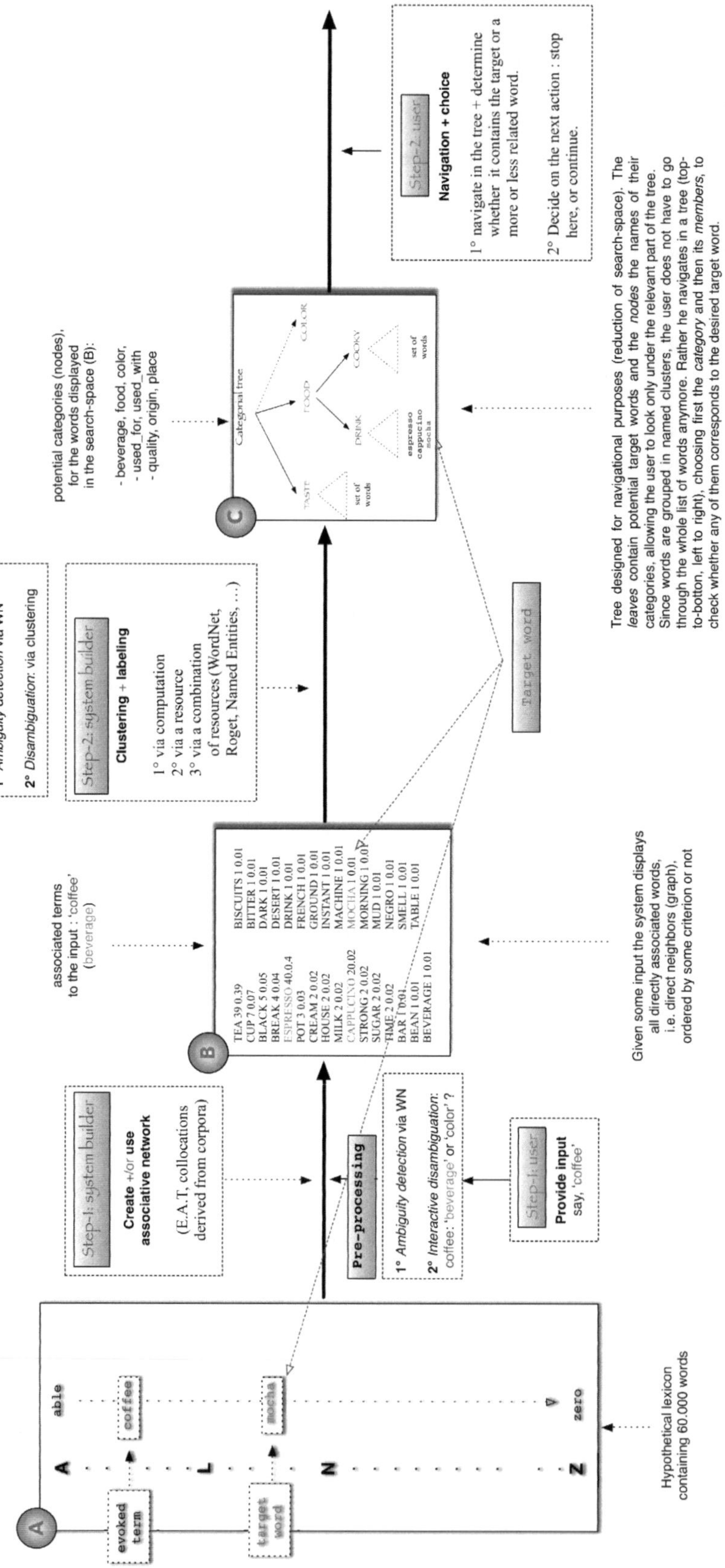

Figure 2: Architecture of the components and information flow

category contains only terms directly associated with the source word. Assuming that the user knows the category of the searched word,[4] he should be able to look in the right bag and take the best turn. Navigating in a categorial tree, the user can search at a fairly high level (class) rather than at the level of words (instances). This reduces not only the cognitive load, but it increases also chances of finding the target, while speeding up search, i.e. the time needed to find a word.

Remains the question of how to build this resource and how to accomplish these two steps. I have explained already the first transition going from A-B. The system enriches the input by taking all associated words, words he will find in the EAT. Obviously, other strategies are possible, and this is precisely one of the points I would like to experiment with in the future : check which knowledge source (corpus, association thesaurus, lexical resource) produces the best set of candidates, i.e. the best search space and the best structure in order to navigate. The solution of the second step is quite a bit more complicated, as putting words into clusters is one thing, naming them is another. Yet, arguably this is a crucial step, as it allows the user to navigate on this basis. Of course, one could question the very need of labels, and perhaps this is not too much of an issue if we have only say, 3-4 categories. I am nevertheless strongly convinced that the problem is real, as soon as the number of categories (hence the words to be classified) grows. To conclude, I think it is fair to say that the first stage is clearly within reach, while the automatic construction of the categorical tree remains a true challenge despite the vast literature devoted to this topic or to strongly related problems (Zhang et al., 2012; Biemann, 2012; Everitt et al., 2011).

7 Outlook and conclusion

I have started from the observation that words are important and that their accessibility can be a problem. In order to help a dictionary user to overcome it I have presented a method showing promise. In particular, I have shown how to reduce the search space, how to present a set of plausible candidates and what needs to be done next (clustering and naming them) to reduce the search space and to support navigation. In particular, I have proposed the creation of a categorial tree whose leaves contain the (potential target) words and the nodes the names of their categories. The role of the latter is to avoid the user to search in non relevant parts of the tree. Since words are grouped in named clusters, the user does not have to go through the whole list of words anymore. Rather he navigates in a tree (top-to-botton, left to right), choosing first the category and then its members, to check whether any of them corresponds to the desired target word.

Even if the details of this work turn out to be wrong (this is just preliminary work), I believe and hope that the overall framework is of the right sort, allowing for a rich set of experimentation in particular with respect to determining the search space and the clustering. Concerning evaluation, the ultimate judge will be, of course, the user, as only s/he can tell us whether our resource fits his/her needs or goals.

References

Jean Aitchison. 2003. *Words in the Mind: an Introduction to the Mental Lexicon (3d edition).* Blackwell, Oxford.

Morton Benson, Evelyn Benson, and Robert A Ilson. 2010. *The BBI Combinatory Dictionary of English.* John Benjamins, Philadelphia.

Theodore Bernstein. 1975. *Bernstein's Reverse Dictionary.* Crown, New York.

Chris Biemann. 2012. *Structure Discovery in Natural Language.* Springer.

Jean Baptiste Prudence Boissière. 1862. *Dictionnaire analogique de la langue française : répertoire complet des mots par les idées et des idées par les mots.* Larousse et A. Boyer, Paris.

Roger Brown and David McNeill. 1996. The tip of the tounge phenomenon. *Journal of Verbal Learning and Verbal Behaviour*, 5:325–337.

Allan S. Brown. 1991. The tip of the tongue experience a review and evaluation. *Psychological Bulletin*, 10:204–223.

[4]A fact which has been systematically observed for people being in the 'tip of the tongue state' who may tell the listener that they are looking for the name of "a fruit typically found in *PLACE*", in order to get 'kiwi'.

Vannevar Bush. 1945. As we may think. *The Atlantic Monthly*, 176:101–108.

Phebe Cramer. 1968. *Word association*. Academic Press, New York.

Ferdinand de Saussure. 1916. *Cours de linguistique générale*. Payot, Paris.

James Deese. 1965. *The structure of associations in language and thought*. Johns Hopkins Press.

Gary Dell, Franklin Chang, and Zenzi M. Griffin. 1999. Connectionist models of language production: Lexical access and grammatical encoding. *Cognitive Science*, 23:517–542.

Zhendong Dong and Qiang Dong. 2006. *HOWNET and the computation of meaning*. World Scientific, London.

David Edmonds, editor. 1999. *The Oxford Reverse Dictionary*. Oxford University Press, Oxford, Oxford.

Brian S. Everitt, Sabine Landau, Morven Leese, and Daniel Stahl. 2011. *Cluster Analysis*. John Wiley and Sons.

Christiane Fellbaum, editor. 1998. *WordNet: An Electronic Lexical Database and some of its Applications*. MIT Press.

Thierry Fontenelle. 1997. *Turning a Bilingual Dictionary into a Lexical-Semantic Database*. Max Niemeyer, Tübingen.

Siegmund Freud. 1901. *Psychopathology of everyday life*. Payot, Paris, 1997 edition.

Victoria Fromkin, editor. 1973. *Speech errors as linguistic evidence*. Mouton, The Hague.

Victoria Fromkin. 1980. Errors in linguistic performance: Slips of the tongue, ear, pen and hand.

Victoria Fromkin. 1993. Speech production. In J. Berko-Gleason and N. Bernstein Ratner, editors, *Psycholinguistics*. Harcourt, Brace, Jovanovich, Fort Worth, TX.

Francis Galton. 1880. Psychometric experiments. *Brain*, 2:149–162.

Hans Hörmann. 1972. *Introduction à la psycholinquistique*. Larousse, Paris, France.

Lori James and Deborah Burke. 2000. Phonological priming effects on word retrieval and tip-of-the-tongue experiences in young and older adults. *Journal of Experimental Psychology: Learning, Memory, and Cognition*, 6(26):1378—1391.

James Jenkins. 1970. The 1952 Minnesota word association norms. In L. Postman and G. Kepper, editors, *Norms of Word Association*, pages 1–38. Academic Press, New York, NY.

Carl Jung and Franz Riklin. 1906. Experimentelle Untersuchungen über Assoziationen Gesunder. In C. G. Jung, editor, *Diagnostische Assoziationsstudien*, pages 7–145. Barth, Leipzig, Germany.

John Kahn. 1989. *Reader's Digest Reverse Dictionary*. Reader's Digest, London.

Adam Kilgarriff, Pavel Rychlý, Pavel Smrž, and David Tugwell. 2004. The Sketch Engine. In *Proceedings of the Eleventh EURALEX International Congress*, pages 105–116, Lorient, France.

George Kiss, Christine Amstrong, and Robert Milroy. 1972. *The associative thesaurus of English*. Ediburgh University Press, Edinburgh.

William Levelt and Herbert Schriefers. 1987. Stages of lexical access. In G. Kempen, editor, *Natural Language Generation: New Results in Artificial Intelligence, Psychology, and Linguistics*, pages 395–404. Nijhoff, Dordrecht.

William Levelt, A. Roelofs, and A. Meyer. 1999. A theory of lexical access in speech production. *Behavioral and Brain Sciences*, 22(1):1–75.

William Levelt. 1989. *Speaking : From Intention to Articulation*. MIT Press, Cambridge, MA.

William Levelt. 1999. Language production: a blueprint of the speaker. In C. Brown and P. Hagoort, editors, *Neurocognition of Language*, pages 83—122. Oxford University Press.

Igor Aleksandrovič Mel'čuk and Alain Polguère. 2007. *Lexique actif du français : l'apprentissage du vocabulaire fondé sur 20 000 dérivations sémantiques et collocations du français*. Champs linguistiques. De Boeck, Bruxelles.

Rada Mihalcea and Dragomir Radev. 2011. *Graph-Based Natural Language Processing and Information Retrieval.* Cambridge University Press, Cambridge, UK.

George A. Miller, Richard Beckwith, Christiane Fellbaum, Derek Gross, and Katherine Miller. 1990. Introduction to WordNet: An on-line lexical database. *International Journal of Lexicography, 3(4)*, pages 235–244.

George Armitage Miller. 1990. Wordnet: An on-line lexical database. *International Journal of Lexicography*, 3(4).

Adilson E. Motter, Alessandro P. S. de Moura, Ying-Cheng Lai, and Partha Dasgupta. 2002. Topology of the conceptual network of language. *Physical Review E*, 65(6).

Douglas Nelson, Cathy McEvoy, and Thomas Schreiber. 1998. The university of South Florida word association, rhyme, and word fragment norms.

Ted Nelson. 1967. Xanadu projet hypertextuel.

Ross Quillian. 1968. Semantic memory. In M. Minsky, editor, *Semantic Information Processing*, pages 216–270. MIT Press, Cambridge, MA.

Stephen Richardson, William Dolan, and Lucy Vanderwende. 1998. Mindnet: Acquiring and structuring semantic information from text. In *ACL-COLING'98*, pages 1098–1102.

Paul Robert, Alain Rey, and J. Rey-Debove. 1993. *Dictionnaire alphabetique et analogique de la Langue Française*. Le Robert, Paris.

Peter Roget. 1852. *Thesaurus of English Words and Phrases*. Longman, London.

Michael Rundell and G. (Eds.) Fox. 2002. *Macmillan English Dictionary for Advanced Learners*. Macmillan, Oxford.

Roger Schvaneveldt, editor. 1989. *Pathfinder Associative Networks: studies in knowledge organization*. Ablex, Norwood, New Jersey, US.

Bennett Schwartz. 2002. *Tip-of-the-tongue states: Phenomenology, mechanism, and lexical retrieval.* Lawrence Erlbaum Associates, Mahwah, NJ.

Gerardo Sierra. 2000. The onomasiological dictionary: a gap in lexicography. In *Proceedings of the Ninth Euralex International Congress*, pages 223–235, IMS, Universität Stuttgart.

Manfred Spitzer. 1999. *The mind within the net: models of learning, thinking and acting*. MIT Press, Cambridge, MA.

Joseph Paul Stemberger. 1985. An interactive activation model of language production. In A. W. Ellis, editor, *Progress in the Psychology of Language*, volume 1, pages 143–186. Erlbaum.

Della Summers. 1993. *Language Activator: the world's first production dictionary*. Longman, London.

Piet van Sterkenburg. 2003. Onomasiological specifications and a concise history of onomasiological dictionaries. In *A Practical Guide to Lexicography*, volume A Practical Guide to Lexicography, pages 127—143. John Benjamins, Amsterdam.

Gabriella Vigliocco, Tiziana Antonini, and Garrett Merrill. 1997. Grammatical gender is on the tip of italian tongues. *Psychological Science*, 4(8):314–317.

Michael Vitevitch. 2008. What can graph theory tell us about word learning and lexical retrieval? *Journal of Speech, Language, and Hearing Research*, 51:408—422.

David Wilkins. 1972. *Linguistics and Language Teaching*. Edward Arnold, London.

Ziqi Zhang, Anna Lisa Gentile, and Fabio Ciravegna. 2012. Recent advances in methods of lexical semantic relatedness – a survey. *Journal of Natural Language Engineering, Cambridge Universtiy Press*, 19(4):411–479.

Michael Zock. 1996. The power of words in message planning. In *Proceedings of the 16th conference on Computational linguistics*, pages 990–995, Morristown, NJ, USA. Association for Computational Linguistics.

Author Index

Association for Computational Linguistics
209 N. Eighth Street
Stroudsburg, Pennsylvania 18360

CURRAN ASSOCIATES INC
proceedings
.com

14th Conference of the European Chapter of the Association for Computational Linguistics 2014

(EACL 2014)

Gothenburg, Sweden
26-30 April 2014

ISBN: 978-1-63266-396-2